Weapons of Mass Deception...
How Billionaires Plan to Destroy Our Public Schools
and What You Can Do to Stop Them

David Spring M. Ed. and Elizabeth Hanson M. Ed.

Weapons of Mass Deception (dot) org

Coalition to Protect Our Public Schools (dot) org

To Jeff! Thank you for being a thinker and a fighter + free!

Copyright, March 9 2015

your friend, Elizabeth Hanson

Dedication

This book is dedicated to the 50 million school aged children in the United States who are counting on the rest of us to provide them with a good education. And to their parents and teachers who need to better understand why our schools are under attack... and what they need to do to fight back. Knowledge is power. We can and must take urgently needed steps to protect our kids and our public schools.

Disclaimer

We are not funded by the Bill and Melinda Gates Foundation and we are not responsible for the billionaire takeover of our public schools. We are just a couple of teachers and parents trying to get the word out about the war against our public schools. We hope you will refrain from the tendency to kill the messenger.

Weapons of Mass Deception...
Table of Contents

Preface... Why We Hope You'll Read This Book on the Dangers of Ed Reform Scams...v

1 The First Weapon of Mass Deception... Drill and Kill Fake Tests.............1
   1.1 How the War Against our Schools and our Kids Began..........................2
   1.2 Rise of the Toxic Test Scammers...19
   1.3 NAEP Proficiency... How High Stakes Tests were Designed to Fail.........37
   1.4 NCLB... How Drill and Kill Fake Tests Harm our Kids............................57

2 CCSS... Common Core Fake Standards...75
   2.1 The Real History of Common Core..76
   2.2 Common Core Standards are Not Age Appropriate..............................93
   2.3 Common Core Math is Insane..107
   2.4 Support for Common Core Plunges..115

3 Why Fake Charter Schools are Kid Prisons...133
   3.1 Ten Reasons Charter Schools Harm Children....................................134
   3.2 The Crooks Behind the Charter School Scam...................................143
   3.3 Why Charter Schools always turn into Fraud Factories.....................165
   3.4 Kids in Prison Program..181

4 How K12 INC Online Fake Schools Harm Our Kids..............................193
   4.1 All Parents Need to Know About the Drawbacks of K12 INC................194
   4.2 K12 INC From Junk Bonds to Junk Schools.......................................204
   4.3 K12 INC Distortions, Deceptions and Outright Lies...........................224
   4.4 Free Open Source Alternatives to K12 INC..245

5 Teach for Awhile Fake Teachers..253
   5.1 Why replacing real teachers with fake TFA teachers harms our kids......254
   5.2 How Teacher Bashing has Harmed Real Teachers..............................269
   5.3 VAM Scam... Firing Teachers based on Student Test Scores................281
   5.4 If you can't measure it, does it still exist?...290

6 Billionaire Funded Fake Grass Roots..301
   6.1 Stand for Children Turns into Stand for Billionaires..........................302
   6.2 The Biggest WMD is the Billionaire Controlled Fake Media................311
   6.3 Exposing the Gates Foundation Tax Evasion Scam............................323
   6.4 Meet the Real Bill Gates..331

7 Billionaire Controlled Fake Government..**349**
   7.1 How Billionaires Buy Elections..350
   7.2 Corrupt Corporate Takeover of the GED Exam...359
   7.3 Consequences of the Pearson Takeover of the GED Test......................368
   7.4 The College and Career Ready Marketing Slogan is a Scam..................378

8 Real Education Reform... Options for a Better Future............................**391**
   8.1 Twelve Steps to Achieve Real Education Reform....................................392
   8.2 How to Get Your State Party to Oppose Common Core..........................399
   8.3 How to pass a bill in your State legislature..407
   8.4 Active Activism... Join the Fight to Protect our Public Schools...............415

About The Authors..**424**

Preface... Why We Hope You'll Read This Book on the Dangers of Ed Reform Scams

> We can have democracy,
> Or we can have concentration of wealth
> In the hands of a few.
> But we can not have both.
> Louis Brandeis
> US Supreme Court Justice
> 1916 - 1939

Welcome to our website and book on how weapons of mass deception are being used to destroy and take over our public schools. We are two teachers in Washington State. Together we have more than 50 years of experience teaching public school and community college courses. We are also both parents concerned about the future of our children and the future of all children. As parents and teachers, we believe every child deserves a real school, a real teacher and a quality education.

Our goal is to explain the dangerous drawbacks of privatizing our public schools and provide parents and teachers with options for REAL education reform. Our purpose is to alert you to the many attacks on our public schools and the horrific harm these attacks are currently inflicting on millions of school children. Our mission is to arm you with useful ideas on what you can do to fight back against these attacks.

A child learns To Hate School... After 5 HOURS of Kindergarten Common Core High Stakes High Failure Rate Tests!

Child psychologists have a term for the harm inflicted on this little girl... It is called CHILD ABUSE.... It is up to those of us who care about children to put an end to this insanity!

Why We Decided to Write This Book... A Personal Story

According to the National Center for Educational Statistics, there are about 52 million school age children in the United States. Each of the 13 grades has about 4 million students. The average graduation rate for the past 40 years has been about 75% - meaning that about one in four students – or nearly one million students – do not get a high school diploma each year. About 90% of these one million drop outs (or 900,000 young adults) eventually attempt to get a High School Equivalency Diploma each year, called a **GED certificate** – which is pretty much required to get a good job or go to a good college. Historically, for the past 40 years, the exam questions were selected so that about 60% or about 540,000 of these 900,000 mostly low income young adults got their GED certificate every year.

However, in spring, 2014, we became aware of a shocking decline in the pass rate of GED students at local community colleges here in Washington State. The cause of this decline was a new GED test called the 2014 Pearson GED test. This new GED test has exam questions that are much more difficult than the previous GED test. In March of 2014, based on our analysis of the difficulty of these questions, we estimated that this new GED test would result in the pass rate falling from 540,000 students (a 60% pass rate) to less than 90,000 students (a 10% pass rate) - preventing nearly 500,000 students across the US from receiving their GED certificate in 2014. Sadly, we were proven correct. Here is an article from December 17 2014 with that exact headline!

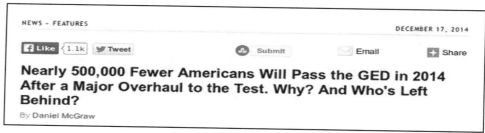

http://www.clevescene.com/cleveland/after-a-major-overhaul-to-the-ged-test-in-2014-18000-fewer-ohioans-will-pass-the-exam-this-year-than-last-along-with-nearly-500000-across/Content?oid=4442224

Here is a quote from the article: "The numbers are shocking: In the United States, according to the GED Testing Service, 401,388 people earned a GED in 2012, and about 540,000 in 2013. This year, according to the latest numbers obtained by Scene, only about 55,000 have passed nationally. That is a 90-percent drop off from last year."

This ongoing disaster with the GED led us to research the sample questions on the new Pearson GED test. We found that, compared to the prior version of the GED test, the new test asked questions that were significantly harder. Based on our data, in May 2014, we created this chart to alert people in our state to this educational crisis:

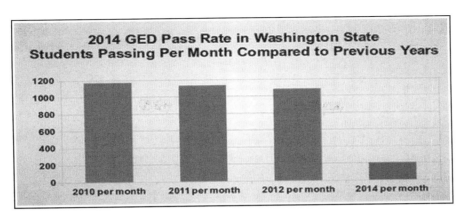

We gave a new Pearson GED practice math test to over 50 people, most of whom had college degrees and only 4 people could pass it. Pearson, the designer of this new test, claimed that the new GED test has to be harder because it is "aligned to Common Core standards." This led us to research the Common Core standards and their relationship to high stakes testing. What we found was so appalling, we decided we needed to write this book in order to expose the scam of common core fake standards and its high stakes high failure rate tests. Specifically, of the 30 million school children who will take the new Common Core tests in the spring of 2015, we predict based upon the difficulty of the new test questions that **more than 20 million students will unfairly be labeled as failures by the new Common Core tests (called SBAC and PARCC).** In fact, none of these kids are failures. It is the Common Core system that is a failure.

Seven Weapons of Mass Deceptions of the Ed Reform Scam
This book exposes seven blatant lies used by the ed reform movement. These seven weapons are Drill and Kill fake tests, Common Core fake standards, Charter School kid prisons, K12 INC online fake schools, TFA Fake Teachers, Billionaire Funded fake grassroots and Corporate Controlled Fake Government.

We call these lies "weapons of mass deception" because they have been used to fool millions of parents and harm millions of children. Common Core High Stakes High Failure Rate tests will harm more than 20 million students just in 2015. But we are not the first to point out that the Ed Reform scam is based on a series of blatant lies. For nearly 20 years, there have been a series of good books exposing the crimes of the ed reform scam and how these crimes harm our kids.

Past books documenting these crimes against our children include:

1995: The Manufactured Crisis: Myths, Frauds, and the Attack on America's Public Schools by David Berliner and B.J. Biddle

1999: One Size Fits Few: The Folly of Educational Standards by Susan Ohanian

1999: Standardized Minds: The High Price of America's Testing Culture by Peter Sacks

2000: The Case Against Standardized Testing by Alfie Kohn

2001: The War Against America's Public Schools: Privatizing Schools, Commercializing Education by Gerald Bracey

2002: Education Inc., Turning Learning into a Business Alfie Kohn

2002: What You Should Know about the War Against America's Public Schools by Gerald Bracey

2003: The Death of Childhood and Destruction of Public Schools by G. Bracey

2004: Failing Our Children by Monty Neill, Lisa Guisbond and Bob Schaeffer

2006: School Reform, The Great American Brain Robbery by Don Orlich

2007: Collateral Damage: How High Stakes Testing Corrupts America's Schools

2009: Education Hell: Rhetoric and Reality by Gerald Bracey

2011: The Death and Life of the Great American School System by Diane Ravitch

2013: Reign of Error by Diane Ravitch

2013 Children of the Core by Kris Nielsen

2013: The School Reform Landscape: Fraud, Myth & Lies by Tienken & Orlich

2014: 50 Myths and Lies that Threaten America's Schools by David Berliner

2014: A Chronicle of Echos by Mercedes Schneider

2014: The Educator and the Oligarch by Anthony Cody

2014: More than a Score, Uprising Against High Stakes Tests by Jesse Hagopian

Despite the mountain of evidence that school reform has caused severe harm to our students (and hundreds of billions of wasted tax payer dollars), the billionaires war against our public schools continues unabated.

Because of the insane dictates of "No Child Left Behind" combined with its terrible twin "Race to the Top," nearly every school in America is now rated as a failure while our children are subjected to toxic "Common Core" tests designed to fail at least 66% of them. This failure to protect our public schools is not the fault of any of the brave authors listed above. It is difficult to see through the propaganda blitz of billionaires who are able to buy off the media, buy up the government and create a massive hoax of fake foundations, fake think tanks, fake non-profits and fake educational organizations to deceive the public into believing that there is merit to the billionaire plan to take over and privatize our public schools. Our goal is to expose the billionaires plan by exposing all of the weapons they are using against our kids and our schools.

We intend for this book to be unique in at least four ways:

#1 We want to use images to expose these weapons of mass deception in a more reader friendly manner
As teachers with more than 50 years of experience between the two of us, we know that images matter. We want a book that tells the story as much through images as through text. There are more than two hundred images in this book. This has doubled the length of the book from 200 to 400 pages. But our hope is that adding these images will help more readers better understand how they are being manipulated by the mass media propaganda paid for by the billionaires.

#2 We hope to connect the dots to expose the fact that the billionaires actually to have a real plan to destroy our Schools
Many folks mistakenly assume that all of the actions of the billionaires are simply a bunch of unrelated random errors made by billionaires who are simply misinformed. But the things that may appear on the surface to be merely just unlucky coincidences actually work together to achieve a real goal which is to privatize and take over our public schools. The billionaires want to destroy our public schools so that we parents will be forced to send our kids to "charter schools" controlled for and by billionaires - rather than public schools controlled by parents through our locally elected school boards.

Here is a diagram of how this plot works:

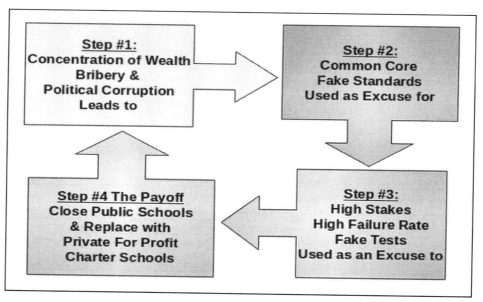

This may seem like a conspiracy theory to some. But read our book and we think you'll discover as we did that a deliberate billionaire takeover of our public schools is exactly what is going on.

We intend to expose how each of their 7 weapons of mass deception used to take over our public schools are connected. Parents, teachers, school administrators, PTA members, school boards and community members need to understand the connections between high stakes tests, common core standards, charter schools, online schools and fake teacher scams like Teach For America. In this book we explain not only what is happening – but why it is happening and how each leg of the elephant is connected to every other leg of the elephant.

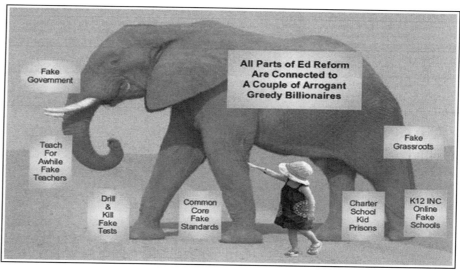

Our research indicates that the Ed Reform movement is being driven by a few billionaires interested in maximizing their corporate profits.

Are we being to harsh on the billionaires?
Throughout this book, you will see example after example of disastrous ed reform scams being funded by billionaires. It would not be accurate to discuss these ed reform scams without talking about the billionaires funding those scams.

Some people have protested that we are being too harsh on the billionaires. They claim that the billionaires are simply misguided and do not realize that they are harming millions of children in their efforts to privatize our public schools. However, we believe that there is a deliberate pattern to the actions of the billionaires. Naomi Klein refers to this pattern as the "shock doctrine." The idea is that the wealthy promote chaos and then use chaos to make changes that benefit the wealthy. Noam Chomsky also sees a familiar pattern to privatization of public schools.

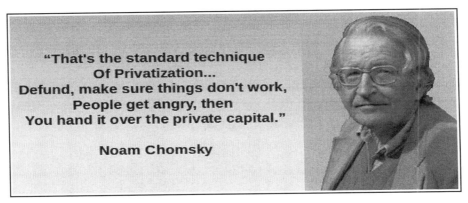

Our research has taught us that there has been a massive transfer of wealth over the last several decades. This wealth transfer is what is hurting our children and overcrowding our schools. There is plenty of money. It's just not moving among the people. Below is a chart showing that while the percentage of people in the work force is at a 30 year low, corporate profits are at an all time high.

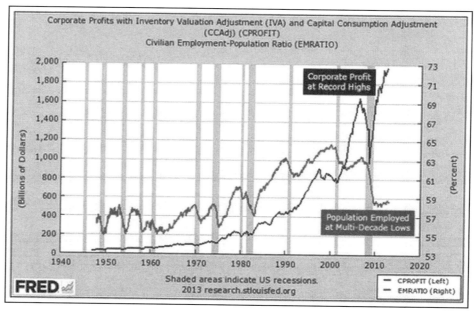

#3 We want teachers and parents to know that we are at war

Many people assume that billionaires have good intentions and all we need to do is explain to the billionaires why what they are doing is wrong and how much it harms kids and then the billionaires will stop. Unfortunately, not everyone in the world shares our values. Billionaires, as we will expose in this book, think much differently than the rest of us. They are so arrogant that they think our schools, our economy and even our political system would be better off if they ran them. We also falsely assume our elected leaders will care if they are made more aware of the harm fake ed reform inflicts on our kids. Sadly, this is not the case as most elected officials only care about keeping the billionaires who paid for their elections happy.

So we need a book which more realistically addresses the war that is being waged against our kids and our public schools. There are hundreds of billions of dollars at stake – as well as the future of 52 million school children. So we wrote a book which realistically addresses the war that is being waged against our kids and our public schools. Our book is more direct in tone than most of the other books. We name names across the political spectrum and from the halls of corporate America. Many of these are names you'll recognize.

#4 We want to arm you with the information you need to fight back

Finally, we want to arm you with the specific and credible information you need to combat each of the seven weapons of mass deception in order that we can keep and strengthen our public schools. Our public schools represent the future of our children and of our democracy. But in the eyes of the greedy and powerful, our schools are a "market" worth nearly one trillion dollars annually. Let's not allow our children to be made into commodities to buy and sell. It will take all hands on deck if we are to to defeat the billionaires. We hope you'll join us!

How this book is organized
This book is divided into 8 chapters with the first seven chapters focusing in on helping you better understand the billionaires "weapons of mass deception." These seven most harmful weapons of mass deception are:

#1: Drill and Kill Fake Tests... A program of endless high stakes tests intended to unfairly and dishonestly brand every public school in America as a failure by forcing our kids to take tests deliberately designed to fail as many students as possible.

Condemning kids to endless hours of computerized testing is child abuse!

#2: Common Core Fake Standards... A poorly designed set of national standards that were developed by billionaires rather than educators and intended to act as a smoke screen to force new "impossible to pass" tests on our public schools.

#3: Charter School Kid Prisons... Charters not only rob tax payers of billions of dollars, but also rob young children of their childhood. We will describe just a few of the many shocking abuses created by unregulated and out of control charter school greed, including KIPP schools – the Kids In Prison Program.

KIPP Charter Schools... Big Prisons for Little Minds

#4: K12INC Online Fake Schools... In this Wall Street scam, half the kids drop out every year, teachers are forced to monitor 300 students every day and the graduation rate is only 22%. Fake Online Schools severely harm millions of children.

Half of K12 online students fail to make it through their first year. 80% drop out within two years. Only 22% of online students graduate from High School!

#5: Teach for America Fake Teachers. Also known as TFA, this scam program gives young adults only 5 weeks of training and then sends them off to experiment with our children. Half of these fake teachers drop out their first year which is why many people call this program "Teach for Awhile."

#6: Billionaire Funded Fake Grassroots... Billionaires have spent more than five billion dollars of tax diversion funds through fake non profit groups with deceptive names like "Stand for Children" to build an army of thousands of corporate lobbyists to fool parents and legislators into unwittingly supporting the destruction of our public schools.

Weapons of Mass Deception

#7: Corporate Controlled Fake Government... Corporate control and deregulation has already destroyed our health care system our energy network, our banking system and our economy. It's impact on public schools will be even worse.

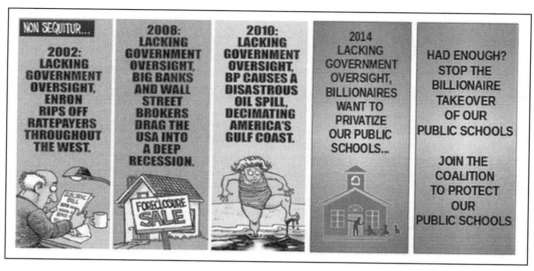

#8... Real Education Reform. In the final chapter, we will explain how to achieve real education reform to improve rather than destroy our public schools. These steps include restoring school funding by rolling back corporate tax breaks and lowering class sizes so struggling students can get the help they need.

What's Next?
We hope you will take the time to learn more about the attacks on our public schools and what you can do to protect them. If you agree with us that our schools are under attack, we hope you will share the link to this book with your friends, family and neighbors. If you have any questions, feel free to post them on our community forum located at **Weapons of Mass Deception (dot) org.**

Regards,
David Spring M. Ed. and Elizabeth Hanson M. Ed.

1 The First Weapon of Mass Deception... Drill and Kill Fake Tests

> "Public school parents value individual talents & know that 'one size fits all 90 minute tests' do not take the full measure of a child. We know, for example, that Albert Einstein – who was dyslexic – Did not perform well on tests as a child. Yet he had one of the Best minds in our history." Dr. Paul Houston, Director, AASA

Welcome to the crazy world of "ed reform" where our children mean nothing and corporate profits mean everything. Fasten your seat belt. We are about to enter the world of bribes and lies used to destroy our public schools – a bizarre world where the truth is the exact opposite of everything you have ever been told.

This chapter, **The First Weapon of Mass Deception... Drill and Kill Fake Tests**, is divided into four sections:

1.1 How the War Against Our Schools and Our Kids Began

1.2 Why Child Poverty Affects Every High Stakes Test

1.3 NEAP Cut Scores... How High Stakes Tests are Designed to Fail

1.4 How Drill and Kill Fake Tests Cause Permanent Harm to Children

1.1 How the War Against our Schools and our Kids Began

The first step in achieving justice Is making injustice visible.
— Mahatma Gandhi

We will begin by briefly examining the history of high stakes tests, what they really measure and how to more accurately compare US student test scores to scores of kids from other nations.

Our Kids and Our Schools are Not Failing... And Never Have Been!
The first lie used as an excuse for testing kids, firing teachers and closing schools is the ed reformer false claim that "our schools are failing" in comparison to schools in other nations. This claim is not true and never has been true. For more than a century, Americans have been the most productive workers in the world. Because of the innovation of American workers, our economy has been the strongest economy in the world. At the heart of the American economic system has been our public schools - which have consistently produced the most highly trained and creative workforce in the world. As just one objective example of how our public schools and colleges excel in innovation, compare the number of Nobel Laureates in Science produced by the United States in comparison to other developed countries in the world. The US has as many Nobel Laureates in Science as the next 20 leading countries in the world combined.

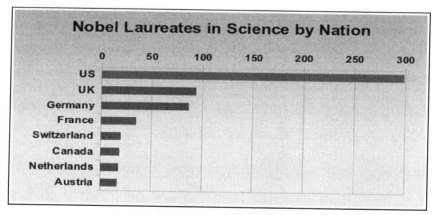

http://en.wikipedia.org/wiki/List_of_countries_by_Nobel_laureates_per_capita

The US Produces More than Enough Highly Trained Workers!
As for the frequently repeated myth that the US does not produce enough computer programmers and engineers, there are more than one million fully qualified computer programmers and engineers in the US who cannot find jobs in the field they were trained for – with more computer programmers and engineers in the US graduating every year and being unable to find jobs in their field.

According to the US Census, only one in four STEM graduates has a STEM job. http://www.census.gov/people/io/publications/table_packages.html?eml=gd&utm_medium=email&utm_source=govdelivery

Hal Salzman, professor of public policy at Rutgers University wrote: "All credible research finds the same evidence about the STEM workforce: ample supply, stagnant wages and, by industry accounts, thousands of applicants for any advertised job. Overall, **U.S. colleges produce twice the number of STEM graduates annually as find jobs in those fields.** Claiming there is a skills shortage by denying the strength of the U.S. STEM workforce supply is possible only by ignoring the most obvious and direct evidence and obscuring the issue with statistical smokescreens – especially when the Census Bureau reports that only about one in four STEM bachelor's degree holders has a STEM job, and Microsoft plans to downsize by 18,000 workers over the next year."

http://www.usnews.com/opinion/articles/2014/09/15/stem-graduates-cant-find-jobs

Sadly, there is a small group of extremely wealthy people who tell us lies like "we Americans are not smart enough" because they want to take over and privatize our public schools. They call themselves "education reformers". But they are really corporate raiders out to destroy the American system of public schools and replace it with a for-profit system of private schools paid for with hundreds of billions of dollars in tax payers funds. The death of our public schools would not only mean the death of our economy, but the death of our democracy.

High Stakes High Failure Rate Tests.. The First Weapon of Mass Deception
High stakes tests are the first and most harmful weapons of mass deception used to destroy and take over schools. Most parents are not aware of how unreliable high stakes tests are. Nor are they aware of how much high stakes tests harm our kids. High stakes tests are based on the simplistic but false assumption that learning can be measured by a number stamped to the foreheads of our children. This magic and extremely deceptive number is then used to unfairly rate children, fire teachers and close schools.

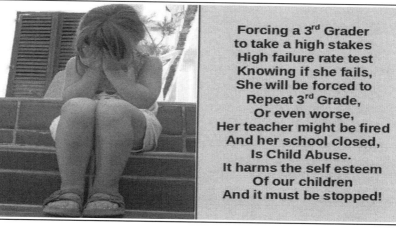

How and when did this insanity of high stakes toxic testing get started? Let's take a journey down memory lane all the way back to 1980.

1980 "Greed is Good" and Public Schools are Bad

Like the decimation of our middle class and the decline of our economy, the destruction of our public schools can be traced back to the election of Ronald Reagan in 1980. In addition to Trickle Down economics, which stole money from the middle class and gave it to the super rich, Reagan promoted the radical ideas of deregulation and allowing the profit motive to over-ride every other factor in the design of our society. In short, he supported the idea that "greed was good." His plan was to starve all public functions of funding (except the military). But one of the most popular public functions was our public schools. Parents valued their public schools and did not want to see funding for their schools cut. The clever solution of the billionaires who elected Reagan was to reduce the popularity of public schools by claiming that they were failing. This was difficult because our public schools were not failing. Thus, the billionaires made up magic numbers based on misleading high stakes tests in a misleading attempt to fool the public into believing that our schools and kids were failing.

A Nation Deceived

In 1981, Reagan publicly advocated eliminating several sections of the US Government including the Department of Education. As with other Departments he did not like, he appointed opponents of the Departments to run them into the ground. Reagan appointed Terrell Bell to preside over the dismantling of the US Department of Education. In August 1981, Bell appointed David Gardner to head the National Commission on Excellence in Education (NCEE). In 1983, this NCEE commission released a report called A Nation at Risk that falsely claimed that the test scores of US students was far below the test scores of students in other countries. The report began with this false claim: "Our Nation is at risk. Our once unchallenged preeminence in commerce, industry, science, and technological innovation is being overtaken by competitors throughout the world." http://www2.ed.gov/pubs/NatAtRisk/index.html

1983 Our Nation was at Risk... But the danger was not our schools, it was at risk of a takeover of our government by billionaires

The beginning of the corporate education reform movement was the 1983 phony report called A Nation at Risk. This report used high stakes test results to claim that the number on the foreheads of students in the Unites States was lower than the number on the foreheads of students in other countries. This deeply flawed report was used as an excuse to begin the destruction and replacement of our public education system with a billionaire-designed, corporate-run, for-profit education system.

The Nation at Risk report is a very short 30 page document that only takes a few minutes to read. The day after it was released, the corporate controlled media put it on the front page of every newspaper and made it the lead story on every news broadcast in America. During the following 30 days, the Washington Post ran two dozen stories about it. It was a propaganda blitz worthy of Joesph Goebbels. Repeat a lie often enough and everyone will believe it.

Ronald Reagan falsely claimed that the report supported his favorite issue, school prayer in order to whip up religious support for his reelection campaign. Ironically, the report did not even mention school prayer. Nevertheless, Reagan gave 51 speeches on the report and the urgent need for school reform during his 1984 re-election campaign. Remarkably, the Nation At Risk attack on public schools failed to provide any actual evidence, charts, graphs or data to back up its many misleading claims. We will therefore briefly review the overwhelming evidence refuting the claim that our public schools were falling behind schools in other nations.

US Students have NOT Lagged Behind Students from Similar Nations

There have been several reviews over the years that have pointed out the problems of the Nation At Risk report. The first of these was a study called the Sandia Report that was commissioned by the Bush White House in 1990. The Sandia Report was supposed to provide evidence supporting the Nation at Risk claims. However, the Sandia Report found that the real evidence did not support the claims in Nation at Risk. The three authors stated: "To our surprise, on nearly every measure, we found steady or slightly improving trends." Instead of American kids doing worse – they were actually doing better! For example, the Sandia report found that high school completion rates in the US are among the highest in the world and that the reason our test scores were lower on international tests was due to the fact that **more poor students took international tests in the US whereas in other countries only the wealthy and top performing students took international tests.**

The Bush White House did not want to hear any of this. They therefore threatened the authors and buried the report. The Sandia report was not published until May 1993 after Bush was safely out of office. The citation for this study is: Carson, C.C., Huelskamp, R.M., & Woodall, R.D., (1993, May/June). Perspectives on education in America. Journal of Educational Research, Volume 86, Pages 259-301. This study has been virtually blacklisted. We were not able to find any link to it on the internet. However, we were able to find and read a copy of this study at the Educational Research library at the University of Washington.

In October 1991, Education Week published an article about the Sandia study and reported that "The researchers who prepared the report could not be reached for comment, and some sources said the researchers had told them that they feared losing their federal funding if they spoke with reporters. The Sandia researchers "were told it would never see the light of day, that they had better be quiet," one source said. "I fear for their careers." The article went on to add that "American participation in higher education is the highest in the world, and there is no shortage of Americans pursuing technical degrees."
Miller, Julie A. "Report Questioning 'Crisis' in Education Creates Uproar." Education Week. (9 October 1991): 1, 32.

Another Report Confirmed that American Students are doing better over time rather than worse

In 1994, the Rand Institute did their own review of test scores of US students. They concluded: "This study does not support the view that schools of the 1970s and 1980s have deteriorated in significant ways with respect to the schools of the 1950s and 1960s in their instruction in mathematics and verbal/reading skills. Moreover, it suggests that schools have made significant progress in decreasing inequalities between minority and non-minority students. The scores of non college-bound students have generally risen even more than those of college-bound students." Rand Institute on Education and Training, Student Achievement and the changing American Family, 1994.

The Problem in the US is Poverty... A disgracefully high child poverty rate in the US is what adversely affects test scores in the US

What the "international comparison" claim ignores is the sad fact that the US is the world leader in child poverty. Only wealthy or high performing students take international tests in other countries whereas nearly all students take international tests in the US. When scores of students at US schools with less than 10% child poverty are compared to other nations which have an average of less than 10% child poverty, US students scored #1 in the world on every area tested by the international PISA test. (Tienken & Orlich, 2013, The School Reform Landscape),

If one compares apples to apples, and controls for poverty, **rich students in the US out perform nearly all other rich students in the world, middle income students in the US out perform nearly all other middle income students in the world and lower income students in the US out perform nearly all other lower income students in the world.** The only way to further increase US test scores is to reduce the poverty rate which means making sure all parents have full time jobs, all families have stable homes and all children have food to eat, books to read and parks to play in.

Evidence that Child Poverty Affects on Test Scores

There are hundreds of studies showing a nearly direct relationship between family income and high stakes test scores. Here is a chart showing the correlation between child poverty and child performance at public schools in Nebraska. http://gfbrandenburg.wordpress.com/tag/iva/

(Note: Each diamond below represents a school district in Nebraska. Note that the poorer the students were in a school district, the worse the test scores were in that school district).

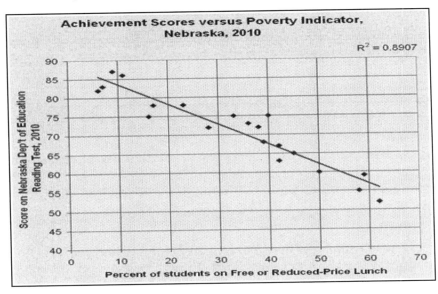

We see the same effect of poverty across all grade levels. Below is a chart comparing the test scores of a low poverty school district (Mercer Island) to a neighboring high poverty school district (Renton). Both school districts are in Washington State and are only a few miles from each other (Source: OSPI Washington State Report Card).

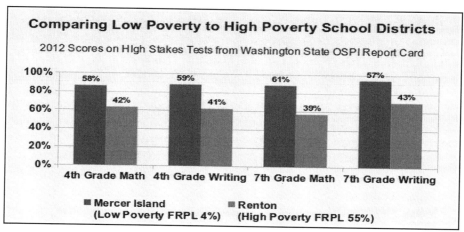

Note that the difference of about 20% in test scores is about half of the difference in poverty rates scores between the school districts. Some low income kids do well. But most low income kids suffer and will continue to suffer until their parents get a job and the children get a stable home.

Failing Students and Failing Schools or Corrupt Leaders and Rigged Economies?

Family income doesn't just determine test scores, it is also the strongest predictor of the dropout rate. Balfanz and Letgers found a strong relationship between poverty and the dropout rate: The higher the percentage of a school's students living in poverty, the higher the dropout rate. When minority students attend schools in low poverty areas, they graduate at the same rate as white students. Balfanz, Robert & Legters, Nettie, (November, 2004) Locating the Dropout Crisis, John Hopkins University.

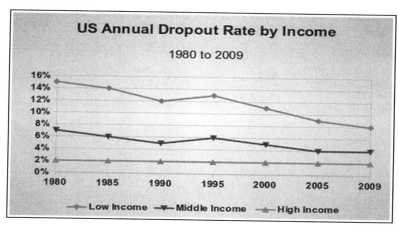

The Four Year Cohort Dropout Rate is about 4 times the US Annual Dropout Rate. Low Income was defined as the bottom 20% of all incomes. High Income was defined as the top 20%. Source: Trends in High School Dropout and Completion Rates in the US 1972 to 2009. US Department of Education Obviously, the best way to increase the graduation rate in the US would be to make sure all low income parents have full time jobs. Sadly, just the opposite has been happening in the US over the past 14 years. Huge numbers of parents have lost their jobs as money has been gradually transferred from the middle class to the billionaires in the US.

Shamefully High Child Poverty Rates in the United States
Now that we understand the role family income plays in test scores and graduation rates, let's look at the poverty rate in the US over time. Poverty is generally defined in the US as living below the US poverty level which is about $20,000 per year for a family of three. In addition, an equal number of children live in low income families which are defined as being below 185% of the poverty level. In 2007, the poverty rate was 21.5% for individuals who were unemployed, but only 2.5% for individuals who were employed full-time. So child poverty means that their parents do not have a full time job. The decline in full time jobs has gotten much worse since 2000.

Dramatic Rise in High Poverty Schools in the US since 2000
In 2000, only 15% of children in the US were living in poverty. By 2012, the child poverty rate has skyrocketrd to 21% of school aged children in the US were in families living in poverty. Put another way, 11 million of the 50 million children ages 5 to 17 were in families living in poverty. The National School Lunch Program is a federally assisted meal program. To be eligible for free or reduced lunch (FRPL), a student must be from a low income household with an income at or below 185 percent of the poverty threshold. In nearly all cases, child poverty is caused by parental job loss or moving from a high paying full time job to a low paying part time job. Free and reduced lunch students are rising rapidly. In 2006, the national rate for FRPL was 42%. In 2013, the FRPL rate was 49%.

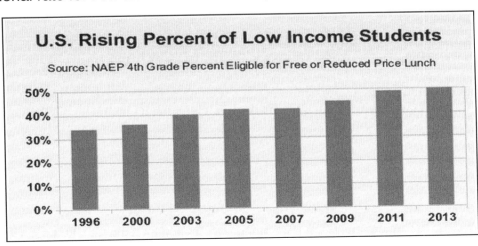

In addition, the percent of high poverty schools was much higher in 2012 than it was in 2000.

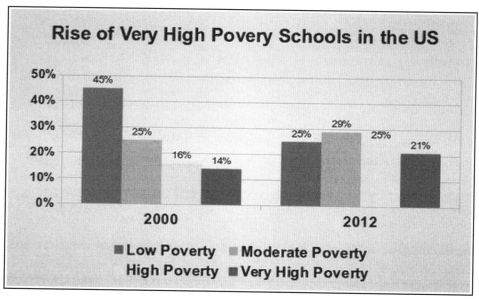

A low poverty school has 25% or less of students eligible for Free or Reduced Price Lunch (FRPL). A moderate poverty school has 26% to 50% of students eligible for FRPL. A high poverty school has 51% to 75% of students eligible for FRPL. A very high poverty school has more than 75% of students eligible for FRPL.

What is shocking about the above chart is that just 14 years ago, almost half of all public schools in the US were low poverty schools – with only 30% being High to Very High poverty schools. Today, only one in four schools are low poverty schools while the percent of high to very high poverty schools has skyrocketed to 46%. SOURCE: U.S. Department of Education, National Center for Education Statistics, Common Core of Data (CCD), "Public Elementary/Secondary School Universe Survey," 1999–2000 and 2011–12. See Digest of Education Statistics 2013, table 216.30.

We have more detailed information for the past 16 years for the State of Washington. The rise in childhood poverty in the US is mirrored in the State of Washington. In 2000, only 30% of the students were eligible for Free or Reduced Price Lunch. Today, almost 50% of all students in Washington State qualify for FRPL. Below is the rate for the past 16 years that OSPI has been posting this statistic as part of the OSPI Washington State Report Card.
http://reportcard.ospi.k12.wa.us/summary.aspx?year=2012-13

The child poverty rate in Washington State is currently at a shocking 46%.

How can this be?

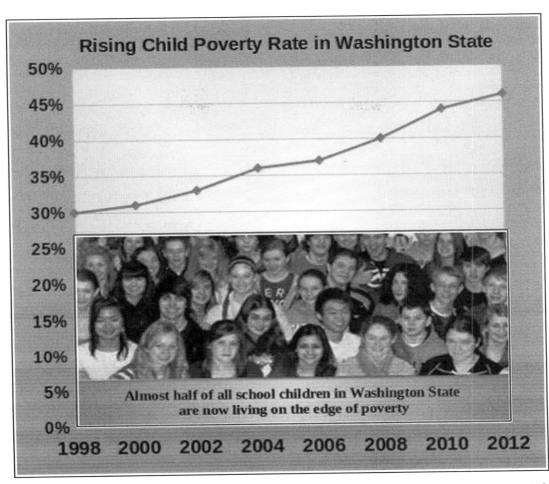

There are two components to this problem. First, Washington State has a total population of about 7 million people. Of these about 1 million are school age children and about 4 million are adults in the workforce. Unfortunately, Washington only has about 3 million jobs. This means the real unemployment rate in Washington State is about 25% - not 6% as reported in the billionaire controlled media.

In addition, of the 3 million jobs, about one million jobs have been cut from full time to part time jobs – which are cheaper for wealthy corporations as part time jobs do not require paying for health care and other benefits. The average family has one child. So one in four children live in extreme poverty because their parents do not have a job. Another one in four children live in borderline poverty because their parents only have part time jobs.

Thanks to billionaires corrupting our political system, deregulating the banks and crashing our economy, nearly half of the children in our State and in our naton are now living in or near poverty. Child poverty in turn is the leading cause of school failure. If we want kids to do better in school, it is time to make sure that their parents have a living wage full time job!

Comparing the Poverty Rate in the US to other Developed Countries

Due to the different values of different currencies and the difference in cost of living in different countries, there are many different ways to determine child poverty. But regardless of the method used, the United States comes in near the worst of all developed countries in the world in terms of child poverty.

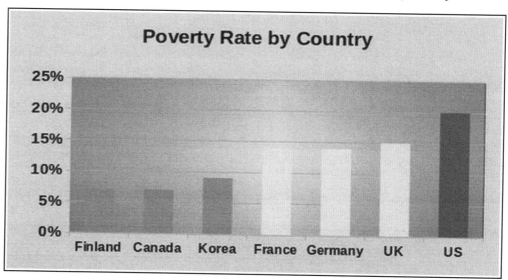

Because the official policy in the US since 1980 has been to focus on deregulation and "drill and kill" testing, rather than creating good paying jobs to reduce poverty, the poverty rate in the US is increasing faster in the US than in any developed country in the world. In November 2012, the US Census Bureau said more than 20% of American children lived in poverty up from 18% in 2009. Meanwhile, the poverty rate in so-called "socialist" countries like Finland is only 7%. This is a major reason students in Finland do so well in school. It is because their parents are also doing well at home.

https://en.wikipedia.org/wiki/Poverty_in_the_United_States#cite_note-Census:_U.S._Poverty_Rate_Spikes.2C_Nearly_50_Million_Americans_Affected-7

The National Center for Child Poverty concluded that the child poverty rate in the US is even higher putting it at 22% in 2010 and 24% in 2012.
http://www.nccp.org/

A 2013 UNICEF report ranked the U.S. as having the second highest relative child poverty rates in the developed world. UNICEF defines childhood poverty as living in a household where the family income is half of the national median income. Since the median income in the US is about $50,000 per year, this would mean a US household surviving on less than $25,000 per year. Below is the 2013 UNICEF childhood poverty rates of the world's richest countries. Using this measure, 23% of the children in the US are living in poverty. http://www.unicef-irc.org/publications/pdf/rc11_eng.pdf

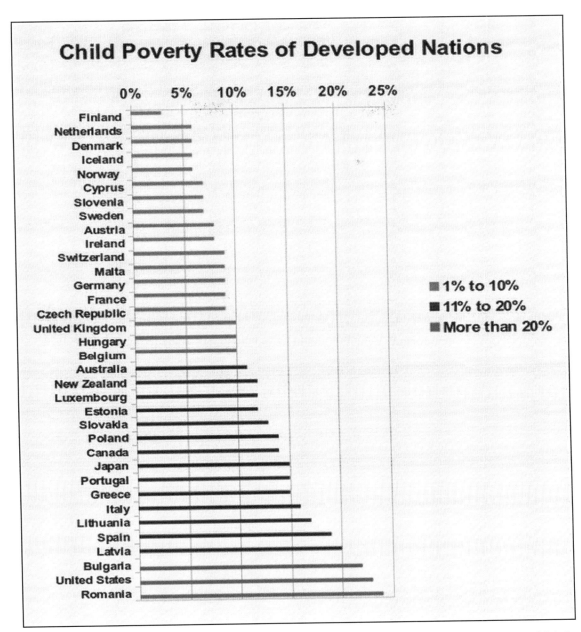

Why does the US have among the highest poverty rates in the world? Could it be because we spend more on wars and military than all other nations in the world combined? Could it be that we have unfair trade agreements that allow for the outsourcing of millions of jobs? Or is it because we simply have the most billionaires in the world? Or is it that we have the most corrupt political system in the world – one where billionaires are allowed to buy elections and bribe politicians who then give billions of dollars in tax breaks to the super rich who elected them?

How are US kids doing compared to other countries when controlled for poverty?

Now that we know where the US stands in the developed world in terms of poverty, let's see how this poverty rate affects our students scores on international tests. US Education Secretary Arne Duncan has been the lead spokesperson for the billionaires in their attempt to take over our public schools. Arne's claim to fame was his destruction of Chicago Public Schools before being given the job of destroying public schools all across the nation. He is the inventor and promoter of a $4.5 billion snake oil scam called Race To The Top. We will cover more of Arne's scams in the chapters on Common Core and Charter Schools. Here is one of Arne's most recent false statements: "Even with the modest increases in math and reading performance on the 2013 NAEP, US students are still well behind their peers in top-performing countries."

What Arne conveniently ignores is that the US has one of the highest poverty rates of any developed nation. When one adjusts for child poverty, the US is about even in most areas to other similar nations and is ahead of other countries in many areas. For example, despite the huge burden of poverty, even when not adjusted for child poverty, US students substantially outperform Finnish students in algebra. http://www.epi.org/publication/us-student-performance-testing/

This is remarkable as Finland has a child poverty rate that is one third of the poverty rate in the US. Finish students also get more experienced teachers and smaller class sizes than our students have in the US. In addition, all Finnish students receive three years of free preschool. Far from failing, US public schools are doing a remarkable job of preparing students compared to other nations. When Arne Duncan says our schools are failing our kids, he is simply wrong. It is Arne Duncan who is failing our kids by refusing to even discuss the issues of childhood poverty and skyrocketing class sizes.

To justify their campaign, ed reformers like Arne Duncan repeat, over and over again, that U.S. students are trailing far behind their peers in other nations, that U.S. public schools are failing. The claims are false. Two of the three major international tests—the Progress in International Reading Literacy Study and the Trends in International Math and Science Study—break down student scores according to the poverty rate in each school. The tests are given every five years. The most recent results (2006) showed that students in U.S. schools where the poverty rate was less than 10 percent ranked first in the world in reading, first in science, and third in math. When the poverty rate was 10 percent to 25 percent, U.S. students still ranked first in reading and science. But as the poverty rate rose still higher, US students ranked lower and lower.

Below is a chart showing international math test results for two states in the US where they are known – Massachusetts and Florida. Massachusetts has a poverty rate below the US average at 15% while Florida has a child poverty rate above the US average at 25%.

Take a close look at how each State would rank in the developed world if they were an independent nation. Massachusetts has international math scores near the highest in the developed world while Florida has among the lowest math scores in the developed world. The reason Florida is doing much worse than the rest of the nation is that it has been subjected to toxic testing and other billionaire Ed Reform scams for a longer period of time.

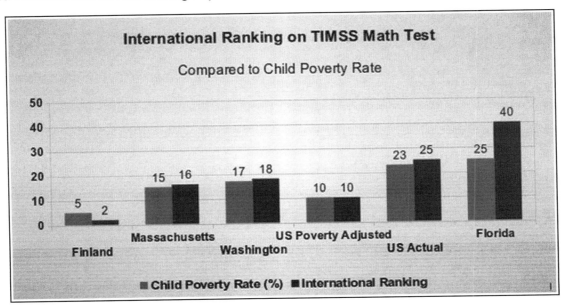

Sources: Child Poverty Rate from
http://nces.ed.gov/programs/digest/d13/tables/dt13_102.40.asp
International Test comparisons
http://phys.org/news/2013-01-poor-international-student.html

How are US Kids Really Doing Compared to Other Nations?

In 2013, Martin Carnoy with the Stanford Graduate School of Education and Richard Rothstein with the Economic Policy Institute produced a highly detailed study breaking down how different income levels of students would perform in the United States on various international tests. The authors provided extensive data confirming that "If U.S. adolescents had a social class distribution that was similar to the distribution in countries to which the United States is frequently compared, average reading scores in the United States would be higher than average reading scores in the similar post-industrial countries we examined (France, Germany, and the United Kingdom), and average math scores in the United States would be about the same as average math scores in similar post-industrial countries... This re-estimate would improve the U.S. place in the international ranking of all OECD countries, bringing the U.S. average score to sixth in reading and 13th in math." Source: Carnoy, Martin & Rothstein, Richard (January 2013) What Do International Tests Really Show About U.S. Student Performance? Economic Policy Institute, Washington DC.

One country that is doing much better than the US and everyone else, even one segregated by family income status is Finland. The authors state: "Great policy attention in recent years has been focused on the high average performance of adolescents in Finland. This attention may be justified, because both math and reading scores in Finland are higher for every social class group than in the United States."

Many have concluded that Finland must have better schools than the US. But it could also be that Finland has almost no child poverty and this has resulted in better scores on international tests. Finland takes better care of kids. Whatever it is, we should try to be more like Finland. The authors pointed out some of the advantages of low poverty noting, "Children whose parents read to them at home, whose health is good and can attend school regularly, who do not live in fear of crime and violence, who enjoy stable housing and continuous school attendance, whose parents' regular employment creates security, who are exposed to museums, libraries, music and art lessons, who travel outside their immediate neighborhoods, and who are surrounded by adults who model high educational achievement and attainment will, on average, achieve at higher levels than children without these educationally relevant advantages."

The authors also compared two low poverty states in the US, Massachusetts and Minnesota, to three other similar countries, the UK, France and Germany. The authors concluded: "Massachusetts and Minnesota outperform the three similar post-industrial countries, in some comparisons substantially." Nevertheless, under the insane standard of "No Child Left Behind," every public school in Massachusetts and Minnesota (and every other State in the US) are now considered "failing" schools! The problem is not public schools in the United States or public school teachers in the United States or public school students in the United States; it is childhood poverty in the United States. If we could only get billionaire tax evaders to pay their fair share of State and federal taxes, we could hire more people to be teachers and build schools which would greatly reduce poverty and thereby increase the achievement levels of all students in the US.

The PISA International Test was Deliberately Rigged in 2009 to Reduce the Scores of US Students

In analyzing the percentage of various income groups of US students taking an international math and reading high stakes test called the PISA test in 2009, the authors found a rather suspicious "sampling error." The authors stated:
"Forty percent of the PISA sample was drawn from schools where half or more of the students were eligible for free or reduced-price lunches. Only 32 percent of all U.S. students attended such schools in 2009–2010 when the PISA test was given. Sixteen percent of the PISA sample was drawn from schools where more than 75 percent of students are FRPL-eligible, yet fewer than half as many, 6 percent of U.S. high school students, actually attend schools that are so seriously impacted by concentrated poverty.

Likewise, students who attend schools where few students are FRPL-eligible, and whose scores tend, on average, to be higher, were undersampled. This oversampling of students who attend schools with high levels of poverty and undersampling of students from schools with less poverty results in artificially low PISA reports of national average scores." Put another way, the US Department of Education used a sample of very low income schools they knew would get lower test scores in an obvious attempt to rig the results so that they could report that US schools were doing worse than schools in other nations. All other nations submitted a more accurate sample of their student population. A few even used a sample of higher income students by having lower performing students not take the test. Why would Arne Duncan and his Department of Education rig the PISA test scores? Could it be because their real goal is not to help our kids but to destroy our schools so that they can reap billions in profits from privatizing them?

More Evidence of the Link Between Family Income and Test Scores
In addition to using misleading data on international test scores, the Nation at Risk reported used misleading data on the SAT test.

Another Nation At Risk False Claim: The Scholastic Aptitude Tests (SAT) demonstrate a virtually unbroken decline from 1963 to 1980.
Once again, the Nation at Risk authors deliberately ignored the known link between family income and test scores in order to deceive the American people into believing that schools in the US were getting worse. The SAT test is a very poor test that has never been shown to be related to college achievement or any other factor other than parental income. Nevertheless, the reason the SAT scores fell from 1963 to 1980 was due almost entirely to the fact that many more poor and middle class students took the test in 1980 than took the test in 1963. Because SAT test scores are directly related to family income, the scores in any given year are also directly related to the family income of those who took the test that year. A better way to judge the performance of schools would be to compare test takers of the past and present who were alike in class ranking. This is what researchers at the Sandia Laboratories did (Carson and others 1993). They selected a group of students from the 1990 SAT test takers who matched in gender and class ranking those students who took the test in 1975. When the researchers compared the two groups' average scores, the 1990 group outscored the 1975 group by 30 points.

There was an important study done by my former advisor at Washington State University, Dr. Donald Orlich. Professor Orlich has been providing research on this issue ever since I was an undergraduate – more than 30 years ago. He was right 30 years ago and he is even more right today. Here is the citation and link for his 2006 study: Test Scores, Poverty and Ethnicity, Orlich, Donald C. And Gifford, Glenn. WSU Summit on Public Education (2006)
http://www.cha.wa.gov/?q=files/Highstakestesting_poverty_ethnicity.pdf

Dr. Orlich states: "For the SAT, 97% of the variance ($r^2 = .97$) in test scores may be explained by family income of the test takers." Let's put this sentence in plain English. Variance or the correlation between one variable and another can run from 0% - which means a random or no relationship to 100% which means a direct one to one relationship. Due to the huge variation of children, there is almost nothing in child development research than has a variance of more than 50%. So an explained variance of 97% means that the only factor that influences SAT test scores is the family income of the test taker. Here is a graph of Dr. Orlich's study:

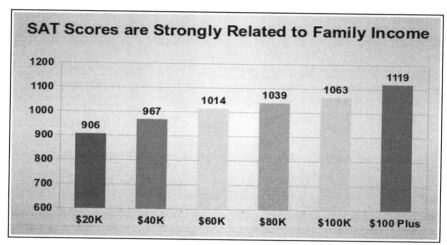

For students coming from families with an income of less than $20,000, the median score was about 900. For students coming from a median income family of under $40,000, the median total SAT score was under 1000. For students coming from extremely wealthy families, the median score was more than 1100. So imagine a college with a minimum SAT cutoff score of 1100. Nearly all of the applicants who qualify will come from very wealthy families. These are also the only families who can afford the skyrocketing college tuition rates.

SOURCE: College Board, College-Bound Seniors 2005: A Profile of SAT Program Test Takers. Retrieved from http://www.fairtest.org/nattest/SAT%20

Scoresn%202004%20Chart.pdf

The truth is that SAT scores – or any high stakes test scores – do not accurately measure what children know. Instead, they merely measure the wealth of a child's parents. But if one did want to raise scores on high stakes tests, the best way to do it would be to give the parents of low income children better jobs, give the family a home and give the children some food and a safe, local park to play in. The one real benefit of high stakes tests is that they create billions of dollars in profits for the scam artists that promote them. In the 1990s' these scam artists used the fake Nation at Risk report to create a multibillion dollar industry. We will therefore next look at the Rise of the Toxic Test Scammers.

1.2 Rise of the Toxic Test Scammers

> "We live in the most perilous time ever in the history of Public education. Powerful forces are arrayed together in A concerted effort to privatize our schools and dismantle The teaching profession." Diane Ravitch July 17 2014

In the previous section, we looked at the lies and deceptions in a scam report called "A Nation At Risk." In this section, we will look at some of the people involved in promoting high stakes testing as the fake "solution" to the fake "problems" claimed by the Nation At Risk report.

History of High States High Failure Rate Tests

The "theory" of Toxic High Stakes Testing education reform is that if school standards are raised (often called raising the bar), and students are tested often enough, students will work harder to jump over the higher bar. Thus, their achievement will go up— even if those kids are hungry and living in the back seat of a car! A second part of this theory is that students will be motivated to work harder if there is a high stakes standardized test they will have to pass at the end of the course. Neither of these claims has ever been supported by any scientific research on child development. Yet these claims are now being used to drive the education (or abuse) of 50 million students in the US. These claims are popular among the billionaires because they allow the super rich to ignore the fact that test scores are related to poverty. There is no need for the billionaires to worry about giving poor parents a job or giving poor kids a stable home. All they need to do is give low income kids more and harder tests. In fact, billionaires are blaming the victims of their concentration of wealth and power so that folks will be distracted from the fact that billionaires are robbing working families of a fair living.

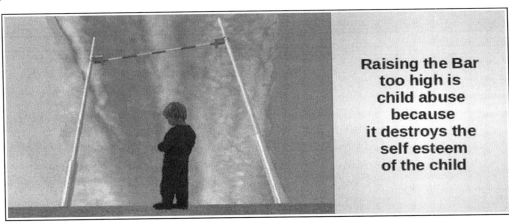

The Toxic Testing scam (also called Standards Based Education) is based on Pavlovian Punishment and Reward conditioning. But this theory applies more to training dogs than teaching children. So how did this theory of unattainable standards and high stakes tests come to take over all schools in the US? To understand how this happened, we need to look no further than one single person... Marc Tucker, President of a billionaire funded outfit called the National Center for Education and the Economy (NCEE).

Marc Tucker... The Godfather of Toxic High Stakes Testing

Marc Tucker has no degree in education and has never been a public school teacher. So why have his views on public schools taken over our entire nation? How was Marc able to promote Standard Based Education into what we now call Common Core State Standards (CCSS)? This summary is based on an article in Democrat and Chronicle, Rochester, New York, March 14, 1993.

Marc grew up in an affluent suburb of Boston Massachusetts called Newton where he attended high quality public schools. Unfortunately, according to Marc's brother, Roger, their mother had "several stays in mental hospitals." Because their father for some reason could not take care of the two boys, they were sent to foster homes and were "adopted by other families." Marc had a teacher who hosted a show on PBS in Boston. This lucky connection helped Marc obtain a job as a camera man for PBS in Boston in 1962 – where Marc worked until 1970.

Marc Tucker, The Godfather of Toxic High Stakes Tests, Explains why Kids Should be Tested until they drop.

In 1971, something very strange happened. Despite having no degree or background in Education, Tucker was hired to be the Assistant to the Executive Director of the Northwest Regional Education Laboratory (NW-REL) in Portland Oregon. NW-REL is a very strange outfit that on the surface claims to be a combination of school systems in five NW States (Washington, Oregon, Idaho, Montana and Alaska). In fact, according to the "About" page on the NW-REL website, it is one of ten regional education laboratories (RELs) that are all "sponsored by the Institute of Education Sciences (IES) at the U.S. Department of Education." According to the IES website, they are the "research arm of the US Department of Education."

So Marc was hired by the US Department of Education in 1971 for an educational research job he was certainly not qualified to do. Marc only worked at this position for a single year. However, since this group strongly supported Outcome Based Education (OBE) – which is based on Pavlovian Conditioning and Skinnerian Behavioralism – It is likely that this is where Marc picked up his regressive educational beliefs that he would later morph into an even more radical approach to education reform that he called Standards Based Education (SBE) – whereby a bunch of standards like Common Core were dumped on teachers from the top down based upon an irrational and overwhelming need to control others. It was also likely that at NW REL in 1971, Marc made connections with Washington State educators – connections he would later use to change education in Washington State and eventually in the entire nation.

In 1972, Marc moved to Washington DC where he became the Associate Director of the National Institute of Education, another arm of the US Department of Education. Marc stayed in this position until 1981. From 1981 to 1984, Tucker worked on a project at the billionaire funded Carnegie Corporation on how to use computers in education. He then created the Carnegie Forum on Education and the Economy in 1985. Keep in mind, this guy just has a college degree in Philosophy – not education or psychology or computers. But he was clearly advocating for a theory that is music to the ears of the billionaires who were backing him.

1986 Marc Tucker Writes "A Nation Prepared"
From 1985 until 1987, Tucker was the Executive Director of the Carnegie Forum on Education and the Economy. There Marc wrote a report called "A Nation Prepared" which was published in 1986 – in response to and three years after the fake report called "A Nation At Risk." Marc's 168 page report, "A Nation Prepared" recommended raising standards for students and teachers – raising the bar – and using high stakes tests to hold teachers and students accountable. It was the beginning of blaming teachers for the made up shortcomings of our public schools that were listed in the fake report "A Nation At Risk."

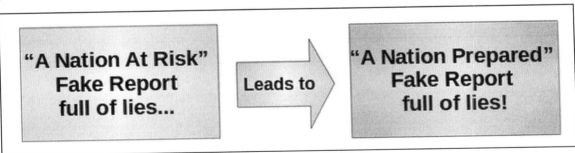

Billionaires and politicians naturally hailed "A Nation Prepared" as the holy grail of education reform and Marc Tucker became their new Messiah (or new Snake Oil Salesman depending on how wealthy you are).

In 1987, Tucker used funding from these billionaires to create a new group called the National Center for Education and the Economy (NCEE) to promote his report "A Nation Prepared." Not so coincidentally, Marc's new group had the same initials as the group that wrote "A Nation At Risk," the National Committee on Excellence in Education (NCEE).

It was therefore easy for folks to mistakenly assume that these were the same group and that "A Nation Prepared" was simply a follow up report to "A Nation At Risk". In fact, the two groups had similar agendas (raising the bar) and were backed by the same wealthy interests.

Here is how one reporter described NCEE:

"NCEE is the multimillion-dollar Gates Foundation-funded advocacy (read: "lobbying") group founded by Marc Tucker, the godfather of Common Core-style schemes and top-down control masquerading as "reform." He has dominated the D.C. education-lobbying scene since before Bill Clinton was in office. Tucker's NCEE is a 501(c)(3) nonprofit that crusades for ever-increasing federal involvement in every aspect of education while denying its brazen lobbying activities." Michelle Malkin, cnsnews.com April 4 2014

One group that bought into the nonsense pitched by Tucker in "A Nation Prepared" was the billionaire funded National Governors Association (NGA), the group that would later help draft the Common Core State Standards. Two governors in particular were thrilled with this report – Governor Bill Clinton in Arkansas and Governor Booth Gardner in Washington State. First, we will look at Booth's involvement in this scam – and then we will look at Bill's involvement.

1985 to 1993: Marc Tucker, Booth Gardner and the Failed Ed Reform Scam in Washington State

The Failed Ed Reform program in Washington State is important because it is the model Marc Tucker created for Washington State that would later be used as a model for national reform by Bush One, Bill Clinton, Bush Two and Barack Obama. So let's quickly look at what happened in Washington State in the 1980s and 1990s and how it failed.

In 1980, Washington was 11th in the nation in school funding. However, by 1990, it had plunged to 20th in the nation – despite doubling the local portion of school funding (called the levy lid) from 10% of total school funding to 20% of total school funding. Thus, as local property taxes went up, school funding went down. One reason for this was the billionaire takeover of government in Washington State in the 1980's. Billionaires like Bill Gates bought elections for their cronies in order to create tax breaks for billionaires. As more tax breaks were given to wealthy multinational corporations, taxes on everyone else went up even as school funding went down – all to pay for the billions in tax breaks for the rich.

Booth Gardner was the perfect example of wealthy people taking over politics in Washington State. He was the wealthy heir to the Weyerhaeuser fortune – which was one of the largest logging operation in Washington State and in the nation. Booth's family made their fortune by wiping out Old Growth Forests. From 1985 to 1993, Booth Gardner was Governor of the State of Washington. During this time, his primary accomplishment was to advance **"standards based education and standardized testing"** in Washington State. However, in 2005, a terminally ill Booth Gardner apologized for pushing toxic tests saying he was wrong and that he had been misinformed. He therefore supported eliminating the test he created - the high stakes test called the WASL.

"I was wrong.
I am willing to admit I was wrong.
I was naïve. I was new to the subject,
And time has shown me
That there is a better way.
A single test should not be
All that matters in a students education."

Booth Gardner to the Seattle Times
December 9 2005

History of the Schools for the 21st Century $21 Million Scam
In early 1985, Booth Gardner was taken in by the magical claims of the Ed Reform Messiah/ Snake Oil Salesman Marc Tucker. Booth allowed Marc to craft an Ed Reform scam called "Schools for the 21st Century." In February, 1987, Marc Tucker addressed the Washington State legislature advocating for this scam. In May 1987, the legislature passed SSB 5479 establishing "Schools for the 21st Century." The initial cost of this program was set at $21 million dollars to do a pilot program in several school districts in Washington State to see if "Standards Based Education" reform really worked.

Later in 1987, Marc started NCEE to be the lead consultant for this new program. Naturally Marc was paid to be the "expert consultant" for this project, "Schools for the 21st Century" which later became a model for Bush One's America 2000 Ed Reform program and Clinton's Goals 2000 Ed Reform program (which were all essentially the same thing). So it is fair to say that the entire national Ed Reform scam got its start in Washington State. Our state owes the nation an apology for the "Standards Based Education" disaster that has since been inflicted on 50 million children.

From 1990 to 1991, Booth Gardner was Chairperson of the National Governors Association and thus worked closely with Bush One and Marc Tucker in creation of the America 2000 Corporate led Ed Reform program. In 1991, Washington State Governor Booth Gardner formed the Governor's Council on Education Reform and Funding. (GCERF). On October 4, 1991, GCERF signed a deal "giving exclusive reference to Marc Tucker, and the New Standards Project (NSP) — another NCEE program." Put in simpler terms, Booth Gardner handed education reform in Washington State over to NSP and NCEE – both of which were ran by Marc Tucker. Governor Gardner and Washington Superintendent of Public Instruction Judith Billings were on the governing board of NSP.
http://www.learn-usa.com/education_transformation/er020.htm

While working on this project, Tucker recommended a school restructuring plan for Washington State that in 1992 became Washington State Senate Bill 5953 – creating a new student assessment and school accountability system in Washington State. On February 2, 1992, Booth Gardner signed a Memorandum of Understanding with Marc Tucker to oversee the "design of 'break the mold' public schools" in Washington State. In 1993, this was supplemented with Washington State Bill number 1209 – yet another ed reform bill. The lead sponsor on this bill was Randy Dorn – the current Superintendent of Washington State Schools. The assessments known as the Washington Assessment of Student Learning or WASL – was to begin between 1996 to 1997 and passing the WASL was to be required for graduation (high stakes testing). Having to pass the WASL to graduate never actually happened, but that is besides the point.

The Billionaire Funded Brainwashing Begins... "Good Ideas are At Work Out There in the State of Washington"
On July 9, 1991, according to an article in the Seattle Times, President Bush announced a new national educational initiative called America 2000:

"President Bush yesterday said he would ask corporate leaders to raise between $150 million and $200 million to finance a school program based on Gardner's Schools for the 21st Century..."Good ideas are at work out there in the state of Washington", Bush said at the White House. Bush's national schools campaign called America 2000 was announced in April."

About America 2000, President Bush said, "We will unleash America's creative genius to invent and establish a New Generation of American Schools...A number of excellent projects and inspired initiatives already point the way. These include Washington State's Schools for the 21st Century. The mission is to help create schools that will reach to National Education Goals and the World Class Standards."

Below is a picture of Washington Governor Booth Gardner, President George Bush and Arkansas Governor Bill Clinton at the National Governors Education Summit. What Bush and Clinton apparently failed to realize is that the Ed Reform pilot program they were both promoting was actually failing badly in Washington State. http://govinfo.library.unt.edu/negp/reports/negp30.pdf

September 27 1989 Washington Governor Booth Gardner with President George Bush And Arkansas Governor Bill Clinton at the National Governors Education Summit.

How did the "Schools for the 21st Century" Experiment Turn Out?
A group called Citizens United for a Responsible Education (CURE Washington) wrote a report about how the pilot program turned out. The group said they were exposing "a human experiment, which may have damaged the academic future of 52,000 children who participated in the "Schools for the 21st Century Program." The 52,000 children whose academic futures were damaged were attending 111 elementary schools in Washington State in 27 school districts. The pilot school districts were allowed to change (required to change) to Standards Based Assessments and programs from 1987 through 1994 (when the pilot program money ran out).

Most of the pilot programs continued with the experiment when both the pilot program elementary schools and the normal elementary schools took the 4th grade WASL test in 1996. Since the experiment had been going on since 1987, the 4th grade kids subjected to "more rigorous standards" had been forced to endure these standards their entire school career and the teachers using these "raise the bar" standards had been drilling kids with these standards for about 9 years before the WASL test was finally given. Meanwhile, the kids in the normal schools were doing normal stuff like reading stories, drawing in picture books and hanging out with their friends on the monkey bars at recess.

So what were the results? How did the Drill and Kill Ed Reform kids compare to the 4 R kids (Reading, Riting, Rithmetic and Recess). Here is a quote from the study: "The statewide percentiles of students meeting or exceeding the standards were: math, 21%; reading, 47%; writing, 42%. These are the kids who haven't had ten years of the harder questions. Compare those scores with the "21st Century school" Drill and Kill students who met or exceeded the same standard: math, 15%; reading, 38%; writing, 36%. **The (Drill and Kill) students who were trained with harder questions performed 5-to10 percentage points worse on standardized tests."** http://www.curewashington.org/archives/371

This is important. So here is a graph of the above 1996 WASL data for readers who are more visual learners:

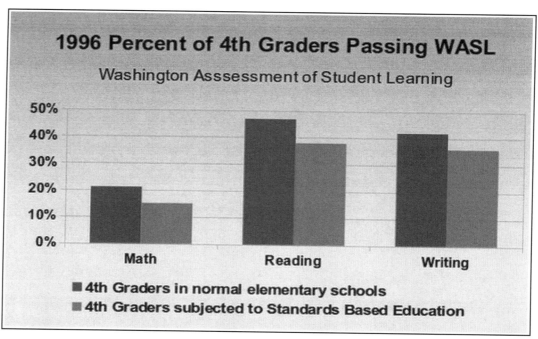

Shocking as it may seem, the project administrators for the 21st Century Schools project lied to the legislature about the progress of kids in the pilot schools. In 1993, they told the legislators that the pilot schools were doing much better than they had done in the past.

Again in 1995, the State Board of Education also lied to the legislature and reported to the Washington State legislature that the "Kids in Schools for the 21st Century Project were performing above the academic level of traditional schools." However, on an independent elementary school test called the Comprehensive Test of Basic Skills (CTBS), the kids in the pilot elementary schools were doing much worse than they had done in the past. In short, after 9 long years of subjecting elementary school children to a much higher bar, the students inflicted with this chronic punishment model of education did significantly worse on the very test intended to measure how much better they would do. Even after years of practice taking high stakes tests, kids exposed to drill and kill education did worse rather than better.

There are many other studies that confirm that small children do not handle high stakes testing and high stress schooling very well. So why did the high stakes movement continue and even expand after Marc Tucker's disastrous failure with over 50,000 students in Washington State and after wasting nearly $21 million dollars? The answer is because Standards Based Education aka Common Core has never been about helping students learn. It has always been about using weapons of mass deception to convince the public into allowing private corporations to take over our public schools.

There are even more shocking problems with the WASL – which we will get back to in a moment. First, we need to update ourselves in the relationship between Marc Tucker and the Clintons and what was happening at the national level in the 1990s while thousands of school children were being severely harmed by Marc Tuckers High Stakes testing scam in Washington State.

Marc Tucker, Bill Clinton and the Dear Hillary Letter
In 1983, Bill Clinton became Governor of Arkansas where he was Governor until 1992. During this time, his wife Hillary served on the Board of Directors of a wealthy billionaire owned corporation called **Walmart** from 1986 to 1992. Hillary also made hundreds of thousands of dollars working for the law firm that represented the Walmart billionaires – the Waltons. Thus, Hillary became good friends with the Walton family billionaires who have since worked with another billionaire Bill Gates to push for a corporate takeover of our public schools.

In 1983, Hillary used the "Nation At Risk" study as an excuse to create a task force called the "Arkansas Educational Standards Committee" to reform Arkansas's education system. Like nearly all other corporate ed reformers, Hillary does not have a degree in Education and has never taught in a public school.

In 1984, Hillary Clinton supposedly wrote her own response to A Nation At Risk. She called it the "Education Reform Report." In this report, she called for higher standards and statewide teacher testing across the State of Arkansas.

Hillary Clinton was on the Board of Directors for Walmart – a group of billionaires promoting the privatization of public schools.

To pay for the Teacher Testing, Bill Clinton passed a sales tax increase of $180 million – the largest tax increase in the history of Arkansas. This money did not go to hiring more teachers. Instead, it went to private corporations that tested students and teachers. Many of the recommendations in Hillary's Education Reform report in 1984 made it into the Tucker "A Nation Prepared" report in 1986 - which also focused on blaming teachers for poor student test scores. Some have claimed that the reason the two reports were so similar is that Bill Clinton had hired Marc Tucker to restructure the Arkansas education system in 1984 and **the Hillary Clinton report had actually been ghost written by Marc Tucker.**
http://www.learn-usa.com/relevant_to_et/ctd01.htm

In any case, it was not surprising that Marc Tucker hired Hillary Clinton from 1990 to 1991 paying her a total of $101,630 to do essentially nothing (while she was still making hundreds of thousands of dollars working for the Walmart law firm). Hillary did not really need the money, but it would look good on her resume. In fact, **Hillary Clinton was also on the Board of Directors for Marc Tucker's group NCEE.**

1992 Marc Tucker Writes the Infamous Dear Hillary Letter
In November 1992, 18 days after the election of Bill Clinton, Marc Tucker wrote the famous 18 page "Dear Hillary" letter in which he outlined his plan for a federal/corporate takeover of our nation's public schools and his desire to **control the education of US citizens "from the cradle to the grave".**

The plan basically involved getting rid of local school boards and having all schools comply with a common core of national standards. Naturally, these new standards would require high stakes tests based on the new national standards to determine the fate of students, teachers and schools.

The infamous "Dear Hillary letter" is posted at
http://www.eagleforum.org/educate/marc_tucker/marc_tucker_letter.html.

> **NATIONAL CENTER ON EDUCATION AND THE ECONOMY**
>
> ---
>
> BOARD OF TRUSTEES
>
> MARIO M. CUOMO
> Honorary Chair
>
> 11 November 1992
>
> Hillary Clinton
> The Governor's Mansion
> 1800 Canter Street
> Little Rock, AR 72206
>
> Dear Hillary:
>
> Marc Tucker's
> Dear Hillary Letter
> Summarizing his plan
> For a private takeover
> Of our nation's public schools.
>
> I still cannot believe you won. But utter delight that you did pervades all the circles in which I move. I met last Wednesday in David Rockefeller's office with him, John Sculley, Dave Barram and David Haselkorn. It was a great celebration. Both John and David R. were more expansive than I have ever seen them — literally radiating happiness. My own view and theirs is that this country has

Note from the above image that another famous politician, Mario Cuomo, the former governor of New York was heavily involved in the Ed Reform scam and his son Andrew Cuomo is also heavily involved in the Ed Reform scam. It pays for politicians to align themselves with the billionaire funded Ed Reform team.

As a result of Marc's connection to the Clintons and as a result of a new report he wrote called America's Choice, Marc was able to inflict his Standards Based Education nonsense on the children of the following nine states in the 1990s: Indiana, Kentucky, Maine, New York, North Carolina, Oregon, Texas, Vermont and Washington. Keep in mind that this is a guy with no background at all in educational research, child development or teaching who has the arrogance to design the schools for the entire nation!

1996 Terry Bergeson Becomes the New School Superintendent in Washington State

If Marc Tucker was the person who designed the plans for education reform in Washington State, Terry Bergeson is the person who built the ed reform house and eventually burned it to the ground. I know the following is going to sound crazy. But when you think about it, Terry Bergeson's amazing rise to stardom is no harder to believe that Marc Tucker rise from a stage hand at PBS in Boston to designing education reform for the entire United States. I am including this information about Terry Bergeson as it is one more example of the kind of crazy people that have run education reform and the American public schools over a cliff in the past 30 years. You really need to know what kind of nuts and charlatans we have promoting education reform in the US. Much of the information about Terry Bergeson and her staff comes from this website: http://www.thefactsaboutwaedreform.org/

From 1988 to 1996, Judith Billings was the Superintendent of Public Instruction in Washington State. Judith was therefore the head of public schools throughout the Marc Tucker experiment. But in 1994, Judith discovered she had AIDS. She therefore decided not to run for re-election.

This left the Superintendent spot open for Terry Bergeson, who in 1993 had been appointed by the legislature to run the Commission on Student Learning – the group responsible for developing the WASL assessments with Marc Tucker. Like Marc Tucker, Terry Bergeson was an extremely unusual and "lucky" person. She had gotten her PhD from the University of Washington in 1982. Her thesis paper was called "A Comparison of Two Methods of Improving Math Attitudes in Intermediate Teachers and Counselors."

Terry's PHD thesis is important because she used the strange ideas in her paper as the foundation for creating a very unusual WASL test. The title of her thesis sounds innocent until you look at the two methods Terry chose to improve math attitudes. Terry set out to prove that a treatment based on something called the "Carkhuff Human Resource Development skills" was superior to the "Eclectic Counseling Curriculum." See page two of the following link.
http://thefactsaboutedreform.homestead.com/The_Unveiling_Part_1.pdf

Terry based her PhD thesis on the strange ideas of a person named Robert Carkhuff. So, to understand what Terry is claiming, we need to take a look at the extremely controversial work of Robert Carkhuff, a New Age Spiritual leader who claims that folks who follow his teachings are able to reach the "Fifth Dimension."

Here is a quote from one of Carkhuff's books called "The New Science of Possibilities": "God is The Great Montessori Teacher: He co-processes only with those of us who use His most precious gift—the intellect with which He has endowed us. We came to know God only when we came to generate human and phenomenal possibilities, for God is in the phenomena He presents to us."

Like billionaires, Carkhuff divides people into groups from low performers to high performers. The low performers include those who are physically sick or just plain poor. Like the billionaires who support his work, Carkhuff blames the poor for the fact that they are poor while he compliments the rich for having "God given intellectual potential." The reason we need assessments and endless testing is to separate the smart humans from the dumb ones. The smart humans are "pure of mind, pure of body and pure of spirit."

What is perhaps most disturbing about Carkhuff is that he advocates for a top down model in which the "smarter" rich people set the standards for the dumber poor people. Rather than a democratic decision making model in which all ideas are given respect, he advocates an elitist framework in which only ideas aligned to his model are worthwhile. Carkhuff conveniently ignores the responsibility of the community in creating poverty conditions or in creating better schools or learning conditions. His is a "pull yourself up by your boot straps" approach to education. It is easier for the wealthy to pull themselves up by their boot straps than for the poor – who may not even have boots – much less boot straps.

We warned you that things were going to get a little strange. Carkhuff has kind of a cult following – or did in the 1970s and 1980s. Two things put a damper on his rise to fame. First, he apparently got booted out of medical school for trying to brain wash other interns at the medical school. Second, his book was "peer reviewed" in 1973 by more normal psychologists who concluded that he had misquoted some sources and his theories lacked any scientific basis. In short, Carkhuff was a bit off his rocker. So it seems odd that Terry Bergeson, who had the responsibility for insuring the future of one million school children in Washington State, had fallen for this snake oil salesman with her 1982 thesis.

Before writing her PhD thesis promoting Carkhuff's ideas about math attitudes, Terry was a school counselor in Tacoma for about 8 years. While in Tacoma, and despite having very little actual teaching experience, Terry was elected to be the chair of the National Education Association Women's Caucus. In 1981, Terry was elected to be Vice President of the Washington Education Association and in 1985, she was elected to be President of the Washington Education Association. This rapid rise to power is almost as surprising as writing her PHD thesis promoting the theories of a cult leader.

As head of all public schools in Washington State, Terry Bergeson (left) gave Robert Carkhuff (right) Over One Million Dollars to help design the Washington State High Stakes Test called the WASL. Eventually, the WASL was abandoned and Terry Bergeson was voted out of office.

In 1992, Terry ran for Superintendent of Public Instruction against Judith Billings and lost. But in 1993, Terry managed to be appointed to a prime job as Executive Director of the Washington Commission on Student Learning. In this role, Terry led the development of new learning standards and a new assessment and accountability system as part of Washington State's educational reform law.

Bergeson ran for State Superintendent again in 1996 and won. This gave Terry control over awarding contracts to develop WASL assessments. She wasted no time in giving Dr. Carkhuff contracts totaling over one million dollars to serve as a consultant in designing the WASL test. These grants were for $400,000 on October 1, 1998 and $667,500 on May 1 2000. The money came from a federal grant so at least Washington State tax payers did not have to foot this bill. Carkhuff did next to nothing to earn this windfall profit.
http://thefactsaboutedreform.homestead.com/TheUnveilingoftheBergesonAdministration_Part2.pdf

After Terry became Superintendent, she ordered 500 copies of Carkhuff's books with a State contract and began passing them out to attendees at educational conferences. Washington State also paid Carkhuff about $75,000 for a few educational videos that were never produced.

In addition, Bergeson hired two of Carkhuff's followers – Shirley McCune and Andrew Griffin – both appointed as Assistant Superintendents. Shirley McCune was so into Carkhuff that she co-wrote a couple of books with him. Shirley also wrote a book based on his teachings called "The Light Shall Set You Free." This book went into more detail about the "interconnectedness between humanity and the universe." The book "channeled" an ascended master named Kuthumi who came to earth from the "stars and seventh dimensional frequency as the Ambassador of Love and Light." Back in the 1990s, Kuthumi told Shirley the "date of entry for the Fifth Dimension is scheduled for the year 2012 and that beginning in 2012 "we will have an entirely new curriculum that we must master." (See page 7 of Shirley McCune's book, The Light Shall Set You Free, 1996).

According to the Ascended Master Kathumi, "The date of entry for the Fifth Dimension is Scheduled for the year 2012. Beginning in 2012, We will have an entirely new curriculum That we must master."

From Shirley McCune's book, "The Light Shall Set You Free."

Given that the Common Core Curriculum started coming out in about 2012, and that it is sending both teachers and students and parents to a whole new level of mind altering frustration, perhaps there is something to this ascended master stuff after all!

The Temple as a Tribute to God the Creator of All

In 2002, a mom in Washington State named Nancy Vernon found out about all of this mystical stuff going on at the Superintendent of Public Instruction's Office. Nancy began writing a series of reports about the strange leaders of education in Washington State. On page 6 of her second report, Nancy Vernon begins writing about her discovery of a yellow 14 inch notepad that was in a series of OSPI documents she was reviewing. The yellow note pad described a plan to create a "Temple." The purpose of the temple was as a "Tribute to God, the Creator of All." The temple was to have four underground passages and be built in the desert. The massive temple would hold all knowledge and control everything. This temple in the desert sounds a lot like the new NSA mass surveillance data center in Utah – which actually was built to hold data on every student in the US from "cradle to grave".

Nancy Vernon eventually uncovered the million dollars given to Dr. Carkhuff and filed a complaint with the Governor and the State Attorney General over misuse of funds. She accused Terry of using her new age religion to brainwash the children of Washington State. Amazingly, even 15 years later, some of Dr. Carkhuff's theories and materials are still on the Washington State OSPI website. Personally, I think his New Age theories are not that much stranger than the claims of Marc Tucker that we can raise the learning of children simply by subjecting them to a never ending series of high stakes tests. With that in mind, let's get back to the real problems with high stakes tests.

1996 Problems with WASL Extremely High Failure Rates

You may recall that only 20% of the Fourth Graders in Washington State were able to pass the 4th Grade Math WASL in 1996. This meant that 80% of the Fourth Graders were labeled as failures. This was pretty upsetting to tens of thousands of parents in Washington State who thought their kids were "at Grade Level." In fact, their kids were normal and at Grade level – but Grade level was no longer good enough for the billionaire funded Ed Reformers. It was also upsetting to thousands of elementary school teachers in Washington State who also thought their students were "at grade level."

The fact was that the WASL test was simply too hard and the standards the test was based on were too high. Things only got worse when the 7th Grade WASL was put into action in 1997.

1997 First Review of the WASL.. The "Assessment from Hell"
Teachers students and parents were all upset about the 7th Grade math WASL. Here is a comment from an upset middle school math teacher, Arthur Hu:

"When I first saw the 1997 sample math problems, I was alarmed upon comparing the problems to the published grade level academic learning requirements. Judging which bag of marbles was more likely to have a white marble requires high school level proportions, comparing fractions and probability. There was a series of scales which was to be used to order blocks, which would be a complex logic problem that I was not even taught how to solve up to my master's degree at MIT. We just need a BASIC FREAKING EDUCATION. ARGH." http://hu1st.blogspot.com/2009/01/perfect-wasl-test-score-scam.html

A young girl was so worried about her WASL score that she asked her mom: "If I fail the WASL, will you still love me?"

In 2000, a Washington State newspaper published a drawing by a 4th Grade boy who was asked to draw his impression of the WASL. The boy drew a picture of a monster. The 4th Grader was partially correct. There was a monster who fed on the fear of children. But it wasn't the WASL test. It was a billionaire who was out to destroy our public schools.
http://www.spokesman.com/photos/2008/jun/04/49311/

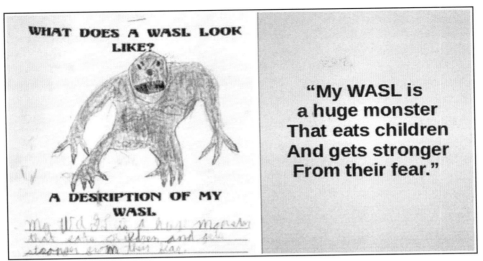

1996 Achieve Incorporated is Formed to "Demand More from Students"

Meanwhile, back in the other Washington (DC), in March 1996, the nation's governors and top corporate leaders came together at the National Education Summit. They decided to create a new kind of quasi-government-corporate organization called Achieve, Incorporated. It was led by six governors and six corporate leaders. But the Governors were mere figureheads to fool the public.

In the old days, this merger of government and corporations was called "Corporate Fascism." It is now called Education Reform. Frank Shrontz, the head of the Boeing Military Machine was one of the six corporate leaders appointed to head this new organization. On March 28, 1996, The Washington Post published "Corporations Vow to Favor States That Boost Academic Standards." This article stated: "Most of the nation's governors and more than 40 corporate chiefs approved the idea at their national education summit here to put pressure on states to demand more from students."

Achieve INC did not have a single teacher on their staff when they started in 1996. Achieve INC still does not have a single teacher on their staff or national board in 2015. Achieve's website in 1997 confirmed its commitment on the part of businesses to increase the pressure on students. To this end, Achieve vowed to establish national academic standards and achievement levels. Businesses such as Boeing vowed to not locate in states considered to have unacceptably low standards and test scores. However, as least for Boeing, what actually determined where they located was the amount of tax breaks they could rob from the public schools – not the grades of students in those schools. Despite receiving billions in tax breaks from Washington State, Boeing has outsourced tens of thousands of jobs to sweat shops South Carolina – ignoring the fact that test scores and standards in South Carolina were much lower than they are in Washington State. Boeing is a wealthy corporation that made more than $20 billion in 2014. Rather than demanding more from our students, we ought to be demanding that Boeing pays their fair share of State and federal taxes.

Terry Bergeson Moves to San Francisco and Gambles Nonprofit Away in the Stock Market

Despite spending hundreds of millions of dollars, the WASL high stakes test was an utter disaster in Washington State. This led to Terry Bergeson being defeated in the 2008 election by Randy Dorn – who promised to replace the WASL with something less costly and time consuming. After being defeated, Terry moved to San Francisco and took a job as the Executive Director of an educational non-profit called San Francisco School Alliance. The San Francisco School Alliance is another strange billionaire funded organization that develops strategic partnerships and advocates for policies to ensure that each student has access to world-class learning opportunities – and that each young person is career and college ready.

Unfortunately, in 2012, Terry quickly got caught up in a complex "grant" money laundering scheme. "We had people that were in positions of trust that were taking money, who were diverting this money for personal use," one of the School Alliance officials said. "This is one of the worst kinds of corruption." San Francisco School Alliance took between $5.5 to $6.3 million and charged about $1.2 million in administrative fees. They even lost about $250,000 in the stock market.

"We are mortified at the thought that trusted employees would conceive of such a scheme to divert funds from the children for whom they are intended," said another official. A call to Terry Bergeson, executive director of the alliance, was not immediately returned. While the other two nonprofits involved in the scandal have returned more than $4 million, San Francisco School Alliance has not returned any money yet, according to one of the investigators. The investigation is ongoing.

http://www.huffingtonpost.com/2013/05/14/san-francisco-schools-embezzlement-scheme_n_3274916.html

Sadly, the WASL was just the beginning of the high stakes testing scam. There was an entire industry being created just to measure student achievement. Of course what they were really measuring was family income.

What is Next?

In the next section, we will look at the history of a little understood national test called NAEP – the National Assessment of Educational Progress. It is essential to understand NAEP because the NAEP "proficiency" standard is now being misused to destroy the lives of millions of students all across America. After we review NAEP, we will look at the disaster called No Child Left Behind and explain how this corrupt law is actually a severe form of child abuse.

1.3 NAEP Proficiency... How High Stakes Tests were Designed to Fail

In this article, we will show that the real purpose of high stakes tests is to create unfair tests that are 'designed to fail" the vast majority of students who take them in order to turn the public against our public schools. This scam was done by changing the passing standard on a national test called NAEP from "Basic" which originally meant "At Grade Level" to "Proficient" which originally meant "Above Grade Level." This simple change meant that instead of 70% of all students passing the NAEP test, only 30% of students would pass the test. No longer was a student being "at grade level" good enough. Instead, every student needed to be "above grade level."

We will also show that in order to prevent students from passing these new high stakes tests, called SBAC and PARCC, their creators specifically chose NAEP "hard" questions that they knew in advance that the vast majority of students would not be able to answer. The bar on the new high stakes tests has been raised so high that the new tests are deliberately designed to fail and destroy the lives of over 20 million children across America of two thirds of the 30 million kids schedule to take these fake tests in 2015.

It is vital to understand the NAEP Proficiency Standard and how NAEP "hard questions" were chosen as these are the basis of all of the current high stakes tests. These grossly unfair scams are the reason that two thirds of the students in New York State failed their Common Core tests. They are the reason two thirds of the students in Washington and 27 other States will fail their SBAC and PARCC tests in 2015. They are the reason nine out of ten GED students are currently failing their GED exams.

The unfair NAEP Proficiency standard and the despicable use of NAEP "hard" questions are two of the main "weapons of mass deception" being used by billionaires to destroy and take over our public schools. So it is very important to understand how these two scams work.

NAEP is the National Assessment of Educational Progress (also known as the Nations Report Card)

The NAEP test was first administered in 1969. Federal law specifies that NAEP is voluntary for every student, school, school district, and state. However, federal law also requires all states that receive federal education funds to participate in NAEP reading and mathematics assessments at fourth and eighth grades. So NAEP is not really voluntary. NAEP results were initially used for two main purposes: monitoring trends in student achievement over time and making state-by-state comparisons. Of course, what NAEP really measures, like all high stakes tests, is the income level of parents in each of the states. It is important to note than not all students in each state take the NAEP test. Also not all grades take the NAEP test. It is only administered in Grades 4, 8 and 12. In general, the test is considered reliable for grades 4 and 8, but not for grade 12. Because 12th graders know that the results of this test "do not count" towards their graduation, 12th graders tend to fail to answer questions that they actually know the answers to. High School seniors get so fed up with taking tests, that they tend to blow off any test that does not go on their permanent record.

Because **student test scores vary too much** from day to day and year to year to be an accurate measurement of any individual student, individual teacher or individual school achievement, NAEP school and student level results are never reported. At least that was how the NAEP test was sold when it first started in 1969. Today, NAEP test results, questions and standards are being used for an entirely different purpose – a purpose that they were never intended to serve. They are being used as an excuse to destroy our kids and our public schools. This is because **the new Common Core high stakes tests, called SBAC and PARCC, are nothing more than NAEP tests with a thin coating of lip stick.**

NAEP Terminology... The Problem with Arbitrarily Defining the word "Proficiency"

The most controversial part of high stakes testing and the NAEP test is called the cut score. This is an arbitrarily set number which determines what percentage of students will pass a test and what percentage of students will fail a test.

All High Stakes Tests are based on a Strange and arbitrary concept called the "Cut Score"		
Below the Cut Score You Fail.	**The Cut Score**	**Above the Cut Score You Pass!**

A common cut score is that a student needs to get 70% of the questions correct to pass the test. Ironically, even the legislators who demand a higher cut score often are unable to pass tests they insisted on administering to our children.

It is important to understand that almost everything involving Common Core and other high stakes tests is completely arbitrary. The new tests are designed to fail two thirds of all children. How they are designed to fail is by manipulating the term "proficiency." At the bottom of this scam is the misuse of "Cutoff Scores" also called "Cut Scores". All one needs to do to increase the percentage of kids who fail a high stakes test is to increase the cut score.

In the old days, before the billionaire takeover, teachers used a term called Mastery. The idea was that all students could pass the test. If they scored above 70% on a test, then they were at grade level and had achieved Mastery of the subject. Now, according to NAEP, there are four levels, **Below Basic, Basic, Proficient and Advanced.** Cut score are set so that very few kids can achieve a score of Proficient or Advanced. Basic used to be considered as passing because kids were at Grade level. Now Basic is defined as failing. Moreover, nearly all tests were teacher-created not billionaire-created.

How Billionaires Misuse Cut Off Scores to create a Designed to Fail Test
The usage of arbitrarily defined levels such as "proficiency," which can mean almost anything, has been rejected by nearly everyone who understands the scientific method, including the National Academy of Sciences, the National Academy of Education, the Center for Research in Evaluation, and Student Standards and Testing. Unfortunately, most politicians and most parents do not understand the scientific method. Thus, there is a great deal of confusion about terms such as proficiency - which is greatly worsened by the current focus on "test mania." For example, in the 1995 Trends in International Mathematics and Science Study, or TIMSS, assessment, American 4th graders finished third in the world among 26 participating nations in science, but the NAEP science results from the same year stated that only 31 percent of US students were "proficient or better." How can our students be among the best in the world in science, yet only 31% of them are "proficient" on the NAEP test? It all has to do with how NAEP defines the word "proficient." We will therefore look at what the term "Proficient" actually mean. http://www.aasa.org/SchoolAdministratorArticle.aspx?id=5096

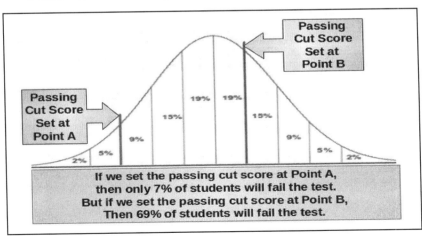

Weapons of Mass Deception

How Billionaires Misused the term Proficient

Achievement on NAEP tests is reported using four levels of cut scores: Below Basic, Basic, Proficient and Advanced. We will now look at how NAEP defines what each of these terms mean.

Below Basic (also known as Level 1) is a student who is below grade level in a particular subject. In normal school language, this would be a student who would get a D or an F. The cut scores for this group are arbitrarily set at about 30% to 40% of all students. This is extremely controversial and has led to the misleading claim that "40% of all students in the US are "failing." In fact, rarely do 40% of any group of students fail any particular course. More commonly, about 10% of students fail any given course. Below is a graph showing the 2005 Grade 8 Math NAEP scores for a few states.

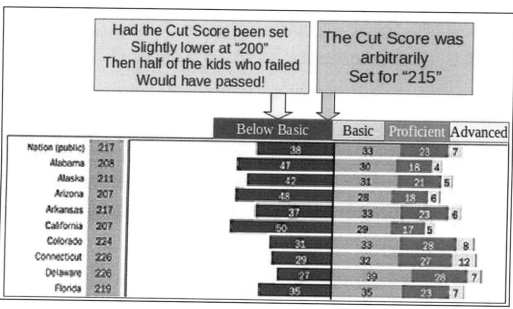

You can see that in some states, like California, half of the students were "Below Basic" while in Colorado, only 31 percent were below basic. The average score in California was 207 and the average score in Colorado was 224. Put another way, for every ten questions the Colorado students answered correctly, the California students answered nine of those same questions correctly. With about 50 math questions on the test, the Colorado "Basic" students got about 20 correct and the California students got about 18 correct. The dividing line in the table above or the cut score was 215. However, if the cut score had been lowered a mere ten percent to 200, **allowing 2 more wrong answers, then the failure rate would have been cut in half**. Less than 10% of the kids in Colorado would have failed the test and only 20% of the kids in California would have failed the test. The key fact to understand is that **the percentage of kids who fail the NAEP test – or any other high stakes test - is not determined by the kids. It is determined by the person who sets the Cut Score.**

Since the designers of the NAEP test set the cut score so that 40% would fail, then 40% of the students failed. What is ironic about this is that international tests have placed US students as Number One in the world on Algebra tests! The problem is not with US kids, it is with the setting of the cut scores of the NAEP test. The billionaires want you to believe our kids are failing so they can take over our public schools. **Any test that is designed to fail 40% to 70% of the students that take it is simply an unfair test.**

Basic (also known as Level 2) means partial mastery of a subject in that a student has learned most but not all of the NAEP standards for their grade. In normal language, this is **a student who is at "grade level"** and would get a passing letter grade of C. The cut score for this group is arbitrarily set for about 30% to 40% of all students. This translates into an actual score of 260 out of 500 for 8th grade Math. Thus, by design, 70% of all students will get either a C, D or F on the NAEP test. While Basic would be good enough to pass any subject or any grade in school during the past 100 years, Basic is not good enough for the billionaires pushing Common Core. Instead, the billionaires insist on a standard that no group of students in any nation has ever achieved... Namely that "All students must be proficient." This is why 70% of all students will fail Common Core tests. It is because **the test is designed to fail 70% of all students.**

Proficient (also known as Level 3) means almost complete mastery of a subject in that a student has learned nearly all of the NAEP (or Common Core) standards for that grade. In normal school language, this is a student who would get a letter grade of B or A. The cut score for this group is arbitrarily set for about 20% of all students. This translates into an actual score of 300 out of 500 for the NAEP 8th grade Math test. Even though US students are among the top performing students in the world on Algebra tests, only 20% to 30% of them will be rated as proficient on the NEAP or Common Core tests because that is how the test cut scores were set. **The NAEP Cut Scores were set so that anyone other than a B or A student will fail the test.**

Advanced (also known as Level 4) means complete mastery of a subject in that a student has learned all of the NAEP standards for that grade and is in the top 10% of all students. In normal school language, this is a student who would certainly get a letter grade of A+. The cut score for this group is arbitrarily set for about 10% of all students. This translates into an actual score of 300 out of 500 for 4th grade and 480 out of 500 for 8th grade.

> Diane Ravitch, a person who used to serve on the NAEP board explain NAEP's four levels of student performance this way:
> "**Advanced** is truly superb performance, like getting an A+.
> **Proficient** is akin to a solid A.
> **Basic** is akin to a B or C performance. Good but not good enough.
> **Below Basic** is where we really need to worry and get kids the help they need."

The problem with No Child Left Behind (passed by Bush 2) and Race to the Top (passed by Obama) is that they both require "all students to be proficient." This is like requiring that all students get either a B or an A in school. Any school with a single C or D student is a failing school. **This is why every school in every state is a failing school under No Child Left Untested.** The law was designed to label every school in every state to be a failure. Put another way, it is like requiring that "all students be above average." This is magical thinking which only happens in imaginary places like Lake Woebegone.

Who set these ridiculously high cut scores?
The NAGB (or National Assessment Governing Board, a group that oversees the NAEP) subcontracts achievement level setting to a private contractor called the American College Testing, Inc. (ACT). ACT set cut scores so high that very few students scored at or above the proficient level and few students scored at or above the Advanced level. **Act, Inc and the Act Foundation have received almost $2 million from the Gates Foundation** to "implement the Rigor and Readiness initiative." ACT is hardly an unbiased source. Previously, the NAGB had outsourced the creation of math items to the College Board, makers of the SAT and AP exams and exam questions. The College Board (aka College Entrance Examination Board) is also private corporation that has received millions of dollars from the Gates Foundation. The same scam artists who ran ACT and the College Board would later go on to write a precursor to the Common Core called the American Diploma Project (ADP) and then write the Common Core standards and tests. This is why there is such a close relationship between the NAEP tests and terms and the Common Core tests and terms.

The National Governors Association, which owns the copyright on Common Core had been reluctant to reveal the members of the Standards Work Groups. However, in July 2009, it did so. The members of the "work" groups chiefly represented three agencies: Achieve, ACT, and College Board. Here is a quote from the NGA: "The initiative is being jointly led by the NGA Center and CCSSO [Council of State School Officers] in partnership with Achieve, Inc, ACT and the College Board." NAEP and CCSS were written by essentially the same group!

No private agency should be allowed to set cut scores for all US children. One reason why parents in New York refused to accept the results of the Common Core PARCC test was that they correctly believed it was not reasonable to give students a test where 70% of the students failed the test. Parents might be willing to believe that 20% of students are failures. But they will never believe that 70% of students are failures. Instead, they will rightly conclude the problem is not with their child, the problem is with the test.

How do State Proficiency Standards Compare to the NAEP Proficiency Standard?

Recall that on 8th Grade math, a NAEP score of 260 is "Basic" or "At Grade Level" and a NAEP score of 300 is "Proficient." NAEP defines "At Grade Level" and "Proficient" as being two different things. However, for the past 100 years, nearly all States have defined the words "proficient" and being "At Grade Level" as the same thing! This change in the meaning of the word "Proficient" is behind the Common Core scam. It is therefore not surprising that nearly all States have learning standards set at "Basic" or "At Grade Level." The following chart and graph compare the various State Proficiency Scales to the NAEP Basic and Proficiency Scale for 8th grade math.

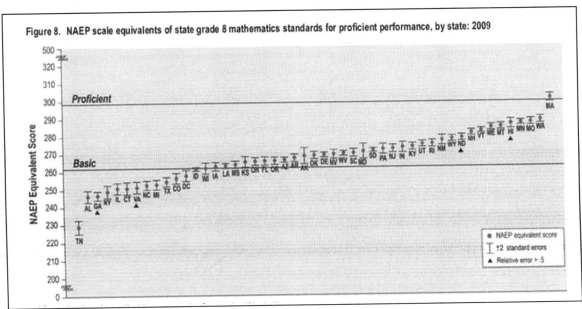

Source: Mapping State Proficiency Standards onto the NAEP Scales
http://nces.ed.gov/nationsreportcard/pdf/studies/2011458.pdf

In grade 8 mathematics, 12 of 49 states included in the analysis set standards that were lower than the Basic performance on NAEP, 36 were in the NAEP Basic range, and one in the Proficient range. 33 States properly viewed "Proficiency" as being at a "Basic" level of competency or being a student being "At Grade Level." An average 8th Grade Math score of 260 to 270 was considered good enough to pass to the next grade and thus 70% or more of all students were allowed to pass to the next grade and/or graduate from high school. There were 11 States that allowed an even lower score of 240 to 250 to be considered "Proficient" or passing their State's high stakes 8th Grade math test. Only one State (Tennessee) allowed an extremely low score of 230 to be labeled "Proficient." Only one State (Massachusetts) required a score of 300 to be labeled "Proficient."

NAEP Test Scores are related to the Income Level of the Parents

NAEP scores show a clear relationship to the poverty level of different States. The NAEP scores for 4th and 8th Graders showing that the poorest kids score much worse on the NAEP test than the richest kids. The poor kids got a 250 on the NAEP 8th Grade test while the rich kids got a 275. Like all other high stakes tests, what NAEP is really measuring is the income of the parents. The following chart are States listed in the order of child poverty. States with the highest child poverty rates (red bars) also have the lowest NAEP test scores (green bars).

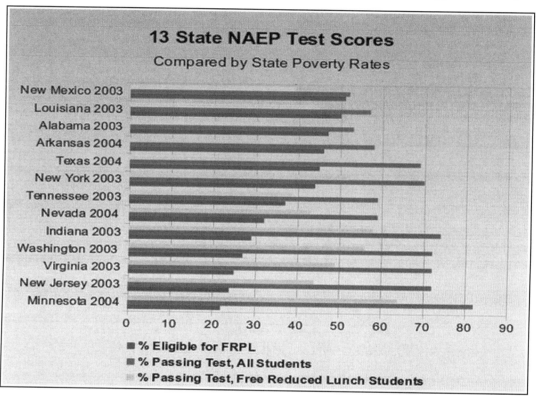

NAEP 2003 Scores 8th Grade Math Test, using At or Above Basic as a Passing Score. If billionaires really wanted to increase student test scores, they should focus on reducing the childhood poverty rate by making sure that every parent had a good job and every child had a stable home and adequate food.

Our kids are actually doing much better on math than past generations

The billionaire controlled media has issued a lot of false claims that "our schools are failing." This is a lie. In fact, the test scores of American students have been rising consistently for the past 30 years. For example, the National Assessment of Educational Progress Long Term Trend test has been administered in the US since the 1970s. For the past 20 years, the NAEP trend assessment (also called the NAEP LTT) has used nearly the same framework and the same test questions. It is therefore the closest thing we have to an "apples to apples" comparison.

The average score for 13 year olds (8th graders) was 265 in 1978. It rose to 273 by 1998. It is currently at 285. Since 10 points on the NAEP math test scale is a rise of about one grade level, 13 year old students in the US today have math skills that are about one full grade level above 13 year olds in 1998 and about two full grade levels above 13 year olds in 1978.

In other words, an 8th Grader today performs about as well on the NAEP math test as a 10th grader did in 1978. Clearly students are doing better in math today than they were doing 20 years ago. But you would never know it from the billionaire controlled media. Source: NAEP Nation Report Card
http://nationsreportcard.gov/ltt_2012/age13m.aspx

NAEP 8th Grade Math Scores have increased gradually

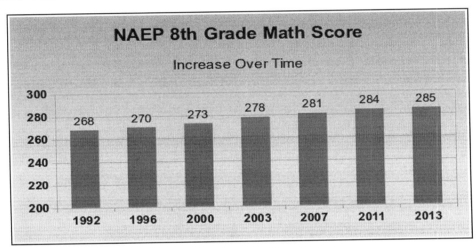

How many students would pass if every State changed to the NAEP/Common Core Definition of Proficiency?
We can tell this simply by comparing the NAEP Basic and Proficiency ratios for the past several years. The percent of 4th Graders who would have "passed the NAEP Math test" if the standard was set for "NAEP Basic" or "At Grade Level" has been about 82% for the past several years. However, **the percent of 4th graders who "pass the NAEP Math test" if the standard is set at "NAEP Proficient" is only about 40%.** Therefore, the percentage of students who fail the CCSS test will be about 40% higher than the percent of students who failed previous non-CCSS high stakes tests.
http://www.nationsreportcard.gov/reading_math_2013/files/Results_Appendix_Math.pdf

The switch to the "NAEP CCSS Proficiency Standard" instead of the "NAEP Basic At Grade Level" Standard will harm poor students much more than it will harm wealthy students. Using "NAEP Basic" as a passing grade, 73% of 4th Grade students eligible for Free or Reduced Lunch passed the NEAP test and 93% of those not eligible for Free or Reduced Lunch passed the test – a difference of 20%.

Using "NAEP Proficient" as a passing grade, only 25% of students eligible for Free or Reduced Lunch would pass the test while 60% of those not eligible for free and reduced lunch would still pass the test – a difference of 35%. Therefore switching to the NEAP CCSS Proficiency standard for a passing score will disproportionally harm low income 4th Grade students.

The 8th grade math test shows a similar effect. The percent of 8th Graders who "passed the NAEP Math test" if the standard was set for "NAEP Basic" or At Grade Level has been about 75% for the past several years. However, the percent of 8th graders who "pass the NAEP Math test" **if the standard was set at "NAEP Proficient" was only about 35%** for the past several years. Therefore, the percentage of students who fail the CCSS test will be about 40% higher than the percent of students who passed previous non-CCSS high stakes tests.

Using "NAEP Basic" as a passing grade, 60% of 8th Grade students eligible for Free or Reduced Lunch passed the NEAP test and 86% of those not eligible passed the test – a difference of 26%. However, using "NAEP Proficient" as a passing grade, only 20% of 8th Grade students eligible for Free or Reduced Lunch would pass the test while 50% of those not eligible for free and reduced lunch would still pass the test – a difference of 30%. Therefore switching to the NEAP CCSS Proficiency standard to define a passing score will disproportionally harm low income 8th Grade students. Below is a graph of the above data.

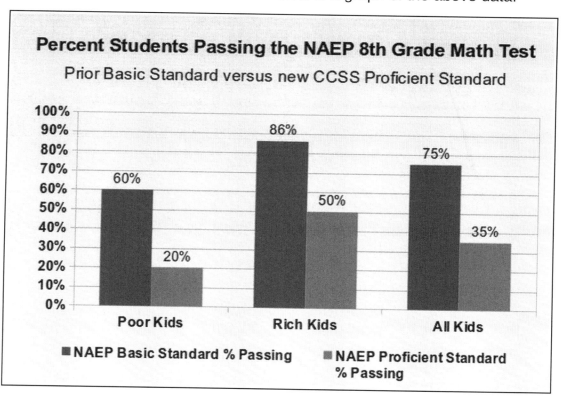

It should therefore come as no surprise that in New York State after 2 years of using Common Core/NEAP Proficient Cut Scores, the average pass rate of their new CCSS high stakes test was only 35%. The test was designed so that only 35% of students could pass it. Similarly, on November 17, 2014, the SBAC CCSS high stakes test scam artists released their cut scores for the 2015 SBAC test that will be taken by millions of students in 17 States around the nation in 2015. (Apparently 5 of the 22 SBAC States will not be using the SBAC test in 2015).

Here is a quote from their press release: "**Smarter Balanced estimates that the percentage of students who would have scored "Level 3 or higher" in math ranged from 32 percent in Grade 8 to 39 percent in Grade 3. See the charts below for further details.**"
http://www.smarterbalanced.org/news/smarter-balanced-states-approve-achievement-level-recommendations/

Note that the percent pass rate predicted by the SBAC scam artists is nearly identical to the pass rate for using the NEAP Proficiency standard. We will look at actual test items shortly to better understand how this scam works. Here is the chart that came with the SBAC press release:

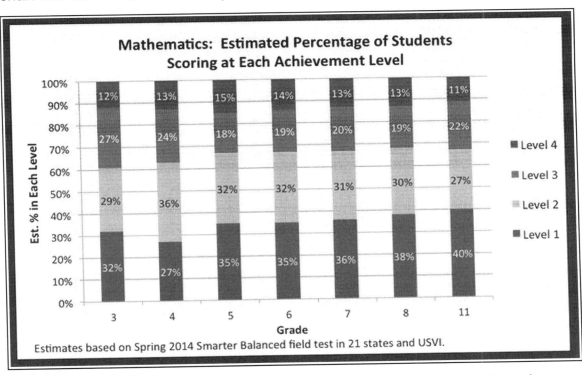

Only one third of all students will pass the 2015 Common Core SBAC Math test. The following is a more understandable chart showing the percent of students who will pass the 2015 SBAC test at various grade levels.

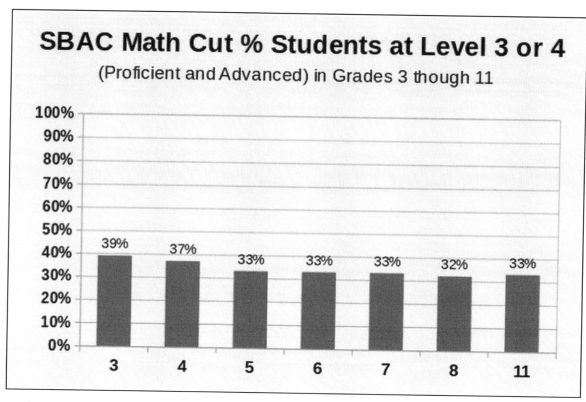

Only 4 in 10 students will pass the 2015 Common Core SBAC English Test.

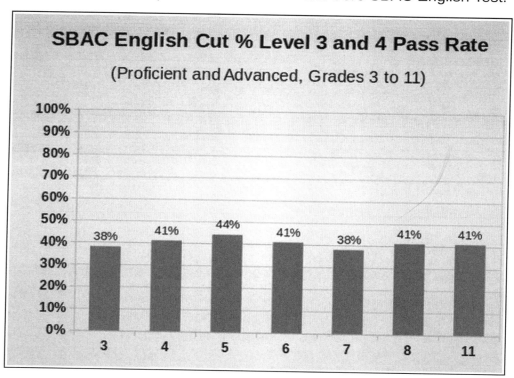

Why Common Core tests are much worse than the prior High Stakes Tests

Common Core and the tests connected to it will artificially cause test scores to collapse. Common Core standards and Common Core tests (SBAC and PARCC) will label many more children as "failures" who are not failures at all. Most students, and especially poor students, will be stigmatized by "designed to fail" tests aligned with an absurd standard of proficiency (aligned with NAEP proficiency, which is equivalent to an A).

How do we solve this confusion about the term Proficient?

Some have suggested changing the word "Basic" to "At Grade Level" so that more people would understand that NAEP Basic actually means a passing grade. This would automatically raise the percentage of passing students so that about 70% of all students would pass. However, we would still be left with deeply flawed tests that measure the income level of the parents of a student rather than the actual ability of the student. The real solution is to understand that high stakes tests are harmful to students because they do not accurately measure what a student knows or can do. We simply need to **eliminate all high stakes tests** including not only Common Core tests, but also the NAEP test, the SAT Test, the ACT test, the AP tests and the entire extremely corrupt and dishonest high stakes testing industry. Since billionaires currently control our elections, it is doubtful that we can get rid of all high stakes tests in the near future. Another alternative would be to insist on "fair standards" for high stakes tests. This would include setting the cut score for Advanced so that at least 10% of all students could get a score of Advanced or A. The cut score for Proficient or B should be set so that at least 30% of all students could get a B or an A. The cut score for Basic or At Grade Level should be set so that at least 90% of all students could get a C or passing grade. This would mean that only 10% of all students would have to suffer the embarrassment and shame of being labeled "failing students" and in need of remedial assistance.

Drill and Kill Fake Tests... All kids must score above average

In Lake Woebegone, all kids may be above average. But in the real world, it is not statistically possible for all kids to be above average. Thus, high stakes tests are designed to fail.

How NEAP was Transformed into SBAC and PARCC

While we will look at the history of Common Core standards in the next chapter, we will look at the two Common Core high stakes tests, SBAC and PARCC here. This is because these two tests were adapted from the NAEP tests.

SBAC supposedly stands for the Smarter Balanced Assessment Consortium. In fact, it can be more accurately thought of as the **Scam Betrayal Against Children Test.** While the marketing department of the billionaires like to call us to call this the Smarter Balanced test, we will simply call it the SBAC test. SBAC is one of two options for the Common Core High Stakes Test. The other is PARCC (see below). SBAC is a computerized "adaptive" test meaning that if a student gets a question correct, the test changes and the next question is harder. Thus, there is no way to statistically or scientifically determine its reliability and/or validity. In addition, it is supposedly based on Common Core national standards. However, there is no evidence that it actually is based on anything other than maximizing corporate profits while failing as many students as possible.

PARCC supposedly stands for the Partnership for Assessment of Readiness for College and Careers test. In fact, it can be more accurately described as the **Pretty Awful and Ridiculous Common Core** Test. This is an awful test that has already failed 60% of the students in Kentucky and 70% of the students in New York. **A multinational corporation called Pearson is the sole vendor for PARCC which is currently being used as the official Common Core High Stakes test in 13 states.** PARCC is being used in States that wanted a lower cost test than the SBAC tests and States that understood the insanity of trying to analyze a computerized adaptive test. In fact, both tests were so horribly designed that there is little difference between them. They were both deliberately designed to fail as many kids as possible.

Despite the fact that both of these tests basically copied the NAEP test, Arne Duncan gave private corporations $360 million in federal funds to develop these two tests.

General Design Flaws of the SBAC Adaptive Test

The chief difference between the two tests is that he SBAC test is an "adaptive" test while PARCC is not. With PARCC, all students receive about the same types of questions. Thus, the number of correct answers is relevant. However, "adaptive" means that if a student gets the first few answers on the test right, the computer adapts and gives the student progressively harder questions until the computer finds questions that the student misses. While this may seem like a good idea, it is actually horrible for students in that there is no way for any student to feel a sense of mastery and accomplishment by getting most of the questions right. Therefore it lowers the self esteem of all students.

Equally important, there is no way to statistically and/or scientifically analyze individual questions to determine if they are fair questions – or even to know what percent of students would get the question correct – since not all students are given the same questions!

There is a basic principle of science that conclusions require the limiting of variables. Since the SBAC test has over 42,000 possible questions given in an infinitely large number of possible combinations, child development researchers cannot analyze SBAC questions the way we can analyze NAEP questions or even PARCC questions (both of which are traditional "fixed question" tests). Even if one supports Common Core, at the very least Washington State should dump the SBAC test and use the PARCC test – and then release the results of the correct percentage for every PARCC question. This will allow researchers to determine which PARCC questions are fair questions and which are not.

A final drawback of adaptive tests is that many students have figured out how to game the test. If they deliberately miss the first two questions, then their remaining questions are much easier and they end up getting a higher total score on the test. None of this matters to the billionaires. All that matters is to create a test that is impossible for parents to understand and impossible for researchers to analyze. If either parents or researchers were ever able to figure out what was going on, they would realize that the test was simply an unfair test and demand that the whole process be terminated.

Looking at Individual Test Questions to Understand How SBAC and PARCC Can Know in Advance How Many Students will fail their tests

We will next look at individual test questions to better understand how high stakes tests can be constructed to pass or fail whatever percentage of students the creators of the test want to fail. With the SBAC and PARCC math tests, increasing the failure rate is done by increasing the number of "hard" questions. NAEP math questions have been studied for more than 20 years. We therefore know in advance what percent of students can answer any particular math question! To better understand the relationship between Common Core High Stakes tests and the NAEP test, we will compare some actual math questions from both tests.

How difficult are NAEP Questions?

In addition to understanding NAEP basic versus proficiency ratings, it is important for parents to understand that NAEP questions are statistically divided into three groups, Easy, Medium and Hard. The reason this is important is because how billionaires make tests harder is simply by reducing the number of NAEP medium math questions on the SBAC and PARCC test and **increasing the number of NAEP hard math questions.**

The makers of the SBAC and PARCC and GED tests claim that they have to ask harder questions in order to measure the new Common Core standards. But this claim is not true. With any standard, one can ask an easy, a medium or a hard question depending on the wording of the question. Once you understand and can tell the difference between Easy, Medium and Hard questions, it becomes much easier to understand how billionaires are pulling off the SBAC and PARCC high failure" rate tests! So let's review the differences between NAEP Easy, Medium and Hard math questions.

Easy Questions mean that about three in four students answered the question correctly on past tests. Put another way, Basic, Proficient and Advanced students can answer these "Easy" questions, but Below Basic students generally do not.

Medium Questions mean that about half of all students can answer the question correctly. Put another way, Proficient and Advanced students can answer these questions, but Basic and Below Basic students generally do not.

Hard Questions mean that about one in four students can answer the question correctly. Put another way, Advanced students can answer these questions, but Proficient, Basic and Below Basic students generally do not.

Here is the most shocking fact of all: If the goal of Common Core was to identify NAEP "proficient" students, then the average question on a Common Core test (SBAC and PARCC) would be similar to the Medium questions on the NAEP test. But as we will show below, the average question on the Common Core test is nearly identical to the NAEP hard questions! Therefore, those who pass Common Core tests are not merely proficient, they are NAEP advanced students!

Put another way, while NAEP tests are unfair and label too many students as failures, the Common Core tests are much more unfair, and label even more students has failures. Every trick in the book has been used to get as many students as possible to fail the Common Core tests. That is why parents, teachers and students say that "Common Core tests are designed to fail."

Comparing the 2014 SBAC math test to the 2013 NEAP Math Test
Now that we have a better understanding of the NAEP test terminology, we will compare a new SBAC Common Core high stakes 8th Grade Math Test, to the national NAEP 8th Grade Math test. The reason we have chosen SBAC is that this test was "field tested" in many school districts in Washington State in May 2014 (including my 8th grade daughter's school district). The SBAC test will be required for all school districts in Washington State and 17 other States in the coming year. Unlike the other Common Core test, called PARCC, which has been tested and failed 60% of all students in Kentucky and 70% of all students in New York, there is currently very little information on the difficulty of SBAC test questions. We will therefore attempt to objectively assess the difficulty of SBAC 8th grade math test questions by comparing them to National Assessment of Educational Progress (NAEP) 8th grade math test questions.

Many parents and teachers mistakenly assume that Common Core tests are much harder than former high stakes tests because Common Core standards are mistakenly believed to be higher than prior standards. But as we will show here, Common Core tests have almost nothing to do with Common Core standards. Instead, Common Core has been used as an excuse to artificially make tests that are much harder to pass. And that is the real purpose of Common Core... to change to unfair tests that are 'designed to fail" the vast majority of students who take them. The NAEP test is the most well researched math test in the US. It has been offered annually to millions of students across the US since the later 1970s. As we described above, its math question database is divided by grade into three types of questions called Easy Medium and Hard questions. The Easy questions can be answered by about three in four students, the Medium questions can be answered by about half of the students and the Hard questions can be answered by less than one in four students. The NAEP database allows us to determine the approximate level of difficulty of the new SBAC Common Core math questions.

Step One... Get your feet wet by taking the SBAC 8th Grade Sample Test
Studies have shown that people think they can answer many more math questions than they can really answer and that people think math questions are easier than they actually are. So it is important at this point that you go online and complete the SBAC 8th grade practice math test above – without looking at the answer sheet first. Then write down your actual score before reading the next article. Keep in mind that you need to get about 18 of the 25 questions correct in order to pass the test. So you are not allowed to miss more than 7 questions. When you are done, write down how many you got right. After you have finished the SBAC one hour sample test, and have recorded your score, you are ready to read the next section. The SBAC 8th Grade sample test and its answer sheet are available online at http://sbac.portal.airast.org/practice-test/

Click on **Student Interface and Training Tests**. Then click OK. Then click Sign In. Then select the 8th Grade. Then click Yes. Then click State G8 Math Practice Test. Then click Select. Then click Yes, Start My Test.

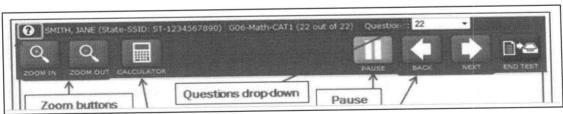

Then click **Begin Test Now.** There are 25 Questions in the SBAC Grade 8 Practice Math Test. The scoring guides for all of the SBAC practice tests are at the following link. http://sbac.portal.airast.org/practice-test/resources/#scoring

The 8th Grade Practice Test and Scoring Guide is also available as a PDF at the following link in case you want to print it out and give it to your legislators.
http://sbac.portal.airast.org/wp-content/uploads/2013/07/Grade8Math.pdf

This 28 page PDF includes all 25 questions and their correct answers. However, it is not as difficult as the online version because one does not have to learn how to manipulate the SBAC interface with the PDF version. Even my rather smart 8th grade daughter had problems with the SBAC computer interface. Another major difference between the Sample test and the real test is that the real test is "adaptive" meaning that if you get a correct answer to one question, the next question is harder. Finally, the Sample test is only 25 questions and takes about one hour to complete while the real test has more than 50 NAEP Hard questions and takes two hours for 8th grade students to complete – if they are able to complete it at all.

If a person designed a building to fail and the building failed and several people were killed, wouldn't this person be sent to prison – or at least lose their license for professional negligence? But Pearson has created a test designed to fail struggling students and destroys the lives of a half million young adults seeking a GED every year and they are rewarded with billions of dollars in government contracts and millions of dollars in grants from the Gates Foundation.

Step 2: Examine the NEAP 8th Grade Math Test Questions

Now that you have completed the SBAC 8th Grade Math Practice Test, we will compare these questions to the 25 hardest NEAP 8th Grade Math questions by going to the new NAEP Home page. http://nationsreportcard.gov/

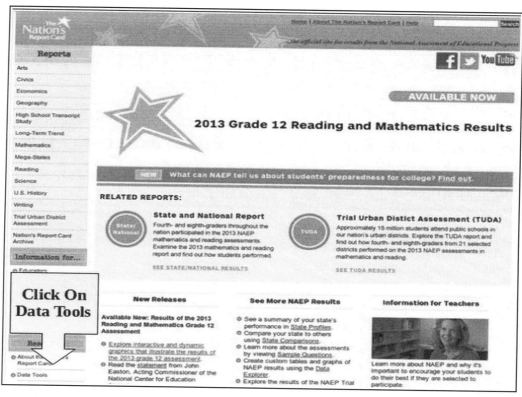

Then click on **Data Tools** in the left side menu.

Then click on **Question Tool.** Then click on **Questions Tool** again. Then click on **Main NAEP Mathematics**. For Grade, uncheck Grades 4 and 12 to only select Grade 8 questions. For Type select Multiple and Short. For Difficulty, uncheck Easy and Medium to only select Hard questions. (You can later check just the Easy or Medium box to better understand what NAEP Easy and Medium questions look like).

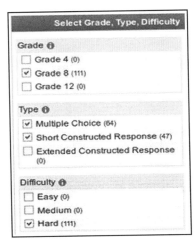

This will place 111 Hard 8th grade questions in the Workspace.

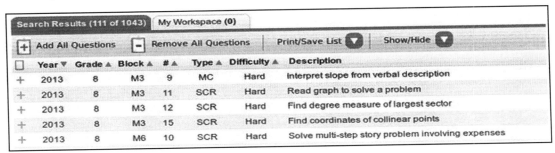

Click on **Add All Questions.** This will transfer all 111 questions to My Workspace. Then click on **My Workspace.**

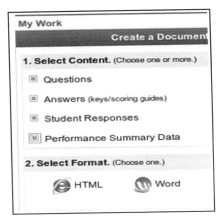

Select all four boxes in Select Content. Then click on **HTML** to view the questions in a web browser. We will examine these 111 questions and look for the **25 most difficult questions on this NAEP test** (questions in which less than 25% of students were able to answer the question correctly) in order to make comparisons to the 25 SBAC questions in order to assess the difficulty of the SBAC questions and predict the percentage of 8th graders that will be able to pass the SBAC test.

The first NAEP 8th grade "hard" question is about the slope of a function.

Q1: In which of the following equations does the value of y increase by 6 units when x increases by 2 units?

a) $y = 3x$ b) $y = 4x$ c) $y = 6x$ d) $y = 4x + 2$ e) $y = 6x + 2$

The correct answer is A. **Only 20% of all US 8th graders were able to get this question correct.** One might claim that American 8th graders do poorly in Algebra. However, as we noted previously, they do better on Algebra tests than almost any nation on earth. It is likely that less than 20% of 8th graders around the world could answer this question. Thus, algebra slope questions are just hard questions for 8th graders because "slope" is an abstract concept. If you look at the next 24 NAEP "hard" questions, you will see that only one of them involves slope. By contrast, out of the 25 SBAC 8th grade math questions, 5 of them deal with slope. This has nothing to do with Common Core standards because Common Core does not emphasis the slope of the function any differently than the current standards. **So what is the purpose of having 5 out of the 25 SBAC questions involve slope?** Could it be that the authors of the SBAC test know that only 20% of all US 8th graders can answer slope questions – and thus they can create a test which 80% of students will fail these five slope questions?

Of the 25 questions on the SBAC 8th Grade Practice Math test, 15 of them were "NAEP" hard questions, leaving only 10 questions that were NAEP medium and easy questions that the majority of 8th graders could answer correctly.

We have also analyzed the recently released NY PARCC test questions and found a similar disturbing trend... Both SBAC and PARCC appear to have deliberately chose NAEP "hard" questions in order to increase the failure rates on these new Common Core tests. If you go back and look at NAEP "Medium" and "Easy" questions, you will see that they tend to be different from typical SBAC and PARCC questions.

Now that we understand how the new Common Core SBAC and PARCC tests were deliberately designed to fail, in the next section, we will look at one of the greatest crimes ever inflicted on our children, a federal law called "No Child Left Behind" or simply NCLB.

1.4 NCLB... How Drill and Kill Fake Tests Harm our Kids

> "By relentlessly testing children, pitting schools
> Against schools, teachers against teachers
> Parents and children against children,
> We have diminished the quality of learning."
> Amrien, A.L. & Berliner, D.C. (2002 March 28)
> High Stakes Testing, Uncertainty and Student Learning

We all want to improve our public schools. But school improvement should not come at the expense of harming millions of children. In this section, we will look at a crime called "No Child Left Behind" and the severe harm inflicted on millions of children by its mandated wave of high stakes tests. Below is just one of these millions of children. It is a five year old girl who was originally excited about attending Kindergarten. But after five hours of testing, she was reduced to tears because she did not know how to answer the questions on her high stakes test.

A child learns To Hate School... After 5 HOURS of Kindergarten Common Core High Stakes High Failure Rate Tests!

Child psychologists have a term for the harm inflicted on this little girl... It is called CHILD ABUSE.... It is up to those of us who care about children to put an end to this insanity!

Needless to say, her mother is now an opponent of high stakes tests.

How the No Child Left Behind Act Got Started
The No Child Left Behind Act, commonly called NCLB, was passed in the US House of Representatives on May 23 2001 on a vote of 384 to 45. It passed in the US Senate on June 14 2001 on a vote of 91 to 8. It was signed into law by George Bush on January 8 2002. This federal law violates the US Constitution which specifies that powers such as education that are not specifically given to Congress in the US Constitution are reserved for the States. Education has for more than 200 years been accepted as a right of each State. However, the billionaires have such a tight grip on Congress that they were able to convince nearly the entire Congress to ignore the US Constitution and do their bidding.

Insane Provisions of No Child Left Behind (NCLB)

NCLB requires that every student in every state be given a standardized test every year. Moreover, every year, every group of students must do better than the previous year's group of students. This is called Annual Yearly Progress or AYP. If a group of students fails to improve over the test scores of the previous years students for three years in a row, a series of punishments are inflicted on the school. These punishments can include firing the entire staff of teachers and administrators, and/or closing the school and/or turning the school over to a for profit corporation to be run as a "charter" school.

The eventual goal was to have all students in all schools in every State at full "proficiency" within 12 years (by the end of the 2013-2014 school year). In short, NCLB required that all students in all schools become "A" students by June 2014.

No other nation on Earth expects every child in every school to meet every standard in every subject! It is insane. NCLB makes it obvious that the US has the most corrupt political system on Earth. Otherwise the bill never would have passed. It should come as no surprise that hardly any schools in the United States were able to turn all of their students into A students in 12 years. Schools would not be able to turn all students into A students if they had 100 years. Thus, nearly every school in America and nearly every student in America has been labeled as a "failure" by the lunacy of the NCLB Act.

The Real Reason for NCLB High Stakes Toxic Tests was to Destroy Schools

In a June 8 2008 Time magazine article, former assistant education secretary under Bush II, Susan Neuman, explained the real reason for the insane NCLB testing mania. It had nothing to do with helping children succeed. Instead it was viewed as a way to destroy public education so that the populace would support school choice, vouchers, and privatization. The law was used as a Trojan Horse to drive a wedge between the public and public education. "No Child Left Behind was nothing more than a cynical plan to destroy American faith in public education and open the way to vouchers."
http://content.time.com/time/nation/article/0,8599,1812758,00.html

How the NCLB Act and High Stakes Testing Harms Children

There are many ways this greedy plan by billionaires and corrupt politicians has severely harmed our kids. Below we will summarize just a few of the harms of NCLB and high stakes tests.

First, NCLB forces teachers to "teach to the test" rather than focusing on meeting the needs of each child.

Instead of helping children explore subjects with their natural curiosity, schools are turned into prisons that focus on "drill and kill" direct instruction and memorization of an endless series of facts that might appear on the next high stakes test.

Second NCLB has forced teachers to change from child centered inquiry learning to corporate centered Drill and Kill Direct Instruction

Below is a link to brief 3 minute video of a billionaire designed Direct Instruction Kindergarten math curriculum in action (Warning: This video looks more like a military indoctrination boot camp than a Kindergarten class. If you are a sensitive person, you may want to skip this video. (It still gives me nightmares.) Below is a scene from the video. https://www.youtube.com/watch?v=Ru9yrYQiVhA

These students are being drilled Into chanting the "Math Way"
Ten... One...
Ten... Two...
Ten...Three..
Ten... Four...
Ten... Five...

Third, NCLB has forced schools to spend more time on tests and less time on learning

NCLB testing requirements forced schools to devote months to drill and kill test preparation. This left no time for art, music, recess, physical education, critical thinking, creative writing or support of independent questioning and learning. Time for physical development, PE, and recess has been shortened in many schools to increase time for drill and kill instruction and testing. This is harmful because brain development in young children requires physical activity. Young children were never designed to sit strapped to chairs all day. Reducing physical activity has led to an epidemic of childhood obesity in the US. Some schools even shorten their school lunch period to have more time for test preparation!

Fourth, NCLB has lead to "cheating scandals" in schools all across America as students, teachers and administrators who did not want to see their beloved school closed down altered the test scores of their students. Cheating is so common that the federal law became known as **"No Cheater Left Behind."**

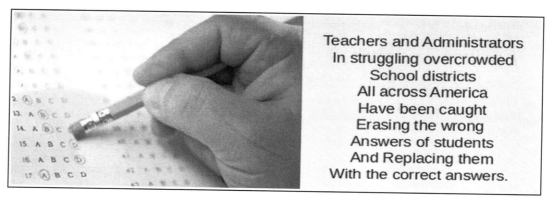

Fifth, forcing elementary school children to take high stakes tests is especially harmful to elementary school children.
A Third Grade girl in Florida started crying when she got a score of 181. She needed a score of 182 to go on to 4th Grade. Prior to this, she had all A's in school. Her twin brother went on to 4th grade while his sister was required to repeat 3rd Grade. Of course, the mother of the twins is outraged. "My heart breaks for her, nobody wants to see their child cry," said her mother. "When she found out she had to go back to third grade again she was crying bad, I mean she was devastated."

Sixth, NCLB increase student anxiety and reduced student motivation to learn. A basic principle of child development is that motivation precedes academic learning. Killing a child's desire to learn harms a child's ability to learn.

Seventh, NCLB test failure lowers self esteem and leads small children to believe they are "too dumb to learn."
Failing NCLB high stakes tests harms a child's self esteem and sense of self worth. Children internalize these negative beliefs and later fail to even try to learn. This kind of harm failed to take into account that children develop at different rates.

One reason some kids drop out of school is they are not given the help they need to pass high stakes tests. They fail a math test and conclude that they are simply "no good at math" or have no chance of passing a course needed for graduation. Dropping out of school leads to all kids of problems like drug abuse, crime and going to prison. Failing high stakes tests can also lead to teen suicide as the child's self worth becomes so low they no longer believe life is worth living. In particular, young boys develop academically at a rate that is one to two years behind young girls. An entire generation of normal young boys as been labeled as failures by the insanity of NCLB. High Stakes Tests create High Risk Kids!

Eighth, the uncontrollable anxiety of raising the bar too high harms kids by Triggering a Stress Response called Learned Helplessness

One of the claims of school reform billionaires is that most American students are not "college and career ready" when they graduate from high school. They claim that the way to solve this problem is to raise the bar by forcing all states to adopt higher common core standards. The claim is that these higher standards combined with increasing the number of high stakes tests will insure that all US students are college and career ready. These claims are not supported by any credible scientific research. This is the danger of exposing our children to guinea pig experiments like Common Core that were developed without any input or review from child development specialists. What ed reformers are ignoring in their drive to raise the bar higher and higher is a principal of child development called the ceiling effect. If you give a child a task that is too difficult and they experience repeated failure, the child will eventually give up and get worse rather than better. For example, if you have a child 5 feet tall and you insist that they jump over a bar that is 10 feet high, the child will eventually stop trying to jump over the bar. They will internalize a sense of failure and develop what some psychologists call "learned helplessness."

Dogs exposed to random severe shocks Eventually give up trying to escape Even when escape is possible. Dr. Seligman called this response To uncontrollable stress "Learned Helplessness"

Learned helplessness is a specific consequence of one particular form of psychological stress: being given an impossible task. The problem in giving small children tests that most cannot possibly pass is that small children and small dogs lack the coping responses to uncontrollable stress (also called self regulation and self esteem) that we adults have.

Instead of responding positively to stress as a challenge to improve, small children are much more likely to internalize the message that they are no good and give up trying to learn at all.

Learned Helplessness
When a bar is set
So high that a
Child cannot
Achieve success
No matter how hard
They try...

They will internalize
A sense of Failure
Shame and
Lack of Self Worth
That can permanently
Harm their ability to
Learn for the rest
Of their life.

This is why
Common Core
Is often called
"Child Abuse"
By many Child
Development
Specialists

Ninth, Chronic Stress leads to a downward spiral that permanently harms a child's emotional, social and academic development.

Threats, penalties and punishment demoralize teachers and students. We know from brain imaging studies that the emotional development of the brain precedes cognitive development. Anything that harms the emotional development of the child also permanently harms the cognitive development of the child. This is why subjecting kids to the chronic stress of high stakes tests is a form of child abuse.

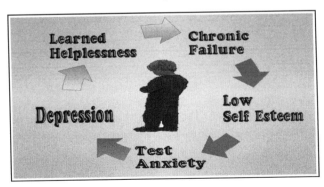

Children blame themselves and are forced to live with the guilt that their poor performance on a single test caused their beloved school to be closed and their beloved teacher to be fired.

The purpose of flunking students is to erode support for public schools and thereby make it easier to close and privatize public schools. According to the National Center for Education Statistics, about 2,000 public schools per year have been closed in the US since the push for privatizing schools began in 2004. This is double the rate of school closures in the 1990s where about 1000 public schools closed every year. These school closures affected the lives of over 300,000 students per year who now live with the guilt that because they failed a test, their school was closed. In ten years, 3 million children have been subjected to losing the school they love. https://nces.ed.gov/fastfacts/display.asp?id=64

During this same time, the number of privately controlled scandal ridden charter schools rose from under 2,000 schools to more than 5,000 schools – with enrollment skyrocketing from under 500,000 students to nearly 2 million students. https://nces.ed.gov/programs/digest/d12/tables/dt12_108.asp

Children internalize the Messages they get from adults. If a child is told that they Are a failure... The child will believe they are Are a failure... And are incapable of learning... Even if the real problem was that The child was given an unfair test!

Tenth, endless meaningless high stakes tests are degrading to students.
The high stakes testing movement is led by Pearson, one of America's three largest textbook publishers and test-assessment companies. Pearson will, at least in part, be using the automated scoring systems of Educational Testing Services (ETS), proprietor of the e-Rater, which can "grade" 16,000 essays in a mere 20 minutes. Pearson will make more than one billion per year by rapidly grading high stakes tests of students. The Pearson machine should have been called the D Grader since what it really does is degrade students.

High Stakes Testing Math Problems:
If the D Grader machine can grade 16,000 essays in 20 minutes, how many can it grade in 2 minutes? If the D Grader machine can grade 1,600 essays in 2 minutes, how many can it grade in one minute? If the D Grader machine can grade 800 essays in 60 seconds, how many can it grade in 6 seconds? If the D Grader machine can grade 80 essays in 6 seconds, about how many can it grade in one second? If the average 3rd grader takes 30 minutes to write their high stakes essay on which their passage to 4th grade depends, how many seconds will the Pearson Degrader spend making this decision about the child's life?

How many years in prison should the wealthy charlatans at Pearson get for degrading the lives of millions of children just to make a quick buck?

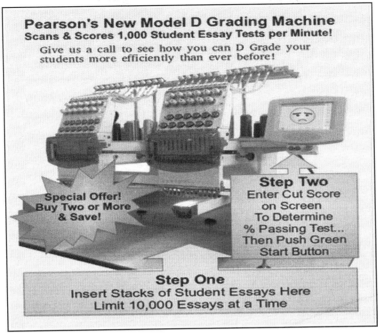

Eleventh, focusing on high stakes tests fails to address the most important reason many kids fail in school... childhood poverty

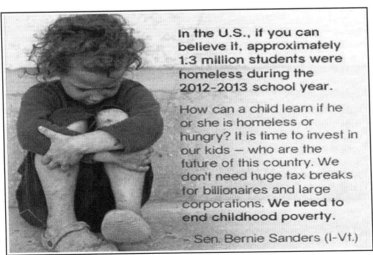

High Stakes testing harms poor kids most by ignoring the real cause of school failure which is childhood poverty. Again, poor kids are most likely to do poorly on standardized tests because they do not have the advantage of a stable home and educational resources enjoyed by rich kids. The issue with students in poverty is that they are in poverty. They don't need their schools closed. They need their parents to have jobs.

It is tough for a kid to do well in school when they are hungry and living in the back seat of a car. The real problem we are facing as a nation is a lack of good paying jobs – not a lack of smart hard working kids!

Twelfth, high stakes tests fail to meet the emotional needs of kids
This is the danger in accepting an education reform agenda developed by billionaires and Wall Street Hedge Fund Managers rather than by child development specialists. A child development specialist would know there is a huge difference between a real child and a computer program. As Psychologist Abraham Maslow pointed out, children have emotional needs for acceptance, attention, affection and approval. A computer has none of these needs.

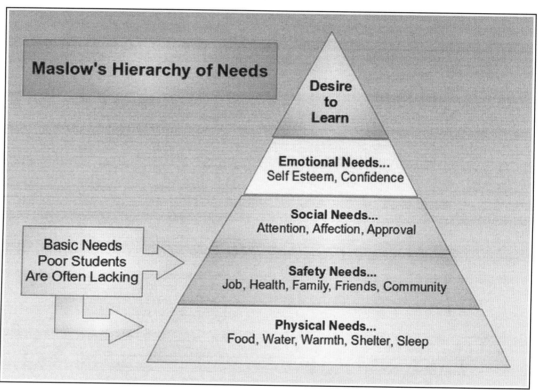

Poor kids need a safe learning environment
As we have seen throughout this book, the greatest threat to child well being and academic success is poverty. However, because high stakes tests remove a safe learning environment and replaces it with a high stress learning environment, these tests turn our public schools into a toxic danger that causes permanent long term harm to children. Those who advocate high stakes tests are not only wrong. They are committing child abuse and should be put in jail where they can no longer inflict harm on our children.

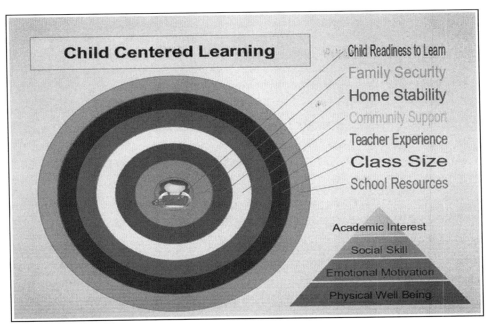

Thirteenth... High Stakes Tests Ignore the fact that each child has a unique learning potential called the Zone of Proximal Development (ZPD)

Those familiar with the child development theories of Lev Vygotsky call the assessment of task difficulty the Zone of Proximal Development or ZPD. You can think of it as a Goldilocks Principal in that a task can be either too easy or too hard. This principal states that children learn best when assisted by a more knowledgeable other (typically a parent and/or teacher) who helps the child learn a task that is just out of the reach of a child. In other words, raising the bar will only result in improvement if the bar is set at the correct height and if the child has the assistance of an experienced teacher. Common Core fails to set the bar at the right height and fails to provide children with an experienced teacher. This is why it is so harmful to children.

There is a corollary to the ZPD. First, each child has a different ZPD. One of the tasks of a teacher, and one of the benefits of smaller class sizes, is that the teacher can better assess the ZPD of each child. Forcing all children to jump over the same bar or pass the same high stakes test harms more children than it helps. Individualized instruction is important because if a task is set too far beyond the child or outside of the child's zone of proximal development, instead of improving, the child's self esteem will be so badly harmed by a sense of failure that the child will regress into a sense of "learned helplessness." An important and overlooked aspect of child development is that if a parent or teacher or other adult figure tells a child they are a failure, then the child will believe them and internalize this belief.

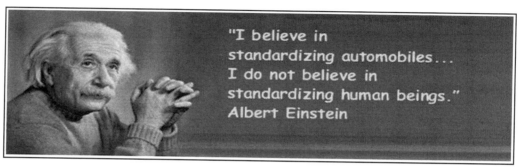

One can think of the ZPD as being like the child's story of Goldilocks and the Three Bears. Standards can be too low. But they can also be too high. And damage from standards that are set too high are much worse than standards that are set too low because in harming the self esteem of the child, excessively high standards permanently harm a child's natural desire to learn and their belief that they are capable of learning. High stakes tests that set the bar too high harm the child today and tomorrow and for many years to come.

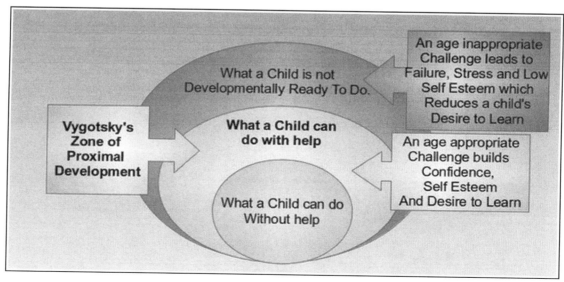

Fourteenth High Stakes Testing Ignores a Child's Stage of Development

Piaget found that children go through stages of development where young children go through a period of magical thinking followed by concrete thinking using real world examples before eventually reaching a stage of abstract or formal thinking sometime in high school or college.

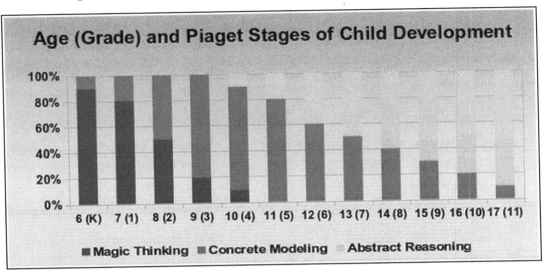

This process varies from child to child. Sadly, standardized testing often asks young children abstract questions that their brains literally have no way of understanding. Nor does raising the bar and shaming children and subjecting them to unfair high stakes tests lead to a quicker transition from concrete to abstract thinking. Instead, raising the bar too high merely harms the child by making them think that they are stupid and not capable of learning. Children deserve fair testing that recognizes the complexity of child development and respects each child's current level of development and provides them with appropriate and individualized learning goals.

Fifteen, High Stakes Tests promote a Punishment Model of Public Schools instead of a Nurturing Model of Public Schools

High stakes tests bring in hundreds of millions of dollars a year to the handful of corporations that produce the tests, grade the tests, and supply materials to raise students' scores on the tests. They also promote acceptance of a corporate-style of external rewards and punishment, which children then internalize as natural and even desirable. Tests are not used to help students improve. Instead, they are used to rank children and label children as failures.

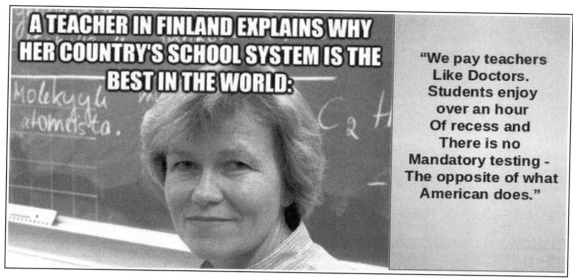

This corporate driven view of education is the opposite of a child centered view of education wherein the goal of public schools is to foster a child's natural desire to learn and help every child succeed in school and in life. Caring, empathy and love are not listed in any educational or business standard, but they are found in the best of schools.

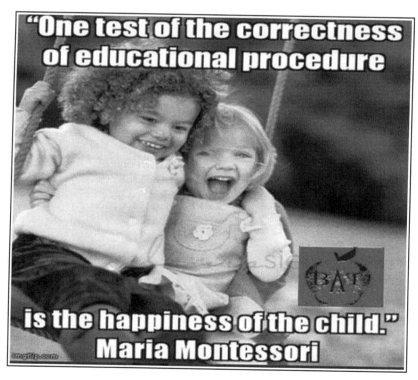

Sixteenth, attempting to grade mountains of high stakes tests done by children they never met is also degrading to thousands of "Test Graders"
High Stakes Testing is not only Degrading for Students, it is Degrading for the thousands of Adults forced to give scores to students who they have never met.

> "There is more oversight of the pet industry
> And the food we feed our dogs
> Than there is for the quality of tests
> We make our kids take."
> Walt Haney, Boston College

Sadly, the high stakes testing industry is completely unregulated. The high stakes testing industry is not accountable for the tests that are used to hold schools accountable. Unqualified evaluators operating in sweat shops grading factories use scoring methods lacking any scientific validity to pass judgment on our children. This is a job that should only be done by experienced classroom teachers who know their students well.

A room full of overworked and underpaid temporary graders Who review hundreds of tests per day. The graders spend 2 minutes per test scoring the writing of students whose future will depend on the score they receive.

Seventeenth, data mining of small children ought to be illegal.
Even worse than the lack of reliability or validity of student test scores is what happens to these test scores after they are reported. Data for small children is placed on easily hackable servers where it can become part of a child's permanent record affecting not only their ability to get into a good college, but even their ability to get a good job later in life. Data mining small children is a violation of their constitutional right to privacy.

Eighteenth, forcing children to endure 13 years of high stakes testing leads to self centered adults who see the world as a competition instead of a caring community who understand that we are in in this together.

Students are conditioned into the greed/competition model from an early age – making competition appear quite natural to them, and so fully indoctrinated they step into the marketplace to perpetuate and inflict this model on others who are viewed as both the competition and the enemy. The focus on winning at all costs and seeing others as 'the competition' fuels divisions between people, leading to conflict, suffering, dehumanization and even war. Instead of viewing children as unique individuals, with innate gifts and talents, they are viewed by billionaires as merely cogs in the corporate profit machine... robots to be made "career and college ready" as quickly as possible. The drive to compete and avoid failure leads to harmful hidden consequences... stress, anxiety and depression. Instead of freedom to learn there is only the slavery to conform.. to get the right answer on the next high stakes test.

Fear of failure is the weapon used to keep children in line. The whip of competition leads to an early death of the soul.

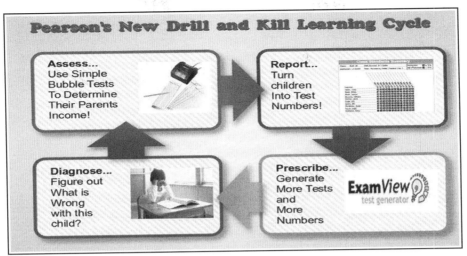

Try Cooperation instead
Competition sets people against each other. For harmony and social justice, cooperation and sharing encourages trust and builds relationships.

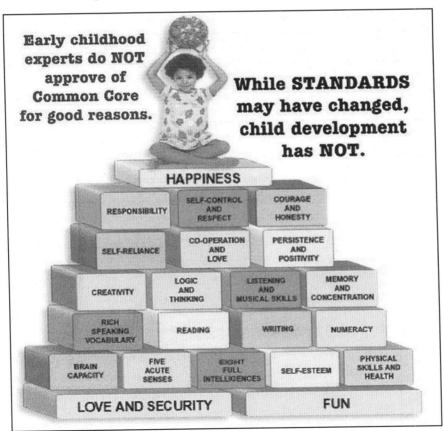

Conversely, there can be no enduring happiness for all as long as our children are taught to accept the nonsense that competition and judging children by fake test scores is all that is possible.

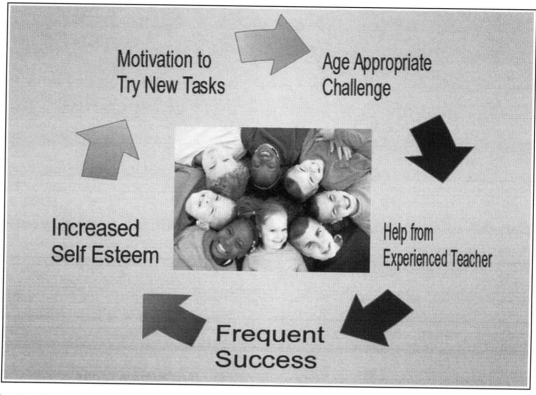

Help Us Stop the Toxic Testing Madness... Opt Out!
Every parent has a Constitutional Right to control the education of your children. Every public school district is therefore required to allow you to opt your child out of any and all high stakes testing without punishment to you or your child. If all parents refused to allow their children to take high stakes, high failure rate tests and every teacher refused to give these toxic tests, we could quickly end the entire high stakes testing scam – allowing more time for real positive learning rather than teaching kids how to take the next toxic test. For more information on the latest developments in the Opt Out movement and to download a form on how to opt your students out of toxic tests, visit our website,
http://optoutwashington.org/

What's Next?
In the next section, we will look behind the curtain and expose the billionaires who are out to destroy our public schools. Then we will look at their latest weapon of mass deception – a truly evil scam called Common Core.

2 CCSS... Common Core Fake Standards

> "The wisest move all states could make to ensure that students learn To read, understand and use English language appropriately before They graduate from high school is first to abandon Common Core Standards." Dr. Sandra Stotsky, Former Assistant Superintendent For the State of Massachusetts & expert on Standards Development

By January 2015, almost half of all Americans had heard the innocent sounding slogan of how Common Core State Standards (CCSS) will prepare our kids to be "career and college ready." In this chapter, we will explain that CCSS has nothing to do with improving State Standards or getting kids career and college ready. CCSS is simply a corporate corruption sucker scam secretly funded by billionaires to rob tax payers of billions of dollars and rob children of their future. This second chapter is divided into four sections:

2.1 The Real History of Common Core

2.2 Common Core Standards are Not Age Appropriate

2.3 Common Core Math is Insane

2.4 Support for Common Core Plunges

2.1 The Real History of Common Core...

How Bill Gates Concocted the CCSS Scam

What is Common Core... Myth versus Fact

Common Core is often written by its initials CCSS which stands for Common Core State Standards. The idea of national standards may seem like a good idea. Unfortunately, these national standards have turned into a nightmare for students, parents and teachers. The marketing slogan factory for Common Core is that CCSS is a set of "State led national standards which prepare students to be career and college ready." In fact, Common Core is Gates led not State led. The standards were hastily written by a few corporate consultants – not by teachers or child development specialists. The Common Core standards were so poorly written that they have been condemned by many educational professionals as being not as good as the prior State standards that CCSS replaced. This is a problem because Common Core standards are patented and do not allow for more than minor changes. Worst of all, Common Core Standards do not prepare students for college or careers. For example, even if a student passed all of the math standards by completing the fake common core tests, they would not be ready to take college level courses. So the whole Common Core program is nothing but a scam based on a series of lies. The real purpose of Common Core is first to create billions of dollars in profit for the Education Industrial Complex and then second to destroy public schools and public school students to such an extent that the general public will demand that public schools be closed and replaced with private for profit schools that are exempt from the Common Core standards.

Who Owns CCSS?

The Common Core standards are copyrighted by a couple of fake non-profit groups called the National Governors Association (NGA) and the Council of Chief State School Officials (CCSSO). Both of these groups are unelected, private organizations who get most of their funding (millions of dollars) from Bill Gates through the Gates Foundation. Because these two groups are private organizations, there is no public record of how they make decisions.

Bill Gates speaking at the National Governors Conference Congratulates them on creating Common Core fake Standards.

If the Common Core standards were so poorly written, why did over 40 States adopt the CCSS?
In order to receive billions of dollars in federal funding through a corrupt federal program called Race to the Top (RTTT), States were forced to quickly adopt Common Core tests and standards. In other words, States were forced to adopt Common Core through a series of bribes and punishments. Most States adopted CCSS before the standards were even written! The states caved to federal blackmail because they needed the money due to the recession.

What is the Common Core plan?

The plan is to subject children to endless Common Core high stakes tests in every grade from Kindergarten through High School. The two official tests are SBAC and PARCC. Like all high stakes tests, these tests will really simply measure how wealthy the child's family is rather than how much they know about the Common Core standards. Most of these test questions were adopted directly from a prior voluntary national test called NAEP or the National Assessment of Educational progress. Thus, the CCSS test questions have almost nothing to do with the Common Core standards. The Common Core plan is simply an excuse to declare two thirds of all kids to be "failures."

Who is Promoting Common Core?

If Common Core is so harmful to children, why would anyone even promote it? Billionaires like Bill Gates promote Common Core because they stand to make billions of dollars by privatizing our public schools. Bill Gates has spent several billion dollars starting and funding hundreds of fake grassroots groups to produce fake reports about how wonderful Common Core is. He has also spent billions of dollars bribing corporate news organizations like NPR to promote Common Core. He has even spent millions more bribing both teachers unions, the National Education Association, the American Federation of Teachers and the National Parent Teacher Association to promote Common Core. Given this blizzard of propaganda, it is no wonder that even well meaning teachers and parents have been taken in by the many false statements promoting Common Core. We will provide more details about Bill Gates and the Gates Foundation in a later chapter. But for now, it is worth noting that the Gates Foundation is one of the most corrupt money laundering and tax evasion schemes the world has ever known. Through this and other schemes, Bill Gates has avoided paying billions of dollars in State and federal taxes. Money that should have gone towards hiring teachers instead went towards bribing politicians, paying off the corporate media and setting up hundreds of fake organizations all in an effort to destroy and then privatize our public schools. To see who has been bribed or owned by Bill Gates, just go to the Gates Foundation website. http://www.gatesfoundation.org/
Then in the top menu, hover the cursor over "How We Work" and select a menu item called "Awarded Grants." This will take you to the following page:
http://www.gatesfoundation.org/How-We-Work/Quick-Links/Grants-Database

Type in **National Governors Association** into the Search Box, then click on the blue "Search Grants" button to see how much Bill has given to the National Governors Association and when the grants were given. The phrase "College Ready" means Common Core. There were 13 direct grants totaling **$24 million.** There have also been hundreds of hidden grants to various fake groups working with the NGA.

GRANTEE	YEAR	ISSUE	PROGRAM	AMOUNT
National Governors Association Center for Best Practices	2014	Postsecondary Success	US Program	$598,705
National Governors Association Center for Best Practices	2013	College-Ready	US Program	$750,000
National Governors Association Center For Best Practices	2012	Strategic Partnerships	US Program	$37,674
National Governors Association Center For Best Practices	2011	College-Ready	US Program	$1,293,904

Next type in the **Council of Chief State School Officers**. There were 21 grants to the CCSSO totaling about **$85 million**. There were also hundreds of other more hidden grants to hundreds of fake organizations promoting Common Core.

GRANTEE	YEAR	ISSUE	PROGRAM	AMOUNT
Council of Chief State School Officers	2014	College-Ready	US Program	$6,148,749
Council of Chief State School Officers	2013	College-Ready	US Program	$1,958,500
Council of Chief State School Officers	2013	College-Ready	US Program	$3,197,931
Council of Chief State School Officers	2013	College-Ready	US Program	$400,000
Council of Chief State School Officers	2013	College-Ready	US Program	$4,000,000

While NGA and CCSSO own the copyright to Common Core, the Common Core standards were supposedly written by a group called **Student Achievement Partners.** Type this into the search box and you will get three grants totaling **$5 million.**

The bribery extends way beyond fake education groups. Type in **National Public Radio** into the Search Box. There were 11 grants totaling **$14 million**. It should come as no surprise that NPR has had dozens of programs promoting Common Core as a wonderful program for American children! Type in **NEA** which is the largest national teachers union. There are 9 grants totaling **$8 million**. No wonder the NEA supports Common Core. Type in **AFT** which is the other national teachers union. There are 8 grants totaling **$11 million**. No wonder AFT supports Common Core!

"We all know that CCSS wasn't state led. It was developed by NGA and CCSSO and Achieve. They're not representing the states. These are trade organizations."

Dr. Sandra Stotsky, English Language Professor who resigned from the Common Core Evaluation Committee in disgust and is now a leading opponent of Common Core.

Supported by billionaires... What can possibly go wrong?
The takeover of our public schools via Common Core has been a process shrouded in secrecy with no public hearings, no public comments, almost no involvement by parents or teachers, no scientific testing and no scientific research – peer reviewed or otherwise. The rush to implement Common Core has been a deeply flawed process filled with corruption, bribes, lies and distortions at every stage in the process.

The Gates foundation has spent hundreds of millions of dollars setting up hundreds of fake "grassroots" organizations and bribing everyone from the corporate media to the Congress to State legislators.

In 2013 alone, the Gates Foundation gave over $200 million to encourage the creation and adoption of the Common Core.

Arne Duncan and the U.S. Department of Education
Unfortunately, many corrupt State legislators still promote Common Core because that is how they get money for their reelection campaigns. They use the excuse that we need to keep Common Core in order to get the Federal funding associated with **Race To The Top** – a corrupt program run by a crook named Arne Duncan – a former basketball player and current snake oil salesman who knows nothing about education or children but was appointed as the person to run the US Department of Education.

Arne Duncan used to be in charge of Chicago Public Schools – where he closed an average of ten public schools per year, fired all of the teachers and turned all of the schools into private for profit charter schools. Thousands of parents and teachers in Chicago adamantly protested the closing of these schools and thousands of children were harmed by these school closures. But their protests fell on deaf ears because Arne was doing the bidding of his corporate billionaire masters.

There is a very close relationship between the US Department of Education and the Gates Foundation. Nearly all of the upper managers in the US Department of Education used to work for or received grants from the Gates Foundation. The US Department of Education, under the leadership of Arnie Duncan, has spent roughly $4.5 Billion dollars in "Race to the Top" tax payer dollars (money that was supposed to be part of the 2009 stimulus funds) bribing state governments into adopting the Common Core. Only 5 States were able to resist the onslaught of bribery and propaganda. Between 2009 to 2011, 45 States adopted Common Core. Not a single State allowed a vote of the people on the standards that would determine the future of their children. Most legislators never even read the Common Core standards.

Even today, with school districts forced to fire teachers by the thousands in order to spend billions of dollars on new "Common Core" textbooks, new Common Core computer networks and new Common Core tests, there is still no evidence that Common Core will benefit students. But there is plenty of evidence that Common Core harms students.

How much does this fake Common Core program cost taxpayers?

Common Core tests are costing States billions of dollars. But the real big money is in the Common Core text books which are supposedly "aligned" with the Common Core standards and Common Core tests. In fact, the Common Core text books were also hastily written and often have little to do with Common Core standards and are merely an excuse to dump billions of dollars worth of poorly written fake tests books on cash strapped local school districts. There is also many billions that must be spent upgrading computers and computer programs. A state by state Cost analysis was released in 2012 by the Pioneer Institute. The report, "National Cost of Aligning States and Localities to the Common Core Standards", estimates that it will cost US tax payers **$16 billion to implement Common Core!**

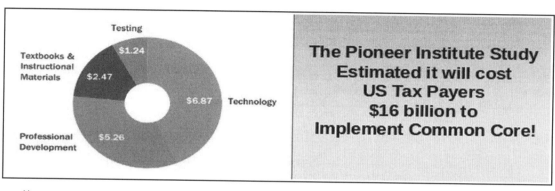

http://www.accountabilityworks.org/photos/Cmmn_Cr_Cst_Stdy.Fin.2.22.12.pdf

All of these billions of dollars is money taken away from hiring teachers and placed in the pockets of corporate leaders and Wall Street hedge fund managers who bribed corrupt elected officials into passing laws mandating Common Core. In Washington State, Common Core will cost over $482 million – nearly all of it paid for by local school districts.

WA Five Year Estimated Costs for CCSS Implementation January 2011

	Five Year Total	Percent
State Level Costs	$17,100,000	9.4%
District Level Costs	$165,500,000	90.6%
State Level and District Level Costs	$182,600,000	Totals
State Level and District Level Costs		$182,600,000
Add Textbooks and Curriculum Materials		$300,000,000

Common Core History... The Marketing Myth of the Miraculous Conception of Common Core

Corporate America would like you to believe that Common Core is a recent idea that resulted from a meeting of Bill Gates with a couple of promoters in the summer of 2008. According to a June 7 2014 article written by Lyndsey Layton in the Washington Post, the involvement of Bill Gates in the Common Core scam was due to a brief two hour meeting Bill Gates had with Gene Wilhoit and David Coleman in Seattle in the summer of 2008.

Here is how this myth was described by Lynsey Layton, reporter for the Washington Post:

"On a summer day in 2008, Gene Wilhoit, director of a national group of state school chiefs, and David Coleman, an emerging evangelist for the standards movement, spent hours in Bill Gates's sleek headquarters near Seattle, trying to persuade him and his wife, Melinda, to turn their idea into reality. Coleman and Wilhoit told Bill and Melinda Gates that academic standards varied so wildly between states that high school diplomas had lost all meaning, that as many as 40 percent of college freshmen needed remedial classes and that U.S. students were falling behind their foreign competitors. The pair also argued that a fragmented education system stifled innovation because textbook publishers and software developers were catering to a large number of small markets instead of exploring breakthrough products. That seemed to resonate with the man who led the creation of the world's dominant computer operating system... "Can you do this?" Wilhoit recalled being asked. "Is there any proof that states are serious about this, because they haven't been in the past?

Wilhoit responded that he and Coleman could make no guarantees but that "we were going to give it the best shot we could...

After the meeting, weeks passed with no word. Then Wilhoit got a call: Gates was in. What followed was one of the swiftest and most remarkable shifts in education policy in U.S. history. The Bill and Melinda Gates Foundation didn't just bankroll the development of what became known as the Common Core State Standards. With more than $200 million, the foundation also built political support across the country, persuading state governments to make systemic and costly changes."

http://www.washingtonpost.com/politics/how-bill-gates-pulled-off-the-swift-common-core-revolution/2014/06/07/a830e32e-ec34-11e3-9f5c-9075d5508f0a_story.html

The story sounds good... It is such a wonderful story about how two people can make a difference in the world if only they can get a two hour meeting with the richest man in the world to pitch their idea. The story was so good that it fooled the Washington Post reporter. But it is actually not true. The fix was in on the Common Core long before 2008.

Follow the Money to the Gates Foundation Database

The way to get at the real history of common core is to follow the money through the Gates Foundation database. The money trail confirms that David Coleman and Gene Wilhoit did not in fact launch Common Core in 2008. Instead, they had been working on Common Core clones with funding from Bill Gates and other billionaires for years before they came up with the name Common Core. We described the early history of this school privatization scam in Chapter One. We will now describe the rest of the history of Common Core.

Who Actually Wrote the Common Core Standards?

Typically, state learning standards are written by a committee of up to 100 highly experienced teachers. However, our research indicates that the Common Core standards were written by two Wall Street consultants – neither of whom was an experienced teacher. This is why the Common Core standards are so poorly written.

There is considerable disagreement over exactly who wrote the Common Core standards. Some have claimed that it was written by a committee of 24 people on the 2009 "work group" – nearly all of whom were from the billionaire funded Ed Reform scammers. Some say there were a couple of teachers who "reviewed the standards" and then refused to sign the final document. But these were merely review committees. The actual standards had been written in secret long before being seen by any review committees. The decisions about any changes to the Common Core standards were also made in secret by a very small group of individuals – none of whom were teachers.

So, while our research indicates that only two people created the standards, there is really no way of knowing how the standards were written or when they were written or who wrote them. It is all a big secret.

However, we do know more about who the "lead writers" of the Common Core standards were. If we limit the definition of lead writers to the people who controlled what standards were included or excluded from the Common Core standards, then there was only 2 to 3 lead writers. Some have claimed there were 6 lead writers – 3 for English and 3 for math. Others have claimed there were only two leader writers for English: David Coleman and Susan Pimentel.

The three claimed lead writers for Common Core math standards were Jason Zimba, William McCallum and Phil Daro. However, our conclusion is that there may have been only one lead writer for the math standards, Jason Zimba. And there may have been only one lead writer for the English standards, Susan Pimentel. We base this conclusion in part on the history of how the Common Core standards were written. As we describe below, the standards evolved from other previous standards. It does not take more than one person to copy/paste standards from other lists of standards. We also base this conclusion on the poorly written nature of the final product. It appears there were no checks or balances. This is a characteristic of standards that were written by only one person. We also base this conclusion on statements made by the claimed authors. David Coleman has publicly stated that he knows little about creating English standards. His resume confirms this fact. By contrast, Susan Pimental does have a background in compiling English standards. Finally, we base this conclusion on researching early pre-CCSS documents that appear to indicate that only Susan Pimental selected the English standards and only Jason Zimba selected the Math standards.

1993 Susan Pimentel, Achieve INC and the American Diploma Project

As we will soon explain in the section on Student Achievement Partners, Susan Pimentel was one of the three primary writers of the Common Core standards. Some have written that she was added to Student Achievement Partners in 2009 to add a "woman's face" to a set of Common Core standards that was mainly written by two men (David Coleman and Jason Zimba). In fact, Susan had much more experience writing education reform standards than either David Coleman or Jason Zimba.

Susan had been working on ed reform standards since 1993. Susan got her start in the fake ed reform movement with a grant from the Walton billionaires in 1993. (In the last chapter, we explained how the Walton Billionaires were associated with Marc Tucker and Hillary Clinton and their effort to privatize our public schools in the 1980s and early 1990s).

Susan got her law degree from Cornell University and then worked for the Maryland State legislature and then a school district in Maryland implementing a "student tracking" program. In 1993, thanks to a grant from the Walton billionaires and shortly after Bill and Hillary Clinton took office, Susan founded a fake ed reform group called **Standards Work** (registered trademark) in Hanover New Hampshire. The goal of this group was to write and implement a set of national education standards and align instruction and textbooks to these standards – very similar to what Marc Tucker and Hillary Clinton had wanted to do.

On the history page for the Standards Work website, they explain: "Following a change in leadership at the White House (after the 1992 election), education reform issues continued but under slightly different names.

In 1993, America 2000 (Bush I) became Goals 2000 (Clinton), and the America 2000 Coalition (Bush I) became the Coalition for Goals 2000 (Clinton)... In 1993, the Walton Family Foundation, a long-time funder of Coalition activities asked the Coalition to manage a two-year grant funding the development of a How To book. Published in 1995 and co-authored by Denis P. Doyle and Susan Pimentel, **Raising the Standard: An Eight-Step Action Guide for Schools and Communities,** was written not only for schools and school districts but also for parents and business and civic leaders who want to move beyond setting standards to implementing them." http://www.standardswork.org/history.asp

Therefore, Susan is backed by the same billionaires who backed Bill and Hillary Clinton and for the same reason: to privatize our public schools. It was not long before Susan hooked up with the private corporate backers of a key private trade organization, **Achieve INC,** that was also working to privatize our public schools. According to her professional resume, Susan began working as a consultant for Achieve in 1996 – the year after she published her book and the same year that Achieve INC was founded. In a previous chapter, we described the corporate funded group Achieve INC that in 1996 grew as a cancer out of the National Governors Association to include corporate leaders and lacked even a single teacher. In 1998, Achieve INC began what it called the Academic Standards and Assessments Benchmarking Pilot Project. In October 1999, Bill Gates gave Achieve INC one million dollars to "support comprehensive benchmarking and review of academic standards and assessments between states." Thus, the beginning of Common Core goes all the way back to the beginning of the Gates Foundation. Bill Gates did not suddenly start promoting Common Core in the summer of 2008. He had been funding it since 1999.

Achieve Inc

Date: October 1999
Purpose: to support comprehensive benchmarking and review of academic standards and assessments between states
Amount: $1,000,000

In 2001, Achieve started the American Diploma Project (ADP) to create a set of National Learning standards and associated tests to determine if high school students were ready for college and careers in corporate America. ADP was the obvious precursor to Common Core. Sadly, not a single teacher was involved in writing the ADP national standards. Instead, Susan Pimentel was a consultant to the American Diploma Project, which was heavily funded by the Gates Foundation. The American Diploma Project (ADP) was given $12.6 million by the Gates Foundation to come up with its high stakes testing standards.
http://www.achieve.org/history-achieve

In May, 2004, Bill Gates gave Achieve INC another $7.7 million to get "certain states" to join the effort to adopt higher graduation requirements:

> **Achieve Inc**
>
> **Date:** May 2004
> **Purpose:** to assist and encourage specific states to adopt high school graduation requirements that align with college entry requirements
> **Amount:** $7,747,861

Also in 2004, ADP released an article called "Ready or Not: Creating a High School Diploma That Counts." This report described a "common core" of English and mathematics academic standards that American high school graduates needed for success in college and the workforce. The history of ADP magically turning into CCSS is described in several documents posted on the Achieve Press Release Archive which goes back to 2004. Here is the link: http://www.achieve.org/press-releases

Here is the oldest press release on ADP:

"WASHINGTON — Feb. 10, 2004 — High school graduates must master more English and math for their diplomas to signify readiness for jobs and college, says the American Diploma Project (ADP), which today released new graduation benchmarks. The three ADP sponsors — Achieve, Inc.; The Education Trust and the Thomas B. Fordham Foundation — call upon higher education, employers and policymakers to tie admissions, placement and hiring decisions to solid new 12th grade high school exit standards."

In October 2004, Bill Gates gave ADP $7.8 million to "adopt high school graduation requirements that align with college entry requirements." There were several more grants after that. All of these ADP grants confirm that the story about the Common Core idea coming up in 2008 is purely a marketing myth and utter nonsense. Sue Pimentel, or more accurately Sue Pimental Incorporated (also incorporated in Hanover New Hampshire) was hired by Achieve to write ADP standards in 2006, 2007, 2008 and 2009. Sometime between 2009 to 2010, Susan switched from Achieve to Student Achievement Partners. But her job remained the same... to help write the ADP/CCSS English standards. In 2007, Sue was appointed to the National Assessment Governing Board (NAGB) the Oversight Committee for the National Assessment of Educational Progress. (NAEP). This gives Susan a role in picking NAEP test questions.

In 2008, ADP released an article called "Out of Many, One: Toward Rigorous Common Core Standards from the Ground Up." The report described how to combine all of the various state learning standards into a single national standard.

Sometime in 2008, the name for ADP was changed to Common Core State Standards (CCSS). Also in 2008, ADP – now known as CCSS – was **subcontracted by Achieve to Student Achievement Partners.** Some articles have claimed that Susan was a co-founder of Student Achievement Partners, along with David Coleman and Jason Zimba. In fact, SAP was started in 2007 and Susan joined the group a couple of years later in 2009. She and Coleman were the lead writers for the Common Core English standards. Now that we know how the Common Core ELA standards were written, let's turn to the Common Core Math Standards.

2006 Gene Wilhoit and the Council of Chief State School Officers
From 2006 to 2012, Gene Wilhoit ran a scam outfit called the Council of Chief State School Officers. Bill Gates gave this outfit $25 million in 2004 to develop the program which eventually became Common Core. Eventually, Bill gave this scam outfit 21 grants totaling $85 million. Here is an image taken directly from the Gates Foundation website showing that the first three year $25 million grant was not in 2008 – it was in 2004:

Council of Chief State School Officers

Date: April 2004
Purpose: to provide states with sophisticated, web-based data tools that will strengthen accountability and improve results through data-driven decision making
Amount: $25,000,000
Term: 36
Topic: College-Ready

Then in March 2007, Bill Gates handed Gene Wilhoit another $21 million grant for Phase Two of the project.

Council of Chief State School Officers

Date: March 2007
Purpose: to support Phase II of the National Education Data Partnership seeking to promote transparency and accessibility of education data and improve public education through data-driven decision making
Amount: $21,642,317
Term: 36
Topic: Global Policy & Advocacy
Regions Served: GLOBAL|NORTH AMERICA
Program: United States
Grantee Location: Washington, District of Columbia
Grantee Website: http://www.ccsso.org

Bill Gates is still handing this fake outfit millions of dollars every year to "implement Common Core and develop curriculum aligned to Common Core standards." Clearly Gates was into the Common Core project at least four years before 2008.

In fact, the whole Common Core scam may have been Bill's idea rather than the idea of Coleman and Wilhoit. And rather than starting in 2008, the idea of national standards attached to high stakes tests started with the failed WASL test in Washington State in the 1980 and 1990s. But someone decided that having Common Core start as a "miracle meeting" between David Coleman and Bill Gates would sound better. So that was the myth promoted by the corporate media ever since.

Who is Gene Wilhoit?
Gene Wilhoit is one of the few Common Core scammers who has actually taught in a public school. Gene got a Bachelor of Arts degree in history and economics from Georgetown College and a master's degree in teaching and political science from Indiana University. He then was a Social Studies teacher in Indiana and Ohio for a short period of time. He next was a program director in the Indiana Department of Education before getting a job with the US Department of Education during the Reagan administration. In 1986, at the beginning of the school privatization movement, Gene became the director of the National Association of State Boards of Education (NASBE) where he was the director until 1993. Gene was then appointed the Education Commissioner in Arkansas. In 1997, he was appointed the Education Commissioner in Kentucky. Gene has also been the chairman of the Advisory Commission of the Education Commission of the States and is currently on the Pearson PARCC test board. In 2013, Wilhoit became a partner in Student Achievement Partners, replacing David Coleman – another Ed Reform scammer we will cover next. Nearly all of the groups Gene was involved with received funding from the Gates Foundation. For example, the National Association of State Boards of Education has received 6 grants from Bill Gates totaling $2 million and the Education Commission of the States has received four grants totaling $3 million.

Who are these groups?
The **Education Commission of the States** appears to be a group promoting high stakes testing. It was originally started in 1965 by the Carnegie Foundation – the same group that funded Marc Tucker and the Nation at Risk scam in the 1980s. Booth Garner, who we reviewed in a previous chapter was the chair of this group from 1990 to 1991 – the same time when Gene Wilhoit was the Executive Director of this group.

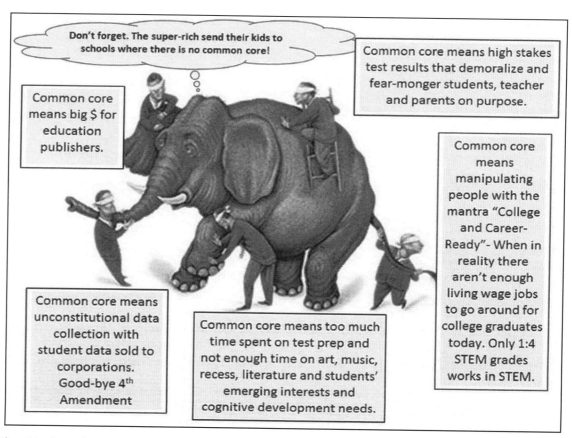

The National Association of State Boards of Education is more obscure. The group was started in 1958 but it is unclear where it gets its funding from. It appears to be funded by a series of private foundations including the Gates Foundation and the Carnegie Foundation and other fake groups for billionaires.

2007 David Coleman and Student Achievement Partners (SAP)

David Coleman was the son of wealthy highly educated parents. In 1991, he graduated from Yale with a Bachelor of Arts degree in Philosophy. He went to England as a graduate student. When he returned to the US, he worked at an international marketing and consulting firm called McKinsey and Company for five years. This firm has close connections to other Wall Street corporations like GE and IBM. According to a Wikipedia summary of this company, it was the most "disliked management consulting firm on earth... It is ruthlessly competitive... the hours are long, expectations high and failure is not acceptable." The firm charges an average of one million dollars for a few months work. Eventually some of the leaders of this firm were convicted of insider trading.

David worked for McKinsey during the dot com bubble where McKinsey helped set up more than 1000 Ecommerce firms between 1998 to 2000. After the crash of the dot com bubble, the firm switched over to the safer public sector to help with "knowledge management." In 2001, David Coleman left McKensey and set up a new corporation with a college friend, Jason Zimba, called **Grow Network**.

Despite a complete lack of experience, they immediately got consulting contracts with Pennsylvania, California, Nevada, New Mexico and New Jersey as well as New York City and Chicago public school districts to analyze student test data. David therefore worked as a testing consultant for the Chicago Public Schools while Arne Duncan was the chief executive. While at Grow Network, Coleman work with Vicki Phillips while she was education commissioner of Pennsylvania. Vicki later played a major role at the Gates Foundation. In 2004, Grow Network was sold to McGraw Hill for about $14 million dollars. McGraw Hill in turn is closely connected with the Bush family dynasty. Therefore David was well connected to both Bill Gates and George Bush.

In 2007, David Coleman and Jason Zimba started a new corporation called **Student Achievement Partners (SAP)** which was immediately funded by Bill Gates and the Gates Foundation. These two people, along with Sue Pimentel, were the "lead writers" for the Common Core standards. In other words, they basically wrote the common core standards... or more accurately they copied and pasted them from a variety of prior learning standards. For this work, Student Achievement Partners received $6.4 million from the Gates Foundation.

It has been claimed that David Coleman was in charge of writing the English Language standards with help from Sue Pimentel. But, as we just described earlier, it is more likely that Sue Pimentel wrote the English standards without any help from David Coleman. Jason Zimba pretty much assembled the Common Core math standards without any help from anyone. The name of the website for SAP pretty much says what their goal was: **achievethecore.org.**

David was once quoted as saying that he did not "give a shit" what students thought. He just wanted them to read and write corporate propaganda text.

Common Core Scam Artist, David Coleman, explains to 1st Graders why they are not allowed to write about themselves...

Unfortunately, David Coleman has no real background in teaching English literature and is an outspoken opponent of narrative writing and classic literature. This is why Common Core English standards focus on learning to read and write corporate propaganda (also called informational text) rather than biographies and classic literature. This radical change in how English should be taught led Dr. Sandra Stotsky to resign from the Common Core review committee in disgust. Dr. Stotsky had played a major role in writing the highly respected Massachusetts State English Standards. By June 2009, 45 states signed legally binding contracts to support CCSS. Most states did this without a single vote of their State legislature. More than 40 States had adopted the standards sight unseen in order to get a share of the $4.5 billion in Race to the Top federal funds. The final draft of the Common Core standards was released in June 2010 – nearly a full year after many states had already signed on.

What is next?
We will next take a closely look at Common Core standards, Common Core Curriculum and Common Core "Designed to Fail" tests. This is one more concrete example of the lies, fraud, corruption, bribery, scandals and theft of billions of tax payer dollars associated with the corporate takeover of our public schools. We will then explain how billionaires and Wall Street hedge fund managers have used the ideas of vouchers, charter schools, virtual schools, closing schools, firing teachers, No Child Left Untested, Race to the Bottom, Common Core and testing mania to destroy public confidence in public schools in order to line their own pockets.

2.2 Common Core Standards are Not Age Appropriate...

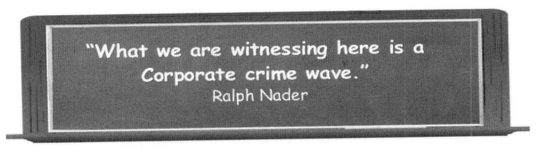

The Real Reason for Common Core is to give Billionaires another weapon to Destroy our Public Schools
Despite the fact that Common Core is now the official education standard for more than 40 States – and has been since 2010 - a 2013 Gallop Poll found that more than 60% of all Americans had "never heard of the Common Core standards". This is still true today. Fewer than half of all Americans have any idea what Common Core standards mean or how they might adversely affect their children. Even those who support Common Core typically have no idea what Common Core is, how it evolved, what its drawbacks are, how much it will cost or what effect it will have on our kids and our public schools. Common Core based testing began in 25 states in 2014 (including most school districts in Washington State). Nearly every state and school district will be subjected to Common Core in 2015. Now is the time for anyone who cares about the future of our children and our nation to become better informed about Common Core. In this article, we will look at one of the chief drawbacks of Common Core, the fact that the standards ignored 100 years of research on child development.

One Common Core Standard to Rule Them All... A Single National Curriculum and an Unfair National Test... Any child who does not pass this test is a branded a failure and so is his teacher and so is his school
The marketing claim used to promote Common Core is that there should be one rigid set of national education standards determined by a few billionaires as being what is needed to prepare every student to be "career and college ready." Common Core is a "one size fits all" approach to education that makes about as much sense as offering shoes that comes only in Size 11. It does not matter how well the shoe is designed. No size 11 shoe will fit every foot. No national standard will fit every State, every school and every student. But the fact that it is an obviously bad idea is not relevant to the corporate raiders. The real point of Common Core is that it can be used to introduce new and more difficult Common Core tests. What is very difficult for many of us to understand is that the **Common Core tests are not related to Common Core standards.** So Common Core standards are LESS complete than prior standards and yet at the same time Common Core tests are much harder than prior tests. Hang in there for a few minutes and we will explain this apparent contradiction.

What is a Common Core Standard?

Common Core standards are similar to the prior State Learning Standards. They are simply statements about what a student should know to graduate from a given subject or grade.

Here is what a Common Core Standard looks like:

CCSS 4.04.17a... All students will _____. Then fill in the blank as to what a Wall Street Hedge Fund manager (or Bill Gates) thinks all students must be able to do by a given year in school such as in the 4th month of the 4th Grade.

Multiple this times 1,620 statements of what all children should be able to do and you have the Common Core standards. Note that the standards are the same whether the student is rich or poor or whether the student has a learning style, interest or motivation that favors the subject. The standard also ignores the class size of the school or the crime rate in the neighborhood. The standards were never reviewed by early childhood educators or experienced classroom teachers. But the biggest problem with Common Core standards is that they cannot change from State to State or from year to year. Unlike previous State Standards, there is no mechanism to revise, correct and improve the standards over time.

Many of the Common Core standards are very poorly written and much worse than prior State standards. The reason for this is that the prior State standards were typically written by groups of teachers who would then have to teach using these state standards.

Teachers want a logical set of standards that are developmentally appropriate for the children they will be teaching. Many of the teachers who wrote the prior State standards had more than 20 years of experience working with students. But the common core standards were written by three people who had no experience at all in teaching either elementary school, middle school or high school. This is why the standards and teaching methods often border on the absurd.

Comparing Common Core Billionaire Standards (CCBS) to Prior Educational Achievement Regulations and Learning Standards (PEARLS)

To see the real purpose of Common Core, we should understand how Common Core standards are different from prior educational standards in the United States. In the past, most States essentially had three high school learning standards. There was a "college prep" standard which included college prep courses and college prep tests such as the SAT test for the one in four students who planned to attend a four year college. We also had general high school courses and requirements to receive a general high school diploma and prepare students for a vocational technical career or attending a two year community college. This middle track worked well for the 50% of students who graduated from high school but did not go on to a four year college. Finally, we had a GED or high school equivalency test standard for the one in four students who failed to graduate from high school. This third track allowed late bloomers to prove to employers that they had mastered basic skills of math, reading and writing. A GED also allowed any late bloomer to qualify to enter a community college.

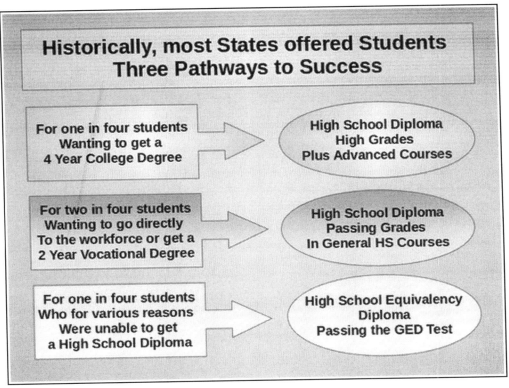

Common Core eliminates these three sets of standards and replaces them all with one uniform set of standards that apply to all students. Thus, the developers of Common Core created the phrase "prepare all students to be College and Career Ready." You will see this marketing phrase used on nearly all Common Core propaganda.

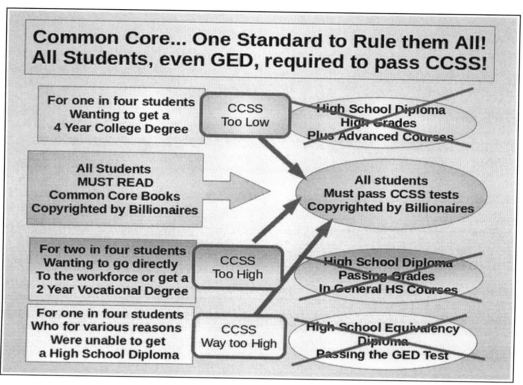

The problem with one standard to rule all students is that it does not really work for any of these three groups of students. Common Core standards, as currently written, are too low to prepare students for a four year college. Thus, you will hear some complain that Common Core is "dumbing down" our colleges which are being forced to accept students who pass the Common Core math test but who lack essential college level math skills and in the past would have been required to take remedial math courses at college. Others fear that Common Core standards may be too high for non-college track students. However, the truth is that Common Core standards are either the same as or LOWER than the prior high school learning standards used in many states.

To better understand Common Core, we will begin by comparing Common Core standards to the prior standards in my home state of Washington. We will then see how these standards were ignored the 8th Grade Common Core math test called SBAC was created. In other words, the Common Core standards have little to do with the Common Core tests. The high stakes tests were not created to align with Common Core standards. They were created simply to flunk as many students as possible.

Finally, to confirm that this is the rule rather than the exception, we will see how Common Core was used as an excuse to change the Washington State GED math exam, also with the goal of failing as many students as possible. My hope is that after seeing these examples, you will better understand the real purpose of Common Core. Like vouchers, charter schools, virtual schools, Leave No Child Untested and Race to the Bottom, Common Core is "designed to fail." None of these programs were ever intended to succeed. They are simply intended to undermine and destroy public schools in order to create hundreds of billions of dollars in new profits for Wall Street hedge fund managers.

Comparing Common Core Standards to Prior Washington State Standards
Common Core marketing propaganda promotes the myth that Common Core standards are more "rigorous and well researched" than prior State standards. Nothing could be farther from the truth. The Common Core standards were hastily written by people who obviously know nothing about child development or how children learn. At first glance, there appears to be almost no difference between the new Common Core standards and the prior learning standards in Washington State. For example, a detailed November 2010 comparison study by a group of 25 educators in Washington state, called the Washington Alignment Analysis – which compared all 332 prior State math standards word for word to the wording of the new Common Core math standards found that **95% of the Common Core standards matched the prior standards!**

Here is the link to the 80 page report:
http://www.k12.wa.us/Corestandards/pubdocs/WAAlignmentDocumentmathematics.pdf

However, the other 5% of the Common Core standards miss important educational tasks and replace them with tasks that are confusing, ambiguous and developmentally inappropriate. For example, Common Core standards fail to introduce the number line and number pattern comparison until the Second Grade. This is a huge mistake that will not work.

These are essential number comparison skills which should be introduced – and historically have been introduced – in Kindergarten. Instead, Common Core has students verbally act out situations involving addition and subtraction – even though many Kindergarten children lack the needed verbal and social skills. Common Core also demands that very young children engage in abstract reasoning even though young children are not capable of abstract reasoning and require instead concrete examples using actual objects. Rather than helping young children learn math, Common Core appears to be designed to reduce the chances that young children will learn math. In short, Common Core is designed to fail because the corporate raiders want our schools to fail.

Arne Duncan Magic Thinking

As bad as Common Core treats math in Kindergarten, its standards for English are even worse. The new standards require that **half of all reading in Kindergarten through Grade 8 be non-fiction.** Any child development specialist or Kindergarten teacher knows that young children are magical thinkers. They thrive on stories of super heroes and princesses in Magic Kingdoms. Fictional stories with lots of well chosen images are how we motivate children to learn to read. Arne Duncan thinks he can just wave a magic wand and have young children instead want to read the latest stock market news in the Wall Street Journal. In a way, Arnie is behaving just like a Kindergartner. He is engaging in Magic Thinking – a kind of thinking that runs throughout the Common Core standards.

An example of Arne Duncan's magical thinking is the claim that it is good for 3rd graders to spend three hours a day on high stakes tests under the extreme stress that their beloved teacher will be fired or their beloved school will be closed if they fail the test. This is similar to telling a child that they will lose their parents if they fail to pass a test. It is a form of child abuse and Arne Duncan should be put in jail.

Confusing Kindergarten Students with Hidden Partners

Here is a Common Core Kindergarten math example. It is a "finger" assignment which involves hidden partners. The problem with this is that Kindergarten students are concrete thinkers. They have a very difficult time describing or using hidden objects.

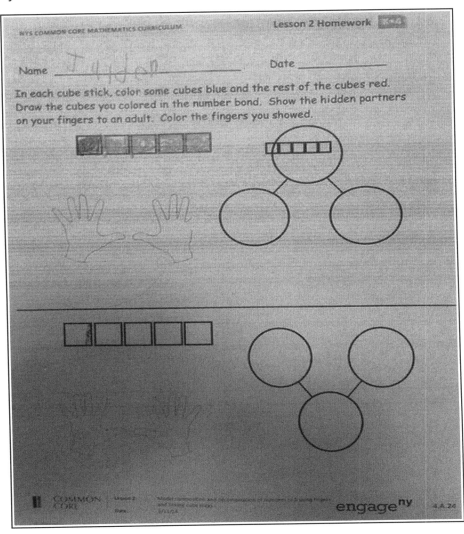

Jaiden was not able to complete the finger assignment. So he asked his dad to help him. The dad has a PhD in Chemistry but was not able to do this beginning Kindergarten assignment either. The dad is now an opponent of Common Core.

Shocking Fact: Not a single person on the Common Core Development Committee was a K-3 classroom teacher or early childhood professional

Here is what one Kindergarten teacher wrote: "Because of Common Core — despite being in tears, these innocent 5 and 6 year old children — children who used to be finger painting, learning nursery rhymes, engaging in dramatic play with miniature kitchens, role playing with costumes and puppets, and building forts with large wooden blocks — endured FIVE hours of standardized testing. FIVE hours of standardized testing of 5 and 6 year olds? Do you really think American parents and teachers are going to allow this testing abuse?
http://teacherslettterstobillgates.com/

Another one wrote: "As a kindergarten teacher teacher with 20 years experience in early childhood education, I am outraged! Every early childhood expert I know will be as well, but I want more than that! I want parents to be outraged! I want teachers and administrators to be outraged! I want them all to call Congress and demand Test Hearings Now! And then I want Congress to be outraged enough to put a gate up between corporations and public education to preserve public education for our children, our parents, our teachers, our communities, and our very democracy." http://teacherslettterstobillgates.com/

Here is another one: "What is developmentally appropriate is being eliminated by high stakes and testing: Five year olds should be playing, exploring, running, jumping, climbing, painting, modeling out of clay, creating, solving real world problems with their clear sense of innocent social justice, learning how to interact with large diverse groups through play, using Montessori-like hands-on materials from nature to learn math, reading, science, etc. Their interests and talents should be foremost, not canned scripted curriculum and "rigor". Five year olds should be free of high stakes, labels of "failure", culling, and standardized testing except in the few instances when we use these for evaluative purposes to get children the special education services they need, period."
http://teacherslettterstobillgates.com/

Here is another one: "Kindergarten children who barely know how to hold their pencil, write the alphabet or add 2 and 2 are expected to write topic sentences and use diagrams to illustrate math equations??? It is time to stop this insanity! We need a firewall between corporate education reform and public schools. We need a firewall between privatizers and public schools. We need a firewall between predatory philanthropists and public education!" Susan DuFresne – Full Day Kindergarten Teacher and Co-Author of Teachers' Letters to Bill Gates
http://teacherslettterstobillgates.com/

Here is another one by Angie Sullivan, Nevada Kindergarten Teacher:
"As a primary teacher, I speak out against common core because it is not developmentally appropriate. Obviously, no one was involved from the Early Childhood Community in writing these standards.

For Example: There are no writing standards in common core for Kindergarten. So they pushed down third grade standards to teach in Kindergarten. My writing standard for my at-risk 5 year olds is... write a fact and opinion paper. Yep - one standard, write a paper. There is not one good kindergarten teacher out there that thinks THAT should be the standard for five year olds who need to learn to hold a pencil and write their name first. Across the nation Kindergarten Teachers are protesting against common core. Something is very wrong when you push down standards for second and third grade and they end up in a Kindergarten classroom. The testing connected with these standards is ridiculous and useless. And this is what we spend our limited funds on now? Millions of dollars spent to test and fail - rather than to support and instruct students. And yes - common core and testing are a package deal... and both do affect curriculum - and it's a lie to state otherwise. And all of the above leads me to fully believe this is about money and not about kids. I am convinced that there has been a huge national campaign to invalidate educators and years of real education research -- so that corporations can make a profit implementing junk science like common core. Someone is making millions and billions -- it is not helping my Nevada students."

http://m.thenation.com/article/181762-venture-capitalists-are-poised-disrupt-everything-about-education-market

A Long Island parent writes: "Recently, my 10-year-old daughter asked me what it would take for me to let her stay home from school forever," she said. "Not tomorrow. Not next week. Forever. She said: 'I'm too stupid to do that math.' Your child is broken in spirit when they have lost their confidence and internalized words like stupid. That damage is not erased easily."

A NY superintendent described a new childhood mental health problem called the "Common Core Syndrome":

"And as a result of our rigorous, gritty approach, students will experience increased anxiety, stress, behavioral problems, sleep deprivation, respiratory issues, self-destructive and self-abusive behaviors."

"The people who wrote these standards do not appear to have any background in child development or early childhood education." Stephanie Feeney, University of Hawaii Childhood Development Professor and chair of the Advocacy Committee of the National Association of Early Childhood Teacher Educators.

The age inappropriate and confusing nature of Common Core standards was ridiculed by Stephen Colbert on the Colbert report. Here is the sample Common Core math problem Stephen used in his report.

> Mike saw 17 blue cars and 25 green cars at the toy store. How many cars did he see? Write a number sentence with a ▢ for the missing number. Explain how the number sentence shows the problem.
>
> 17+25 = ▢ I got the answer by talking in my brain and I agreed of the answer that my brain got.

"Common Core testing prepares our students for what they'll face as adults: Pointless stress and confusion." Stephen Colbert, The Colbert Report April 2014

Shaming a Second Grader for Failing to Show their Work

Second graders are still in the magic thinking phase of childhood. But Common Core ignores the research on child development and treats children as if they were little robots to be filled with facts rather than human beings to be filled with hopes and dreams. Here is an example of a Common Core problem given to a Second Grader who was labeled a failure for getting the problem wrong.

"Irini has a favorite day of the week. She chose this day because it is the only day that has an i in it. What is Irini's favorite day? Show your work in the tank." Math, Grade 2, c) 2013 by Scholastic Teaching Resources

The Second Grader got the correct answer (Friday) but was marked down for "failing to show his work."

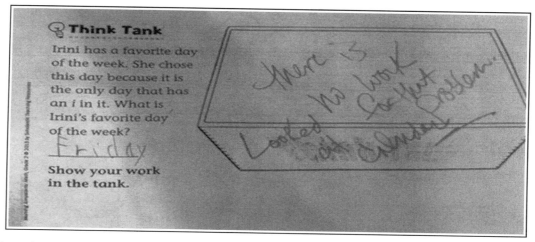

In the above example, a second grader got the correct answer but she failed the problem because she failed to show her work in the Think Tank. What would you have put in the Think Tank? The teacher gave the Second Grader a clue which was to "Look at calendar."

Apparently what the teacher wanted the student to do was list all of the days of the week in the Think Tank by looking at a calendar. The student was then supposed to circle the "i" in Friday indicating that Friday was the correct choice. Such a task of showing such logical detailed work might be appropriate for a high school student. But asking a Second Grader to do this task is developmentally inappropriate – especially for little boys who are as much as two years behind little girls in brain development in the Second Grade.

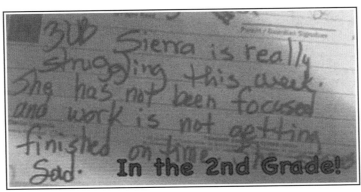

Common Core sets academic standards that very few children can meet.

Sadly, any teacher who fails to go along with this Common Core child abuse program is labeled as being against education reform and is in danger of losing their job.... Many caring teachers simply quit rather than subjecting their students to such abuse. This is why Ed Reform is also about attacking experienced teachers.

Early Childhood Educators Speak Out Against Common Core
Common Core promotes a military boot camp style of instruction called Direct Instruction also known as Drill and Kill. Two recent studies show that direct instruction can actually limit young childrens learning by turning them against school at an early age.

More than 500 early childhood professionals signed a statement opposing Common Core. The <u>Joint Statement of Early Childhood Health and Education Professionals on the Common Core Standards Initiative</u> was signed by educators, pediatricians, developmental psychologists, and researchers, including many of the most prominent members of those fields. Their statement reads in part: "We have grave concerns about the core standards for young children…. The proposed standards conflict with compelling new research in cognitive science, neuroscience, child development, and early childhood education about how young children learn, what they need to learn, and how best to teach them in kindergarten and the early grades…."
http://www.edweek.org/media/joint_statement_on_core_standards.pdf

The statement's four main concerns are based on abundant research on child development—facts that all parents and policymakers need to be aware of:
1. The K-3 standards will lead to long hours of direct instruction. This kind of "drill and kill" teaching will push active, play-based learning out of many kindergartens.
2. The standards will intensify the push for more standardized testing, which is highly unreliable for children under age eight.
3. Didactic instruction and testing will crowd out other crucial areas of young children's learning: active, hands-on exploration, and developing social, emotional, problem-solving, and self-regulation skills—all of which are difficult to standardize or measure but are the essential building blocks for academic and social accomplishment and responsible citizenship.
4. There is little evidence that standards for young children lead to later success. Many countries with top-performing high-school students provide rich play-based, nonacademic experiences—not standardized instruction—until age six or seven.

The National Association for the Education of Young Children is the foremost professional organization for early education in the U.S. Yet it had no role in the creation of the K-3 Core Standards. The Joint Statement opposing the standards was signed by three past presidents of the NAEYC—David Elkind, Ellen Galinsky, and Lilian Katz—and by Marcy Guddemi, the executive director of the Gesell Institute of Human Development; Dr. Alvin Rosenfeld of Harvard Medical School; Dorothy and Jerome Singer of the Yale University Child Study Center; Dr. Marilyn Benoit, past president of the American Academy of Child and Adolescent Psychiatry; Professor Howard Gardner of the Harvard Graduate School of Education; and many others.

The harm that Common Core is inflicting on children and elementary schools is enormous. Dr. Carla Horwitz of the Yale Child Study Center notes that many of our most experienced and gifted teachers of young children are giving up in despair. "They are leaving the profession," says Horwitz, "because they can no longer do what they know will ensure learning and growth in the broadest, deepest way. The Core Standards will cause suffering, not learning, for many, many young children."

This is a 25 minute video by Dr. Megan Koschnick a Child Developmental Psychologist at Notre Dame explaining why Common Core standards are not developmentally appropriate for young children.
http://www.youtube.com/watch?v=vrQbJlmVJZo

Common Core Standards & Tests being Developed for Preschool Children

Not content to control merely Kindergarten through 12th Grade Learning, Common Core advocates are planning a "cradle to grave" set of education standards to include both preschool and college level national standards. According to the billionaires, it is never too soon to get your toddler career and college ready. Arne Duncan has said that we should be able to look a Second Grader in the eye and tell them if they are "career and college ready." Of course, we will also need to explain to them what a college is and what a career is.

Public Openness versus Corporate Secrecy

Under the prior Washington State learning standards and high stakes tests, parents had a legal right to review the standards and review the test questions given to their child. Teachers also had a right to review the questions that their students would be subjected to. However, because Common Core is copyrighted and so are the Common Core tests, neither parents or teachers are allowed to see the actual test questions of the two Common Core tests (SBAC and PARCC).

The State of New York actually had to pay private corporations to get them to realize just some of the Common Core test questions given to students in New York in the past couple of years. Keep in mind that the federal government paid these private corporations (SBAC and PARCC... both of which are basically Pearson) hundreds of millions of dollars to develop the Common Core tests. So the idea that we need to pay again for a test that we as tax payers have already paid for is absurd.

Common Core is Set in Stone

Here is a quote from Diane Ravitch on this inability to revise bad standards: "Another problem presented by the Common Core standards is that there is no one in charge of fixing them. If teachers find legitimate problems and seek remedies, there is no one to turn to. If the demands for students in kindergarten and first grade are developmentally inappropriate, no one can make changes. The original writing committee no longer exists. No organization or agency has the authority to revise the standards. The Common Core standards might as well be written in stone." Diane Ravitch
http://www.washingtonpost.com/blogs/answer-sheet/wp/2014/01/18/everything-you-need-to-know-about-common-core-ravitch/

Summary

Common Core standards, curriculum and tests force all kids into the same academic track... a track that does not actually serve any students. The standards are very poorly written and are developmentally inappropriate... especially for very young children. The standards are missing many important components. Finally, the standards are set in stone and there is no way to fix them.

What is Next?

Now that we understand that Common Core is not developmentally appropriate, it the next section we will take a closer look at the actual common core math standards and curriculum. Take a deep breathe... Things are about to get pretty ugly.

2.3 Common Core Math is Insane

As many parents and teachers have discovered, the new Common Core math standards and curriculum are often quite different from prior math standards and curriculum. For example, the following is a new math method for elementary schools based on the Common Core Elementary School Math Standards:

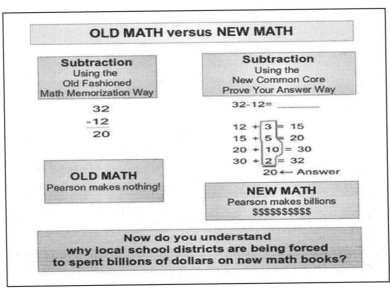

This new math method is based on something called set theory which is used a lot with Computer Programming. Sets are any group of numbers... for example, even numbers are one set of numbers and odd numbers are another set of numbers. Any group of numbers can be a set and you can define a series of any operations for any set of numbers. This process is also called **Number Transformation.** For example, understanding that the number 8 can also be expressed as "10 minus 2." The problem with math transformations is that they are abstract and beyond the cognitive development of young children. Here is an example of Common Core Math Transformation:

Question #8: Tell how to make 10 when adding 8 + 5:

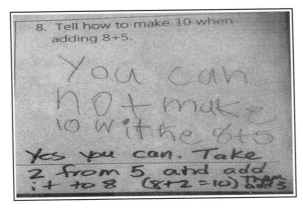

More is Less... Subtracting by Adding

Another confusing part of Common Core Math is that to subtract you need to add and to add you need to subtract. Here is an example.

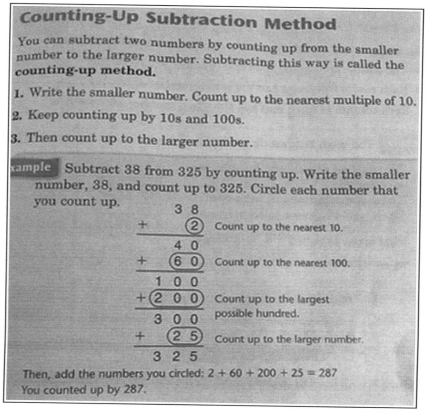

George Orwell warned us that "New Think" would involve convincing us that war is peace and bad is good. With Common Core New Think, now to subtract, we must add and to add we must subtract. Welcome to the insane world of Common Core math!

Set theory is not merely limited to real world examples. This is what makes set theory so useful for computer programming. The problem is that set theory is extremely abstract and well beyond the brains of most young children to understand. Remember that young children are "concrete thinkers." The old style of teaching math is based on concrete thinking and concrete reasoning. Even many adults (parents) are not able to understand the new type of abstract math. It is not merely children who are forced to start crying when confronted with this new form of math, it is also their parents. This new math is not supported by any child development research. Instead, it is largely the produce of one person, David Coleman's friend and college buddy, Jason Zimba, the person with Student Achievement Partners who wrote the insane Common Core math standards.

Common Core also uses confusing word problems and puzzles which are confusing even for math experts to solve.

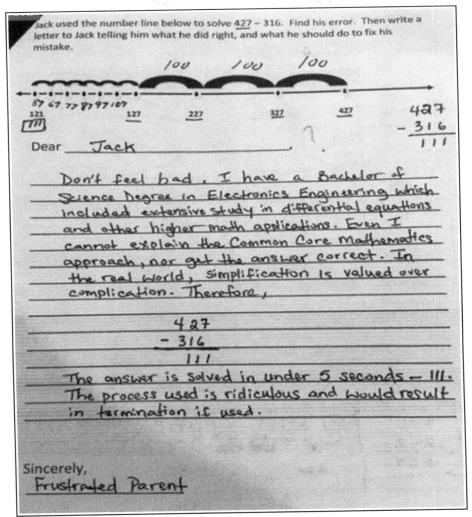

Common Core Math Shortcomings run all the way through 12th Grade

Setting aside the problems with Common Core assignments and Common Core tests, the problems with the Common Core standards are not merely limited to Kindergarten and the First Grade. According to the detailed comparison study in Washington State, in the Second Grade, Common Core standards fail to address days, weeks, months and years when calculating time. Instead Common Core only covers hours and minutes. In the Third Grade, Common Core fails to cover the relationship between multiplication and repeated addition and/or the relationship between division and repeated subtraction. Common Core also fails to cover the concept of equality. (can it be billionaires don't want kids to know about the concept of equality?).
http://web.archive.org/web/20111124022641/http://k12.wa.us/Corestandards/pub
docs/WAAlignmentDocumentmathematics.pdf

In the Fourth Grade, Common Core fails to compare fractions to decimals and/or decimals to fractions. I guess if you are rich enough, you do not need to learn about fractions of a dollar. In the Fifth Grade, Common Core does not have students determine the formula for the area of a triangle. (See page 37).

In Sixth Grade, Common Core fails to cover the inverse relationship between multiplication and division. (See page 40). Nor does it cover 3.14 as the common approximation of pi. Nor does it cover the important concept that probability should be expressed as a percent. (See page 43).

In the Seventh grade, Common Core includes histograms, line plots and box plots – but not stem and leaf or circle graphs. (See page 50). Ironically, circle graphs are on the Common Core test. Perhaps including items on the test that are not part of the standard curriculum is intended to keep the kids on their toes and get them used to being judged on things they were never taught.

In the Eight Grade, Common Core Algebra One standards are about the same as prior Algebra One standards. However, Common Core Algebra One tests are much harder than the prior Algebra One tests. For Algebra Two, Common Core standards only include linear inequalities and not quadratic inequalities. But kids are still tested on quadratic inequalities!

Geometry also is pretty strange with Common Core. Common Core standards basically ignore Euclidean Geometry and move right into Cartesian geometry.

This is a major mistake because Euclidean Geometry is much easier for kids to grasp (because it relates better to the real world) that Cartesian Geometry.

Cartesian geometry may better relate to computer programming - but it is more abstract than Euclidean geometry. There are many critiques of the Common Core Geometry standards posted on the Internet written by Geometry instructors which explain the need for Euclidean Geometry and make it clear that Common Core does a bad job with Geometry.

Common Core Math Tests are even more confusing than Common Core Math

In March 2015, math educator, Steven Rasmussen, wrote a detailed report condemning numerous flaws in the Common Core SBAC math test. His report can be found at this link:
https://dl.dropboxusercontent.com/u/76111404/Common%20Core%20Tests%20Fatally%20Flawed%2015_03_07.pdf

He found that the SBAC test math questions did not comply with and in many cases completely contradicted the Common Core math standards. Even worse, with some questions, it was impossible to provide the correct answer while in other cases incorrect answers were accepted as being correct! Here is a quote from his report:

> "No tests that are so unfair should be given to anyone. Certainly, with stakes so high for students and their teachers, these Smarter Balanced tests should not be administered. The boycotts of these tests by parents and some school districts are justified. In fact, responsible government bodies should withdraw the tests from use before they do damage."

You you still think there is nothing evil about Common Core and the SBAC test, we urge you to read and download Steven's shocking report. Steven wondered how a test that was funded with over one hundred million dollars in tax payer funds – one of the most expensive tests ever created – could have been constructed in such a deeply flawed manner. Certainly, if the goal of SBAC is to actually promote the Common Core standards, it is a complete failure. However, if the goal is to create mass confusion and chaos among teachers and students – resulting in flunking as many students as possible, then the fatal flaws in the SBAC test make more sense. While Steven attributed the flaws of the SBAC test to reckless incompetence, we have a different theory. We think that the flaws in the SBAC test were deliberately included as a feature – part of the "designed to fail" nature of the test. It is simply not possible to teach students how to pass a test where the wrong answer is the right answer and the right answer is the wrong answer!

Thus, the marketing hype around Common Core that it "raises the bar" or "is more rigorous" than prior State standards is simply not true. Those who have supported Common Core under the false belief that it would "raise the bar" and thereby motivate students to achieve higher standards should rethink their support of Common Core. Common Core does not raise the bar.

Instead, it is merely an excuse to artificially lower student test scores. We advocate a return to the higher standards that preceded Common Core. Our students deserve fair standards that were created by educators and child development specialists – not incomplete and sloppily written standards that were written by billionaires and Wall Street Hedge Fund Managers intent on destroying schools and increasing corporate profits.

Specific Concerns about the Common Core Math Curriculum
In addition to the general concerns that Common Core is not needed, harms students and takes control of curriculum and testing away from teachers and local school districts, there are many specific concerns that upset parents and teachers. We will only look at four of them here.

First, Common Core ignores child development research by assigning tasks to very young children before their brains are ready to do the task. Specifically, very young children are "concrete" learners who use physical objects to understand the world. The billionaire developers of Common Core failed to understand this and included many abstract concepts and tasks for very young students. In short, Common Core curriculum is designed to fail.

Second, Common Core new math techniques are not backed by any scientific research. This is in part because Common Core was adopted so quickly that there was no time to do research before Common Core was implemented. But the lack of research was also likely due to the fact that the developers of Common Core KNOW it will not work. The last thing they want is research.

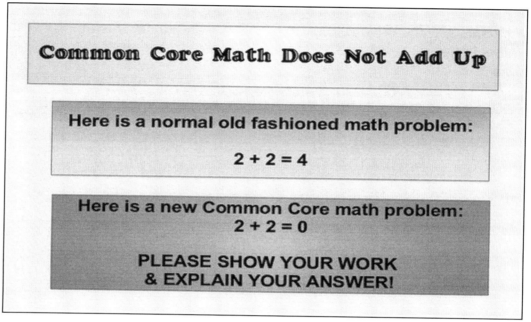

Those familiar with set theory understand that sets of numbers can have any result depending on how the properties of the set are defined. Just like with the rest of the Common Core standards, one is not limited to reality. Also, when billionaires calculate their taxes, no matter how much they make, the amount of taxes they pay is always zero. All they need is a fake non-profit like the Gates Foundation to set up a tax evasion and money laundering scheme. This is why it is so important to teach kids new math – so they will better understand how our modern tax code works.

Third, Common Core math curriculum devalues Euclidean Geometry and replaces it with Cartesian Geometry. This makes it harder for young students to learn geometry because Euclidean geometry is more concrete and related to the "real world" than Cartesian Geometry. For hundreds of years, students were first taught Euclidean Geometry and then Cartesian Geometry. Many math instructors fear that skipping this step will make it harder for some students to learn geometry.

While Cartesian Geometry does lend itself better to computer learning on a two dimensional (X, Y axis) grid, the real reason for this change is to make geometry harder to learn. Just as the change away from addition and multiplication tables is to make basic math harder to learn. The underlying goal is that Common Core has been "designed to fail."

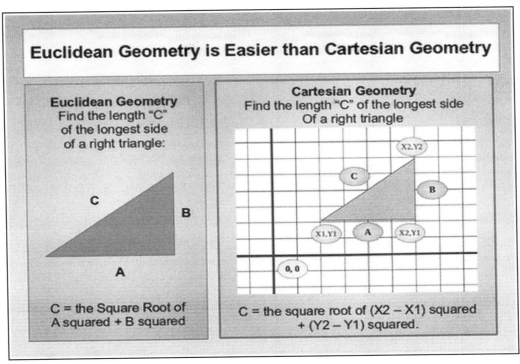

In other words, the goal is not to improve math instruction. It is to destroy math instruction and therefore increase the chances that students will fail standardized tests. The real plan is that increasing the failure rate in public schools will increase public acceptance for a private for profit takeover of the public schools.

Fourth, Common Core does not include any Precalculus standards. Massachusetts was forced to discard their Precalculus standards in order to adopt the much weaker Common Core standards. The problem here is that with a Common Core "teach to the test" mentality, it is less likely that Precalculus will be offered in high schools in the future meaning that students will not be ready to take Calculus during their first year of college. Because Calculus is required to start engineering programs, colleges are pretty upset about Common Core "dumbing down" their Engineering programs.

"It is astonishing that Massachusetts adopted Common Core's standards without asking the engineering, science, and mathematics faculty at its own higher-education institutions (and the mathematics teachers in its own high schools) to analyze Common Core's definition of college readiness and make public their recommendations. After all, who could be better judges of what students need for a science, technology, engineering and math major? Massachusetts should revise or abandon its Common Core's mathematics standards as soon as possible." Dr. Sandra Stotsky was a member of Common Core's Validation Committee from 2009-10. She is professor emerita at the University of Arkansas.

University of Washington instructor, Cliff Mass, wrote the following about the Common Core Math Standards: "Are the new Common Core standards better than the current ones enjoyed in our state? The answer is a clearly no. A review by the state math watchdog group, wheresthemath.com, has documented a number of problems with Common Core compared to our current standards. Common Core standards are extraordinarily difficult to read and decipher, a critical requirement for any standard. It is will be very difficult for most teachers to understand what they need to be teaching--which is a huge problem. Want an example? Here is an example of a fifth grade Common Core standard: Interpret the product (a/b) × q as a parts of a partition of q into b equal parts; as the result of a sequence of operations a × q ÷ b. For example, use a visual fraction model to show (2/3) × 4 = 8/3, & create a story context for this equation. Do the same with (2/3) × (4/5) = 8/15. (In general, (a/b) × (c/d) = ac/bd.)

There have been no pilots or tests of these new Common Core standards. No proof that they enhance student performance. Can you imagine pushing a new national math standard without insuring that students learn better with them? Common Core Math Standards: Worse for Our Kids and Millions of Dollars Wasted
http://cliffmass.blogspot.com/2011/01/common-core-math-standards-worse-for.html

What is next?
Now that we better understand the drawbacks of the Common Core math standards and curriculum, in the next section, we will look at the decline in popularity of Common Core standards, curriculum and tests as more parents and teachers have become aware of the shocking nature of this war against our children.

2.4 Support for Common Core Plunges

So far, we have shown that the Common Core standards, curriculum and high stakes tests are a mess. They were written in secret by a small group of people with no background in education and then forced on States who were desperate to get billions of dollars in "Race to the Top" federal funding. Common Core has been corrupted by political manipulation, corporate profiteering and an unfair scoring system designed to ensure that two out of three children will fail the new high stakes tests they will be forced to take in 2015. Currently young children in over half of the States are being subjected to Common Core standards and curriculum. In the Spring of 2015, more than 30 million children will be subjected to the Common Core tests (SBAC and PARCC). Thus, in 2015, more than 20 million children will be severely and permanently harmed by being unfairly labeled as "failures." This will go down as one of the worst crimes against children in history.

Despite the horrific nature of this crime against our children, a June 2014 Poll showed that nearly half of all Americans have never even heard of Common Core. Only one in four Americans said that they had heard "a lot" about it.
http://msnbcmedia.msn.com/i/MSNBC/Sections/A_Politics/14463%20JUNE%20NBC-WSJ%20Poll%20%286-18%20Release%29.pdf

Even those one in four Americans that have heard a lot about Common Core have been badly misinformed about them thanks to a multibillion dollar mass media propaganda campaign paid for by Bill Gates. This misinformation campaign includes a series of "push polls" that have made false statements about Common Core in order to drum up support for Common Core.

For example, the poll taken in June 2014 included this misleading question: *"Just to make sure that everyone has the same information, let me describe the Common Core standards in a bit more detail. The Common Core standards are a new set of education standards for English and math that have been set to internationally competitive levels and would be used in every state for students in grades K through 12. Based on this information, do you support or oppose the adoption and implementation of the Common Core standards in your state?"*

The above statement is simply a lie. The Common Core standards have NOT been set to internationally competitive standards. No other nation on earth uses standards so high that two thirds of their students are unable to achieve the standards! Despite this obvious attempt to manipulate the public, **only one in four people said they "strongly supported" Common Core. One in four strongly oppose it and the remaining half have yet to make up their minds.** As is typical of most polls, the average respondent was much more wealthy that the average American with an annual family income of $50,000 to $75,000. Only one in four of the respondents had a child living in their household.

Thankfully, despite all the lies, deceptions, misinformation and push polls, resistance to Common Core standards, Common Core curriculum and Common Core testing by parents and teachers is growing. Despite the fact that we are going up against the richest and most powerful people in the world, who have used four billion dollars in "Race to the Top" blackmail money to corrupt education in 45 States, there are several reasons to believe that parents and teachers are beginning to wake up to the threats facing our kids and our schools.

First, a November 2013 national poll found that 56% of Americans now oppose standardized tests as the primary way to determine how schools, teachers and students are doing. Only one in four still support this insane practice.

http://www.rasmussenreports.com/public_content/lifestyle/education/56_oppose_use_of_standardized_tests_as_chief_measure_of_school_performance

Second, in May 2014, the Chicago Teachers Union voted unanimously for a resolution opposing Common Core. Equally encouraging, polls in Chicago show that the leader of the Chicago Teachers Union is much more popular than the current Ed Reform mayor of Chicago.
http://www.substancenews.net/articles.php?page=4967

The above may seem like a joke. But Duncan actually said this. Here is the link.

http://cityroom.blogs.nytimes.com/2009/02/19/new-education-secretary-visits-brooklyn-school/?_php=true&_type=blogs&_r=0

Third, a June 2014 poll taken in New York in the wake of the Common Core test disaster of 2013. This poll showed that **82 percent of New Yorkers now oppose Common Core Standards and their associated high stakes tests**. In March 2014, the Governor of New York was forced to place a several year hold on Common Core testing in New York. This shows that once kids are harmed by Common Core tests, parents start to wake up.
http://wnyt.com/article/stories/s3474870.shtml

Fourth, a national June 2014 poll found parents with school aged children were rapidly turning against Common Core. Only 34% believe the federal government should set education standards for the entire nation. That is an 18-point drop from 52% who supported federal education standards in a November 2013 poll. Meanwhile, parents who oppose Common Core rose from one in four in November 2013 to one on two in June 2014.
http://www.rasmussenreports.com/public_content/business/general_business/june_2014/common_core_support_among_those_with_school_age_kids_plummets

Fifth, in July 2014, the **National Education Association** voted to call for the resignation of US Department of (Corporate) Education and Chief Snake Oil Salesman, Arne Duncan. Similar resolutions had failed in past years, but the passage of this one is an indication that teachers are finally starting to wake up.

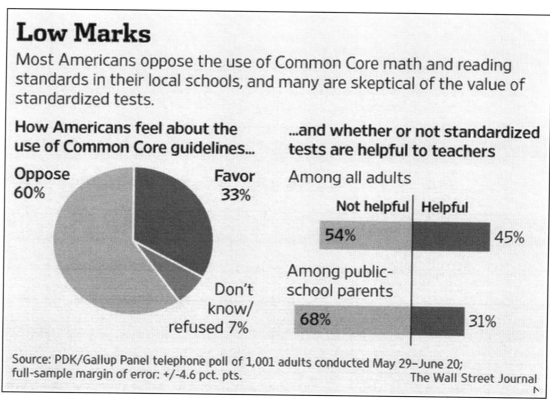

Sixth, in August 2014, a national poll found that 60% of the public and 62% of public school parents now oppose Common Core. This same poll showed that 68% of public school parents now oppose high stakes standardized tests as a waste of time and money. This same poll found that Americans preferred their local schools to be controlled by a local school board instead of the federal government by a margin of 4 to 1. http://pdkintl.org/noindex/PDK_Poll_46.pd

Seventh, in August 2014, our home state of Washington became the first State to stand up to Arne Duncan by refusing to implement his phony teacher evaluation program. Arne responded by revoking the NCLB waiver for Washington State. http://www2.ed.gov/policy/elsec/guid/esea-flexibility/index.html

The result of our State standing up to Arne Duncan was that every parent in Washington State received a letter telling them that their local school is a failure. This includes some of the most highly rated schools in the United States!

This crazy letter from Arne Duncan has sparked almost as much anger in Washington State as the despicable Common Core test results sparked in New York State – as many parents are learning about ed reform scams. Parents in Washington State want to know why their beloved local schools were declared a failure. The research of these parents will hopefully help wake them up to the scam of fake education reform.

> In August 2014, every parent and every child
> In Washington State received a letter
> Warning them that their beloved local school
> Had been declared a failure by Arne Duncan.

In October 2014, a poll of 27,000 teachers in Tennessee found that after three years of bad experiences with the Common Core, 56% of teachers want to abandon it completely. "Support for Common Core among Tennessee teachers has waned so much since last year that a majority now opposes the academic standards." Just a year earlier, 60% supported Common Core. By October 2014, only 31% still supported Common Core.
http://www.tennessean.com/story/news/education/2014/09/24/common-core-losing-support-tennessee-teachers-survey-finds/16171421/

Some polls have indicated support for Common Core. However, every one of these was a "push poll" that first lied to the public about the advantages and drawbacks of Common Core and then asked for the opinion of the public based upon the assumption that the lies they were told were true! Here is an example of one such push poll taken in Washington State in 2014.

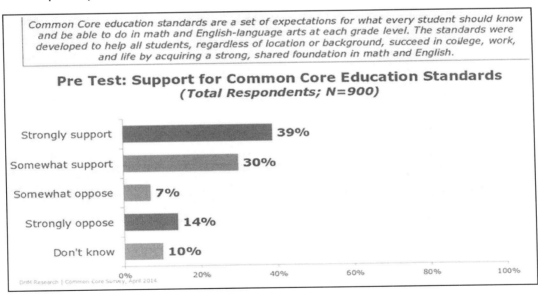

There is no evidence that any of the benefits described in this poll are true. But making these false claims biases the results. Very few parents would support Common Core if they knew the tests would unfairly label 700,000 of our one million school children as failures.

States Leaving Common Core like Rats Deserting a Sinking Ship
In the past couple of years, State after State has dropped out of the Common Core nightmare. Like rats deserting a sinking ship, States have dropped the Common Core Standards or the Common Core tests or both.

In September 2010, Arne Duncan awarded $330 million to PARCC ($170 million) and SBAC ($160 million). According to a USDOE press release, 46 States signed up for either or both of the two Common Core testing scams. But given Minnesota's resistance to the assessments, we will list it as one of the five non-adopter States:

2010 PARCC ONLY – 14 States: Arizona, Arkansas, California, Florida, Illinois, Indiana, Louisiana, Maryland, Massachusetts, Mississippi, New Mexico, New York, Rhode Island, and Tennessee.

2010 SBAC ONLY – 19 States: Connecticut, Hawaii, Idaho, Iowa, Kansas, Maine, Michigan, Missouri, Montana, Nevada, North Carolina, Oregon, South Dakota, Utah, Vermont, Washington, West Virginia, Wisconsin, and Wyoming.

2010 BOTH PARCC and SBAC (observers only) – 12 States: Alabama, Colorado, Delaware, Georgia, Kentucky, North Dakota, New Hampshire, New Jersey, Ohio, Oklahoma, Pennsylvania, and South Carolina. This meant that PARCC originally had a total of 26 States and SBAC had a total of 31 States.

2010 Never Adopted – 5 States: Alaska, Minnesota, Nebraska, Texas, and Virginia. Only 5 States resisted the propaganda and bribery.

Here is a map of the various States Common Core Tests in 2010.

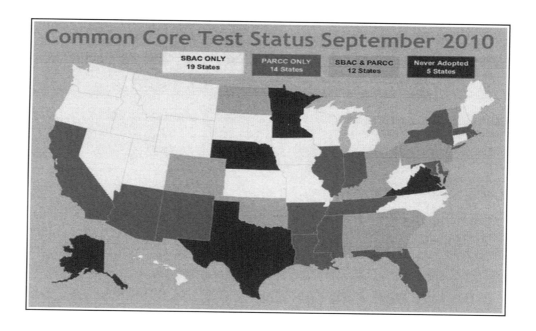

Both Common Core Testing Scams Have Fallen Apart

The biggest loser has been PARCC – which is a test made by a terrible corporation called Pearson. As of January 2015, of the original 25 States in the PARCC camp, with 31 million students, there are only 10 States that have not yet abandoned the PARCC ship. These remaining states have only 5 million students. So PARCC total test takers have fallen by more than 80%:

PARCC Test down from 26 States to 10 States

A minimum of 15 States is required to get $186 million in federal funding. However, PARCC is now down to 10 States. In December 2014, Congress killed the remaining Race to the Top funding – which was funding both the PARCC and SBAC Common Core tests. It is therefore uncertain what Arne Duncan will do or how PARCC will be funded in the future. The first to leave PARCC was California which switched to SBAC on June 9 2011. This was followed by South Carolina in August 2012. In 2013, Alabama left in February, Pennsylvania left in June, Indiana left in July, Georgia and North Dakota left in August and Florida left in September. In Florida in 2013, a furor erupted when only 27 percent of fourth-graders passed the PARCC writing test. The state Board of Education promptly, and retroactively, lowered the score required to pass the test - and in a flash, the pass rate jumped to 81 percent. So much for the magic of high stakes tests!

In 2014, Oklahoma left in January, Kentucky left in March, Florida left in May, Arizona, Louisiana and Tennessee left in June, New York made "special arrangements" in July. In New York, after two years of public outrage over the PARCC test (that only had about a 33% pass rate), the State legislature voted to delay the consequences of the Common Core test and to set up a different State controlled test. All of the above revolts meant that by the August 2014 deadline to pay Pearson for the 2015 PARCC test, only 10 States were left: AR, CO, IL, MD, MA, NJ, NM, OH, and RI. Mississippi withdrew from PARCC in January 2015 and will soon be out of Common Core. Delaware and New Hampshire are now both SBAC States. Indiana, Oklahoma Louisiana and South Carolina have repealed the Common Core standards altogether. In New Jersey, a bill that would slow down the introduction of the Common Core education standards and the use of test scores in teacher evaluations passed the Assembly Education Committee with unanimous support. So it is likely New Jersey will shortly be out of PARCC. This would drop the number of PARCC States down to 8. The PARCC contract in New Mexico is also in dispute after a Pearson connected "bidding scandal." If this lawsuit succeeds, PARCC/Pearson would be down to 7 States. Massachusetts has put PARCC on hold with a 2 year phase in. This would drop PARCC to only 6 States.

http://truthinamericaneducation.com/common-core-state-standards/states-fighting-back-map/

SBAC Test also losing States like Rats leaving a Sinking Ship
In 2010, SBAC started with 31 states, 17 of which were designated as governing states. As of July 21, 2014, SBAC still lists 22 states on its website. Unlike PARCC, SBAC appears to still be above the 15-state mark for federal funding.
http://www.smarterbalanced.org/

Here is a map of the States from the SBAC website:

According to the SBAC website, the 17 governing States are: CA, CT, DE, HI, ID, ME, MI, MT, NV, NH, ND, OR, SD, VT, WA, WV, and WI. The 3 remaining affiliated Members are IA, NC and WY. This would indicate that SBAC still has 20 States. The map incorrectly shows Missouri. But they are developing their own test for 2016.

In 2012, Utah withdrew from SBAC. In 2013, Pennsylvania opted out in favor of its own test. In December 2013, Kansas jumped ship. Missouri defunded Common Core testing in favor of their own State test. Missouri still owes SBAC $4.2 million for a test it has now disavowed. So there is still a chance it will use the test in 2015 but then get a different test for 2016. Wyoming joined SBAC in late 2010. However, it has decided to not sign the SBAC agreement and will not administer the SBAC test in 2015. So they are effectively opting out. In August 2014, Iowa also withdrew from SBAC. This brings SBAC down to the following 18 States: CA, CT, DE, HI, ID, ME, MI, MT, NV, NC, NH, ND, OR, SD, VT, WA, WV, and WI. North Carolina and Michigan may be the next two States to pull out of SBAC. Combined with the 8 States still actively in PARCC, there will be about 25 States giving the SBAC and PARCC tests in 2015.

http://www.realcleareducation.com/articles/2014/12/09/common_core_future_elections_heat_map_1140.html#map

Here is a map of where things likely stand as of January 2015:

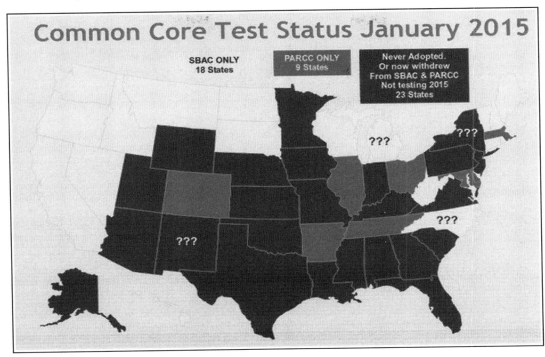

Below is a table summarizing all of these changes.

State	2010 CCSS Test	2015 January Common Core Status
Alabama	Both	Neither national test now debating CC
Alaska	Not adopted	Joined SBAC. Then withdrew in 2014. Now neither.
Arizona	PARCC	Pulled out of PARCC & pledged to pull out of Common Core
Arkansas	PARCC	Bill to pull out failed so still a PARCC State.
California	PARCC	Switched from PARCC to SBAC on June 9 2011
Colorado	Both	Repeal vote failed. Now PARCC.
Connecticut	SBAC	Still SBAC
Delaware	Both	Now just SBAC.
Florida	PARCC	Pulled out of PARCC and CC.
Georgia	Both	Was PARCC only. Then pulled out of PARCC and CC.
Hawaii	SBAC	Still SBAC
Idaho	SBAC	Repeal vote failed. Still SBAC.
Illinois	PARCC	Still PARCC
Indiana	PARCC	Pulled out of PARCC and CC.
Iowa	SBAC	Pulled out of SBAC and CC.
Kansas	SBAC	Pulled out of SBAC but still has CC.
Kentucky	Both	Then just PARCC. Then pulled out of PARCC and CC.
Louisiana	PARCC	Governor signed order to withdraw from PARCC June 2014.
Maine	SBAC	Still SBAC but considering repeal.
Maryland	PARCC	Now lead PARCC state after Florida withdrew.
Massachusetts	PARCC	Delayed PARCC testing for two years in November 2013.

State	2010 CCSS Test	2015 January Common Core Status
Michigan	SBAC	Still SBAC but will replace with their own test in 2016.
Minnesota	Not adopted	Neither PARCC or SBAC
Mississippi	PARCC	Canceled PARCC in January 2015.
Missouri	SBAC	Delayed for 2 years in June 2014, making own standards.
Montana	SBAC	Repeal vote failed. Still SBAC.
Nebraska	Not adopted	Neither PARCC or SBAC
Nevada	SBAC	Still SBAC.
New Hampshire	Both	Now SBAC.
New Jersey	Both	Now PARCC but Assembly Ct. voted unanimously to leave.
New Mexico	PARCC	Still PARCC but lawsuit is pending.
New York	PARCC	Arranged for special test & delayed most until 2022.
North Carolina	SBAC	Still in SBAC for 2015 but will replace SBAC and CC in 2016.
North Dakota	Both	Now SBAC. But likely to replace with State test & standards.
Ohio	Both	Now PARCC but debating options.
Oklahoma	Both	Withdrew from CC & CC tests. Using State tests & standards.
Oregon	SBAC	Still SBAC.
Pennsylvania	Both	Withdrew from CC & CC tests. Using State tests & standards.
Rhode Island	PARCC	Still PARCC
South Carolina	Both	Withdrew from CC & CC tests. Using State tests & standards.
South Dakota	SBAC	Still SBAC.
Tennessee	PARCC	Pulled out of PARCC and is debating CC.
Texas	Not adopted	Neither PARCC or SBAC
Utah	SBAC	Pulled out of SBAC & changed name of CC to Utah Core.
Vermont	SBAC	Still SBAC.
Virginia	Not adopted	Neither PARCC or SBAC
Washington	SBAC	Still SBAC.
West Virginia	SBAC	Still SBAC.
Wisconsin	SBAC	Still SBAC.
Wyoming	SBAC	Never signed SBAC agreement and will not use in 2015.

How many kids will take either the SBAC or PARCC test in 2015?
When you combine the New York Pearson test, which is similar to the Pearson PARCC test, it is likely that up to 60 percent of US 50 million students will take the SBAC or PARCC tests in 2015. This would mean 30 million students will be exposed to these toxic unfair "designed to fail" tests in 2015 and that 20 million of these 30 million children will be unfairly labeled as "failure" - including students that would be among the top performing students in the world. Most of these "failures" will be from poor families. There is now a rapidly spreading national revolt against Common Core standards as more folks become more aware of the drawbacks of this scam. There are bills opposing Common Core standards and Common Core tests in nearly every State in the nation.

While the Common Core tests are being rejected, what about the Common Core Standards they are supposed to measure?

While some states are repealing the standards and replacing them with their own in-house standards, others have simply chosen to continue using the Common Core standards, but under another name. Arizona, Florida and Iowa have all renamed the standards as "Arizona's College and Career Ready Standards," the "Next Generation Sunshine State Standards" and "The Iowa Core," respectively. Upon signing the executive order to change the name of Arizona's standards, Gov. Jan Brewer said the move was "reaffirming Arizona's right to set education policy," although the Common Core standards will still be used.

Parents Protest Punitive High Stakes Tests

Clearly, a backlash against high-stakes standardized testing is sweeping through U.S. school districts as parents, teachers, and administrators protest that the exams are unfair, unreliable and unnecessarily punitive. **This is not a left vs right issue. It is not a Republican vs. Democrat issue. It is a propaganda vs. truth issue**. The closer we get to a billionaire takeover of our public schools, the more parents and teachers are waking up and starting to fight back. Our goal is to give parents and teachers the information they need to fight back and win

What does the future hold for Common Core Blackmail?

Given the reaction of parents to Common Core after test results were announced in Kentucky, New York and Florida during the past two years, and given that Congress recently defunded Arne Duncan's Race to the Top blackmail scheme, it would be reasonable to conclude that Common Core tests and standards will disappear in the next couple of years. As we've explained, 30 million students in 26 States will be subjected to Common core tests in 2015. 20 million of these students will be falsely and unfairly labeled as "failure" thanks to the inflated Common Core cut scores and manipulated Common Core test questions. This will result in 40 million angry parents – most of whom are also voters.

How will 40 million Upset Parents affect the 2016 Congressional and Presidential Elections?

Given how close Congressional and Presidential elections have been in recent years, 40 million upset parents and the issue of Common Core privatization of our public schools could be a major issue in the 2016 elections and opposition to Common Core by either major party could tip the election towards one or the other of the two major political parties.

But this assumes that at least one of the parties and their Presidential candidate is wise enough to oppose Common Core. Unfortunately, billionaires have backed both of the likely presidential candidates for the 2016 election – Jeb Bush and Hillary Clinton and both candidates support Common Core. Billionaires have been controlling our Presidential elections since at least the 1980s.

Five Presidents all promoting Common Core

Common Core is closely linked to the Reagan testing craze that began in the 1980s and continued with the Bush and Clinton administrations in the 1990s and with the Bush II and Obama administrations after that. There is a direct link from the National Governors Association in 1990 to Achieve in 1996 to the American Diploma Project and No Child Left Behind in 2001 to Student Achievement Partners in 2007 to Common Core and Race to the Top in 2009. It is not just a coincidence that all of the States that were "early adopters" of Common Core were previously part of the American Diploma Project Network (ADP). In fact, there was no difference between ADP and CCSS.

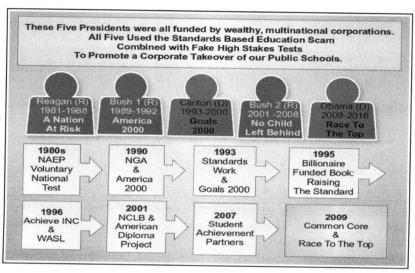

Why did NGA, CCSSO and Achieve insist on writing new national standards when there were already many States that had standards superior to Common Core Standards?

Many commentators had observed that States such as Massachusetts had spent years developing their own State Standards that were written by teachers and had broad acceptance by teachers. So why was Student Achievement Partners contracted to basically re-invent the wheel? Some have claimed new standards were needed so that NGA and CCSSO could own and copyright the Common Core Standards. But this just leads to the question: Why did the billionaires behind NGA and CCSSO feel like they needed to own the standards?

The corporate propaganda was that none of the State standards were good enough to get kids "career and college ready." But this claim is nonsense. Many state Standards had a long track record of getting students career and college ready. Another common claim is that the billionaires wanted to own the national standards so that they could control the text books and tests associated with these standards – and make money selling these CCSS aligned tests and books. This explanation is slightly more plausible because corporations like Pearson are making billions of dollars on CCSS books and tests.

However, "CCSS aligned" tests and books are so bad that they are not really aligned to CCSS standards. So this is only a partial reason for wanting to "own" and control the standards. Our view is that the billionaires want bad standards and bad tests. This is why there was no field testing of the new standards and why the CCSS standards and CCSS aligned books and tests have turned out so bad. It is because they are supposed to be bad. This is also why the Common Core standards are so developmentally inappropriate.

The goal of Common Core has nothing to do with getting students career and college ready. Instead, the goal all along has been to raise the bar of high stakes testing so high that few students can pass the tests. This allows billionaires to falsely label American schools as failures so they can close public schools and replace them with private for profit corporate run schools. This is a clearly different history than the fake history put out by Bill Gates and the Gates Foundation and the corporate run American fake news media. Common Core did not start after a 2 hour conversation with Bill Gates in 2008. Instead, it was the culmination of a project to destroy and privatize our public schools that began in the early 1980s. Nor were the Common Core standards produced in a few months between 2009 and 2010. Instead, Achieve had been working on these standards for several years via the American Diploma Project. CCSS was in part simply prior State Standards all stirred together by three people who did not know what they were doing. This is what made Common Core standards worse than the prior State standards. This history of Common Core is clearly different from that being promoted by the corporate media and may be difficult for many Americans to believe. We have all been taught by the corporate media that there was a change from the Republican presidencies of Reagan and Bush One to the Democratic Presidency of Bill Clinton and then back to the Republican presidency of Bush Two followed by the Democratic presidency of Barack Obama. In fact, since 1980, there has been only one party, the billionaire party, that controls the leadership of both the Republican and Democratic parties. Recently George Bush Two referred to Bill Clinton as his "brother by a different mother." It is looking like 2016 will be another presidential election in which the likely leading candidates of both major parties, Hillary Clinton and Jeb Bush, both support Common Core and High Stakes testing.

In November 2014, Bill Clinton and George Bush Two joke about whether Hillary will beat Jeb. Either way, whoever wins, the billionaires will win and the corporate assault on our public schools will continue. In a previous chapter, we covered Hillary Clinton's relationship with Marc Tucker and the Walton billionaires in setting up the Goals 2000 Ed Reform scam. Jeb Bush is equally up to his eyeballs in the Ed Reform scam. He has a group called Foundation for Excellence in Education (FEE) which has collected over six million dollars from the Gates Foundation to promote Common Core, Charter Schools and other privatization scams. Bill Gates also gave Bill Clinton's foundations more than $20 million. In short, the billionaire attack on our public schools will continue if either Hillary or Jeb win the 2016 Election because both represent the billionaires:

Why State Standards are Better than National Standards

The 10th Amendment to the United States Constitution states that any powers not expressly given to the federal government are reserved to the State governments. Because education is not a power given to the federal government, it is a process reserved for the States. This was how Thomas Jefferson and other founders of our nation wanted it to be. They wanted each State to be an experiment in Democracy. They believed in strength through diversity.

They opposed rigid national standards. Having different education systems in each State allows parents to have more local control over the education of their children. Encouraging different states to try different curriculum allows us to observe what works versus what does not work. Forcing Texas standards, Texas Curriculum and Texas High Stakes tests on Washington State children deprives Washington State parents of a voice in the education of their children.

> "The powers not delegated to the United States
> By the Constitution, nor prohibited by it to
> The States, are reserved to the States
> Respectively, or to the people."
> Thomas Jefferson, 10th Amendment to the US Constitution

There are also numerous federal laws that prohibit the federal government from dictating national standards, national curriculum or national tests on individual states. So Common Core standards, tests and curriculum are clearly not legal. But because Bill Gates and other billionaires believe they are above the law and because they have enough money to bribe our corrupt elected officials, most State legislatures voted to adopt Common Core sight unseen without any analysis or testing to confirm that Common Core standards were better than the previous educational standards that already existed in nearly every State.

Thankfully, some parents and teachers have seen first hand how Common Core texts and tests harm children. These caring parents and teachers have banded together to oppose Common Core. They are starting to put the dots together and realizing that Common Core is part of a much bigger plan to destroy and privatize our public schools.

What about Student Mobility... Don't We Need National Standards to Help Children who move from one state to the next?
One of the most common arguments billionaires use as a reason for imposing national educational standards on all 50 states is that we need national standards and tests for every student in every grade in order to help students who move from one state to another. However, according to a 2011 US Census Report, only 200,000 students move between States every year. This is less than one half of one percent of the 50 million students who attend public schools in the US. Is it right to cause severe harm to 49,800,000 students in order to make schools more uniform for the tiny fraction of students who migrate from one state to another? http://www.census.gov/hhes/migration/data/cps/cps2011.html

Common Core Standards, Curriculum and Tests have already harmed millions of children

As we have shown, the Common Core High Stakes tests have almost nothing to do with the Common Core Curriculum or Common Core standards. Instead, the goal of the new tests is simply to flunk as many kids as possible. In Kentucky in 2012, 60% of 670,000 students failed the new billionaire designed Common Core tests. The total number who failed the test was about 402,000. In New York State in 2013, over 70% of 2.7 million students failed the new high stakes, high failure rate tests. The total number who failed the test was 1.9 million. Thus the total number of students tested so far has been 3.3 million and 2.3 million failed these high failure rate tests. Here is a link to the 2000 page report with the failure rate in New York State broken down by individual school and grade. http://www.p12.nysed.gov/irs/ela-math/2013/2013ELAandMathemaitcsDistrictandBuildingAggregatesMedia.pdf

Again, the purpose of flunking students is to erode support for public schools and thereby make it easier to close and privatize public schools. According to the National Center for Education Statistics, about 2,000 public schools per year have been closed in the US since the push for privatizing schools began in 2004. This is double the rate of school closures in the 1990s where about 1000 public schools closed every year. These school closures affected the lives of over 300,000 students per year who now live with the guilt that because they failed a test, their school was closed. In ten years, 3 million children have been subjected to losing the school they love. https://nces.ed.gov/fastfacts/display.asp?id=64

During this same time, the number of privately controlled scandal ridden charter schools rose from under 2,000 schools to more than 5,000 schools – with enrollment skyrocketing from under 500,000 students to nearly 2 million students. https://nces.ed.gov/programs/digest/d12/tables/dt12_108.asp

Cradle to Grave Data Tracking of every child

Another harm being inflicted on all students as a result of Common Core standards and Common Core tests is the frightening increase in database monitoring of students from "cradle to grave." On June 9, 2009, Arne Duncan gave a speech in which he explained why he wants to use Common Core tests and standards to track student data from the cradle to the grave: "We need robust data systems to track student achievement and teacher effectiveness... We want to see more states build comprehensive systems that track students from pre-K through college and then link school data to workforce data."

http://www2.ed.gov/news/speeches/2009/06/06082009.html

This problem with high stakes high failure rate Common Core testing is about to get much worse in 2015 as over 30 million school children in States around the nation will be subjected to the insanely difficult standards of the two Common Core tests (SBAC and PARCC).

One of the goals of public education is to help students learn how to separate deception from truth and reality from myth. Knowledge is the antidote to propaganda. Research is the cure for ignorance. Our goal is to help students, parents and teachers better understand the extent to which we are all being bombarded with weapons of mass deception in a war against our public schools.

Fair Assessment should Help not Harm Students
There has always been testing in public schools. Historically, the tests were developed by teachers. The theory was that an experienced teacher - who had spent the entire year observing a child and knew whether that child had completed their homework and how the child scored on an entire series of tests given throughout the school year – that teacher was in a better position to judge whether a child was ready to move onto the next grade than a "one size fits all" standardized test written by some far away bureaucrat. Some have politely referred to those trying to destroy our public schools as "corporate reformers." The truth is that the goal of Wall Street billionaires is not to reform public schools but to destroy them. Those involved in this hoax should more accurately be called "corporate raiders."

The Real Goal of Corporate Raiders
Corporate raiders know their "reforms" have not worked and will not work. Shocking as this may seem, they do not care. In fact, they have deliberately promoted one hoax after another because they want public schools to fail. They want teachers to fail and they want kids to fail. In this article, we will show that their reform efforts, including the new Common Core tests are "designed to fail." The reason these corporate raiders want kids to fail is that corporate raiders truly believe in the power of greed, competition and privatization. They want to destroy public schools and shrink them until they are so small that they can "drown them in a bathtub." They see public schools as a giant waste of money. We currently spend $10,000 per child per year in operating public schools and another $4,000 per year in building and repairing schools. Multiply $14,000 per year times 50 million students in our nation's public schools and you get $700 billion dollars per year. According to the National Center for Educational Statistics, 5% of the entire GDP of the United States is spent on public schools. In other words, five cents out of every dollar you earn goes towards the education of our children. Wall Street wants this money transferred from public hands to private hands. They want it all. The only way to stop this evil plan is to fully expose it for what it is – a corporate takeover by corporate raiders. In the eyes of Wall Street, there is actually a benefit in driving a company (our public schools) out of business prior to the takeover as the stock price or purchase price will be much less if the public values the product (public education) much less. Destroy the brand name of public education and it is easier to take over the business. The only problem with the corporate takeover plan is that public schools have proven to be remarkably resistant to their takeover attempts.

Despite all of the attacks on public schools during the past 30 years, student test scores on the National Assessment of Educational Progress (NAEP) math and reading tests have actually gone up – to the point that students today are one to two grade levels above what they were 30 years ago. The success of our public schools creates a real problem for corporate raiders. It is difficult to claim that schools are failing and scores are falling, when student test scores are actually going up and the graduation rate is going up. If you are a corporate raider out to destroy and takeover public schools, what you need is some way to greatly reduce student test scores and thereby artificially increase the number and percentage of students who are "failing." To understand how this diabolical plot all works, we first need to consider an important but not so simple question: What exactly is the purpose of Common Core? Common Core is the bullet billionaires are firing into the heart of our public schools in order to "prove to parents" that our public schools are a failure and should be privatized and turned over to the billionaires.

What to Put in Place of Common Core?
Instead of Common Core what we really need is common sense. It is common sense that replacing thousands of experienced teachers with poorly trained "TFA" recruits will not help our students. It is common sense that forcing 3rd graders to take high stakes tests knowing they will lose their teacher and maybe even their school should they fail the test is harmful to 3rd graders. It is common sense that tests which fail 70% of the students are simply unfair tests. Thankfully, there is a simple solution to this problem. That solution is to honor the US Constitution and encourage every state to set their own learning standards. Learning standards should be written into clear language that the public can understand.

To see what clarity looks like, read the mathematics standards of Finland. They are clear, concise and jargon free. They explain what students should know,

Learning standards should also be transparently and openly reviewed and revised by experts in child development. Children deserve standards that respect their cognitive growth. Equally important is to completely end the barbaric practice of giving high stakes high failure rate tests to young children.

What is Next?
In the next chapter, we will learn about charter schools – the third weapon of mass deception. We will show in the next article that Common Core is the weapon being used to introduce new Common Core tests. What parents need to understand is that these new tests have almost nothing to do with the new Common Core standards. The goal of the new tests is not to raise standards, but simply to sharply lower test scores by any means necessary. This includes asking test questions that are not even part of the Common Core standards. This will give the billionaires the excuse they need to close our public schools and replace them with for profit charter schools – schools run by the billionaires.

3 Why Fake Charter Schools are Kid Prisons

> "Going to school is not the same as going shopping. Parents should Not be burdened with locating a suitable school for their child. They should be able to take their child to their neighborhood public School as a matter of course and expect that it has well-educated Teachers and a sound educational program." Dr. Diane Ravitch

While many Americans now oppose billionaire funded fake high stakes tests and fake Common Core standards, they still support billionaire funded fake charter schools. This is not surprising given that charter schools have been promoted for more than 20 years by our fake billionaire backed corporate media as being the "miracle cure" schools filled with poor kids whose parents do not have living wage jobs. In this chapter, we will show that charter schools are simply one more of the billionaires weapons of mass deception. The real purpose of charter schools is not to improve education but to allow billionaires to rob tax payers of billions of dollars and rob children of their future. This third chapter is divided into four sections:

3.1 Ten Reasons Charter Schools Harm Children

3.2 The Crooks Behind Charter Schools

3.3 Charter Schools are Fraud Factories

3.4 The Kids in Prison Program

3.1 Ten Reasons Charter Schools Harm Children

This is a quote from a First Grade teacher who transferred from a Charter School to a Public School after just one year of teaching:

"The kids in my Charter School First Grade class were never allowed to be children. Instead they were stuffed into little invisible straight-jackets all day long, from which outbursts and tantrums were frequent.... I am now teaching at a public school where my First Graders have play center time and lots of choice; our curriculum isn't scripted, the children are allowed to talk, sing, breathe, and be themselves. It's truly a different world, one my former students will most likely never know." http://maryannreilly.blogspot.com/2011/04/guest-blog-miss-c-recounts-teaching-at.html

Two decades ago, not a single penny of taxpayer money was spent on charter schools. This year, public funding for charters will run into the billions of dollars. This massive waste of tax payer funds is despite the fact that dozens of studies have concluded that charter schools do no better than traditional public schools – and often do worse. The few studies falsely claiming that charter schools do better than public schools use statistical manipulations such as ignoring the massive student attrition and drop out problem at charter schools. Charter schools suspend, weed out and expel struggling students rather than helping them. Many charter schools expel over half of their students. The suspension rate for normal public schools is under 5%. Dumping their most struggling students back into the public schools is what allows some charter schools to make exaggerated claims about the select students that remain in their program. Charter schools also use discredited "drill and kill" military boot camp teaching methods that destroy a child's desire to learn – shortening the school to prison pipeline into a "school is prison" pipeline.

Obviously, dumping the kids that need the most help does not result in the education of ALL children. But the purpose of charter schools has never been about helping children. The real purpose of the charter school weapon of mass deception is the same as the purpose of high stakes fake tests and Common Core fake standards – to privatize public schools and transfer billions of dollars from the tax payers into the pockets of greedy billionaires.

Three Weapons of Mass Deception are Designed to Work Together to Privatize Schools

As we described in earlier chapters, first billionaires impose inappropriate Common Core standards and confusing Common Core curriculum. Then they force kids to take high stakes high failure rate tests – unfair tests that two out of three kids are certain to fail. Then when the kids fail the fake tests, the billionaires move in to close the "failing" public schools and replace them with privately run but publicly funded for-profit charter schools – schools controlled by the billionaires. This clever deception is designed to gradually phase out public schools like a block of ice that slowly melts away.

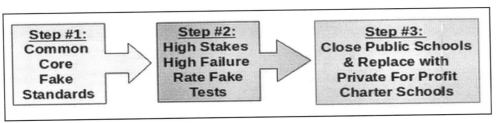

Charter schools then create huge profits for the billionaires by firing experienced and certified teachers and replacing them with untrained and uncertified and poorly paid "staff." Second, charters weed out any struggling and special needs students to allow them to dramatically increase class sizes. The profits then go to out of State "administrators" who are accountable to stock holders rather than to the parents of students. Some of the profit is diverted into huge bribes for the re-election campaigns of corrupt politicians who promote charter schools. This is the corporate model of education reform.

This is why billionaires have spent billions of dollars trying to convert every public school in America into private for profit charter schools. This is ironic because the main reason our children are forced to attend some of the lowest funded most overcrowded schools in the nation is that billionaires are not paying their fair share of state taxes.

Diverting public dollars to charter schools managed by private corporations will make our public schools even more overcrowded as more money is diverted away from classrooms and into huge profits for Wall Street corporations. In short, charter schools are just like Common Core... They are a marketing scheme whose real goal is to privatize our public schools.

Below are ten reasons charter schools harm children.

#1 Charter Schools are NOT Public Schools... Public Schools are Child Centered... Charter Schools are Profit Centered

Charters are publicly funded, but privately operated schools. Because they are privately operated schools, charter schools are not accountable to the public or to a publicly elected school board. Instead, they are run by a small group of unelected corporate managers who sub-contract to private for profit corporations. Put more bluntly, charter schools are a corporate takeover of our public schools.

The billionaire bought mass media propaganda has falsely claimed that billionaire run charter schools are just like public schools only with more "flexibility." What they fail to mention is that "flexibility" means not accepting all children, not using trained teachers, not having available administrators for parents to talk with and not having elected volunteer school board members who oversee the budget and who parents can talk with to get their concerns addressed.

Here is the structure of our public schools – a transparent structure with many checks and balances which has fostered public schools for more than one hundred years. The best education is made democratically, in the local community by parents and teachers with the oversight of a publicly elected school board – all working together to meet the needs of their children.

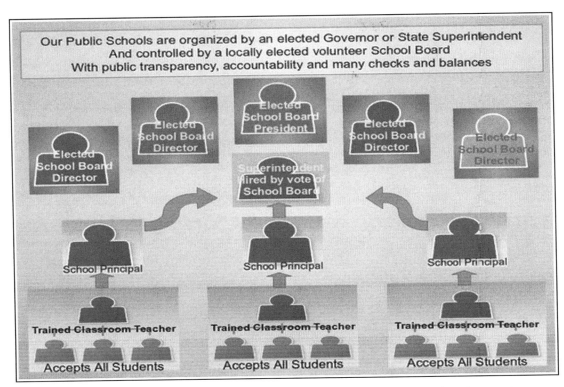

Here is the structure of billionaire run charter schools with no checks and balances – leading to rampant fraud and corruption:

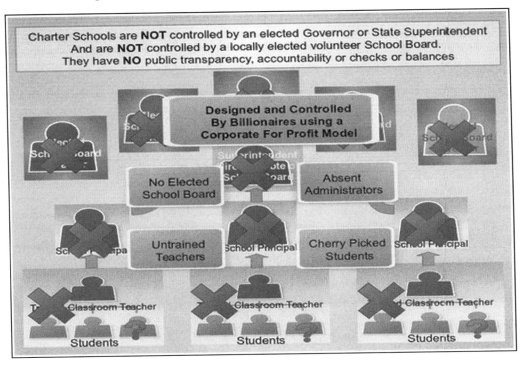

#2 Charters Harm Children by Robbing Public Schools of Public Funds
Charter schools siphon off money from public schools. The whole point of charter schools is to use tax payer money to increase corporate profits. Diverting funds away from our public schools makes our school funding situation even worse!

#3 Charter Schools are NOT Non-profits. Instead the need to make a profit makes them much more expensive than comparable public schools
Charter school con artists mislead the public into thinking that charter schools will be run by a non-profit. However, the non-profit typically sub-contracts the operation of the school to a private, for-profit corporation.

#4 Charter Schools are Fraud Factories
There are several reasons that privatization of public schools has led to rampant fraud and outright theft of tax payer dollars. The first is the profit motive. Billionaires cannot help themselves. They are used to taking whatever money they can get their hands on. Second, charter schools are a toxic mix of deregulation combined with lack of accountability. Since there is no elected school board to watch over how public funds are spent, charter school operators are free to divert public funds to themselves and their friends.

> **$400,000 embezzlement suspected at Kid Street Charter School**
> Finance director arrested on embezzlement, burglary, forgery and drug violations

Even when the fraud is uncovered, there is no elected school board to kick out of office and replace with a better group. Parents have literally no voice once their school has been replaced by the fraudsters. The third problem is that charter schools like to measure how they are doing simply by high stakes test scores. This inevitably leads to cheating scandals and many other attempts to manipulate the system – such as having low performing students call in "sick" and not take the test – and even handing students the answer sheet before the test or having administrators change students test answers in the dead of night. There are many websites that have documented thousands of cases of fraud and abuse at charter schools. The fraud is so rampant that we have compiled a few of these stories into a separate article to give you an idea of what a bad idea it is to deregulate public schools and hand them over to for profit corporations.

#5 Charter Schools Cherry Pick the Easiest Students to Teach
Because charter schools are interested in maximizing their profit margins, they frequently weed out students who are more expensive to teach. This includes slower learners, children with special needs, children in rural communities and children from poor or unstable families. Our public schools accept all children and help every one of them succeed.

#6 Charter Schools often use poorly trained, inexperienced teachers
Real public school teachers are required to have at least 5 years of real training in education and child development. However, charter schools often save money and increase their profit margins by hiring "Teach for America" recruits who are given as little as 5 weeks of training. Many of these fake teachers quit in their first year of teaching. The results are predictable. Children fail to learn, there is chaos in the classroom and the unprepared teachers resign within their first year – leaving students and parents to pick up the pieces of a lost school year.

There is a huge turn over of teachers at charter schools. Here is a quote from one teacher who spent a year in a charter school: "Unlike most public schools, charter schools do not offer contracts, tenure, or a union. Teachers sign "letters of intent", stating that they intend to work in a position for the school year, that they can be fired at any time without cause, and that they are free to leave at any time. Staff changes are frequent. At my school, since teachers were more or less viewed as factory drones, replacing them was swift and emotionless--when people quit, it was often not even mentioned at the weekly faculty meeting. A face was absent, a new face was in place, and life continued. During that one year, seven teachers quit between September and May, one was fired, and five more (myself included) resigned in June."
http://maryannreilly.blogspot.com/2011/04/guest-blog-miss-c-recounts-teaching-at.html

#7 Charter Schools do NOT perform better – and often perform much worse than public schools Study after study has confirmed that privatizing schools does not improve student outcomes – despite cherry picking children and booting out kids with problems. For example, the National Center for Education Statistics found that charter-school students performed significantly worse on academic assessments than their peers in traditional public schools. This is why the charter school movement is not about making schools better. It is simply about robbing public schools and diverting billions of dollars to private for profit corporations.

#8 Public Schools already offer many Flexible Reform Options

This debate is not about improving schools. Like all parents and teachers, I am in favor of improving schools using credible scientifically proven reform strategies. Our current State laws already allow innovative schools, alternative schools, cooperative schools, home schooling, Hi Tech schools, Multicultural schools, Flexible Curriculum reforms, Testing waivers, Parent Choice options, College Running Start opportunities, GED options and practically any other changes or experiments that a local school board wants to try. Nearly every school district in King County (where we live) has several different kinds of successful alternative and experimental schools and instructional programs to meet the needs of students and parents. The key is that all of these programs have public accountability to a publicly elected school board.

#9 Charter schools have destroyed the public school system in many cities

Charter schools are like a cancer. By diverting funding away from public schools, and cherry picking the easiest students to teach, they send public schools on a downward spiral making it harder and harder for students and teachers to succeed in the public schools. The drop in funding for public schools has then led to the closures of literally hundreds of public schools in States like Illinois, New York and Pennsylvania. These school closures divide and destroy entire communities – harming thousands of students. We will review some of these school closure disasters in the next section.

#10 We need REAL school reform based on credible scientific research
Public schools are the foundation of our Democracy and the foundation of our economy. Public schools offer equal access and opportunity for all of our children. Two decades of research and experience with charter schools has confirmed that charter schools are not the answer to improving our schools. We should not gamble with the future of our children just to increase corporate profits. What we need is REAL school reform based on credible scientific research. This includes improving school funding and lowering class sizes.

Smaller class sizes give students and teachers A better chance to succeed in school.

We also need stronger efforts to increase retaining good teachers and reducing bullying in and out of the classroom. Mostly, what will help children is reducing POVERTY. The best way to improve test scores is to make sure that the parents of every child have a good job. Sadly, the promoters of charter schools are the very people who are blocking funding our public schools and blocking the kinds of reform that would actually benefit ALL of our children.

Look Who is Backing Charter Schools
Despite all of these drawbacks, Billionaire Bill is backing charter schools with $5.5 million courtesy of his fake non-profit Gates Foundation.

National Alliance For Public Charter Schools

Date: November 2007
Purpose: for general operating support
Amount: $5,500,000

What is next?
Now that we have a basic idea of how charter schools harm children, in the next section, we will look at the history of how the charter school scam started – beginning in Chicago in the 1990s.

3.2 The Crooks Behind the Charter School Scam

One of the first school districts in the nation to use high stakes/ high failure rate test scores to evaluate and close schools - and then replace them with private for profit charter schools - was the Chicago Public School District.

The Chicago Mob and their Hit Man... Arne Duncan
In a 2013 article, New Teachers, New Unions, New Alliances, New Politics, Michael Yates wrote:
"Chicago's financial and political leaders have been trying to destroy the city's public schools and the teachers' union since 1995, when the Illinois State Legislature gave Mayor Daley the power to appoint the Board of Education and choose a CEO to run the Chicago Public Schools (CPS). The appointed board and a succession of CEOs pushed an unprecedented level of high-stakes testing and top-down corporate management. Mayoral control was the lynchpin of this process. By 2012, Chicago Public Schools had closed over one hundred schools and simultaneously opened almost one hundred privately run charter schools. In 2012, Mayor Emanuel proposed closing up to 120 more schools by fall 2013."
http://truth-out.org/opinion/item/17756-public-school-teachers-new-unions-new-alliances-new-politics

The first crook behind the Charter School scam is a con artist named Arne Duncan – the current head of the US Department of Education and a close friend of Barack Obama. Arne Duncan has no training or background in education. Instead, Arne played basketball for Harvard in the 1980s. He then began his career as a professional basketball player in Australia from 1987 to 1991.

Arne Duncan Played Basketball For Harvard University In the 1980s Before moving to Australia from 1987 to 1991.

Despite having no background in education, Arne Duncan moved back to the US in 1992 and was immediately appointed Director of Ariel Education Initiative, a very strange Chicago School that taught kids a stock market based view of the world. Imagine a private religious-based school. Only in this case, the religion being preached to the children was greed and profit.

Each of 40 selected inner city First Graders at the Ariel School was given a $20,000 grant to invest in the stock market through the 8th Grade. The profit from the child's investment fund was evenly divided between the school and a college fund for the child. The plan was that after 8 years, the money would double – returning the original $20,000 to the school and creating a college fund of $20,000 for the child. Back in 1990, thanks to State support for higher education, $20,000 would actually pay for a higher education. It may seem odd giving $20,000 to a First Grader and having them invest it in the stock market. But this is actually what happened. Arne Duncan went from being a professional basketball player to a Wall Street Guru and investment advisor for First Graders. Welcome to the crazy world of charter schools!

This crazy elementary school program continued in 1995 when the mayor of Chicago, Richard Daley, got rid of the locally elected school board and replaced it with dictatorial "mayoral" control. In 1996, Mayor Daley used his new power over kids to close a public school called William Shakespeare Elementary School and give it to Ariel Investments to use as Ariel Community Academy. This was also strange because Chicago supposedly did not get any charter schools (private schools using public money) until 1997. This new school pretended to be a normal public school. But it was clearly a charter school in that it received public school funding, and private funding, but was not under the control of a local school board and had no public accountability. For example, it is unclear what Arne Duncan actually did at this charter/elementary school since there are almost no public records of this supposedly public elementary school (charter schools seem to be exempt from the record keeping rules and accountability standards of public schools). Arne never took a single course in Education and never taught in a classroom. Arne seems to have been more of a politically connected fund raiser and snake oil salesman than a school teacher or school administrator.

Also in 1996, Richard Daley, appointed a corrupt accountant Paul Vallas - who had no background in education - to run Chicago's public schools. After a corruption and kickback scandal, Paul Vallas resigned in disgrace in 2001.

On the other hand, Arne did such a great job at Ariel Community Academy (as a charter school promoter and snake oil salesman) that on June 26, 2001, Chicago's Mayor Richard Daley, one of the most corrupt mayors in American history, appointed Arne to run the Chicago Public Schools, America's third largest school district with over 400,000 students. Arne's idea of school reform was to fire teachers, close public schools and turn some of them into private charter schools with inexperienced and poorly trained and poorly paid charter school "staff" (since charter schools do not have or believe in professionally trained and paid real teachers). By the time Duncan left Chicago to help guide the national program in school destruction, Arne had closed more than 80 public schools and converted them into private charter schools.

Top down punishment driven pressure cooker schools versus bottom up local control nurturing schools
85% of the Chicago School Districts 400,000 students are from low-income families - many are living below the poverty line. Closing schools is almost as traumatic and harmful an experience for children as losing their homes. With a minimum of 500 students per school, Duncan's school closure and conversion program severely harmed at least 40,000 mostly low income students during his 8 year reign of terror in Chicago.
http://www.rethinkingschools.org/restrict.asp?path=archive/23_03/arne233.shtml

During his first year as CEO of Chicago schools, Duncan hired more than 30 managers at salaries of between $90,000 and $115,000 per year. Duncan refused repeatedly to provide the public with the details of the cost, qualifications, or even job descriptions of the members of his widely touted "management team.

Many of the members of the Duncan "management team" were reported to be friends and neighbors of Duncan

http://www.substancenews.com/archive/March02/jordan.html

Arne Duncan Closed more than 80 schools In Chicago During his 8 year Reign of Terror.

What were the results of the Duncan assault on Chicago public schools?
The following is a quote from a 2013 Washington Post article:
"The Consortium on Chicago School Research, a nonpartisan group of researchers at the University of Chicago, released a report in 2009 saying that the school closings during Duncan's tenure as head of the Chicago schools did very little, if anything, to improve the achievement of students who were sent to other schools." http://www.washingtonpost.com/blogs/answer-sheet/wp/2013/05/30/the-biggest-irony-in-chicagos-mass-closing-of-schools/

In September 2011, the Consortium on Chicago School Research and the University of Chicago produced another summary of the impact of the changes in Chicago schools from 1990 to 2010. Here is a quote from this report:
"From 2001 to 2009, Chicago saw 155 new schools open and 82 schools close... More than 70% of 11th graders fail to meet state standards, a trend that has remained flat over the past several years."

Many "failing" schools were closed twice... First by Arne Duncan and then after the private takeover did not succeed in improving test scores, the "charter" schools were closed again. This is clear evidence that the problem with schools in low income neighborhoods is not the school. The problem is poverty. All parents, all children and all teachers need to be treated with respect, dignity, fairness and opportunity. Closing public schools in poor neighborhoods over and over again is not the answer. It is simply another form of child abuse. Closing public schools and turning them all into private, for profit charter schools does not improve outcomes for poor inner city children because this "solution" does not address the real problem faced by poor inner city kids. That problem is poverty – their parents do not have a living wage job.

2002 Joel Klein and the New York City Charter School Scam
At about the same time that Arne was closing public schools in Chicago and turning them into private for profit charter schools, another scam artist, Joel Klein, was closing public schools in New York and turning them into private for profit charter schools. As with Chicago, New York public schools were under dictatorial "mayoral control." In 2001, one of the ten richest billionaires in America, Michael Bloomberg spent $73 million to buy his election to be mayor of New York.

Bloomberg has a net worth of about $37 billion so $73 million meant nothing to Bloomberg. Despite a huge spending advantage, Bloomberg only won the election by a margin of 50% to 48%. In 2002, Bloomberg appointed Joel Klein to be chancellor of New York City public schools. Joel Klein was the head of the New York school system until 2011.

The New York City school district has one million students. Klein rejected the role that poverty plays in educational outcomes. Instead, he advocated a "get tough" approach to poor students claiming that he himself grew up in "working-class, poor" family in New York City and overcame poverty through his own hard work. Neither Bloomberg or Klein had any real background in education... or in poverty. Klein, who was a corporate attorney who served as a legal adviser to Bill Clinton, is fond of saying that "Poverty does not have to be destiny" and "I reject categorically the principle that poverty is an insurmountable impediment" and You'll never fix poverty until you fix education" - as if education was the cause of poverty rather than the lack of jobs and the greed of billionaires.

Joel Klein's Fake "Poor Kid" Biography
Richard Rothstein, who grew up in Queens near Joel Klein and had the same physics teacher as Joel, exposed the fraud of Klein's "poverty" story in an article in October 2012 called Joel Klein's Misleading Autobiography. He states, "in nearly every detail, the story he tells is misleading or untrue... The discrepancies matter because they go to the heart of what is wrong with his reform agenda" Klein's father had a good paying full time job at the post office and Klein's mother was an accountant. Their combined income was well above the national average. By contrast, many families living in poverty do not have any adults with even a single full time job. The family income of the typical child who qualifies for Free or Reduced Price Lunch has less than has the median income – or less than one third of the income of Joe Klein's supposedly poor family. In fact, Joe Klein lived in a community that specifically excluded poor families including excluding "single-parent families and those with irregular employment history, out-of-wedlock births, criminal records, narcotics addiction, or mental illness—in other words, any family with the qualities we now associate with public housing. Neighborhood schools serving complexes like Woodside Houses thus didn't have to contend with unruly adolescents; they had already been weeded out by the Housing Authority...Klein and I both attended almost entirely segregated, white schools...Klein's story has contributed to the demoralization of tens of thousands of teachers who are now blamed for their low-income students' poor test scores."
http://prospect.org/article/joel-kleins-misleading-autobiography

How many schools did Klein change to charters?

During his 9 years as head of New York City schools, Joel Klein closed about 160 public schools – firing teachers and administrators by the thousands. Joel replaced these public schools with more than 160 privately run for profit charter schools – creating chaos and confusion for more than one hundred thousand children in New York City.

http://nycpublicschoolparents.blogspot.com/2014/12/joel-kleins-failed-record-as-nyc.html

What was the result of Joel Klein's Assault on Public School Children?

On May 10, 2010, The New York Times reported: "According to the test [NAEP], New York City eighth graders have shown no significant improvement [in math or reading] since 2003." In fact, New York City students made less progress on the NAEP test than any other major city in the US other than Cleveland.

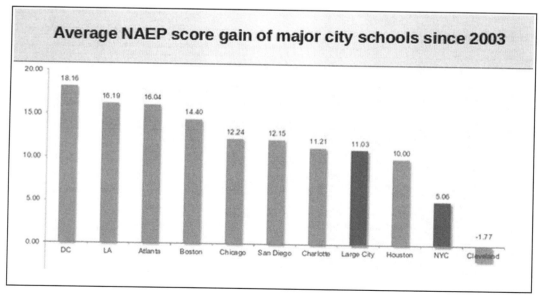

What was left in the wreckage of New York City schools were thousands of angry parents and demoralized teachers who protested the closure and privatization of their community schools. Here is what one angry parent wrote: "Joel Klein is the biggest fake you ever want to meet. This reckless goon gutted the NYC school system and created a situation of pitting people against one another in hope of creating hostile environments. Klein is evil make no mistake - this is why you will read a story just about every day about corrupt principals (put in place by Klein) who treat people like shit - for no good reason and how the schools are a mess with a principal in place who has never taught in a school but rather graduated from the Mike Bloomberg Joel Klein so called "leadership academy" – which is now closed."

We would like to add that the federal tax rate on the income of billionaires in the 1950's when Joe Klein went to school was 90%. Today, it is very close to 0%. The current reform agenda is not just a school privatization agenda, it is a government privatization agenda.

Paul Vallas... Corrupt Accountant and Expert at Converting Public Schools into Private For Profit Charter Schools

It is likely that no con artist in America has closed more public schools than Paul Vallas. During the past 20 years, Paul Vallas has closed public schools in Chicago, Philadelphia and New Orleans – and then converted all of them to private for profit charter schools. As we noted at the beginning of this article, in 1995, after Mayor Richard Daley assumed "mayoral control", he appointed accountant Paul Vallas as the "Chief Executive Officer" of the Chicago public schools were Vallas was the boss for 6 years until he resigned in disgrace in 2001 (to be replaced by Arne Duncan).

Paul's job was to close public schools and turn them over to private for profit charter school operators. He was also charged with balancing the school district budget. He did this by by robbing from the Teachers Pension Fund – a financially irresponsible act that lead to billions of dollars in additional costs 10 years later.

Paul Vallas Riding a Tandem Bike with Mayor Richard Daley.

Paul rode the Chicago Public Schools And their Teachers Pension Fund Into the Ground Between 1996 to 2001.

Paul Vallas... Teacher or Con Artist?
In the above picture, Paul is taking Mayor Daley for a ride. It turns out, Paul was also taking the tax payers for a ride. It seems Paul had trouble telling the truth. Paul Vallas often claimed on his resumes and websites that he was an "elementary school teacher" from 1976 to 1980. However, in a sworn court deposition, he stated that from 1976 to 1979, he worked in his father's restaurant business. Vallas then claimed that he was a teacher in Montana for one year. After an investigation into this claim revealed it was false, Vallas claimed he was an unpaid "student teacher" in Montana for one year. Vallas later changed this story that he spent "ten weeks" as a student teacher in Montana.
http://www.substancenews.com/archive/March02/index.html

Paul also seemed to have had a problem with racism.

"The Paul Vallas that I know misused the resources, authority, and prestige of his office To harass, humiliate, intimidate and attempt to destroy the careers of many Black people."

Grady Jordan,
Chicago SD Administrator
1985 - 1995

"Of the 45 principals who had been removed from their schools by Vallas, 42 were Black. In other words, 93 percent were Black. This clearly is racial profiling... At the same time Paul was undermining the authority of Black principals and administrators, Paul was also terminating tenured teachers, large numbers of whom were Black, the heart of the school system, using equally unfair methods. Sadly, the teachers had fewer resources during those years than the principals who stood up to Vallas. Most have seen their careers finished by his policies." Grady Jordan Chicago School District Administrator

In just a few short years, Vallas flunked over 50,000 Chicago students. Research shows that retention leads to greater academic failure, higher levels of dropping out, greater behavioral difficulties, poor attendance, negative attitudes toward school and feelings of shame and depression. So in creating the now highly profitable "school to prison pipeline", Paul Vallas was one of its primary builders.

Vallas Refined the Art of Teacher Bashing and Teacher Firing
Paul also discharged more than 200 tenured teachers. By 1999, Vallas was firing veteran tenured teachers despite a growing teacher shortage. These teachers were not fired for cause, but because the Vallas administration worked to make sure that principals would not hire them after they had been displaced from their previous schools. In many areas of attacking teachers and their union, Paul and the Chicago School district were pioneers in the art of using chaos to close public schools and convert them into private charter schools.

Paul Vallas Wasted Millions on a Fake High Stakes Test

In the late 1990s, Paul Vallas spent more than $5 million on one of the nation's most ludicrous standardized tests, the "Chicago Academic Standards Examinations" (CASE). Chicago schools wasted another $200 million in teacher time preparing students for this high stakes test. The CASE exam was exposed to be a fraud in 1999 by a highly respected English teacher, George Schmidt, who had more than 20 years of experience teaching in Chicago schools. The teacher published some of the more absurd test questions in his community newspaper. Paul's response was to fire the teacher and launch a 5 year million dollar litigation campaign against the teacher.

The terrible CASE tests were finally ended in 2002 – but not until after having destroyed the life savings of George Schmidt and his wife – despite the fact that more than 2,000 friends and supporters contributed to his defense – including leading opponents of school privatization Monty Neil of Fair Test and Gerald Bracey of the Bracey Reports. Here is one of the confusing CASE American History questions that appeared to be an attack against progressives: "How many U.S. presidents and leaders of the so-called "Progressive" movement in American history were supporters of Jim Crow, the segregation of the armed forces, and other forms of racial discrimination?" This absurd question attempts to link Progressives to being Racists – when in fact, nearly all progressives strongly oppose racism.

Paul Vallas and the Pension Fund Scam

One of the most serious crimes committed by Paul Vallas while he was running the Chicago public schools into the ground was a money transfer scheme that resulted in the bankrupting of the school district pension fund and permanent harm to the school district operating fund. For those who may not be aware, school districts usually have two completely separate funds. The "operating" fund is used to pay short term operating costs like teachers salaries. A different fund called the "capital" fund is used to pay for long term capital needs like building schools. To get money for the capital budget, one either needs to get money from the State legislature capital budget or pass a long term 20 year to 30 year school bond. Paul was unable to get money from the corrupt Illinois legislature and he did not think he could pass a school bond. So he came up with a "creative accounting" plan. He would simply ignore payments to the Chicago School District Pension Fund (a retirement account for teachers who taught for more than 25 years). He then put this money into the Chicago School District "operating" budget.

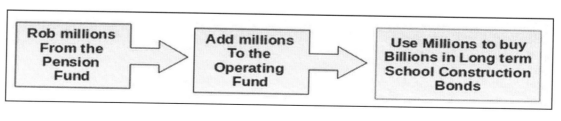

He then took this new revenue stream and used it to purchase long term bonds in order to have money to build new charter schools. Robbing Peter to pay Paul is also called a Ponzi Scheme. The problem is that over time the money needed to pay off the bonds and pay back the money stolen from the pension fund keeps going up. This is exactly what has happened.

Growth of the Chicago Public School Debt Bubble
The percent of general State aid (which was supposed to be the operating budget) going to debt payments was less than 2 % when Paul first started. It has now ballooned to about 20% of the total operating budget. This does not include the repayments to the pension fund – which is now on the verge of bankruptcy.

In total, Paul Vallas and his successor Arne Duncan, have borrowed more than $10 billion in general obligation bonds since 1996, debt that has contributed to the Chicago Public School District's current financial crisis.

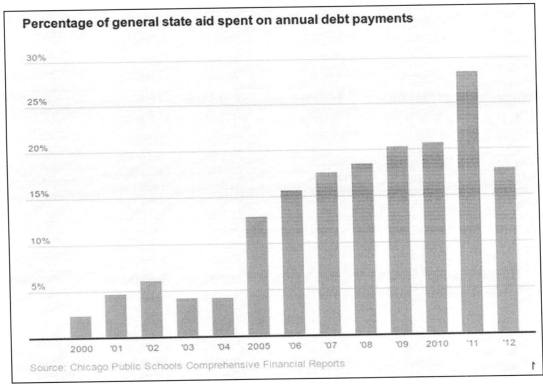

CPS officials have also contributed nothing toward teachers' pensions for a decade, depriving the pension fund of $2 billion and using the money to run the district instead. Annual debt payments on bonds, have grown from $80 million in 1998 to more than $322 million in 2012. This is a great deal for Wall Street bankers who get a huge profit from these bonds – but it means that there is less money available to hire teachers and kids end up with huge class sizes.

Paul Vallas takes his Snake Oil Charter School Scam to Philadelphia
One would have thought that Paul Vallas's school boss career would have been over in 2001 after resigning in disgrace in Chicago. Given his diversion of Teacher Pension funds, he should have been charged with a crime. Instead, he was appointed CEO of Philadelphia Public Schools – a school district with 200,000 students. 70% of these students come from families that are at or near the poverty line. Per Pupil funding for Philly schools was 50% less than for neighboring more wealthy school districts. In 2002, Paul presided over one of the nation's largest and most rapid experiments in privatization. In just three years, Paul closed more than 40 public schools in Philadelphia and turned them into private for profit charter schools. Thousands of experienced teachers were fired and replaced with inexperienced non-certified "staff." No public hearings or public votes were required to close any of these public schools.

How did the Philadelphia School Privatization Scam Turn Out?
In Pennsylvania, charter schools compete for funds with traditional public schools on an uneven playing field that exempt charter schools from serving the full range of student abilities. Charter schools are also exempt from disclosing financial details of their operations to the public. Despite this freedom from regulation, according to the Pennsylvania School Board Association, "Charter schools continue to academically under-perform traditional public schools, with fewer than half of the brick and mortar charter schools meeting acceptable benchmark scores … None of the cyber charter schools met the mark. Nearly three-quarters of traditional public schools, however, earned passing scores in the first year of the new measuring system."

http://keystonestateeducationcoalition.blogspot.com/2012/05/pa-charter-schools-4-billion-taxpayer.html

In March 2013, the chair of the Pennsylvania House Education Committee, James Roebuck issued a scathing report on the corruption and poor performance of Pennsylvania's 157 charter schools – of which 80 are in Philadelphia. Here is a quote from his report: "For 2011-12, 50% of public schools met Annual Yearly Progress (AYP). In stark contrast only 29% of charter schools met AYP and none of the 12 cyber charter schools met AYP." The report also detailed a host of fraud and corruption and cheating scandals at charter schools: "The review of the selected Charter Schools revealed that the lack of Accountability over the Governance and Financing of Charter Schools across the Commonwealth, As a result of this ineffective oversight taxpayer funds are left extremely vulnerable to fraud, waste and abuse as demonstrated in this investigation... Taxpayers could save $365 million with a charter/cyber school reform bill."
http://www.pahouse.com/PR/Charter_and_Cyber_Charter_School_Report.pdf

Parents in Philadelphia Protest the closing Of their Public Schools.

With a disastrous record like this in Chicago and Philadelphia, one would think that this would be the end of Paul's career. But it only got worse. Paul was just getting started closing schools and turning them into charters.

Paul Vallas Takes his Charter School Scam to New Orleans

In August 2005, Hurricane Katrina struck New Orleans flooding the city and led to the evacuation of most of its citizens. While the parents were in another State, the Louisiana State legislature changed the law to allow the State to take over "failing" public schools in New Orleans. The intention was to convert them all into failing private for profit charter schools. However, they could only find charter school operators for about half of the schools. Therefore the State started their own school district called the "Recovery School District (RSD) and ran the schools as deregulated charter schools. As a result of this law, in 2006, 18 of New Orleans 23 public high schools were converted into charter high schools and a total of more than 100 New Orleans public elementary, middle and high schools were converted to charter schools. As a result of this action, which displaced tens of thousands of students, more than 7,500 experienced teachers were fired without any due process. These teachers were replaced by novice teachers with no teaching experience – and often not even any teacher training - the following year.

Many of the new teachers were from "Teach for America" and abandoned their schools and students in less than one year. The salaries paid to TFA recruits and other novice teachers were much less than those paid to real teachers. http://www.researchonreforms.org/html/documents/OliveretalvOPSBetalFOURTHCIRCUITRULINGJAN152014.pdf

In 2007, Paul Vallas arrived in New Orleans to finish the conversion of New Orleans Schools to private for profit charter schools. In New Orleans, Paul Vallas closed more than 100 public schools and fired teachers, custodians and administrators to create a business-friendly citywide charter school experiment.

Thankfully, in nearly every city where charter schools have been used as a weapon of mass deception to destroy and privatize our public schools, a group of concerned citizens has arisen to document the lies associated with the scam. In the case of New Orleans, two educational researchers have written a series of studies to expose the scam. Their names are Charles Hatfield MS and Dr. Barbara Ferguson. Their research is posted for free download on this page: http://www.researchonreforms.org/html/documentreposit.html

Their first post was on November 7 2008 about a report they wrote in July 2008. This was when Paul Vallas was boss of the New Orleans schools and in the process of converting many of the schools into private for profit charter schools. The topic of the first post was the failure of the new charter schools to enroll "at risk" youth. Here is a quote: "Louisiana's Charter School Law, in its first paragraph, seems all about serving at-risk students. Louisiana's charter school law says that "the overriding consideration in establishing this law is to serve the needs of at-risk students." But further into the law, it states that charter schools "can establish admission requirements." These purposes are contradictory. Either a school is required to serve all students who apply; or, a school is allowed to exclude certain students."

In allowing charter schools to restrict who attends them, at risk students do not have access to charter schools because unlike public schools, charter schools in New Orleans are allowed to have "admission requirements." The report discovered that the new charter school district established in New Orleans after Katrina, called the Recovery School District or RSD, failed to submit complete information on students for the 2006 to 2007 school year.

2007 to 2011 Disasters under the leadership of Paul Vallas as the superintendent of the Recovery School District

The second report from Research on Reform was in October 2008. It claimed that two years after the conversion of public schools to charter schools, the "state takeover was not working for New Orleans High Schools." Specifically, the scores on high stakes tests showed almost no change. In English, in 2005, 68% were not proficient and in 2008, 70% were not proficient. In Math in 2005, 70% were not proficient and in 2008, 67% were not proficient.

The report also noted that principals and teachers were being fired in large numbers and without just cause. So despite spending millions of dollars on the new charter schools and giving them the freedom to fire hundreds of teachers, there was no significant improvement in test scores.

Dr. Ferguson was the first female superintendent Of the New Orleans Public Schools where she had Previously served as a teacher, elementary school Principal and High School Principal.
Her primary interest has always been Improving education for at risk children.

In subsequent reports by Hatfield and Fergeson, the authors explained why there was no improvement in test scores. One of the first problems is that nearly all of the experienced teachers had been fired and replaced with first year "Teach for America" teachers. At one middle school, within the first two months, over 70% of these inexperienced teachers had quit. There was also a lack of instructional materials and some schools lacked internet access and even phone access. Another problem has been the massive increase in "expelled" students and held back students. This has resulted in older students being placed in the same classes as younger students and severely disrupted the learning process.

In May 2010, Dr. Ferguson published another report on the New Orleans Ed Reform scams, called RSD High School Test Results Show Alarming Trend. She noted that while the Reform School District (RSD = private for profit charter schools) had three times more students than the normal school district, in the 2009-2010 school year, they each tested the same number of 10th graders. She concluded: "Large numbers of high school-aged students in the RSD did not make it to 10th grade to take the test; and at the same time, crime rates in New Orleans continue to explode. There is a strong relationship between these two factors, and there must be an urgency to address this issue."

It is difficult to imagine that two thousand of the charter school 10th graders simply failed to take the 10th grade test. But that is what happened. There are several possible reasons for the this problem. First, it appears that many of the charter school students were simply expelled from the charter school. Some were sent back to the public schools. But many more simply dropped out of school altogether. Second, it appears that many struggling students were encouraged to not come to school on the days of the tests in order to inflate the scores of the charter schools.

A year after Hurricane Katrina, Schools reopened... But they often lacked Experienced teachers Libraries, Internet access and In some cases even Phone services.

Dr. Ferguson believes the huge expulsion and dropout rate at New Orleans charter schools is a reason the crime rate has exploded in New Orleans. She could be right. However, since there has been a major economic crash that has disproportionately harmed young poor people, the lack of economic opportunity (no living wage jobs for young people – and especially young people without a high school diploma) could also be a factor in the increased crime rate. Either way, there appears to be a lot of corruption in New Orleans charter schools.

In June 2010, Dr. Ferguson published another report. She wrote: "When high school students graduate, the community has greater economic development. When high school students drop out, the community has greater crime. This is the importance of high schools in America. Tragically, the Recovery School District (RSD) has done nothing to improve the standing of New Orleans high schools, especially the seven lowest performing high schools."

Dr. Ferguson presented a series of tables showing that "the percentage of 10th graders taking the test has decreased from 85%, before the State Takeover, to 72%, five years later." She then showed that this problem was due entirely to the charter high schools. The percent of 10th graders tested at the normal high schools had actually gone up. Dr. Ferguson concluded that the charter schools were deliberately not testing struggling 10th graders in order to inflate the average scores of charter schools. Dr. Ferguson states that these results show that charter schools are not helping at risk students – which was the claimed purpose of the charter school program when it was started in 2005. What she fails to realize is that the purpose of the charter school program was not to help students. It was to increase corporate profits. Using this as a measure of success, the charter school program is very successful.

In July, 2010, the Southern Poverty Law Center filed a legal complaint against the Louisiana Department of Education alleging that schools have been turning away parents with disabled children and shirking their responsibilities to ensure that the special-needs students they do serve actually benefit from academic instruction.

The complaint asserts that New Orleans schools are in violation of the federal Individuals With Disabilities Education Act (IDEA), particularly in terms of excessive punishment of children with emotional and behavioral problems.

Under IDEA, all public schools must implement an Individual Education Plan (IEP) for each special-needs student before taking punitive measures. However, suspension and expulsion rates of these students are shockingly high in New Orleans: overall, almost a third of the city's 4,500 special-needs students have been suspended by the Recovery School District.

In November 2010, Dr. Ferguson issued another report, this one called RSD's 2009-10 Performance Report Omits 30% of Schools. She refuted the charter schools claim of success by noting that 30% of the charter schools did not file a report. This was at a time that the New Orleans charter schools were being hailed as a "miracle" by ed reform billionaires around the US. Apparently the miracle was too good to be true.

On April 4, 2011, the researchers issued a press release noting that the children of New Orleans had been the pawns of an education experiment lasting over five years. Here are some of the quotes from the press release: Dr. James Taylor, President of the Louisiana Retired Teachers Association, observed, "What we see in the state leadership is simple, capitalistic ideology, a kind of 'Disaster Capitalism,' not an emphasis on quality education... Why are we letting non-educators tell us how to educate our children?"

Charles Hatfield, Analyst with Research on Reforms, Inc., described the state's posture on education as "market driven propaganda, a sort of 'gain' game with school performance scores perpetuating a myth to the public."

Joe Potts, President Emeritus, Jefferson Federation of Teachers added **"Why should schools be run more like a business when more than half of all businesses fail?"**

"Why should schools be run like a business When more than half of all businesses fail?"

Joe Potts, President Emeritus
Jefferson Federation of Teachers

In July 2011, Dr. Ferguson issued another report. This one was called Dumping Kids Out –The Misuse of Charter Schools in New Orleans. Here is a quote from the report: "Selective retention, called "dumping kids out," gives some New Orleans charter schools an advantage over other schools. Why is this allowed?... States with the highest educational attainment rates have the lowest crime rates and the highest economic development status. Louisiana continues to be at the lowest educational attainment level. And, New Orleans has the highest crime rate in the nation."

Dr. Ferguson notes that New Orleans charter schools have expelled students for minor infractions including: "not being in assigned seats before the tardy bell rings, not bringing pencils or books to class, not raising hands before talking, not following a teacher's directions the first time they are given, sleeping in class, failing to report to the office as directed, disobeying a teacher, cheating, or lying."

In March 2012, Dr. Ferguson issued another report. This one was called. New Orleans Schools Should Not Serve as a National Model. Here is a quote from this report:

"There is a negative relationship between public education and crime in New Orleans. Since the years following the takeover, crime has increased dramatically, with more and more crimes involving juveniles and young adults. For the 2011 year in New Orleans, crime jumped 10 percent from the previous year, with significant spikes in murders, rapes and armed robberies. There has been a steady increase in crime during the past two years, and that increase is continuing into the 2012 year. The city has seen a significant rise in recent months in armed robberies."

"Although the Recovery School District (RSD)'s public relations machine glorifies the tremendous gains made over 6 years, the overall performance of the RSD in New Orleans remains at or near the bottom in Louisiana, i.e., RSD received an overall letter grade of `D' as compared to the overall letter grade of `B' received by the OPSB."

In January 2013, Dr Ferguson wrote another report. This one was called RSD Skews Its Performance Score By Omitting Nearly 20% of Schools. Here is a quote from her report:

"The 2010-11 school year is the most recent year for which the Louisiana Department of Education released the District Composite Reports, and the Recovery School District's Composite Report omits the accountability information for twelve (12) of the seventy (70) RSD schools, thus skewing the RSD's performance score. If these schools had been included in the calculation, the Recovery School District's Performance Score would have declined."

Also in January 2014, the federal court of appeals affirmed the ruling of a lower court that the due process rights of 7,500 New Orleans teachers were violated when they were fired after Hurricane Katrina. Each teacher was awarded three years of back pay and benefits. Sadly, no amount of money could compensate for the loss of their careers and their self dignity.
http://www.researchonreforms.org/html/documents/OliveretalvOPSBetalFOURTH CIRCUITRULINGJAN152014.pdf

In June 2014, Dr. Ferguson issued another report. This one was called Closing Schools, Opening Schools and Changing School Codes: Instability In the New Orleans Recovery School District. Here is a quote from her report:

"During its first few years, the Recovery School District (RSD) simply opened schools in New Orleans, without closing any and without changing any school codes. But, five years ago the RSD began to close schools and change school codes as frequently as it opened schools. These actions compromise the RSD District Performance Score because test scores from students in closed schools are omitted. Also, when the RSD changes a school code, the old code and the test scores listed under that code are often eliminated. In addition, when schools are newly opened, many wait years to receive a School Performance Score, meaning that those students' test scores are not calculated into the RSD District Performance Score. During the last five years, the RSD closed 25 schools, opened 23 new schools, and changed the codes of 21 schools in New Orleans.

The question is whether these actions represent the challenges of the newly created Recovery School District, or if they are a deliberate attempt to thwart research on its progress...Of the 34 schools that the RSD opened during its first full year of operation in 2006-07, only 20 remain opened in 2013-14."

On October 1, 2014, researcher Charles Hatfield issued a report called Analysis of 2014 iLEAP Results for the Recovery School District in New Orleans. After presenting data that the Recovery School District had made little progress in the preceding 10 years, he expressed concern about the likelihood that the new Common Core standards and tests would make the plight of children in New Orleans even worse. Here is a quote from his report:

"The new Louisiana Department of Education (LDOE) goal is predicated on the successful implementation of the Common Core State Standards (CCSS) and the associated new assessments, (PARCC). The LDOE's public relations spiel for adopting the CCSS and PARCC was that the existing standards were not rigorous enough and must be replaced by more rigorous ones in order to better prepare students for college and careers. Yet, no empirical evidence has ever been presented to indicate how and to what extent these new CCSS standards are superior to the LDOE's accountability standards that were established in 1998. Is the LDOE really serious or is this just another example of the hyperboles that have been promulgated by the LDOE, RSD-NO and their advocates to continue to delude the public about the successes of this market-based reform movement? After ten years, the vast majority of the RSD-NO's students have failed to come even close to achieving the 2014 NCLB achievement goal of 100% proficiency under the old standards. Now, the LDOE expects that students will perform at the higher mastery level in another 11 years under these rigorous standards... Sadly, another generation of students will be lost. Indeed, this is the tragedy of the market-based reform movement in New Orleans."
http://www.researchonreforms.org/html/documents/Analysisof2014iLEAPResultsfortheRecoverySchoolDistrictinNewOrleans-Final.pdf

In September 2014, the Recovery School District experiment was ended and the New Orleans schools were handed over to 57 private for profit charter school operators. This will make the Recovery School District the nation's first "all charter" school district. Of the 89 public schools in New Orleans, only five will not be charters in fall 2014, all 5 under the local Orleans Parish School Board. Ten of the schools will be ran as KIPP kid prisons (which we discuss in detail in another article). Thus, New Orleans has the third highest concentration of KIPP schools in the nation (the highest is Houston followed by Washington DC). About 90 percent or about 40,000 of New Orleans 45,000 students are now attending charter schools – despite the evidence that charter schools do no better and often do much worse than normal public schools.

Under Louisiana state law, the Recovery system was supposed to give buildings back to the local Orleans Parish School Board when it no longer needs them. Instead the Recovery system gave the buildings to private charter school operators. The regular school district school board is now suing the Recovery system in an attempt to get their school buildings back.
http://www.nola.com/education/index.ssf/2014/12/who_may_reopen_new_orleans_pub.html#incart_story_package

The Paul Vallas School Closure Virus Spreads to Other States

Even worse, the Louisiana Recovery School System, despite being a disaster for the students of New Orleans, has become a model for State takeovers of urban school districts and conversion to private for profit charter schools in several other States including Michigan, Tennessee and Pennsylvania.
http://www.tennessean.com/article/20131215/NEWS04/312150035

Parents in Tennessee Protest ASD Takeover Of their public schools.

In Tennessee, the new State school district is called the "Achievement School District" or ASD. The Achievement School District charter schools have suffered from the usual problems. These include misuse of tax dollars, lots of Teacher For America fake teachers, plunging test schools, upset kids, upset parents, and upset teachers. But lots of profit for the charter school operators.

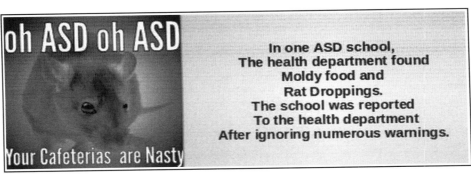

In one ASD school, The health department found Moldy food and Rat Droppings. The school was reported To the health department After ignoring numerous warnings.

Allegations of child abuse have already arisen. In one school, as a form of punishment, students were prohibited from using the bathroom! Welcome to the wonderful world of charter schools!
http://www.tnparents.com/our-voicesblog/category/barbic

2011 to 2013 Paul Vallas Takes his School Closure Scam to Bridgeport CT

In 2011, Paul could see that he was running out of public schools to close in New Orleans. Thankfully, where money is to be made, there is always another target. So in December 2011, he got was appointed to be the new boss of the Bridgeport Connecticut school district by State leaders who had fired the publicly elected school board. The mission as usual was to close all of the public schools and replace them with private for profit schools.

There was only one problem. It turns out that Paul Vallas never bothered to complete "superintendent training" or get a superintendent certificate. Such a minor detail was never required in New Orleans or Philadelphia or Chicago. But it was required in Connecticut.

In April 2013, a group of parents filed a lawsuit – which they won in June 2013. http://www.ctpost.com/local/article/School-s-out-for-Vallas-4637246.php

Here is what one teacher wrote about Paul Vallas: "Vallas is a product of the era of corporate "school reform." He may be one of the more bizarre of those, but he is just another cog in that machine, just as his successor Arne Duncan... The proliferation of these snake oil salesmen and women (let's not forget D.C., Philadelphia and of course Atlanta) is a by-product of an era... Vallas's career is a case study in the arrogance and abuse of corporate power... Looking back on it, from the beginning (Vallas began in Chicago in 1995), it's clear that the whole thing was always about teacher bashing, privatization and union busting...Hopefully, the next generation will be inoculated not only from the Shake-And-Bake nonsense of Teach For America but also the pressure of corporate lies behind the careers of crooks and con artists like Paul Vallas."

Summary... The charter school takeover pattern
Hopefully, you can now see the pattern of charter school takeovers. It begins with billionaires electing corrupt legislators who then change laws to take over public schools when their students are unable to pass high stakes, high failure rate tests. High failure rates are used as an excuse to close public schools. Then after closing public schools, corrupt heartless villains like Arne Duncan, Joel Klein or Paul Vallas act as hit men for the charter school mob. Public schools are closed by the hundreds and converted to charter schools regardless of the poor performance of the charter schools. Experienced teachers are fired by the thousands and replaced with fake "Teacher for America" recruits. Data is manipulated and struggling students are suspended by the thousands to deceive the public into believing that test scores are rising. So the charter school takeover has nothing to do with helping children and everything to do with increasing corporate profits. This is the reason for Common Core and Common Core tests. Their purpose is to fail 70% of all students and then convert every public school in America into a for private for profit charter school. It is up to us to stop them.

What is next?
In the next section, we will briefly review charter school corruption in the US.

3.3 Why Charter Schools always turn into Fraud Factories

In the previous section, we looked at charter school corruption in Chicago, New York City, Philadelphia and New Orleans. In this section, we will look at fraud and corruption in seven States: California, Arizona, Texas, Florida, Pennsylvania, New York and Ohio. But what we may think of as corruption is really the intended payoff of charter schools... just a part of the plan to maximize profits by diverting funding away from public schools to private for profit schools

Four Steps in the Cycle of Ed Reform Corruption

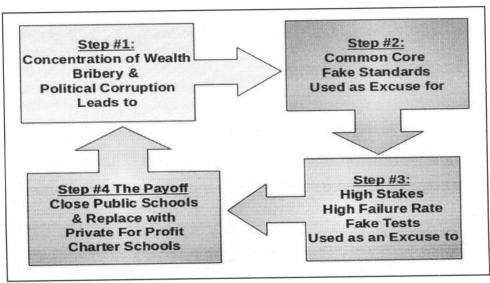

No publicly elected school board means no public accountability
One of the most important purposes of a publicly elected school board is to oversee the spending of tax payer funds to prevent fraud and corruption. This is why one of the most important goals of charter schools is to get rid of publicly elected school boards. Unlike public schools, private profit charter schools are not subject to a public audit of their books. This allows charter school operators to get away with all kinds of fraud and corruption. Charter schools have already robbed American tax payers of billions of dollars – in addition to robbing American children of their right to a good education. The charter school fraud problem is getting worse every year. In this section, we will provide just a few examples. But with charter schools, fraud is not the exception. It is the rule. If tax payers understood the degree of fraud, waste and abuse going on at charter schools, every charter school in the nation would be shut down within a year.

Understanding Charter School Corruption Requires a tour of the US
In order to bring some sense of order to the charter school corruption scams, we have divided them up by States, starting in California and working our way east along the southern United States through Arizona, Texas and Florida and then up the East Coast to Pennsylvania and New York and ending in Ohio.

Here is a picture index of how this section is organized:

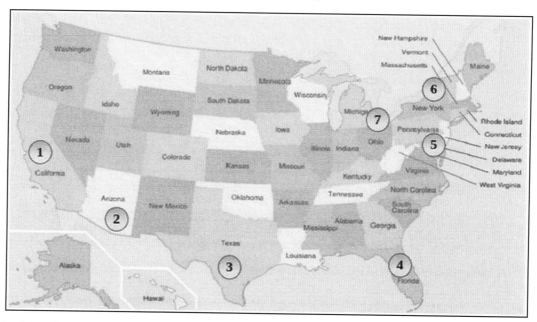

A National Charter School Corporate Crime Wave
In May 2014, the Center for Popular Democracy and Integrity in Education issued a report called Charter School Vulnerabilities to Waste, Fraud And Abuse. This report concluded that fraudulent charter operators in 15 states were responsible for losing, misusing or wasting over $100 million in taxpayer money per year. http://integrityineducation.org/charter-fraud/

Since there are actually charter schools in 45 States, it is likely that the total fraud and abuse of tax payers funds by charter schools exceeds $300 million per year.

The report contains news stories, criminal records, and other documents to detail abuses such as charter school operators embezzling funds, using tax dollars to illegally support other, non-educational businesses, taking public dollars for services they didn't provide, inflating their enrollment numbers to boost revenues, and putting children in potential danger by foregoing safety regulations or withholding services. **These are only a few specific examples of the thousands of cases of fraud involving charter schools nationwide.**

Here is a quote from the report: "Our examination, which focused on 15 large charter markets, found fraud, waste, and abuse cases totaling over $100 million in losses to taxpayers. Despite rapid growth in the charter school industry, no agency, federal or state, has been given the resources to properly oversee it. Given this inadequate oversight, we worry that the fraud and mismanagement that has been uncovered thus far might be just **the tip of the iceberg.**"

In December, 2014, another report was published called When Charter Schools are Nonprofit in Name Only. This report described the common practice of charter schools pretending to be "non-profits" only to sweep all of the money out of the fake non-profit front group and into the pockets of private for profit "management" corporations. These "sweep" contracts divert nearly all of the charter school's public dollars to for profit corporations – with very little left to actually run the charter schools. Once the public money goes into the black hole of a private corporation, there is no way to keep track of how it is actually spent. Here is a quote from the report: "It can be hard for regulators and even schools themselves to follow the money when nearly all of it goes into the accounts of a private company... "We can't audit the (private) management company," said Brian Butry, a spokesman for New York Comptroller Thomas DiNapoli."
http://www.propublica.org/article/when-charter-schools-are-nonprofit-in-name-only

There are several reasons that privatization of public schools has led to rampant fraud and outright theft of tax payer dollars. The first is greed and the profit motive. Billionaires cannot help themselves. They are used to taking whatever money they can get their hands on. The second is deregulation combined with lack of accountability. With charter schools, there is no elected school board to watch over how public funds are spent. Even when the fraud is uncovered, there is no elected school board to kick out of office and replace with a better group. Parents have literally no voice once their school has been taken over by the fraudsters. The third problem is that charter schools like to measure how they are doing simply by high stakes tests scores. This inevitably leads to cheating scandals and many other attempts to manipulate the system – such as having low performing students call in "sick" and not take the test – and even handing students the answer sheet before the test or having administrators change students test answers in the dead of night.

In 2005 Ronald Corwin and Joseph Schneider published "The School Choice Hoax." In this book, they concluded that the number of charter schools that closed due to corruption and mismanagement outnumbered charter schools that closed for academic reasons by a margin of more than three to one.

The only solution to corruption and fraud is to not allow private corporations to make profits off of public schools. The only way this will happen is to ban charter schools. Hopefully, the fraud stories from the following 7 states will help convince more Americans that charter school fraud factories need to be shut down.

#1: California... The Golden State

As of the 2014 school year, California has about 1,000 charter schools affecting about 500,000 students. The entire nation has about 7,000 charter schools controlling the lives of 2.5 million students. So California represents about 20% of our nation's charter school corruption problem. Charter schools are virtually unregulated in California. Thus charter school corruption is rampant in California. It has been rampant since it started in 1999. From 1999 until it went out of business in 2004, the California Charter Academy was the state's largest charter school operation, with more than 4,557 students in kindergarten through 12th grade. In 2004, the State of California Department of Education began looking into allegations of financial fraud at the charter chain. This led to criminal charges against the executives of a charter school operation after an audit found they had **misused at least $25.6 million in public education money**, including $2.6 million for personal expenses. The audit found that executives of the now-closed California Charter Academy used public funds to pay for personal boats, travel, health spa visits, Disney-related merchandise and more. Two employees even paid their income taxes with $42,000 in school funds.

In 2010, the former principal of Northwest Academy Canoga Park charter school plead guilty to embezzlement. Edward Peter Fiszer, 40, pleaded guilty to one count of embezzlement by a public officer and **admitted that the dollar-value exceeded $1.3 million**. Fiszer was sentenced to five years in state prison.

Also in California in 2012, a probe into a charter school was prompted after a former employee blew the whistle on suspicious financial activity between the school and a real estate company owned by the school's founder and "chief executive," Ben Chavis. Chavis's company also owns the building leased to the school in the urban East Oakland Laurel District. The Fiscal Crisis and Management Assistance Team that conducted the investigation has brought into question up to $3 million of questionable transactions over the past three years between the charter school and Chavis's real estate company. The allegation is that Chavis has been embezzling with the aid of his wife, who works as an administrator as well as a consultant to the school. The team concluded that "several companies that conduct business with the charter schools are owned by the founder and/or his spouse, and payment for these services are signed by one or both of these individuals."

In 2011, a charter school finance director faced charges of **embezzling nearly $400,000** to support a prescription narcotics habit, Santa Rosa police officials said. Sheila Accornero is suspected of writing checks to herself and hiding money through accounting techniques during the five years she managed the books for the Kid Street Learning Center Charter School on Davis Street, Sgt. Michael Lazzarini said. **"It appears that all the money went to drugs,"** said Lazzarini, who runs the property crimes unit. "

> **$400,000 embezzlement suspected at Kid Street Charter School**
> **Finance director arrested on embezzlement, burglary, forgery and drug violations**
>
> NOW ENROLLING

In 2013, a jury convicted the founders of the Ivy Academia charter school in the San Fernando of **embezzling public funds and filing filing false tax returns**. Eugene Selivanov and his wife Tatyana Berkovich founded Ivy Academia in 2004 as a state funded charter school. An audit three years later found the couple had not kept public money separate from its for-profit companies. During a three-week trial, prosecutors alleged **the couple filed false tax returns and used $200,000 in public funds to buy groceries, clothes and other personal items - and to fund a separate private school!**

In 2014, according to an investigation by the California State Auditor, the Cato School of Reason Charter School registered and collected **millions of taxpayer dollars** for students who were actually attending private schools. Also in 2014, in California, a charter school con man admitted to stealing **more than $7 million** worth of computers from the US government by creating fake online schools and then selling the computers on Craig's List. The total loss to the tax payers of this scam was more than $30 million since 2007.

Also in 2014, a charter school board member in Newport Beach California was accused of **stealing $750,000**. He took the money telling other school board members he was investing it. It turned out he was investing it in himself through a series of money laundering schemes. Tax payer funds disappeared into thin air. http://www.latimes.com/local/lanow/la-me-ln-charter-school-board-member-charged-theft-20140212-story.html#ixzz2tg0PSWLm

Arizona...

In 2002, Arizona had 422 charter schools – more than any other State in the nation at the time. More than 10 percent of these charter schools have since closed with other charter schools taking their place in a rotating shell game. Currently, Arizona has about 500 charter schools affecting about 200,000 children. In Arizona, in 2012, the Arizona Republic found that board members and administrators from 17 charter schools "profiting from their affiliations by doing business with schools they oversee." Investigators reviewed thousands of pages of federal tax returns, audits, corporate filings, and records filed with the Arizona State Board for Charter Schools. The analysis looked at the 50 largest non-profit charter schools in the state as well as schools with assets of more than $10 million. For-profit schools were not analyzed because their tax records are not public. The Republic's analysis found at least 17 contracts or arrangements, totaling more than $70 million over five years and involving about 40 school sites, in which money from the non-profit charter school went to for-profit or non-profit companies run by board members, executives or their relatives.

http://archive.azcentral.com/arizonarepublic/news/articles/20121016insiders-benefiting-charter-deals.html

Texas...

Like Arizona, Texas has about 500 charter schools affecting about 200,000 students. In April 2008, an investigation by the Dallas Morning News reported that out of 206 charter schools in Texas, 93 of them – or almost half - had been bilking the state out as much as $26 million dollars per year by over counting their enrollment. The Texas Education Agency (TEA) is working to recover $17 million of the $26 million from nearly half of the charters now operating in Texas. TEA records show that 20 schools went out of business before the state could recover its money, leaving taxpayers holding a $9 million bag of debt. Due to the lack of transparency at charter schools, no one knows for sure if the charter school debt is really $26 million dollars. The actual amount of fraud could be much more. http://www.schoolsmatter.info/2008/04/charter-schools-mismanagement-fraud.html

Florida...

Like Texas and Arizona, Florida has about 500 charter schools affecting more than 200,000 children. Pushing charter schools on the children of Florida was one of the main goals of presidential candidate and former Florida governor, Jeb Bush – who also received millions of dollars from Bill Gates.

In a 2007 editorial called "Charter Schools Run Wild," the St. Petersburg Times of Florida noted that in the state of Florida: **"Those lobbyists, and an embarrassingly compliant state Department of Education**, have turned charter education into a $560-million-a-year enterprise that is so immune to oversight that an **Escambia school convicted of fraudulently using its students to work on road crews is still receiving tax money.** A Pensacola school where not a single student has passed the state's standardized reading and math tests in four years is still receiving tax money. A Vero Beach school investigated twice for suspicion of cheating on standardized tests is still receiving tax money."
http://www.sptimes.com/2007/04/01/Opinion/Charter_schools_run_w.shtml

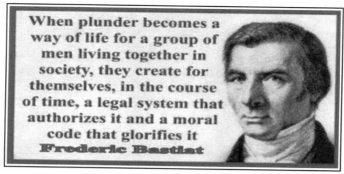

In 2011, the former director of Life Skills Center Charter School in Florida, John Wyche, was sentenced to serve six years in prison for misusing more than $750,000 in state education monies to sustain a failing apartment complex that he owned. In 2012, the former home of a shuttered charter school was auctioned off after Great Florida Bank won a $2.24 million foreclosure judgment. The Miami-Dade County School Board shut down the Balere Academy after parents complained of house parties with alcohol and other distasteful promotions. http://www.bizjournals.com/southflorida/blog/morning-edition/2012/12/charter-school-building-heads-to.html

In April 2014, the League of Women Voters of Florida issued a report on fraud of charter schools. The report was shocking. They found that while public schools spent more than 80% of their funds on classroom instruction, charter schools spent barely 40% on classroom instruction. Charter schools spent much less on teachers and much more on overhead costs, management and rental fees. Charter schools had a closure rate of 20% per year. Numerous members of the State legislature benefited directly or indirectly from charter school kickbacks. http://origin.library.constantcontact.com/download/get/file/1103316066537-1070/LWV+Final+Report+Statewide+Study+1-3.pdf

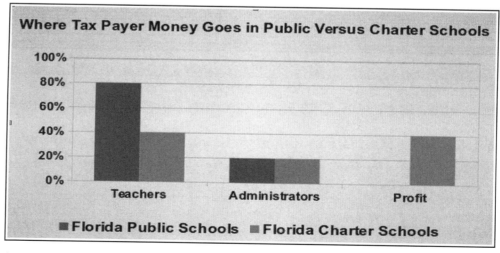

Thus, how charter schools make a profit is by cutting teachers in half. No wonder charter school operators want to get rid of teachers unions!

In June 2014, an investigation by the Orlando Sun Sentinel found, "Unchecked charter-school operators are exploiting South Florida's public school system, collecting taxpayer dollars for schools that quickly shut down." How this scam works is that 56 South Florida charter schools were started and got a lot of public money. Then they closed leaving the local public school district to pick up the pieces. The scam artists included Charter Schools USA – an outfit we will talk more about when we get to Pennsylvania. The scams cost local public school districts more than one million dollars in lost funding. Here are a couple of quotes from the article: "It's almost mind-blowing what's going on," said Rosalind Osgood, a Broward School Board member. "They just get away with it."

"They're public schools in the front door; they're for-profit closed entities in the back door," said Kathleen Oropeza, who co-founded FundEducationNow.org, an education advocacy group based in Orlando. "There's no transparency; the public has no ability to see where the profits are, how the money is spent."

In August 2014, another Florida investigation of charter school operations found millions of taxpayer dollars misdirected from classrooms and students to management companies like charter school chain operator Charter Schools USA. Charter Schools USA uses tax-exempt bonds to build schools that it then rents to its affiliates- basically overcharging them by tens of millions of dollars in extra school rental charges that get passed on to the tax payers.

What Charter School USA does very well is provide campaign funding for State legislators. State records indicate Charter Schools USA spends nearly $2 million per year in bribes/lobbying to the State legislature and the State Governor.

http://www.wtsp.com/story/news/investigations/2014/08/21/charter-school-profits-on-real-estate/14420317/

Pennsylvania...

Pennsylvania has about 170 charter schools affecting more than 100,000 children. In 2010, five Philadelphia charter officials plead guilty to or were convicted of federal fraud charges, and 18 charter schools in the city were under federal investigation based on allegations including financial mismanagement, nepotism, conflicts of interest, unusual salary arrangements for chief executives, and complex real estate deals in which charters leased facilities from related organizations. This was part of a national investigation. Here is a quote from the report: "In the last five years, the Inspector General's Office has opened more than 40 criminal investigations of charter schools nationwide that have resulted in 18 indictments and 15 convictions. The offenses have included embezzling, inflating enrollment to obtain more funding, changing grades, and creating companies to divert money from schools."
http://www.philly.com/philly/education/20100503_U_S__probe_widens_to_18_city_charters.html

In July 2012, the FBI charged charter school promoter Dorothy June Brown with stealing more than $6.5 million in school funds. Dorothy had a habit of stealing from charter schools she had started in Philadelphia. Between 2007 to 2011, Brown robbed $6.5 million from three charter schools she founded. In 2013, the charter school promoter plead guilty to most of the counts.

http://www.fbi.gov/philadelphia/press-releases/2012/charter-school-founder-dorothy-june-brown-charged-in-6-million-fraud-scheme

In June 2014, a study was released showing that Pennsylvania charter schools got $200 million more in tax dollars for special needs students than they actually spent on special needs students.

http://thenotebook.org/sites/default/files/PASBO%20special%20education.pdf

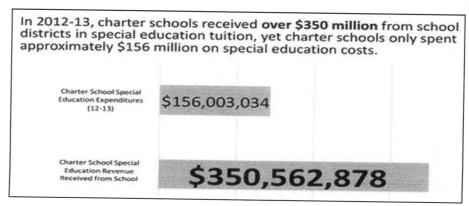

As best we can tell, instead of special ed money serving special needs students, it appears that the windfall has funded things like multi-million dollar CEO compensation, over 19,000 local TV commercials urging kids and their parents to sign up for a charter school that has one of the worst academic records in the nation, a jet and Florida condo, generous political campaign contributions and a 20,000 square foot mansion on the beach in Palm Beach Florida. Here's a three minute youtube video produced by KEYSEC Co-Chair Mark B. Miller that clearly explains how this happens.

https://www.youtube.com/watch?v=WRw5oO02KpA

In September 2014, the Center for Popular Democracy, Integrity in Education, and ACTION United published a report that disclosed charter school officials in Pennsylvania had defrauded at least $30 million intended for school children since 1997.

http://populardemocracy.org/sites/default/files/charter-schools-PA-Fraud.pdf

Examples of charter school fraud described in the report included:
In 2007, one charter operator was caught diverting $2.6 million in school funds to a church property he also operated.

In 2008, another charter school operator was caught spending millions in school funds to bail out other nonprofits associated with the school's parent corporation.

In 2009, a pair of charter school operators stole more than $900,000 from the school by using fraudulent invoices for home improvement expenses.

In 2012, another charter school operator was sentenced to prison for stealing $522,000 to prop up a failing restaurant.

In 2014, another charter school operator was indicted for diverting $8 million of school funds to buy houses and an airplane.

In November 2014, Pennsylvania voters decided they had finally had enough of their corrupt pro-charter school governor Tom Corbett and voted to replace him with Tom Wolf, a governor who pledged to support and protect real public schools.

On December 6 2014, the Philadelphia Coalition Advocating for Public Schools issued a press release calling for the Pennsylvania Attorney General to investigate charter school fraud.
http://wearepcaps.org/2014/12/06/pcaps-calls-on-pennsylvania-attorney-general-kathleen-kane-to-investigate-charter-school-fraud-prevention-practices-requests-by-community-and-parents-for-information-go-unanswered/

Here is a quote from their press release: "After uncovering **$30 Million in fraud by Pennsylvania Charter schools,** members of the community and parents have seen their "Right to Know" requests for information about Philadelphia Charter Schools fraud prevention policies go unanswered. A formal complaint will be filed requesting that the PA Attorney General open an investigation into these private, non-profits and how they care for taxpayer dollars."

The charter school scam in Pennsylvania is being run by a wealthy attorney named Vahan Gureghain. He is the founder of a corporation called CSMI which stands for charter school Management Incorporated.

Managing Charter schools Creates a lot of wealth. This is a drawing Of Vahan Gureghain's Second Home Being built in Florida For more than $30 million. His first home in Pennsylvania is Much bigger...

Gureghain runs Pennsylvania's largest charter school – with more than 3,000 students. He has donated more than one million dollars to political campaigns of pro-charter school candidates including near a half million dollars to former Governor Tom Corbett. Apparently, this was not enough money to get Tom Corbett re-elected.

Merry Christmas Pennsylvania... We are Stealing your Schools!
York (Pennsylvania) School District Takeover by Charter Schools USA
In December 2014, a judge removed the public schools of York City, Pennsylvania, from their publicly elected school board and handed them over to a receiver, business man David Meckley. He has said he will turn the all eight schools over to a for-profit charter chain, Charter Schools, USA. The school district got into financial trouble after former governor slashed $1 billion in State funding for public schools. This meant an $8.4 million cut for the York School District. The Governor then appointed David Meckley to fix the financial problem that the governor had created. When the elected school board refused to go along with the conversion of the school district to charter schools, Meckley got a judge to sign a court order forcing the conversion.

This is what the local newspaper said:

"The community clearly opposes the plan. Yet while they have no say in the matter, city property owners' tax dollars now will be used not only for education but to boost the profits of Charter Schools USA. Since the district is struggling financially, how can anyone justify diverting even a penny away from the students?"

https://gadflyonthewallblog.wordpress.com/2014/12/27/merry-christmas-were-stealing-your-schools/

Below is an image of parents protesting the takeover of their York School District.

As we noted in the section on Florida charters, Charter Schools USA is an extremely corrupt corporation. They spend as much on fees and leases profiting upper management as they do on teachers. Another Charter Schools USA school in Indiana kept more than $6 million of "misappropriated" state funds for 1,800 students who never enrolled in its schools. The CEO of Charter Schools USA Jonathan Hage has become very rich from diverting funds away from students and towards things like his personal yacht which he named "'Fishin' 4 Schools."

New York...

New York has about 250 charter schools affecting more than 90,000 children.

On December 1 2014, the Alliance for Quality Education released an analysis of charter school financial fraud, finding that more than $54 million in tax payer funds had been diverted away from schools by charter school operators in New York state in just the past year.

http://www.aqeny.org/2014/12/release-new-report-reveals-new-york-states-charter-schools-pose-54-million-fraud-risk-to-taxpayers/

Here is a shocking quote from this report: "State agencies have audited just a quarter of New York's more than 250 charter schools since 2005, largely relying on them to police themselves. Yet in a startling 95 percent of the charters examined, auditors found mismanagement and internal control deficiencies that have occasioned $28.2 million in known fraud, waste, or mismanagement."

Put in plain English, in 9 years the State of New York was only able to investigate 62 charter schools. Of these 62 charter schools, 59 were found to have committed fraud or mismanagement! Yet New York taxpayers spend over $1.5 billion on these corrupt charter schools each year.

Examples from the report included:

#1: A New York City charter school operator issued credit cards to its executives allowing them to charge more than $75,000 in unexplained charges in less than two years.

#2: A Long Island charter school operator paid vendors over half a million dollars without competitive bids.

#3: An Albany charter school operator lost as much as $2.3 million by purchasing a site for its elementary school rather than leasing it.

#4: A Rochester charter school operator awarded contracts to board members, relatives, and other related parties rather than get competitive bids.

#5: A Buffalo charter school operator signed a leasing arrangement that paid more than $5 million to a building company at a 20 percent interest rate. It is likely that the actual fraud is three times worse than the known fraud.

Ohio...

Ohio has about 400 charter schools affecting more than 120,000 children. Ohio seems to be the nation's leader in charter school corruption which is why we have saved them for last. In 2013, an Ohio man and his brother plead guilty to an alleged $1.8 million charter school fraud in Cleveland. Both were sentenced to one year probation. Also in 2013, in a similar case, prosecutors charged a charter school operator of diverting at least $1.2 million dollars in public funds away from his charter school and into other businesses and multiple homes. In 2014, the judge gave the operator 5 years of probation. http://www.cleveland.com/court-justice/index.ssf/2014/02/lion_of_judah_charter_school_o.html

In another case, a charter school treasurer plead guilty to stealing $470,000 from 4 Ohio charter schools. The funds were supposed to be used for the education of students at four charter schools in Columbus, Youngstown and Dayton between 2005 and 2011, according to the office of the U.S. Attorney for the Southern District of Ohio.

In 2013, 19 charter schools closed in the State of Ohio, joining 150 other charter schools in Ohio that had already been shut down since 2005. With about 400 total charter schools in Ohio, that is a **failure rate of over 40 percent!** "$1.4 billion has been spent since 2005 through school year 2012-2013 on charter schools that have never gotten any higher grade than an F or a D,"

In 2014, a corporation called White Hat that runs a fake charter school called Life Skills – with one of the worst graduation rates in the nation – began fooling kids and their parents into signing up with a key word advertising campaign aimed at folks who are online. Private charter school companies are advertising on television, radio, billboards, and even automated telephone messages to entice students away from public schools using "key words" like free, flexible, and find your future.

The funds to pay for this massive misleading advertising blitz came from State tax payers. Ohio charter schools enroll less than 7 percent of Ohio's students yet receive 11 percent of all state funds set aside for public education.
http://www.ohio.com/news/local/charter-school-operators-use-key-words-to-entice-families-away-from-public-schools-1.491420

As in Florida, charter schools are closing at a record rate in Ohio and sticking tax payers with the bill

Charter schools are closing in Ohio at a record rate after a series of fraud cases were uncovered. The tax payers are left to pick up the pieces and the kids suffer the loss of their schools and their education.

Charter schools are funded by the state on the backs of school districts and taxpayers. Because charter schools are exempt from most state laws and do not have a publicly elected school board, there is almost no oversight of spending at charter schools. Over $900 million dollars per year is diverted away from public schools to charter schools in Ohio every year. But the bill doesn't stop there. When there is financial mismanagement, charter schools can be closed. But it is almost impossible to get the money invested in charter schools back. Nearly $187 million in tax money spent on failed charter schools is still uncollected.

Conclusion

Fraud, corruption, mismanagement, bribes and kick back schemes... This is what happens when billionaires and their corrupt politicians promote private, for profit charter schools that are not under the control of a locally elected public school board. In this chapter, and in previous chapters, we have described a whole new set of fraud techniques that have developed a whole new charter school language. For example, cream skimming means taking all of the most successful, easy to teach and profitable children away from public schools and putting them into charter schools. Dumping means taking the poorest most challenging special needs students and expelling them from charter schools when they are not able to keep up. What parents need to understand is that charter schools were never meant to work. Charter schools are simply another of the weapons of mass deception that billionaires are using to destroy and privatize public schools.

It does not matter to the billionaires that 95% of all charter schools suffer from fraud and mismanagement. The real purpose of charter schools is to divert public funds away from real public schools to the pockets of corrupt investors in charter schools. Measured through this lens, charter schools are serving their purpose. As evidence of the billionaires plan to divert funds away from public schools and into private for profit charter schools, check out this chart of the change in funding from major foundations (also known as billionaire tax dodges) since 2000:

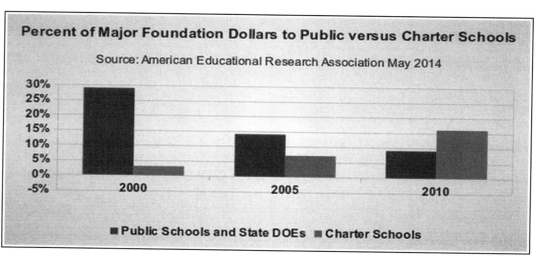

Billions of dollars that used to go towards the improvement of public schools has been shifted towards the funding of private for profit charter schools. Thankfully, because of all of the charter school scandals, public support for charter schools is starting to drop. An August 2014 poll in Michigan found that 73 percent of responders want a moratorium on the creation of new charter schools.

http://www.freep.com/article/20140831/NEWS06/308310070/charter-schools-poll-Michigan

In communities around the nation, announcements about new charter operations opening up have been greeted with public protests. While law markers continue to pass laws promoting charter schools, they do so at their peril. The day will come when parents will blame legislators for the harm that has been inflicted on their children. Hopefully, these corrupt legislators will be voted out of office just as Tom Corbett was in Pennsylvania.

What is next?
Now that we better understand the level of fraud that occurs in charter schools, we will take a closer look at how one particular charter school called KIPP inflicts abuse on children forced to endure its unusual methods.

3.4 Kids in Prison Program
How KIPP Charter Schools Use CIA Torture Techniques to Abuse Children

> "At KIPP, I would wake up sick, every single day. Except Sunday, 'cause that day in didn't have To go to school. All of the students called KIPP The "Kids in Prison Program."
> A former KIPP student

The Start of KIPP Charter Schools

KIPP charter schools started in Houston in 1994 by a couple of "Teach for America" graduates – Mike Feinbery and David Levin - two people with no degree in education or child development with only a 6 week "TFA" course under their belt – and a desire to make a profit off of children.

Mike Feinberg (left) and David Levin started a single charter school in 1994 that has evolved into one of the most well-known charter organizations in the U.S.

Due to massive funding from Bill Gates and his billionaire buddies, KIPP has grown to be among the largest and richest charter school chain in America. For example, in 2009, the Gates Foundation guaranteed $30 million in KIPP bonds so that KIPP could expand its operations. The KIPP network now includes 130 charter schools in 20 states with more than 50,000 students. Bill Gates has given KIPP more than $27 million dollars including $10 million just in 2006!

KIPP, Inc.
Date: September 2006
Purpose: to support the development of a network of Pre-K through 12th grade charter schools in Houston
Amount: $10,000,000
Term: 60
Topic: College-Ready

In addition, KIPP has received $50 million from the US Department of Education.

KIPP- The Kids in Prison Program

KIPP stands for "Knowledge is Power Program." But as the kids themselves have concluded, it really stands for "Kids in Prison Program."

KIPP students attend school 9 hours a day and every other Saturday... and also a big part of the summer. Compare this to public schools where kids only attend school 7 hours a day and not at all on weekends. Goodbye weekends and goodbye summer vacation. So much for a happy carefree childhood.

It's sad for children to get so little free time. You are only young once. And shockingly, at some KIPP schools, students even have to earn the right to sit at a desk! Here is a quote from a former KIPP teacher:

"...during the first week of school 100 fifth-graders were packed into a single classroom without desks, where they sat the entire class time Monday through Thursday learning to earn the right to sit in a desk...It was treating them like animals. Only they weren't animals. They were children."
http://www.substancenews.net/articles.php?page=4679

Speaking of treating children like animals, consider classroom management. At one KIPP school in California, a KIPP principal told a student to get on his hands and knees and bark like a dog. The same principal put a garbage can on another student's head implying that the student was no better than a sack of garbage.

Using shame to control children seems to be the norm at KIPP. A teacher described what happened during high stakes testing time. Many students were not allowed to use the bathroom. This resulted in some students wetting their pants. Also to raise high stakes test scores, students' test answers were reviewed by teachers, and then students were given their tests back and told which answers to correct. (That is one way to increase test scores.)
http://www.markgarrison.net/archives/62

At another KIPP school, small children would be deprived of recess for infractions as small as turning their head around and failing to look at the teacher. Eventually, trouble making children who failed to keep silent and keep their eyes on the teacher either dropped out or were expelled. No individuality is permitted at Kipp and anyone who does not toe the line is ridiculed, punished and/or expelled. This is why an independent three year study of KIPP schools found they have an extremely high attrition rate. Out of every 100 students, more than 60 either drop out or are expelled within three years.
http://www.examiner.com/article/bay-area-kipp-schools-lose-60-of-their-students-study-confirms

An attrition rate of 60% is 10 times more than the attrition rate at a normal public school!

Bad for Kids and Bad for Teachers

More than half of the teachers quit KIPP schools every year. This is in part because KIPP pays teachers less than real public schools pay real teachers – despite the fact that KIPP teachers work much longer hours than normal teachers. KIPP schools also use a lot of Teach For America teachers. TFA teachers have no training and do not intend to keep working as "teachers" for more than a year or two. According to the KIPP website, one in three KIPP teachers is from TFA. In fact, the leader of KIPP, Richard Barth, is married to the leader of TFA, Wendy Kopp. So fraud and corruption run in the family.

The extremely high teacher attrition rate is also due to the fact that teachers can't stand the abuse and torture that KIPP subjects children to. For example, 5 year olds who do not obey have been put into padded cells. According to their parents, 5 year old children were repeatedly placed in this cell for 15 to 20 minutes at a time.

This is a padded cell also known as a "prison for children" used at a KIPP Military Boot Camp Style Charter School to hold Kindergarten students Who did not toe the Line when they Were ordered to obey.

For at least some KIPP students, childhood ends here

"He was crying hysterically," said Teneka Hall, 28, a Washington Heights mom whose son, Xavier, was rushed to the hospital after he panicked and wet himself while he was holed up in the padded room. "It's no way to treat a child."
http://www.nydailynews.com/new-york/education/padded-calm-down-room-causing-anxiety-kids-article-1.1543983#ixzz2nCXqbLiV

Other KIPP schools/prisons, that lack a padded room, use a humiliating style of punishment called "The Bench" to shame small children into keeping quiet. In KIPP schools, kindergartners are shamed and ridiculed for things as innocent as turning their head or chatting with their classmates. Kids/inmates are expected to remain silent for up to 9 hours a day. If a child fails to toe the line, they are taken off of the team for up to two days, isolated and forced to wear a bench sticker. They must eat lunch away from the rest of the team and are keep in detention for an extra hour after school. To get back on the team, they must write a letter of apology and also make a verbal apology at a team meeting. Repeated offenses result in expulsion.

"Those who resisted the rules or were slackers wore a large sign pinned to their clothes labeled "miscreant." Miscreants sat apart from the others at all times including lunch, were denied recess and participation in all other school projects and events. Here we see a young girl on a bench at KIPP school with a sign around her neck that says "CRETIN." Her crime was "chatting" in class.

Chatting is a natural activity for little girls... Unfortunately, it is not allowed in KIPP Schools/Kid Prisons.

Other KIPP Schools Send Trouble Makers to the Basement
Here is a quote about this tactic: "On VIB (Visitor in Building) days, at least one KIPP school puts up to 30 problem students in the empty basement for hours until the visiting investors or politicians have left the building. Also during this time, no class changes occur, even though visits might last three hours. Children are, in essence, in lock down mode in their classrooms so that no infraction or non-compliant behavior during class change may be seen by outsiders."
http://www.schoolsmatter.info/2014/11/kipp-puts-up-to-30-problem-students-in.html

What teachers and child development experts say about KIPP schools
Here is what a couple of teachers said about KIPP: "I've spent many years in schools. KIPP felt like a low security prison or something resembling a locked-down drug rehab program."
http://www.schoolsmatter.info/2010/11/learning-about-kipp-lesson-3-social.html

Childhood education expert, Deb Meier called this "military style" discipline aimed at "humiliating kids into compliance."
http://michaelklonsky.blogspot.com/2013/12/kipps-long-record-of-child-abuse-must.html

"Any system that demands of children that they give up their childhood as a condition for success, which KIPP does, should not be entertained as a viable education intervention. KIPP is education reform on the cheap, where economy is more important than the children who are sacrificed through the unethical excess that we turn our backs to. There are humane ways to run schools and increase academic achievement at the same time. KIPP is not one of them."
http://www.schoolsmatter.info/2009/03/interview-kult-of-kipp-and-abuses-in.html

Another KIPP teacher said: *"I was a teacher at a KIPP school for 1 1/2 years. It was the most horrible experience of my life. The teachers and students are literally in school for 11 hours a day. I saw numerous teachers experience nervous breakdowns from the extreme pressure and harassment of administration. There was a 50% turnover for staff each year."*

http://nycpublicschoolparents.blogspot.com/2012/03/at-kipp-i-would-wake-up-sick-every.html

Another former KIPP teacher agreed: *"I worked at a KIPP school for over a year and saw exactly what the first writer saw. Teachers were bullied and harassed by the school leader living in fear if they spoke up. Students with special needs were not accommodated. The turnover with staff is huge. Two teachers had nervous breakdowns over the stress. Students were under constant control and no freedom of expression. Chants and a cult mentality permeated the school. KIPP robs children of their childhood. Most KIPP teachers in our building were not qualified. Student achievement was very poor. It was a nightmare, beware."*

KIPP College Graduation claims turn out to be nonsense
One common claim to justify all of the child abuse is that 80% of Kipp students go on to college. With 30,000 students, this would imply that 24,000 of them went to college. However, according to the KIPP website, so far only 447 (less than 2%) have gone to college. No word yet about how many have completed college.

No School Board, No Reporting, No Transparency
Go to the KIPP website and you will find their annual report – which is really more of a marketing brochure than a report. It does not list how much is paid to administrators versus teachers or really where any of the tax payer funds have gone. There are no school board minutes or any process for parents to be involved in decision making. It does not list how much is spent per child or the transfers in or out of the program. By comparison, any public school district has a website detailing where every dollar was spent and lists minutes of past school board meetings and when the next school board meeting will be held. The lack of transparency at KIPP ought to offend not just any parent, but any tax payer.

Bill Gates Loves KIPP (just not for his kids)
According to Billionaire Bill: "KIPP is one of the most promising examples of innovative thinking in American education. I find it stunning that the educational schools are not training teachers to use the KIPP way of teaching classes."
Bill Gates January 21 2010

Bill Gates at a KIPP school In Houston TX... Of course, where Bill's three kids attend School at a wealthy Private school in Seattle, Uniforms are not worn And kids are not locked Into closets for chatting In class.

Bill claims we need the KIPP Child Prison program because American public schools are broken and do not do well on international test scores. Yet whenever one adjusts for childhood poverty, American schools do as well as or better than any other schools in the world. For example, two of the three major international tests—the Progress in International Reading Literacy Study and the Trends in International Math and Science Study—break down student scores according to the poverty rate in each school. The tests are given every five years. The most recent results (2006) showed the following: **students in U.S. schools where the poverty rate was less than 10 percent ranked first in reading, first in science, and third in math.** When the poverty rate was 10 percent to 25 percent, U.S. students still ranked first in reading and science. But as the poverty rate rose still higher, students ranked lower and lower.

Twenty percent of all U.S. schools have poverty rates over 75 percent. The average ranking of American students reflects this. **The problem is not public schools; it is poverty. And the true cause of poverty is that all the wealth in America is concentrated in the hands of a few billionaires. Public Schools are not the problem – the real problem is billionaires like Bill Gates.**

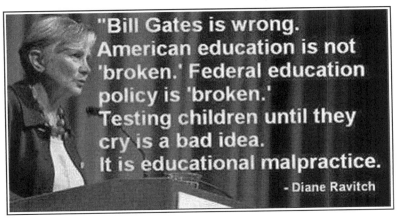

Comparing KIPP to the School Where Bill Gates Sends His Kids
Bill Gates sends his three kids to a private school in Seattle called Lakeside where the annual tuition is $28,500 and where the teacher student ratio is 9 students per teacher and no students are locked in a closet just for having talked during class. Lakeside has no high stakes tests, no Common Core Curriculum and plenty of respect for caring experienced teachers. Our public schools should be more like Lakeside, the private school in Seattle where Bill's kids go and have small class sizes and academic freedom to explore their potential – not like the KIPP schools Bill wants to subject our children to.

Learned Helplessness- How KIPP Schools are related to CIA Torture

(We know this section might be hard to believe. It was hard for us to write. We include the links so you can do your own research.)

One of the two psychologists on whom KIPP bases its strict discipline approach is Martin Seligman. Here he is listed on the KIPP website:
http://www.kipp.org/our-approach/character

FOCUSING ON 7 STRENGTHS

KIPP's innovative approach is grounded in the research of Dr. Martin Seligman and the late Dr. Chris Peterson

---

KIPP claims that Martin Seligman came up with the idea for "Seven Strengths." The 7 Strengths include things like having determination and true grit. However, there is a back story to Martin Seligman's work in psychology and how it relates to the methods used by KIPP to shame and control children. It is a horrifying story all parents considering sending their kids to KIPP should be aware of. Unfortunately, Mr. Seligman, who is the inspiration for KIPP schools, was also the inspiration for the CIA Torture program at Guantanamo Bay. We now know that no useful intelligence was gained by torturing prisoners at Guantanamo Bay. The CIA Torture Program, which was finally exposed by the US Senate, can be read at this link: http://www.intelligence.senate.gov/study2014/sscistudy1.pdf
But as you are about to see, this torture program is still the hidden basis of KIPP's unique style of disciplining and shaming small children.

The Story Begins...Martin Seligman tortures dogs and discovers "learned helplessness" n the 1960's Martin Seligman did research subjecting caged dogs to random severe electric shocks as a way to break the will of the dog. He called his method of training dogs "learned helplessness." From the article, "How Seligman's Learned Helplessness Theory Applies to Human Depression and Stress":

"...he would ring a bell and then give a light shock to a dog. After a number of times, the dog reacted to the shock even before it happened: as soon as the dog heard the bell, he reacted as though he'd already been shocked.

But then something unexpected happened. Seligman put each dog into a large crate that was divided down the middle with a low fence. The dog could see and jump over the fence if necessary. The floor on one side of the fence was electrified, but not on the other side of the fence. Seligman put the dog on the electrified side and administered a light shock. He expected the dog to jump to the non-shocking side of the fence. Instead, the dogs lay down. It was as though the small dog learned from the first part of the experiment that there was nothing they could do to avoid the shocks, so they gave up...

Seligman described their condition as **learned helplessness**, or not trying to get out of a negative situation because the past has taught you that you are helpless."

http://education-portal.com/academy/lesson/how-seligmans-learned-helplessness-theory-applies-to-human-depression-and-stress.html#lesson

How Seligman got involved with human torture

According to the Senate report on torture, released in December 2014, we know that two psychologists were paid a total of $82 million from 2002 to 2006 to design and run the Guantanamo Bay CIA Torture Program. (See page 11 of the Senate Report). Here is the link to this 500 page report:
http://www.intelligence.senate.gov/study2014/sscistudy1.pdf

The two psychologists, referred to by pseudonyms Grayson Swigert and Hammond Dunbar in the Senate torture report, were James Mitchell and Bruce Jessen.

http://www.dailykos.com/story/2014/12/09/1350587/-Properly-Recognizing-The-Crimes-of-Drs-Bruce-Jessen-and-James-Mitchell

Mitchell and Jessen reportedly got their ideas on reducing the self esteem of prisoners and creating a sense of learned helplessness from Martin Seligman and the way he tortured helpless dogs.

Seligman's alarming journey from psychologist working with learned helplessness to his connection with the CIA was revealed in a 2011 book written by law professor and ethics expert M. Gregg Bloche (current co-director for the Georgetown-Johns Hopkins Joint Program in Law and Public Health). In Chapter 7 and 8 of his book, The Hypocratic Myth, Bloche described a meeting between Martin Seligman and James Mitchell during the crucial period when Mitchell was involved with setting up the CIA torture program. Seligman had met both James Mitchell and Bruce Jessen in December 2001 and May 2002.

In his book, Bloche writes that Seligman admitted being invited by the CIA to speak at a May 2002 conference before an audience that included CIA psychologists Mitchell and Jessen: "[Seligman] acknowledged only that he spoke on learned helplessness at a JPRA meeting in May 2002 and that Mitchell and Jessen were in the audience: "I was invited to speak about how American… personnel could use what is known about learned helplessness to resist torture and evade successful interrogation by their captors. This is what I spoke about.""

Bloche goes on to describe another meeting between the CIA psychologists and Seligman: "... in the spring of 2002, according to a CIA source, Seligman met with Mitchell and Jessen in Philadelphia. "The fact that we had a meeting in Philadelphia means that Mitchell and Jessen were at least thinking about interrogation strategies." **Seligman wanted to help and understood what Mitchell had in mind.** But having built his reputation as a clinical pioneer — the man who'd discovered learned helplessness... he didn't want to be seen as telling CIA operatives how to break people by inducing despair... "Seligman", said the CIA source, had a "classic approach-avoidance conflict regarding helping us…"

According to Bloche, Seligman also met with Mitchell literally days before Mitchell was called to fly to Thailand, where the CIA wanted him to torture a prisoner being held there. The new torture method was based on Segilman's learned helplessness torture/experiments.

http://pubrecord.org/torture/11073/psychologist-allegedly-psychologist/

Seligman's involvement with the Guantanamo Bay CIA torture program
Clearly, Seligman was involved with people who had direct connections to the CIA torture program at Guantanamo Bay. And it also turns out that Segilman was paid $31 million by the US Army and the CIA to develop learned helplessness torture techniques to use on caged prisoners at Guantanamo Prison aka Gitmo.
http://michaelklonsky.blogspot.com/2013/12/kipp-guru-seligman-helped-develope.html

The proof that Seligman, the role model of KIPP schools, played a role in CIA torture is made crystal clear in a 2010 Salon.com article: "The Army earlier this year (2010) steered a $31 million contract to a psychologist whose work formed the psychological underpinnings of the Bush administration's torture program.

The contract was a no-bid contract as the Army claimed that Seligman was "uniquely qualified."" Government documents say that the goal of Bush-era torture was to drive prisoners into a psychologically devastated state through abuse. "The express goal of the CIA interrogation program was to induce a state of 'learned helplessness,'" according to a July 2009 report by the Justice Department's Office of Professional Responsibility.
http://www.salon.com/2010/10/14/army_contract_seligman/

The Mitchell/Seligman CIA Torture program at Gitmo subjected detainees to torture techniques such as "water boarding, sleep deprivation, isolation, exposure to extreme temperatures, enclosure in tiny spaces, bombardment with agonizing sounds at extremely damaging decibel levels, and religious and sexual humiliation." **One of their defenseless prisoners was water boarded 183 times.** https://en.wikipedia.org/wiki/Enhanced_interrogation_techniques

Here is a sample of the torture that occurred at Guantanamo Bay in the words of one of its victims, Abu Zabaydahs, in his own words as told to a member of the International Committee of the Red Cross: "After the beating I was then placed in the small box. They placed a cloth or cover over the box to cut out all light and restrict my air supply. As it was not high enough even to sit upright, I had to crouch down. It was very difficult because of my wounds… I was then dragged from the small box, unable to walk properly and put on what looked like a hospital bed, and strapped down very tightly with belts. A black cloth was then placed over my face and the interrogators used a mineral water bottle to pour water on the cloth so that I could not breathe. After a few minutes the cloth was removed and the bed was rotated into an upright position. The pressure of the straps on my wounds was very painful. I vomited…. I struggled against the straps, trying to breathe, but it was hopeless. I thought I was going to die. I lost control of my urine. Since then I still lose control of my urine when under stress."

The Geneva Convention says, "Prisoners of war who refuse to answer may not be threatened, insulted, or exposed to any unpleasant or disadvantageous treatment of any kind." What we need now is a Geneva Convention to outlaw cruel and unusual punishment of small children. Outlaw high stakes tests, outlaw Common Core, outlaw charter schools.

How KIPP Schools are related to CIA Torture
KIPP's program can best be described as an extremely sadistic "drill and kill" style of instruction intended to shame students into submission. This method of shaming and punishing small children in a manner that children have little control over, for natural child behaviors like "chatting" indicates that KIPP's program is based on a cross between dog training and military indoctrination. Many kids claim that KIPP schools are a form of torture. However, few realize that the same person who was the inspiration for KIPP schools, psychologist Martin Seligman, was also the inspiration for the CIA Torture program.

Thus, small children at KIPP schools are now being subjected to similar learned helplessness torture techniques as those used by the CIA. Here is a quote from a 2008 article:

"In the KIPP schools, children are routinely broken down into a state of learned helplessness through inescapable surveillance (by school and parents), academic drudgery, repeated testing, and isolation and labeling as "miscreants" for any infringement of rules."

http://www.schoolsmatter.info/2008/08/apa-cia-seligman-and-kipp.html

Here is a chart that explains the relationship between Seligman's torture of small helpless dogs and KIPP's torture of small helpless children.

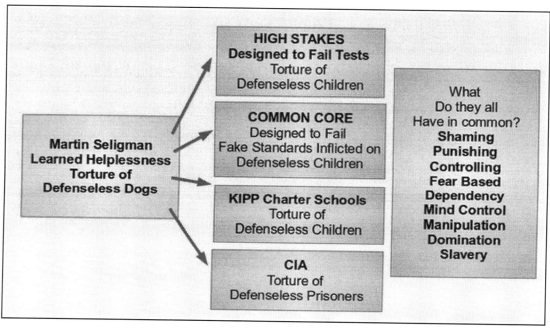

Note that small children also wet their pants when under the stress of high stakes tests and common core standards that they have no hope of meeting. The difference is that small children do not have the coping skills or self esteem of adults. When adults tell them that they are failures, the small children blame themselves for not passing the test – rather than blame the adults for giving them a test that they had no chance of passing. That in a nutshell is child abuse. That is learned helplessness. Whatever else you do, do not allow your kids to go to a KIPP charter school.

What is next?
Now that we understand that charter schools are really nothing more than profit generating child prisons, in the next section we will look at the worst charter school in existence (even worse than KIPP)... a private for profit online charter school called K12 Inc.

4 How K12 INC Online Fake Schools Harm Our Kids

> K12 INC spends millions on advertising to recruit 100,000 students. For every 10 students recruited into the K12 INC online program, One normal public school teacher will have to be fired. In addition, Of these 10 children, 7 will drop out of school and only 3 will Graduate from high school. Only one of the 10 will go to college.

One of the worst charter schools in America is a fake online school called K12 INC. This darling of Wall Street has an annual dropout rate of more than 50% and a graduation rate of less than 30%. In this chapter, we will show that K12 INC is simply one more billionaire weapon of mass deception against our public schools. The real purpose of K12 INC is to rob tax payers of billions of dollars and rob children of their future. This fourth chapter is divided into four sections:

4.1 Why All Parents Need to Learn About the Drawbacks of K12 INC

4.2 From Junk Bonds to Junk Schools

4.3 K12 Distortions, Deceptions and Outright Lies

4.4 Free Open Source Alternatives to K12 INC

4.1 All Parents Need to Know About the Drawbacks of K12 INC

The fourth and perhaps most damaging weapon of mass deception is a vicious Wall Street corporation called K12 INC - a profit-driven corporation that now has branches in nearly every State. This for profit corporation not only destroys the future of children – many of whom actually regress academically after starting this program – but it also destroys the reputation of online education.

K12 INC rarely uses its own bad name. Instead, it hides behind dummy non-profit corporations called "Virtual Academies" such as the Washington Virtual Academy (or WAVA) in our home State of Washington or the Colorado Virtual Academy (or COVA) in Colorado. It is likely that your child's school district has a Virtual Academy and that your child has already been subjected to mass marketing campaigns that target and deceive young children with misleading ads on the Disney and Nickelodeon channels with false claims that online learning is much easier and more fun than attending a normal public school. Both of our children have been subjected to these misleading claims and have friends who have been taken in and severely harmed by K12 INC propaganda. Over 90% of K12 INC enrollees eventually drop out of the terrible program – but are left with even lower self esteem than when they entered the program.

The problem with K12 INC is that it is a for profit corporation. It therefore is driven to lie to increase market share and increase sales and profits. It therefore sells itself as the magic cure to education – just as high stakes tests are sold as the magic cure and common core standards are sold as the magic cure and charter schools are sold as the magic cure. Because the future of our children is at stake, parents have a right to know the full truth about all of these programs. All of them harm children rather than help them. So why do they continue to grow like a cancer destroying our education system? The answer is "Greed." Where there is a profit to be made, some billionaire will be willing to step in and fund the scam in order to get some of the billions of dollars we invest as tax payers in the education of our children. With the case of online education, one billionaire in particular – Bill Gates - has a dream that one day all children will receive the benefits of online education (which just coincidentally benefits his corporation Microsoft). His plan is to turn every school in the US into an online school like K12 INC. We know this sounds crazy. But read on and we will show you.

Four Steps to Converting All Public Schools to For Profit Online Schools

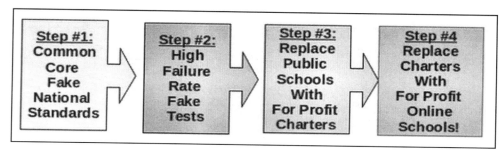

The Real Plan to Takeover and Privatize our Public Schools

The plan to takeover and privatize our public schools is not merely to use Common Core Fake National Standards and high stakes, high failure rate national tests to declare public schools as failures and thereby replace them with private, for profit charter schools – **the real plan is to replace charter schools with for profit online schools like K12 INC.**

There are many "benefits" to this plan in the eyes of the super rich who are backing it. First and foremost is that the billionaires can get rid of those pesky, expensive and hard to control public school teachers. Also, all children, or at least the children of the poor and middle classes, would receive the same online education – a centralized national education where the standards, the curriculum, the tests and the database of results are all controlled by private corporations which are owned by the billionaires.

There would also be no need for other expensive things like brick and mortar schools, school buses,, school secretaries, school principals, school janitors, lunchroom cooks, school counselors, school nurses, school librarians or playground attendants. The entire process of educating the masses could be accomplished much more efficiently for a fraction of the current cost. Best of all, the entire process could be "programmed," controlled and monopolized by a few billionaires – just like the Windows operating system. One operating system for all, one set of national standards for all and one giant online national school system for all.

We realize such a monstrous scheme may seem insane to most parents and most teachers. But billionaires live in a different world than the rest of us. They have so much money that they get detached from reality. They have no idea of what it takes to raise a child or educate a child. And they do not really care.

Real parents and real teachers know that real children were never intended to sit in front of a computer screen to be brain washed hour after hour and day after day. Real children need to interact with each other and interact with real teachers in real time. Real children need to sing and play and draw and build. Real children need to watch real teachers and their classmates as they solve problems and improve skills. Each child is different and unique and learns in a different way and at a different rate. Only a real teacher who knows the child and watches the child on a daily basis will be able to help each child achieve their full potential. There is no way that any computer program will be able to replace a real teacher. But in the eyes of billionaires, their plan is not about maximizing the potential of every child. It is about maximizing the profits of every billionaire. The goal is not high standards for children. It is about high profits for the super rich.

Free Public Education versus Expensive Private Scams
There are two different models about how to share knowledge. One insists that knowledge sharing is a public good and therefore should be free to all regardless of their income. This is why we have free public schools, free public libraries, a free public internet and free public computer operating systems and programs such as the Linux operating system and the 64,000 free public software programs that come with it. Many nations like Germany and Norway also offer free higher education – which is why their economies are in much better shape than the billionaire-based, for-profit, debt-ridden economy in the United States.

The second model sees knowledge sharing as a toll road – a chance to make a buck off of every mile that a student travels on their quest for knowledge. K12 INC is an example of what happens when we allow the quest for knowledge to be privatized and controlled by greed. It should come as no surprise that Bill Gates is behind the privatization of public schools. He has made billions of dollars by forcing folks to pay him for a slow and poorly written Windows operating system when they could have gotten a much much faster and more reliable Linux operating system for free. Bill wants to charge folks for fake education just like he wants to charge folks for his fake operating system. Go to the Gates Foundation website and enter "Online Learning" into the search engine. You will find 36 grants totaling more than $10 million. Here is just one of these grants:

North American Council for Online Learning

Date: October 2013
Purpose: to provide general operating support
Amount: $1,000,000

Free Open Online Education versus Private Monopoly Online Education

In a similar way, there are two different models for online education. There are hundreds of free open source courses and learning systems available to public schools and public school teachers. We will review some of these in the final section of this chapter. Then there are a few for profit closed source learning systems. The most notorious of these is K12 INC. It diverts money away from public schools and public school teachers into a series of scams that harm children. We therefore wonder why any public school system or public school teacher would support such a scam. It is the equivalent of a committing professional suicide as the goal of K12 INC is to destroy public schools and public school teachers. We hope after reading this article that you will agree and ask your school and your State to get rid of scam artists like K12 INC and replace them with free open source education systems.

The Problem with Replacing Public Schools with Private Profits

The problem with allowing private for profit corporations to control our public schools is that all for profit corporations like K12 INC cut corners at every opportunity leaving children with a very low quality education. The problem is not online education – it is that the profit motive corrupts and destroys education. The for profit motive should never be allowed to run our public schools. The profit motive should never be allowed to destroy the future of our children. K12 INC is the poster child of what is wrong with the for profit motive running our schools. Because K12 INC is out to maximize its profits, it recruits children who do not belong in an online program and have no chance of benefiting from an online program.

The above ad may look good. But remind yourself that if there is no publicly elected school board and no public accountability of where all of the tax payers money went, K12 INC is NOT a public school. They are a private corporation pretending to be a public school in order to increase corporate profits.

K12 INC spends millions of tax payer dollars on deceptive TV ads targeting young children

An analysis by USA today found that K12 INC spends about $30 million per year suckering kids and their parents into signing up for the K12 fake school program. Here is a quote from the article: "A look at where K12 is placing the ads suggests that the company is working to appeal to kids: Among the hundreds of outlets tapped this year, K12 has spent an estimated $631,600 to advertise on Nickelodeon, $601,600 on The Cartoon Network and $671,400 on MeetMe.com, a social networking site popular with teens. It also dropped $3,000 on VampireFreaks.com, which calls itself "the Web's largest community for dark alternative culture."
http://www.usatoday.com/story/news/nation/2012/11/28/online-schools-ads-public-/1732193/

Examples of Deceptive K12 TV Ads

In September 2014, K12 INC ran an add on a Nickelodeon cartoon show called Kid Toons. The ad was called "Is Your child happy in School." The video featured happy kids sitting in their parents lap and playing on a computer.
http://www.ispot.tv/ad/7DzG/k12-online-schools

The K12 INC ad fails to mention the fact that their program robs money from public schools (it is not free to tax payers). Nor does the ad mention that the drop out rate at K12 INC is 80% (their online program severely harms most children).

There is an even more deceptive K12 INC ad called "An Introduction to Online Schools" that features a young child extolling all of the wonderful things that will happen to children if they sign up for K12 INC – including becoming an astronaut!

http://video.cdn.ispot.tv/media/001/039/713/7o4S_360.mp4

Every K12 INC TV commercial claims that teachers and parents "enthusiastically endorse" this fake online program. They fail to mention that the vast majority of parents and teachers strongly oppose the program due to the extremely high drop out rate. According to former teachers and call in center workers, K12 INC also targets low income students who have almost no chance of success with the K21 INC program. Here is what one former K12 INC teacher from New Orleans wrote: "K12 Inc. targets poor communities and economically struggling regions; they are easily influenced because they are desperately seeking alternatives to devastatingly under-funded schools. These financially strapped schools are being further bled by the exodus of students who are lured by what I now see are empty promises of marketing experts at K12 Inc. It is a vicious cycle in which, as far as I can see, no one but the corporate profiteers are winning," http://blogs.edweek.org/teachers/living-in-dialogue/2014/01/15_months_in_virtual_charter_h.html?cmp=ENL-EU-NEWS2

Online Programs Only Work with an Available Parent and a Motivated Child
Online programs work best when there the child has a parent who can devote the entire day to helping the child and go through every step of the online program with the child as a one on one tutor. This requires a very special parent who has the time to learn about every subject the child needs to learn about. Very few low income or middle class parents have this kind of free time. Online programs also require students who are self directed learners. Even then, extra efforts need to be made to insure that each child has an opportunity to interact with other children to develop their social and emotional regulation skills.

We should offer our students better online educational opportunities

Online education has the potential to help some students in some situations. But online education also requires very careful oversight to insure that our students are being served and that our tax dollars are being well spent. K12 INC is one of the worst corporate vultures in America. Every year, they rob more than $990 million dollars from our public schools in the US and divert it into the pockets of Wall Street hedge fund managers. https://finance.yahoo.com/q/is?s=lrn

As we will review in more detail in the next section, K12 INC has a dismal record where less than one in four students who enter this program graduate from high school. Half of the students who enter this program quit in their first year! In the past ten years, K12 INC has harmed nearly one million children. By robbing $990 million per year from our public schools, K12 INC has directly caused the firing of more than ten thousand teachers in the US.

What is K12 INC?

We will next examine the history of K12 INC and then explain why students fail in K12 INC programs. K12 INC was founded in 2000 and now sucks nearly one billion dollars per year out of the school budgets of America's cash starved public schools. It has been described as a "Wall Street Cash Cow" because of its ability to suck money out of State tax payers in order to increase Wall Street profits.

K12 INC Founder Michael Milken... From Junk Bonds to Junk Schools

One of the largest initial investors in K12 INC was Michael Milken, the 1980's junk bond king who cost millions of Americans billions of dollars and was convicted of securities fraud and tax evasion in 1990.

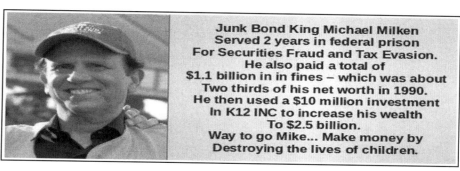

The head of K12 Inc is Ron Packard who makes more than $10 million per year destroying the lives of children. Like nearly all the other Corporate Ed Reformers, Ron has no background or training in Education and has never been a teacher. Ron Packard has a pretty dark background. From 1986 to 1988, Packard worked in mergers and acquisitions for **Goldman Sachs** – the corrupt investment banking and gambling outfit known for bribing Congress into deregulating the banking industry and whose reckless bets crashed the world economy in 2008. Another name for Mergers and Acquisitions is "Junk Bonds" as these are used to finance the mergers and acquisitions – which are often leveraged buyouts. It was likely during this time that Ron met Junk Bond King Michael Milken

In 1989, the same year that Michael Milken was indicted by a federal grand jury, Ron moved to safer job at **McKinsey & Company** – the same company where both Common Core scam artist David Coleman worked and the head of Pearson, Michael Barber worked. Ron Packard worked at McKinsey until 1993, which was the same year that Milken was released from prison. Ron then worked on foreign investments until 1997 when a miracle happened. Despite having no background in Education, Ron joined "Knowledge Universe" owned by the former Junk Bond King Michael Milken.

K12 INC... Rise of the Fake Online School Scam
In 2000, Milken and a couple of other billionaires put up $10 million to start K12 INC with Ron Packard as the CEO. The timing was perfect as this was also the beginning of the high stakes testing, Common Core national standards and charter school scams. K12 INC fit right in because it offered charter schools a fake online curriculum to go with fake online testing. Just sit kids in front of computers all day and there was no more need for a qualified teacher!

In 2001, K12 INC's first contract was with the corrupt State of Pennsylvania. The Pennsylvania Virtual Charter School (PAVCS) was the first school in the country to succumb to the K12 marketing scam. Within months, K12 INC ads were everywhere – encouraging kids to abandon public schools and move to K12 INC.

One blogger Called Mother Crusader Said that "Philadelphia's highways Seem to be littered with K12.COM billboards."

http://mothercrusader.blogspot.com/2013/08/the-false-choice-of-school-choice.html

K12 INC Harms the Youngest Students Just to Make a Buck

PAVCS began with 700 students in grades K-2 in Fall 2001 – just before the 911 disaster. The reason they limited the school to just Kindergarten through Second Grade was to escape the No Child Left Behind testing requirement which began with the 3rd Grade. Sadly, the group of students most harmed by sitting in front of a computer screen all day is the youngest children. For example a 2002 report by the National Education Association concluded: "Our current understandings of the characteristics and needs of learners in earlier grades ... would suggest we exercise great caution in the use of the online environment to deliver instruction to students prior to middle school."
http://www.edweek.org/media/ew/tc/archives/TC02full.pdf

Despite this fact, the first programs K12 Inc set up were for grades K through 2. The reason? No Child Left Behind (NCLB) required testing and reporting from grades 3 and up. So working with the youngest kids meant no need to report for the first couple of years. In other words, K12 Ind wanted to fly under the radar screen – even if it meant focusing on kids for whom online education was least appropriate.

Child Development Experts Warn that very young Children Should NOT Spend extended periods Of Time Sitting In Front of A Computer Screen... Yet this is the very group K12 INC has Targeted in their ads And Programs.

K12 INC Creates Its Own Online Preschool Market

We know this is going to sound like some sort of sick, twisted joke. But in July, 2013, K12 INC announced that it was entering what K12 INC calls the Online Preschool Market! According to K12 INC the goal of their latest online ed scam is to get toddlers from Cradle to Kindergarten Ready (where they can then be made college and career ready). One ed reform scammer called it "from cradle to grave" data tracking (a dream come true for the NSA).
http://www.prweb.com/releases/Kindergarten/Embark/prweb10959407.htm

The founder of K12 INC, the Junk Bond King Michael Milken, already owns a national preschool program called Kinder Care. Looks like these kids are going to have to jump over a higher bar to get Kindergarten Ready. As for marketing, look for K12 INC to put more ads on the Cartoon Channel. Nothing like using tax payer dollars for K12 INC propaganda and promotion.

According to national education researcher, Diane Ravitch, K12 INC keeps "coming up with new ideas to put children in front of computers and absorb public dollars."
http://dianeravitch.net/2014/10/15/bad-news-k12-inc-enters-the-preschool-market/

A wise commenter on Diane's blog wrote the following: "Learning is social...What happened to the teaching that captivates their interest; learning without fear and intimidation; and giving kids the sense of freedom to experiment and explore? The computer can not begin to meet the needs of preschoolers and kindergarteners. Reading stories written by fabulous children's authors, singing... All the basic needs for preschool and kindergarten are met in an interesting and captivating way with literature, music, poems and finger plays: physical, cognitive, social, and emotional...There are countless rich stories, poems and songs to develop cognitive skills... Leave it to the fairy tales... to teach social skills- living and working together, dramatizing, interacting with building and playing. Dramatizing above all provide for their emotional needs- getting positive feed back from classmates and teachers giving them the sense of accomplishment."

What is Next?
Now that we know what kind of monster K12 INC is marketing to our children, in the next section, we will review how K12 INC went from junk bonds to junk schools and then back to junk bonds. It is a story you will not want to miss.

4.2 K12 INC From Junk Bonds to Junk Schools

A History of Fraud and Corruption
In our last section, we noted that K12 INC started its first online school in Pennsylvania in September 2001 – just in time for the 911 disaster. Here we will calculate the cost to tax payers of this and other K12 INC fake online ed scams. The total is now in the billions of dollars and rising every year.

Calculating the Total Harm to Tax Payers
Currently, PAVCS is one of the largest online schools in the country and has about 10,000 students in Grades K through 12. It spends more than one million dollars per year just on advertising! In 2005, K12 INC set up another cyber school in Pennsylvania called Agora. It also has about 10,000 students. Pennsylvania tax payers give these schools about $8,000 per student. The total sucked out of Pennsylvania tax payers is therefore about **$160 million per year – or about 20% of K12 INC's annual revenue.** For this massive amount of money, PAVCS and Agora have among the lowest test scores and highest drop out rates of any school in the nation. Combine this with $140 million sucked out of Pennsylvania by gold digger poorly performing charter schools and the total loss to Pennsylvania tax payers is **more than $300 million per year.**
http://thenotebook.org/blog/125416/pa-auditor-general-blasts-cyber-charter-funding-again/

"There is over $300 million in public taxpayer dollars being lost each and every year due to the flawed funding formula for charter and cyber charter schools"

Jack Wagner, Pennsylvania State Auditor 2012

One former teacher from Pennsylvania's Agora Cyber Charter School, which is run by K12 Inc., said she was assigned 300 students but had no idea how many attended class. Here is a quote from this teacher: "I taught English at Agora from 2010-12. It was a horrible experience. When I started, I was assigned 300 students, which was very, very overwhelming. For each class, I'd have maybe seven out of 30 students attend – and even among those seven, just because their name was there showing them present doesn't mean they were at their computers. A huge portion of my students never showed up or did anything. I have no clue what happened to them, though I have no doubt Agora was charging the state for them. When it came time to give grades, I was told, whatever I had to do, I had to pass every student. I would not say there was much learning going on."

One does not have to look far to figure out why the Pennsylvania State legislature allows K12 INC and other charter scam artists to steal $300 million per year from the State taxpayers. Just since 2007, K12 Inc. has spent $681,000 on lobbying, according to the New York Times. It has 11 registered lobbyists, according to the National Institute on Money in State Politics. K12 Inc. has also used a fake grassroots group called "Pennsylvania Families for Public Cyber Schools" to lobby for it. This fake K12 Inc. funded group spent $250,000 on lobbying in the last five years, with all of the money coming from K12 INC according to the New York Times. The head of K12 INC, Ron Packard, has called lobbying (also known as bribery) a "core competency" at K12 INC. http://www.nytimes.com/2011/12/13/education/online-schools-score-better-on-wall-street-than-in-classrooms.html?_r=0

In 2002, K12 INC added the **Ohio Virtual Academy (OVA)**. OVA currently has about 13,000 students sucking **about $100 million per year** out of Ohio tax payers. It also has extremely low test scores and an extremely high student drop out rate. In 2012, K12's OVA had a 30 percent on-time graduation rate, compared with a state average of 78 percent. K12's Pennsylvania online charter schools did even worse. Their on-time graduation rate was only 12 percent compared with 72 percent statewide in Pennsylvania. One does not have to look long to figure out why the Ohio State legislature allows K12 INC to steal $100 million per year from Ohio tax payers. The New York Times 2012 article also reports that K12 Inc. is connected to a fake grassroots group called "My School, My Choice." This fake group organized protests in Ohio against reforming the state formula for financing charter and online schools. The protesters turned out to be **paid temp agency workers**. Tim Dirrim, the founder of "My School, My Choice," is the board president of the K12 Inc. managed Ohio Virtual Academy!

A sharp reporter interviewed a couple of the protesters – who openly admitted that they were temp workers who had been paid to protest in favor of online charter schools!

Also in 2002, K12 INC added the **California Virtual Academy (CAVA).**

CAVA currently has online programs in 10 different locations in California with a total of about 8,000 students for a total **cost to California tax payers of about $70 million.** Almost half of these students are in the Los Angeles School District – meaning that the loss to the Los Angeles School district is about $40 million per year. At this point, we should explain that in nearly every State, K12 INC offers school districts who "sponsor" them a bribe or kickback of about 5% of whatever K12 INC takes in. So it is likely that the LA school district got about about a $2 million kickback. But K12 INC likely got the other $38 million. It is hard to tell precisely with K12 INC because they have hidden contracts which very from State to State and even from School District to School District.

Also in 2002, K12 INC added the **Wisconsin Virtual Academy (WIVA).** K12 INC made a deal with the Northern Ozaukee School Board and started with 455 students. The school district got four percent of whatever public funding K12 took in. However, because they were advertising in other school districts and robbing kids from other school districts, there was a lot of conflict and eventually in 2008, the whole program temporarily shut down. In 2009, the program was moved to a new school district, the McFarland School District. It currently has about 1,000 students **costing Wisconsin State tax payers about $8 million per year.**

In 2003, K12 INC added **Colorado Virtual Academy (COVA),** which currently has more than 5,000 students and **costs Colorado tax payers about $40 million per year.** A 2011 study found that over half of all K12 INC students in Colorado fail to make it through even a single year before dropping out of the program. The graduation rate is only 25%!   http://gazette.com/article/126009

A former teacher from the Colorado Virtual Academy said, "Three-quarters of my credit recovery kids never logged in, never completed any work, never answered their emails or phone calls, yet they remained on my class rosters. I began wondering about the state-mandated hours for students at the high school level. No one is monitoring this as far as I can see."

We have interviewed many former K12 INC teachers. They all say one of the biggest problems is that Kids are never logged into their computers. Teachers have no way to monitor the children And make sure they are getting their work done.

According to the New York Times, a Colorado state audit found that the Colorado Virtual Academy received money for 120 students whose enrollment could not be verified. The state ordered the online school to reimburse $800,000 dollars.

Also in 2003, K12 INC added the **Arizona Virtual Academy (AZVA)** which currently has about 4,000 students **costing Arizona tax payers about $32 million per year**. This scam operation was caught a couple of years ago outsourcing student essays and other private data to a sweat shop in India.

In 2004, K12 INC added the **Idaho Virtual Academy (IDVA),** which has about 3,000 students and **costs Idaho tax payers about $2 million per year.** Like all of the other K12 INC schools it has extremely low test scores, extremely high turnover of teachers, grossly inflated class sizes and a very high dropout rate. Here is what one former parent wrote: "If I could rate this school any lower I would. We have had nothing but problems with them.

Our children cant access their site most days and when they do get on it runs sooooooo slow...our children are falling behind because half the time they cannot access their site. You can complain till your blue in the face but they don't care. This is a terrible home school company. We're having more problems than I can list. Please do your research and see for yourself. Not worth it...NOT WORTH IT"

Also in 2004, K12 INC and a **corporate profit driven front group called ALEC** proposed "model legislation" for States to use to make it easier for K12 INC to come in and rob from the tax payers. K12 INC is one of ALEC's primary sponsors. This model law was later passed in States all across the US. For example, soon after passage of ALEC law in Tennessee in 2011 - making private virtual school operators eligible to receive public funds - K12 Inc. received a contract allowing it to provide virtual education to any Tennessee student. Tennessee lawmakers also closed down Tennessee's former State-run successful online education program so that K12 INC would not have to compete with the much better state program.

Just 2 years later, in 2013, <u>Tennessee</u>, education commissioner Kevin Huffman threatened to close the K12 INC school. Kevin said that Tennessee Virtual Academy has test results "in the bottom of the bottom tier" and is an "abject failure." Also in 2013, a K12 INC school in Tennessee sent an email to a teacher telling her to simple delete bad grades in order to increase the pass rate of her students. Here is a quote from the article: "NASHVILLE, Tenn. Are leaders of a for-profit public school trying to hide the fact their students are failing? That's the question that some are asking tonight as a result of an email uncovered by News Channel 5 Investigates. At the center of the controversy is the Tennessee Virtual Academy -- a for-profit, online public school that Republican lawmakers touted as a way to improve education in Tennessee. Two years ago, state lawmakers voted to let K12 Inc. open the school, using millions of taxpayer dollars.

But, now, those lawmakers are concerned about standardized test results that put it among the worst schools in the state. In fact, the email suggests that even school leaders are becoming increasingly concerned by how their students' grades may look to parents and the public...

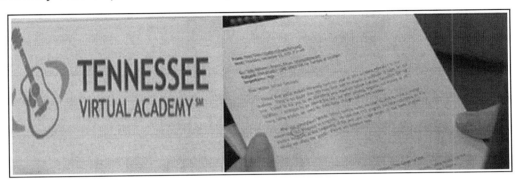

The email -- labeled "important -- was written in December by the Tennessee Virtual Academy's vice principal to middle school teachers. "After ... looking at so many failing grades, we need to make some changes before the holidays," the email begins. Among the changes: Each teacher "needs to **take out the October and September progress [reports]**; delete it so that all that is showing is November progress." http://video.newschannel5.com/story/21129693/email-directs-teachers-to-delete-bad-grades

In 2006, the head of Chicago Schools, Arne Duncan brought K12 INC to the Chicago Public Schools with a "no-bid" contract. The fake charter school is called **Chicago Virtual Charter School (CVCS)**. The school has about 1000 students.

Also in 2006, K12 INC started the Washington Virtual Academy (WAVA) by arranging a bribery and kickback "sponsorship" with the Steilacoom School District in Washington State. In May 2005, the Washington State legislature passed Senate Bill 5828 to allow K12 INC into Washington State. This very bad bill amazingly had the support of the Washington Education Association – the teachers union in Washington State – even though it led to the firing of more than one thousand public school teachers in Washington State as any student in any other school district could sign up for this corrupt program and their home school district would lose $8,000 per student nearly all of which would be passed through the Steilacoom School District to K21 INC! Multiply $8,000 times 8,000 students and the loss to Washington State tax payers is $64 million – or enough to higher 640 normal public school teachers! Within a couple of years, Washington State had several online programs besides the WAVA program. These including Insight Schools (with a bribe and kickback scheme "sponsored by the "Quillayute School district) and Aventa Learning (with a bribe and kickback scheme sponsored by the East Valley School District). However since K12 INC owned all of these programs, there was only the appearance of choice. In reality, nearly all of the money for online education in Washington State goes to K12 INC. In the next section, we will review the terrible results of these programs.

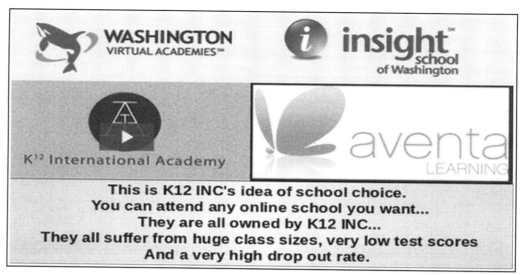

In 2007, K12 INC started the **Georgia Virtual Academy (later called the Georgia Cyber Academy)** which currently has 12,000 students costs the taxpayers of the State of Georgia about $10 million per year. In 2012, after complaints from several parents, the Georgia State Board of Education condemned the Georgia Cyber Academy for enrolling more than one thousand special needs students without the capacity to assess or teach special needs students.
http://www.ajc.com/news/news/local-education/georgia-cyber-academy-assailed-for-missing-special/nS5sH/

2007 K12 INC Goes Public and Makes a Killing
In 2007, K12 INC promotion plan (also known as a bribery and kickback scheme) was working brilliantly. So Ron Packard and Michael Milken decided to take their ponzi scheme public so they could start cashing in their chips before the parents got wise to the scheme and started jumping ship. According to K12's 2007 stock offering prospectus, K12 INC got nearly half of their total revenues from just four States – Pennsylvania, Ohio, Arizona and Colorado. (This is still pretty much the case today as we will show in a few minutes.). 2007 was the height of a stock market bubble fueled by a rapid rise in housing prices. Who could have known that in just a few months, the Housing Ponzi Scheme was going to come crashing down? For now, it was time for Ron and Mike to cash in on the Online Education Ponzi Scheme. To arrange this stock Public Offering (also known as a Public Fleecing), they chose a highly respected investment firm called Bear Sterns – which strangely blew up in 2008 at the hands of none other than Goldman Sachs. Perhaps it was all just an unlucky coincidence.

For awhile, everything looked great. More States were signed up every year thanks to the ALEC Online Charter School Law. Enrollment increased every year.

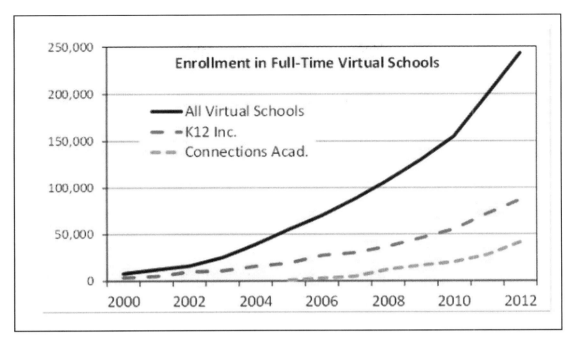

http://nepc.colorado.edu/files/virtual-2014-all-final.pdf

Revenue also increased every year.

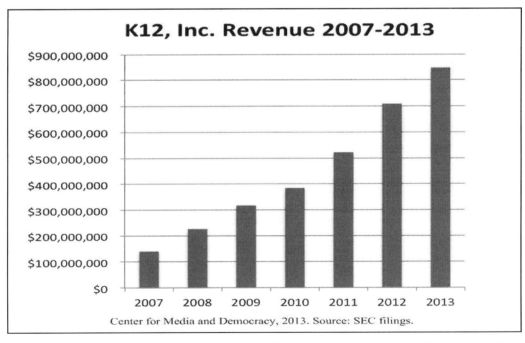

The stock opened at about $25 a share. The stock price took a hit during the Stock Market crash of 2008 reaching a low of about $12 a share. But then thanks to the Federal Reserve Free Money program, also called Quantitative Easing, the stock more than tripled to almost $40 a share on April 24, 2011.

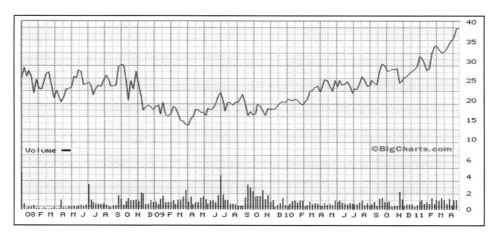

http://www.marketwatch.com/investing/stock/lrn/charts

But then reality started to set in as study after study from State after State consistently showed that the students were not learning from the K12 INC magic learning program – which also meant that the drop out rate was very high. In addition, there was a lawsuit from investors in 2012 claiming they were given false information in 2010 and 2011 by K12 INC CEO Ron Packard.

The Truth About K12 INC "Drop Out Rates" Finally Comes Out

During the summer of 2011, K12 INC CEO Ron Packard made extremely bullish statements about future student enrollment and revenue growth. This caused K12 INC stock to rise sharply. Then in October and early November 2011, Ron Packard sold millions of dollars in stock options. Finally, on **November 16 2011,** Packard admitted for the first time that nearly half of all K12 INC students drop out during their first year (only to be replaced by even more students who also drop out) and therefore the promised profits were not likely to happen.

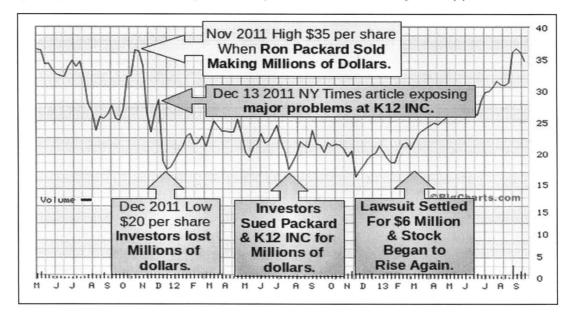

Within days K12 INC stock plunged. Then, on **December 13, 2011** a New York Times article entitled "Profits and Questions at Online Charter Schools" revealed, among other things, that K12's schools had extremely high drop out rates – even higher than what Packard had told investors on November 16 2011. K12's stock price plummeted 23.6% the very next day reaching a low of $20 per share on December 15 2011. This led to an Investors lawsuit in 2012.

Using Lies to Fool Parents and Children into Enrolling at K12 INC
In sworn declarations with the 2012 lawsuit, former sales employees at K12's call centers described high pressure to make huge enrollment quotas in order to get a commission. Sales employees were provided with a "script" of what to say to prospective students and parents, including purported "statistics" showing that K12 students were years more advanced than brick-and-mortar school students.

Here are a summaries of former K12 INC Call Center Workers: CW2 described a toxic work environment where sales staff were pressured to meet unrealistic quotas, frequently being forced to make as many as 200 outgoing calls daily to keep up. Sales staff were never given any actual data of student performance, but were instead fed statistics from K12's website, and were told to tell parents that **students who did the K12 program for 1-2 years performed better than their peers at brick and mortar schools.**

CW4 stated that there was constant pressure to generate sales, describing the Company's sales philosophy as **"enroll, enroll, enroll."** CW4 stated that enrollment consultants were instructed to refer to the performance of K12 students as "comparable [to] or even better" than the performance of students at traditional schools, and to state that students at K12 schools were "on a better tier" than those at traditional schools. Source: K12 INC lawsuit 6/22/12

In fact, as we will show in the next section, half of all K12 INC students drop out during their first year and only one out of four every graduates from high school. The 2012 lawsuit was finally settled in early 2013 for $6 million.

During the summer of 2013, Ron Packard assured everyone that the trouble from 2011 was over and all of the K12 INC problems had been solved. Then a miracle happened. K12 INC stock started to rise again. It was almost as if some billionaire was pushing the stock price up. By early September 2013, the stock price was back up to $36 per share. It was magic! Sadly, the magic did not last long. As the next chart shows, within days of reaching its high of $36 a share in early September 2013, the stock began to plunge. For the rest of 2013 and all of 2014, it continued to plunge. It was as if someone had pulled the rug out from under K12 INC's investors. As we will show next, this is exactly what happened.

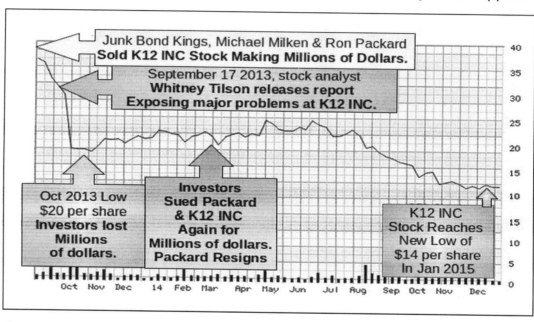

Junk Bond King Michael Milken Jumps Ship - Leaving the Public Holding the Bag

Between September 1, 2013 and October 1, 2013, the stock price of K12 INC fell from $36 a share to $20 a share. There were two reasons for this sudden plunge. The first was that the Junk Bond King had decided to walk away from his Ed Reform Toy. He had been quietly selling his K12 INC stock until by September 2013, he had no stock left in K12 INC. Ron Packard had also been selling his stock. Both Ron Packard and Michael Milken made millions of dollars pumping the stock up and then dumping it. This is actually what market traders call this kind of rigging – pumping and dumping. The rest of us in the general public call this a Ponzi Scheme – and we get left with massive losses. K12 INC stock remained at about $20 per share for nearly a year – even though Ron Packard had announced he was leaving K12 INC in January 2014.

Then in August 2014, the next batch of K12 INC test scores were released by States around the nation. The test scores were horrible. The stock has been in a nose dive ever since. It is currently at a record low of $14 a share. Our advice is to sell now – because eventually this stock is going to be worthless – just like every other Ponzi Scheme.

The Big Short
The other thing that happened in September 2013 was a report released by a major stock analyst and hedge fund manager named **Whitney Tilson** who somehow figured out that Michael Milken and Ron Packard had been selling all of their shares. Whitney did some research and found out that K12 INC was not all it had been cracked up to be. He reviewed the lawsuits and complaints from former teachers, students, parents and looked at the test scores and drop out rates. He then realized why Michael Milken and Ron Packard were jumping ship. It was because the K12 INC ship was sinking.

At the beginning of September, Whitney told his investors about the sinking ship and encouraged them to "short" the stock. "Shorting" is a Wall Street gamble where you bet the stock is going to fall and if it does, then you make a huge amount of money. On **September 17, 2013**, Whitney also went public with a 125-page slide show vividly describing why the K12 INC ship was going to sink. In particular, he spilled the beans about Michael Milken's company (called Knowledge Universe) recently distributed all of their remaining shares in K12 INC and he spilled the beans about Ron Packard selling a huge number of shares. Whitney's slide show made it clear that K12 INC was nothing more than a house of cards that would eventually fall over.
http://www.tilsonfunds.com/K12-Tilson-9-17-13.pdf

Whitney said in an interview, **"When you introduce unlimited government money and virtually no government regulation, the industry will run amok."**

An Analysis of K12 (LRN) and Why It Is My Largest Short Position

Whitney Tilson
Value Investing Congress
September 17, 2013

Whitney noted that K12 Inc. had hired 153 lobbyists in 28 states from 2003 to 2012. But not even 153 lobbyists can save a company from a bad business model. Any school that has a drop out rate of more than 50% per year is eventually going to fail. Parents will eventually find out. And they will no longer send their kids to a program where most were certain to fail.

A Double Whammy... Double Talk from Double Crossers
As if the harsh critique from Whitney Tilson was not bad enough, in a statement on October 8, 2013, K12 INC admitted for the first time that its enrollment and profits would not be as high as it had earlier claimed. In Form 8-K, they **lowered their revenue forecast by about $80 million compared to a forecast they have supported just a few weeks earlier!**
http://investors.k12.com/phoenix.zhtml?c=214389&p=irol-newsArticle&ID=1862757&highlight=#.VKe7A3Wx3UY

Two days later on October 10, 2014, K12 INC released a second written statement admitting that K12 INC would have a projected **operating loss of about $9 million** in the first quarter of fiscal 2014.
http://investors.k12.com/phoenix.zhtml?c=214389&p=irol-newsArticle&ID=1863577&highlight=#.VKe84XWx3UY

Also disclosed in this second statement was the fact that K12 INC was taking a capital expense of $80 million on its software development. In other words, it was writing it off over time. This is not generally how software is accounted for. It is usually accounted as an expense as the software is written. Only things like buildings are written off over time. So **had K12 INC followed normal accounting practices, it would have actually lost $89 million** in the first quarter of fiscal 2014. This was not what investors wanted to here. No wonder Ron Packard and Michael Milken had jumped ship in August 2013. They apparently had some inside information. After the October 8 announcement, K12 INC stock shares fell 38% in a single day.

Meanwhile, since K12 INC's 2007 initial public offering, Packard had made $21 million from share sales and exercising options according to Insider Score in Princeton, New Jersey. In the three months before the share drop in October 2013, Packard made about $3 million in profit from option-related sales according to Insider Score. Milken made even more of a killing. In September 2013, a month before K12's disappointing results were announced, **Milken's companies distributed about $270 million in shares** according to a securities filing.
http://www.bloomberg.com/news/2014-11-14/k12-backed-by-milken-suffers-low-scores-as-states-resist.html

Misleading Claims, Bad News and Two Lawsuits Make for Irate Investors
The shocking revelations in October 2013 combined with the shocking information from Whitney Tilson on September 17 2013 led to the second investor lawsuit in January 2014 – this time by another group of stockholders (the Oklahoma Firefighters Pension and Retirement System – who had lost millions of dollars as a result of Ron Packard's deception). This second lawsuit, like the first one, cited overly optimistic statements made throughout the Spring and Summer of 2013 by company officials, including misleading statements Ron Packard and Nate Davis, K12's current CEO, about the company's ability to grow.

Only later on October 8 2013 - after Milken and Packard had sold their stock – did Packard reveal that K12 INC had missed key enrollment and revenue targets.

The April 2014 lawsuit, like the 2012 lawsuit, alleged that former K12 CEO Ron Packard "reaped the rewards" of the bullish company projections by selling $6.4 million dollars worth of stock in the months before an October announcement of disappointing news sent its stock price plummeting. He sold his stock at a rate that was 8 times higher than his prior rate of stock sales. Below is a table from Page 9 of the January 2014 Complaint:

DEFENDANT PACKARD'S CLASS PERIOD STOCK SALES

Sale Date	Number of Shares	Price	Transaction Value
07/15/2013	18,841	$29.94	$564,099.54
07/16/2013	6,159	$29.97	$184,585.23
07/17/2013	8,000	$29.96	$239,680.00
07/24/2013	8,000	$30.43	$243,440.00
07/31/2013	8,000	$30.84	$246,720.00
08/01/2013	2,000	$32.01	$64,020.00
08/07/2013	8,000	$31.09	$248,720.00
08/14/2013	8,000	$31.65	$253,200.00
08/21/2013	8,000	$30.71	$245,680.00
08/28/2013	10,000	$31.74	$317,400.00
08/29/2013	10,000	$35.01	$350,100.00
08/29/2013	7,000	$35.15	$246,050.00
09/04/2013	27,000	$36.74	$991,980.00
09/11/2013	17,000	$37.43	$636,310.00
09/11/2013	10,000	$37.41	$374,100.00
09/18/2013	13,000	$34.48	$448,240.00
09/18/2013	5,000	$34.68	$173,400.00
09/25/2013	10,000	$31.74	$317,400.00
10/02/2013	8,000	$31.1	$248,800.00
TOTAL	**141,000**	–	**$6,393,924.77**

DEFENDANT PACKARD'S PRE-CLASS PERIOD STOCK SALES
(August 2012-March 2013)

Sale Date	Number of Shares	Price	Transaction Value
11/12/2012	40,000	$19.71	$788,400

Weapons of Mass Deception

2014 Oklahoma Firefighters Pension & Retirement System versus K12

The lawsuit alleges that Ron Packard deliberately inflated the stock price of K12 INC with knowingly false and misleading statements in order to increase his profits from sales of his stock. Many examples of these false and misleading statements were given. After K12 INC finally revealed the truth, K12 stock fell by more than 38%, falling from a closing price of $28.59 on October 8, 2013 to a closing price of $17.60 on October 9, 2013.

http://www.blbglaw.com/news/press_releases/00012/_res/id=sa_File1/K12%20Complaint.pdf

The Seven Hundred Million Dollar Heist

We mentioned earlier that Milken's companies distributed $270 million in K12 INC stock before the stock crashed. However, for every winner on Wall Street, there has to be a loser. In this case, the losers were retired people who belonged to pension funds which invested in K12 INC stock. We will next estimate how much these pension funds lost as a result of the stock crashing from $36 per share in early September 2013 to $16 per share on October 9 2013. As of January 2 2015, the stock is at $11.70 per share and falling.

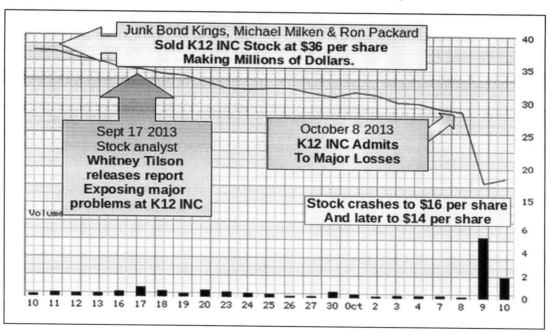

How many shares of K12 INC are there?

The loss from September to October 2013 was about $20 per share. The current market capitalization is $450 million at $11.70 per share. This implies that there currently are about 39 million shares of K12 INC stock. However in 2013, there were only 36 million shares of K12 INC stock.
http://www.marketwatch.com/investing/stock/lrn/financials

36 million share times $36 per share means that the market capitalization of value of all stocks in September 2013 was $1,296 million. The loss to all investors stuck with K12 INC stock in October 2013 was $20 per share times 36 million shares equals **$720 million**. Therefore while Michael Milken made $270 million and Ron Packard made $6.4 million and folks who are clients of Whitney Tilson made hundreds of millions, retired pensioners lost $720 million. Think of this as a transfer of wealth of $720 million from senior citizens living on a fixed income to billionaires like Michael Milken.

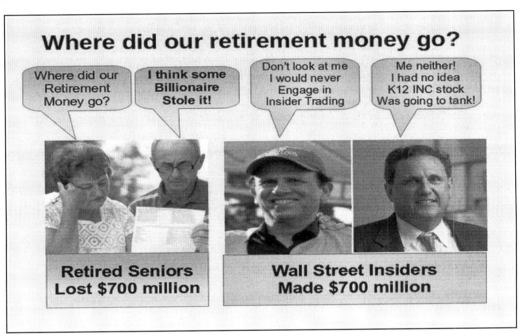

There are at least ten reasons to believe that the K12 INC stock crash and $700 million wealth transfer was a pump and dump operation
First, on August 29, 2013, just 40 days before the October 8 2012 K12 INC announcement that they would lose about $80 million, their chief financial officer (Rhyu) and their chief executive officer reassured investors that **"we are comfortable with the fiscal 2014 estimates posted to First Call through yesterday as follows: revenue of $986.8 million."** Then on October 8 2013, they announced that revenue would only be about $900 million. This was an $80 million change in just 40 days. This was equal to an entire month of revenue.

http://www.blbglaw.com/news/press_releases/00012/_res/id=sa_File1/K12%20Complaint.pdf

Second, in the four months preceding the stock price crash, the person who knew the K12 INC stock value best, Chief Executive Officer, Ron Packard, started selling his stock stock at a rate that was 8 times faster than he had previously sold his stock.

Third, in the two months preceding the stock price crash, the person who was the founder of the company, Michael Milken, cashed in all of his chips.

Fourth, on September 17 2013, stock analyst Whitney Tilson, provided detailed information on the major problems at K12 INC. Even if K12 INC leaders were not aware that they had problems on August 29 2013 when they reassured investors that they were heading for record earnings, they certainly must have known about Whitney Tilson's Presentation which went into devastating detail about the problems at K12 INC.

Fifth, it was obvious from Whitney Tilson's presentation that he spent several months analyzing K12 INC and interviewing former employees of K12 INC. This means that Whitney suspected months before the stock actually crashed that it was going to crash. It was also clear that he told his clients that K12 INC stock was going to crash at least a full week before he told the general public. He admitted that his clients made millions of dollars on his advice by shorting the stock. It is not reasonable to conclude that Whitney knew more about K12 INC than their chief executive officer Ron Packard.

Sixth, Ron Packard had also withheld other key information from investors in the months before the stock price crash. For example, there had been a 9% decline in enrollment in the spring of 2013. This was not disclosed to investors until October 10 2013 – after the stock had already crashed.

Seventh, K12 INC leaders had used a highly questionable accounting trick to hide expenses and hide losses by "capitalizing" $80 million in software development expenses over time rather than declaring them as current expenses. Ron Packard knew they were doing this. But investors did not know until October 8 2013.

Eighth, according to the complaint filed by the Pensioners, on March 11 013, Ron Packard told investors: **"Our customer satisfaction is extremely high. It has been since the very beginning."** We will provide substantial and irrefutable evidence in the next section that this statement was false and misleading and that Ron Packard knew it was false and misleading – and has known for years that it was false and misleading. The truth is that nearly 90% of all customer's – including parents and students – have a very low opinion of K12 INC – which is why K12 INC has to spend $30 million per year every year to recruit a new batch of suckers.

> Out of 190,000 parents involved in the K12 program, 95% – or 180,000 parents - failed to turn in their K12 Satisfaction Survey form!
> Over 50% of these parents pulled their child out of the K12 program in less than one year. Despite these facts, K12 has the audacity to tell us that 88% of all parents were "happy" with the K12 program and would recommend it to a friend!!!

Ninth, this was not the first pump and dump operation pulled off by Ron Packard and Michael Milken. Both have a long history of pump and dump operations going all the way back to the 1980s – including a K12 INC pump and dump that they pulled off in 2011 which led to the 2012 investor lawsuit that was also about hiding important information from investors. The 2013 pump and dump was a mirror image of the 2011 pump and dump.

Tenth, as we will show in greater detail in the next section, the entire K12 INC operation is nothing but one huge fraudulent enterprise. There are literally hundreds of examples of K12 INC leaders lying to students, parents, teachers, legislators and investors with year after year of false and misleading statements going all the way back to the hatching of the K12 INC scam in 1999.

November 5 2014 Judge Anthony Trenga Grants K12 INC Motion to Dismiss

Despite the mountains of evidence that Ron Packard and K12 INC had misled and defrauded investors, on November 5 2014 Judge Anthony Trenga granted K12 INCs motion to dismiss the complaint. Here is a link to his ruling.
https://cases.justia.com/federal/district-courts/virginia/vaedce/1:2014cv00108/302903/49/0.pdf?ts=1415302891

The judge stated: "Plaintiff is required to prove:

(1) a material misrepresentation or omission by the defendant;

(2) scienter (the defendant knew the misrepresentation was false or misleading);

(3) a connection between the misrepresentation and the purchase of a stock;

(4) reliance (by harmed investors) upon the misrepresentation or omission;

(5) economic loss; and

(6) loss causation (that the loss was caused by the misrepresentation)."

The judge then decided that it was theoretically possible that Ron Packard had no idea that K12 INC was in trouble or that the stock would crash. To make it clear, I agree that defendants should be given the "benefit of the doubt" and that the burden of proof is on the person making the allegation. However, the evidence summarized above not only meets the civil standard which is more likely than not – it also meets the criminal standard of beyond a reasonable doubt. It is simply not credible to conclude that Ron Packard had no idea that K12 INC was in trouble and he just happened to sell 43% of his stock in the 3 months before it actually crashed.

If Whitney Tilson knew it was going to crash in the summer of 2013, and many of his investors knew, then so did Ron Packard. It is also beyond belief that the head financial officer of K12 INC did not know that enrollments had been down by 9% just months earlier or that revenue would be down by 9% ($80 million) just 30 days later. This was not just a coincidence. It was a predictable event.

Three Remedies... It is up to all of us to seek and demand justice
The first remedy would be for a new group of harmed K12 INC stockholders to use the evidence I provide in the next section to bring a new class action lawsuit against Ron Packard and K12 INC. The original January 2014 complaint was not well researched and not well presented to the court. Given that the total lost by investors was more than $700 million, one would assume that someone would be interested in getting their money back.

The second remedy is to use the Court of Public Opinion. If the court system will not hold Ron Packard, Michael Milken and K12 INC accountable for defrauding senior citizens of more than $700 million, then it is up to the rest of us to hold them accountable by voting with our feet and with our voices and with our cash. **Do not send your kids or grand kids to any program run by K12 INC!**

The third remedy is to get informed about K12 INC and then share this information with others. Take the time to read the next section. Share the link to our book and our website with other parents, teachers, seniors, legislators and concerned citizens. Together we can hold K12 INC accountable for the educational crimes they have committed against our children and the financial crimes they have committed against our senior citizens.

A Warning... The Goal of K12 INC is to Harm Even More Millions of Children
According to the 2014 Investors Complaint, in early 2013, Ron Packard told investors that K12 INC was planning a massive expansion. Here is a quote from Ron Packard: "if you look at the size of U.S. public education market, its $650 billion or it's about 58 million kids. We have 130,000 kids today. So we can grow at a high rate for a long time. And even if you **double every three years**, which is about 24% growth rate, it's a long time before you can get to the 2 million home school kids that are out there...The last count,(home school) is about 11% of the students who come into our program. The other 89% are coming from that brick-and-mortar component... So believe that high growth rates can be sustained at K12 for a long time."

K12 INC clearly has a goal of using false and misleading advertising to expand their "market" in coming years – as if they have not already harmed enough children. With a planned growth rate of doubling every three years, they apparently want to harm millions of children every year. Below is a graph showing the numbers of children currently being harmed by K12 INC.

18 States with more than 5,000 students attending online charter schools 2012 – 2013 School Year

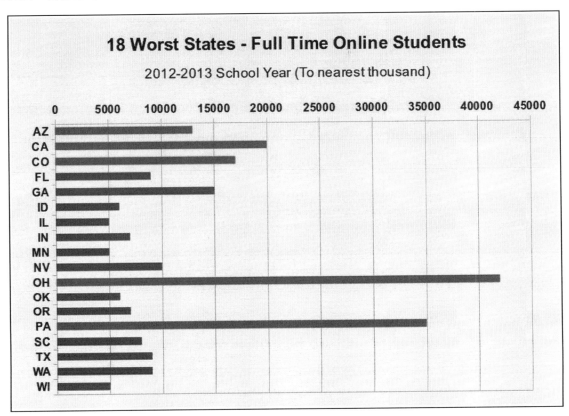

The 5 original K12 INC States, Arizona (2003), California (2003), Colorado (2004), Ohio (2002) and Pennsylvania (2002) are shown in red above. Note that 5 of the 6 worst States for subjecting children to online schools are the original K12 INC States. All five States were subjected to a massive K12 INC propaganda campaign that misled tens of thousands of parents and students into believing that a fake online school was better than a real public school.
http://nepc.colorado.edu/files/virtual-2014-appendix_b-numbers-final_0.pdf

My mom always said "Fool me once, shame on you, Fool me twice, shame on me." K12 INC has been fooling too many parents for far too long. For the sake of our children, we need to stop this corrupt monster before it grows into a cancer that destroys our schools, our kids and our democracy.

What is Next?
In the next section, we will review the bad news between 2011 and 2013 that convinced Michael Milken and Ron Packard that it was time to abandon the K12 INC ship. Given that the future of more than 100,000 children are at risk, this is a topic that every parent should know more about.

4.3 K12 INC Distortions, Deceptions and Outright Lies

In this section, we will present hard evidence of the horrific harm K12 INC has inflicted on the children in its programs here in Washington State as well as evidence that K12 INC leaders know that the marketing information they are giving to students, parents and investors is false.

Why are we using Data from Washington State in this Section?
The reason we are using the state of Washington for our example is first because we have better access to data about students in the State of Washington than we have in other states. Also, there has already been a great deal written and published online about the harm inflicted by K12 INC on children in other States – including the states of Pennsylvania, Florida, Colorado and Ohio (just do a Google Search). As you will see, the story in Washington State is remarkably similar to the story of harm in these other states. This is because all children and all parents in all states will have about the rate of failure if they try to replace a real public school and public school teacher with the fake K12 INC program. The one difference we noted here in Washington State was that K12 INC appears to be targeting wealthy white children rather than poor minority children. The result is still the same – a huge percentage of children fail in this program regardless of their family income level.

Washington Virtual Academy (WAVA)
The Washington Virtual Academy is an online education program being run through the Omak and Monroe School Districts. It is the second largest of about a dozen online schools being run here in Washington State. Each has a different name and is run through a different school district. But in the end, they are all the same online program and they are all actually run by a national for-profit corporation called K12 INC.

What can we learn from K12 INC problems in other States?
Lawsuits and court declarations from more than 20 former K12 teachers and other former K12 employees accuse K12 Inc of using uncertified teachers and having teacher case loads of 300 to 400 students per teacher. They also accuse K12 of lying to parents about the record of K12 in order to deceive parents into signing their children up for the K12 program.

K12 spends $30 million per year (all from the tax payers) to advertise to children on the Disney channel. K12 INC also spends millions more dollars bribing our elected representatives into passing laws making it easy for K12 INC to rob public schools and increase their corporate profits.

> Last year, K12 Inc diverted more than $700 million away from our public schools and into the pockets of Wall Street Hedge Fund Managers. This huge loss of funds led to the firing - either directly or indirectly - of more than 10,000 public school teachers.

Huge Turnover in Students every year

K12 INC gets $6,000 to $9,000 in State tax payer dollars for every student they convince to enter their program. Nationally, over 120,000 students out of our nation's 50 million school children sign up for the K12 program each September. Of these 120,000 children, about 70,000 children – or well over half of these children - drop out during their first year.

Ironically, because K12 Inc continues to recruit more parents and children throughout the school year, the 70,000 children who drop out are replaced by 70,000 more students so by the end of the school year in May, there are actually more students in K12 online classes than there were at the beginning of the school year – despite the fact that more than half of the initial students dropped out and they are all different students!

> Imagine a public high school with one thousand students that was so bad that more than 500 students dropped out of the school in a single year... That is what happens at nearly every K12 online school... over half of the students fail to make it through a single year. 80% drop out by the end of the second year. Only one in ten make it through their third year.

Huge Declines in Test Scores on Washington State Standardized Tests

The test scores of WAVA/K12 INC students are much lower than the Washington State average. (Source OSPI Report Card, Omak SD, WAVA schools)

2011-2012 WAVA students % Passed compared to the State Average

Grade	State Ave Math	WAVA Math	Difference	State Ave Reading	WAVA Reading	Difference
3	65	46	-19%	69	53	16%
4	59	30	-19%	71	49	-22%
5	64	29	-35%	71	52	-19%
6	62	37	-27%	71	50	-21%
7	59	27	-32%	67	53	-14%
8	56	22	-34%	81	41	-40%

The result was similar for the 7th Grade Writing test where 40% of WAVA students passed compared to 71% of statewide students.

On the 8th Grade Science test, 33% of WAVA students passed compared to 66% Statewide. Having a REAL teacher makes a huge difference in helping students learn!

> Less than one in four WAVA students passed the 8th Grade Math Test.
> Only one in three WAVA students passed the 8th Grade Science Test.
> **But the biggest gap between WAVA 8th Graders and the State average was in the Reading Test – where only 41% of WAVA students passed compared to the State average of 81% passing – a gap of 40%!**

Struggling K12 INC Students Disappear on State Testing Days

Note: Most of the information in this section comes from the 2013 OSPI annual report on online programs in Washington State:
http://www.k12.wa.us/LegisGov/2013documents/OnlineLearningAnnualReport.pdf

> The problem with K12 INC is that they place too great a burden on students and parents - because they devalue, abuse and eliminate the teacher – and try to replace the teacher with a computer program.

These very low K12 INC test scores are despite the fact that K12 INC has a known practice of dropping struggling students from their rolls in the weeks before the standardized tests in an effort to raise their test scores- and despite the fact that huge numbers of WAVA students do not even take the tests.

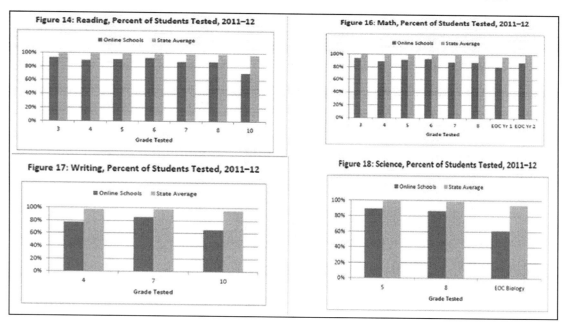

The huge number of K12 INC students who fail to take State testing calls into question even their current meager results. Former K12 INC teachers and administrators have submitted statements in various K12 INC lawsuits that they were instructed to release poor performing students before State testing to try to artificially raise K12 INC test scores!

K12 INC students are much less likely to complete courses

K12 course completion rates are about 80% versus a state average in normal schools of 97%. The following table shows total K12 INC students per school followed by the number who completed courses:

WAVA (Monroe)	10,155	8,619	84.9%
iQ Academy Washington (Evergreen)	3,131	2,648	84.6%
Kent Phoenix Academy (Kent)	1,212	1,003	82.8%
Yakima Online (Yakima)	963	789	81.9%
Washington Virtual Academy (Omak)	3,017	2,261	74.9%

Student Grades in K12 INC completed courses are also much lower:

One in four of these students who completed an online K12 course received an F. This means that the actual pass rate for K12 is now 60% versus a State average of 90%. The following table shows the number of K12 INC students who completed their courses followed by the percent who receive at least a C and the percent who received at least a D.

WAVA (Monroe)	8,619	62.0%	74.4%
Internet Academy (Federal Way)	1,181	71.6%	72.1%
iQ Academy Washington (Evergreen)	2,648	55.1%	67.5%
Insight School of Washington (Quillayute Valley)	18,770	46.3%	63.6%
Bethel Online Academy (Bethel)	1,096	59.4%	59.5%
Washington Virtual Academy (Omak)	2,261	45.2%	58.8%

Below is a graph of the percentage of Grades Earned in K12 INC courses versus traditional non-online courses.

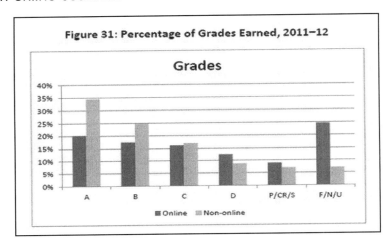

Figure 31: Percentage of Grades Earned, 2011–12

The combination of not completing courses and getting a failing grade in courses they do complete means K12 INC students are much less likely to graduate than students who attend public schools in classes with real teachers.

What is the average graduation rate of K12 INC online students?
According to OSPI, the 2011-2012 Graduation rate for WAVA was only 22%. The Washington State average graduation rate is 75%. In Colorado, the average graduation rate of K12 INC online students was only 20%. In Ohio, the K12 INC graduation rate was 30%. By comparison the average graduation rate for all students in Colorado is about 72%. In Ohio, it is 78%. Below is a chart showing the two year graduate rate of several K12 online schools compared to the average high school graduation rates in the same state:

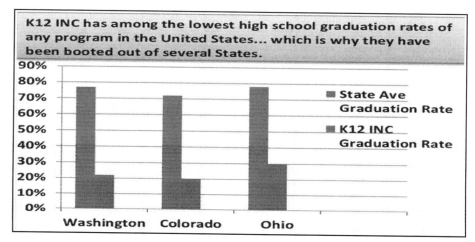

The Washington State WAVA result is based on a small number of students. However, the Colorado and Ohio, K12 INC graduation rates are based upon thousands of students in each state. In general, **the more years a student is subjected to the K12 INC online program, the less likely they are to graduate from high school as students tend to fall further behind every year they are in the K12 program.**

		Graduation Rates (%)			
		2009-2010		2010-2011[a]	
State	K12 Schools	K12 School	State	K12 School	State
AZ	Arizona Virtual Academy[b]	23	76.1	35.2	75.4
CA	California Virtual Academy @ Los Angeles[c]	29.2	78.6	34.8	80.5
CO	Colorado Virtual Academy	12	72.4	21.6	73.9
NV	Nevada Virtual Academy[d]	83.3	71.3	58.3	72.3
OH	Ohio Virtual Academy (OVA)[e]	54.1	83	58.8	84.3
PA	Agora Cyber Charter School[f]	68.5	90	66	91
SC	South Carolina Virtual Charter School[g]	23.2	72.1	7.4	73.7
WA	Washington Virtual Academies[h]	N/A	76.5	22.2	75

So the graduation rate of K12 INC students is much worse than almost any public school – despite the fact that K12 INC students typically come from families with higher incomes and therefore should have a higher graduation rate.

Who are K12 INC aka WAVA students?

Note: Most of the information in this section comes from the 2013 OSPI annual report on online programs in Washington State: http://www.k12.wa.us/LegisGov/2013documents/OnlineLearningAnnualReport.pdf

There are about 8,000 students enrolled in online education programs in Washington State. About 6,000 of these students are enrolled in K12 INC programs such as WAVA. To be clear, this is just the enrollment at the beginning of the school year. During the school year, over 3,000 K12 INC students drop out to be replaced by another 3,000 new student victims. So the total number of students harmed every year by the K12 program is about 9000 students – even though there are only 6,000 students in the program at any given time. The only good news is that the number of K12 INC students in our State fell in the latest report by about 6% - a sign that parents are starting to realize that K12 INC programs are not all they claim to be. K12 INC claims that the reason their students do so poorly is because they are "at-risk" students to begin with.

However, the facts in Washington state show that just the opposite is the case. There is a strong relationship between poverty and low school performance. Yet K12 students typically come from families which are much wealthier than the State and national average. For example, only 15% of WAVA students are from poor families (eligible for free or reduced price lunch) while 42% of all Washington State students are from poor families who are eligible for free and reduced lunch. Because student test scores are highly related to family income, WAVA students should score much higher than the State average. Instead, they score much lower than the State average. Source OSPI Report Cards. Also, only 4% of WAVA students are special education students while the State average is 14% special ed. This also should increase K12 INC scores.

K12 also serves fewer minority at risk students than normal schools:

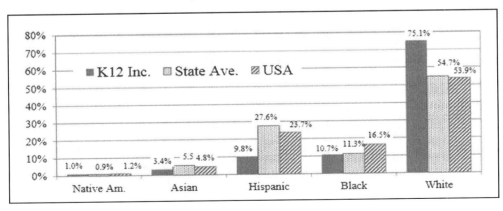

In Washington, lower income minorities make up only 25% of K12 INC programs compared to over 40% of normal schools. This should increase K12 INC scores because upper income students always do better on high stakes tests than lower income students. Instead we see just the opposite. Even high income can not make up for a terrible program.

If the students are not low income or minority at-risk students, then why are so many of them failing in the K12 online program?

There are several reasons. Below we will review the top four reasons so many middle class students fail in the K12 INC online program:

#1: Poorly qualified, over-worked and under-paid teachers.
#2: Overburdened Parents are also not well trained to meet the academic needs of their children.
#3: Overburdened students are not able to handle prolonged "independent study."
#4: K12 has extremely poor Grading and Attendance policies

#1: Poorly qualified, over-worked and under-paid teachers.

K12 INC's entire program is based on devaluing the roll of highly trained and certified teachers and replacing teachers with parent coaches. K12 INC has a court case well documented history of hiring uncertified teachers and abusing them with huge case loads. This is how K12 INC is able to maintain their huge profit margin. In a normal public school, two thirds of our taxpayer dollars go towards teacher salaries and one third goes towards administration. However, with K12 Inc schools, only one third of our tax payer dollars goes towards teachers and the other **two thirds goes towards Wall Street Profits.**

Normal public schools use certified teachers and limit caseloads to 100 to 150 students per teacher per day (5 classes of 20 to 30 students each). For example, North Carolina, state statutes call for no more than <u>150 students per teacher</u> in grades 7 through 12. In both Florida and Colorado, K12 inc teachers were assigned 250 to 300 students per day, two to three times the national average).

In both States, K12Inc teachers were paid a meager $35,000 per year (far below what public school teachers are paid). More than half of these teachers quit in less than one year.

See for example K12 INC under investigation for high teacher case loads

http://pulse.ncpolicywatch.org/2012/09/18/k12-inc-under-more-scrutiny-for-high-teacher-caseloads/

In one documented case in Florida, a K12 manager ordered a certified teacher to sign a class roster of more than 100 students. The certified teacher refused because she only recognized seven names on the list. "I cannot sign off on students who are not my actual students," K12 teacher Amy Capelle wrote to her supervisor. "It is not ethical to submit records to the district that are inaccurate." Many other teachers have also come forward with similar allegations of **K12 falsifying records to increase profits.**

Here is what one former COVA teacher wrote about K12Inc: From what I have personally observed there is one goal, and one goal only and that is making millions of dollars for K12. They have never cared about quality teachers, and in fact, K12 lobbied NOT to have certified teachers, so they could save money on employee salaries. They could care less about the students' education. How can anyone justify **77 cents out of every dollar going to a private for profit company,** when that money is tax payer money set aside for the education of our children? COVA should be shut down immediately and K12 should be held responsible for the tax payer money that they have pocked over the years!!

http://www.kunc.org/post/overworked-and-underpaid-teacher-staffing-colorado-virtual-academy

A 2012 National Study on K12 INC also found that they spent far less than normal schools on teachers, administrators and counselors and almost nothing on facilities. Thus, the bulk of the funds they received went towards corporate profits. Here is a quote from another study: "K12 has more than three times the number of students per teacher compared with overall public school student-teacher ratios. The higher student-teacher ratio and the reduced spending on teacher salaries, as well as on salaries for all other categories of staff typically found in schools, help explain the poor performance of K12's schools "
http://nepc.colorado.edu/files/nepc-rb-k12-miron.pdf

Former employees allege that K12-managed schools aggressively recruited children who were ill-suited for the company's model of online education. They say the schools then manipulated enrollment, attendance, and performance data to maximize tax-subsidized, per-pupil funding.
http://kunc.org/post/ahead-colorado-charter-renewal-embattled-k12-inc-facing-complaints-nationwide

Does the total number of students assigned to a teacher matter?

Those who defend the K12 INC program say it is a different model of education from a normal public school. They therefore claim that the total number of students assigned to a teacher does not matter. However, former K12 INC teachers have said that the total number of students they are assigned does matter and that it is physically impossible for them to meet the needs of their students when they are responsible for 300 kids.

What is the average training, experience and pay of K12 INC teachers?

K12 INC does not release this information. However, reports from former K12 INC teachers confirm that the average K12 teacher has less than one year of teaching experience. Most quit during their first year – leaving students with a constant turnover of teachers to deal with the constant turnover of students. In addition, former K12 teachers report that they are paid less than $35,000 per year – half of what a normal teacher is paid. By contrast, the average teacher in the Snoqualmie Valley School District in Washington State has more than 10 years of experience and a Master's Degree in Education.

#2: Overburdened Parents are not well trained to meet the academic needs of their children

Defenders of the K12 program claim that they do not really need teachers because K12 relies on parents to "coach" their children through the K12 program. Some parents have strong enough social skills to act as their children's teacher and coach. Some parents also have the time to stay home and help their children through their course work. Some parents also have adequate academic knowledge of math and learning methods to help their children. However, many parents lack one of more of these crucial skills. This leaves many children without the resources they need to succeed in school.

Parents often do not have
The time or training
To devote six hours
Per day coaching
Their children through
A complex series
Of online computer
Programs and
Academic Exercises.

#3: Overburdened students are not able to handle prolonged "independent study"

Defenders of the K12 program claim that online courses place less pressure on students because students can study at their own pace. In fact, online courses place much greater pressure on students because any time they fail to perform, their parent will be right there watching them as they fail. Students are therefore under tremendous pressure to retain their relationship with their parents. While home school may help some students, other students are too distracted by other things which are at home but not at school – things such as the TV or video games. They are also quickly bored with the online programs because they lack interaction with their former school friends.

One former K12 INC teacher explained it this way: "When you have the television and the Xbox and no parental figure at home, sometimes it's hard to do your schoolwork." Both young girls and young boys struggle with online programs.

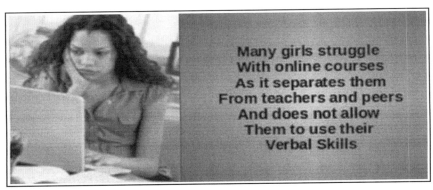

Online programs are particularly hard on young boys who are often cognitively as much as two years behind young girls in their brain development.

#4: K12 Inc has extremely poor Grading and Attendance Policies

In addition to under-paying and overloading uncertified teachers with huge student case loads, K12 Inc inflated enrollment numbers by counting attendance merely by the number of students who logged in rather than the amount of time they spent online.

In a normal public school, a student has to actually be at the school for a minimum of 3 hours in order to be counted in the daily attendance.

The state audit of the Colorado Virtual Academy, which found that the state paid for students who were not attending the school, ordered the reimbursement of more than $800,000.

State auditors found that the K12-run Colorado Virtual Academy counted about 120 students for state reimbursement whose enrollment could not be verified or who did not meet Colorado residency requirements. Some had never logged in. The lawsuit alleges that K12 Inc. used lax grading and attendance practices to maintain and artificially inflate enrollment. One former COVA academic advisor claimed there was a push by administrators to keep students enrolled until the October count date, which determines school funding. Despite having information on date, time and duration of students' engagement with the K12 Inc. software, "the only factor that was taken into account for attendance purposes was whether the student logged in."http://kunc.org/post/institute-reject-colorado-virtual-academy-application-ripples-felt-wall-street

Below are quotes from a lawsuit court filing on June 22, 2012. The quotes are all from former K12 teachers and other K12 employees. http://securities.stanford.edu/1048/LRN00_01/2012622_r01c_12CV00103.pdf

"It was very easy to cheat on exams because there was no way of knowing who was actually taking the online test. Parents or other family members could be taking the test. Students received passing grades on courses for which they had never even logged in. Teachers were threatened with being fired if they did not pass more students."

> One teacher remembered a specific instance in which one of his students failed to attend class for 30-45 days in a row, with no excuse. **Another teacher, a teacher at Agora Cyber Charter School from February 2009 through June 2010, reported that Agora Cyber Charter School continued to bill for one of his students even though the student was absent for 140 consecutive days. Another teacher,** who taught at Ohio Virtual Academy from September 2009 through July 2011, and was responsible for approximately 280 students stated that *over half (of his 280 students) carried a 0.0 GPA* because they never logged in to the system and never took their assigned quizzes or tests.

Several current and former staff members said that a lax policy had allowed students to remain on the rolls even when they failed to log in for days. Officials of the Elizabeth Forward School District in western Pennsylvania complained that Agora had billed the district for students who were not attending. One of them was a girl who had missed 55 days but was still on the school's roster, according to Margaret Boucher, assistant business manager at Elizabeth Forward.

When a student failed to log in for a class day, parents were instructed to log in for the student. When the parents failed to log in, teachers were allowed to log in for the student. When teachers failed to log in for the student, administrators were allowed to log in so that K12 would receive the maximum funding for the student having attended classes that day.

> I am dealing with this [family] with the learning coach and it is not getting anywhere. *They have cleared their attendance but not provided any progress for weeks.* Mom keeps giving the excuse that her daughter is ill or that their computer is in the "shop." ... *they are not doing daily progress.* I have kept a log of our communication. *I really suggest that this student get an administrative withdrawal.* Maybe that is stepping over my authority but I think it's something that would only benefit the student because she would get into a school where she is at least being exposed to schoolwork on a daily basis and not sitting at home losing precious time.

Poor attendance and disengaged students have been such a problem that Agora dismissed 600 students last year for nonattendance, 149 of them just before state tests were administered, according to school board minutes.

It can be difficult to determine whether students are actually doing the work, or getting help from their parents or others. "Virtual schools offer much greater opportunity for students to obtain credit for work they did not do themselves," said a report in October from the National Education Policy Center. Due to rampant reports of cheating on online tests, in 2012, the NCAA announced that they are no longer accepting credits from K12's Aventa Learning.

Fact checking K12 distortions, deceptions and outright lies
Despite all of the above evidence, K12 still falsely claims in their recruitment meetings and in their promotional literature and on their websites that K12 students do significantly better than normal students. We will therefore examine several of their claims:

Claim #1: K12 INC claims that their students do better than normal students

Claim #2: K12 INC claims that parents approve of K12 school

Claim #3: K12 INC claims that their schools have received State and National awards

Let's take a closer look at the deception used in each of these claims.

Claim #1: K12 Inc claims that their students do better than normal students

I attended a K12 recruitment meeting where parents were told that K12 students did much better than normal students. When I asked what evidence this claim was based on, I was told to go to the K12 Inc website and read their 2013 Academic Report. In this report, K12 INC claims that their "norm based Scantron" tests are more reliable than "achievement based" tests approved in most States. According to the Washington State MSP test, K12 students are doing much worse than the State average. However, according to the K12 Scantron test, K12 students are doing slightly better than the Scantron national average:

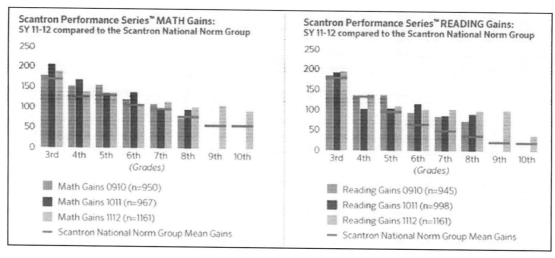

Look carefully and you will see that for three years in a row, less than 1,000 K12 "WAVA" students in our State took the Scantron test. The problem of course is that each of these years, there were over 3,000 total students in the WAVA program. So less than one in three students even took the Scantron test. This indicates that K12 cherry picked the students who would take the test in order to inflate their results.

Below are the Scantron test results for the Insight School of Washington State – another K12 school:

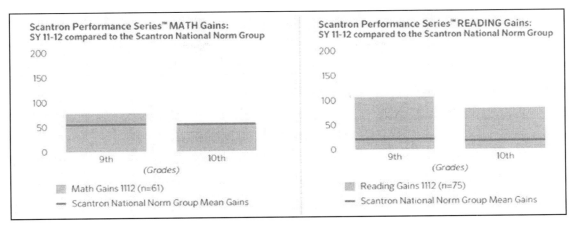

Look closely and you will see that only 75 students took this test. The problem here is that there are 1750 high school students in this online program. **Only 3% of these 1750 students even took the test! What happened to the other 1675 students???**

What exactly is the Scantron Test?
We were curious to read about the K12 Scantron test. What we learned was that there is almost no published data on how the crucial "normed national sample scores" were determined. In fact, there are only a couple of objective scientific studies even done on this test. One was a controlled test in Illinois where the same group of students was given standardized tests and then given the Scantron test. A standardized test, while graded by turning in computer cards, is actually done with the student reading a written test guide and where the student fills in their answers on a multiple choice answer sheet. All questions range in difficulty but are the same questions which are answered by all students. The reason for using a paper test booklet and paper answer sheet and a pencil is to simulate as much as possible how a student normally works – with paper books, paper sheets and a normal pencil.

Students taking a Real Paper and Pencil Standardized Test
With a real standardized test, it is possible for parents to see a copy of the actual test questions that were administered to their child because all test questions for all grades are publicly available. This is not possible with Scantron tests because they use a completely different test process in which every child gets a different test and no two tests are alike. Because Scantron tests are scored online, no parent or teacher can verify the results.

Students adapt easily to paper and pencil tests

Scantron Tests are Online Tests using a computer key board

The Scantron test is radically different from a traditional standardized test. It is done on a computer screen with internet access to the Scantron testing center. Each time a student gives a right answer, the next question is harder. Each time a student gives a wrong answer, the next question is easier.

Elementary School Children about to Take a Scantron Online Test Often do not even Know how to type On a Key Board.

Surprisingly, the following study found that there was very little relationship in the scores received between the normal standardized test and the Scantron test. In other words, a student can score high on one but low on the other. This means that Scantron tests are measuring different skills from standardized tests.

http://www.gocatgo.com/texts/davis.scantron.analysis.pdf

Many students who did well on a standardized test saw their scores drop on the Scantron test by as much as 20%. Strangely, when the students took the Scantron test a second time, their scores rose dramatically.

While student scores generally rise with re-tests, the rises with the Scantron test were much higher.

Middle School Students taking the Scantron Online Test

Here is what the author of the study concluded: "The wide range of gains within classrooms supports the idea that the Scantron test results are not valid or reliable for some students...The Scantron issues raise important concerns for teachers, parents and administrators. If the goal of testing is to accurately assess student learning, then something is amiss with the testing of these students"

> In fact, what Scantron is really testing is not student knowledge of their subject. Instead, **Scantron is testing how comfortable and skilled students are at reading passages from a computer monitor and typing in answers on a computer key board.**

This is why students did much better on re-tests. It is because they had more skill in reading the computer monitor and using the computer keyboard.

Should Scantron testing be called Scamtron testing?
This is why K12 students may do better than normal students on Scantron tests. When you spend your days looking at computer screens and typing answers into computer key boards, you will naturally get more comfortable with this process. The evil geniuses at K12 were quick to realize this. And they have been hyping the Scantron tests ever since. Sadly, these test results do not correlate with standard test results. Nor do they correlate with student knowledge. Nor do they correlate with student SAT scores or student achievement in college.

In fact, the college rate of attendance for K12 students is only 10%. This compares to a 55% rate of college attendance for normal high school students.

Claim #2: Parents approve of K12 schools?

K12 also frequently claims that 88% of all parents report that they are happy with the progress their children make in the K12 online program. On page 67 of their nationwide 2013 Academic Report, K12 presents charts claiming that 88% of their parents are satisfied with the K12 program as indicated by a response of 5, 6 or 7 on a scale of 1 to 7. They do not disclose the percentage of parents who failed to respond to the survey. However, they did list the sample size for the survey. If you look very closely, you will see that only 9,174 parents completed the survey out of 190,000 parents that year.

K12 has 120,000 students at their schools on average at any given time. But because 70,000 drop out and are replaced by 70,000 new students during the year, the total sample size of students is 190,000. So out of 190,000 students, less than 5% of their parents even returned the surveys.

This is a very low response rate. It is unknown what happened to the other 95% of the surveys. It is like having an election where one does not know what happened to 95% of the ballots. What is known is that parents and students voted with their feet. Over half of them left the program in the first year.

> Out of 190,000 parents involved in the K12 program, 95% – or 180,000 parents - failed to turn in their K12 Satisfaction Survey form! Over 50% of these parents pulled their child out of the K12 program in less than one year. Despite these facts, K12 has the audacity to tell us that 88% of all parents were "happy" with the K12 program and would recommend it to a friend!!!

This problem is also true here in Washington State. About 90% of all parents turning in K12 Satisfaction surveys indicate they are satisfied with the K12 program. However, in the Omak WAVA program only 130 parents turned in the form out of more than 2,000 students who started out the school year in the program. Considering that there were actually more than 1000 students who dropped out of the program during the year – only to be replaced by another 1000 new students, the total number of parents was more than 3000. Therefore, the response rate to this survey was less than 5% - with 95% of all parents not turning in the survey and 50% of all parents voting with their feet by pulling their kids out of the program before the end of the first year.

Claim #3: K12 schools have received State and National awards

On the home page of the K12 Washington Virtual Academy, they proudly claim that they were awarded an OSPI School of Achievement Award in 2012. Knowing how badly the WAVA school actually does, it is hard for me to imagine this online school ever getting an award for anything.

So I clicked on the link to see the award. Instead of going to the award, the link led to the K12 national website home page where there was a press release describing the award and what a great achievement it was to have gotten this award in Washington State.

At the bottom of this press release was a link which claimed to go to the award. So I clicked on this link. This link went to the OSPI website which described the award and the process for getting the award.
http://www.k12.wa.us/EducationAwards/WashingtonAchievement/default.aspx

There was a link on this OSPI page to see the actual award winners. Curious to see how many schools got this award, I clicked on this link. This took me to an Excel spreadsheet listing 383 who got this award in 2012. I examined this very long list very carefully. Strangely, **WAVA was not on the OSPI list. Nor was any other K12 Inc school!**

I then went back to the OSPI page and clicked on the PDF version of the list. WAVA was not there either. I then checked 2011 and 2010 to see if perhaps WAVA was on one of these lists. Not there either. So I called OSPI. They said that WAVA – Monroe School District did receive an award for "improvement" in 2011 by having their scores better than they were in 2010. We will therefore look at the Monroe WAVA scores compared to the State average to see how WAVA managed to game the system to get an award that they clearly do not deserve. For reference, here are the most recent test scores Statewide (the average test scores for all students in Washington State):

2011-12 MSP/HSPE Results (Administration Info)

Grade Level	Reading	Math	Writing	Science
3rd Grade	68.8%	65.3%		
4th Grade	71.5%	59.4%	61.4%	
5th Grade	71.1%	63.8%		66.3%
6th Grade	70.7%	61.5%		
7th Grade	71.3%	59.2%	71.0%	
8th Grade	67.3%	55.5%		66.4%
10th Grade	81.3%	See EOC below	85.4%	See EOC below

Grade Level *	EOC Math Year 1	EOC Math Year 2
All Grades	71.1%	79.1%

Grade Level *	EOC Biology	
All Grades		64.3%

Below are the average test scores for students in the Snoqualmie Valley School District:

2011-12 MSP/HSPE Results (Administration Info)				
Grade Level	Reading	Math	Writing	Science
3rd Grade	83.0%	83.0%		
4th Grade	84.6%	85.2%	82.8%	
5th Grade	82.3%	73.5%		87.3%
6th Grade	83.6%	75.8%		
7th Grade	89.3%	81.1%	93.5%	
8th Grade	86.3%	76.2%		86.3%
10th Grade	92.6%	See EOC below	97.3%	See EOC below

Grade Level *	EOC Math Year 1	EOC Math Year 2
All Grades	87.8%	87.6%

Grade Level *	EOC Biology
All Grades	74.5%

Students in the Snoqualmie Valley School District are far above the State average in every category. Now here are the Monroe School District WAVA program test scores. Because it is only a 9-12 program, they do not list test scores for the lower grades:

2011-12 MSP/HSPE Results (Administration Info)				
Grade Level	Reading	Math	Writing	Science
10th Grade	67.3%	See EOC below	64.4%	See EOC below

Grade Level *	EOC Math Year 1	EOC Math Year 2
All Grades	54.1%	68.0%

Grade Level *	EOC Biology
All Grades	50.8%

Monroe WAVA students are far below the State average. This is very sad considering that there are 900 students in this program. Half of them are failing.

Below are the charts of the WAVA performance for the past three years in Reading and Writing:

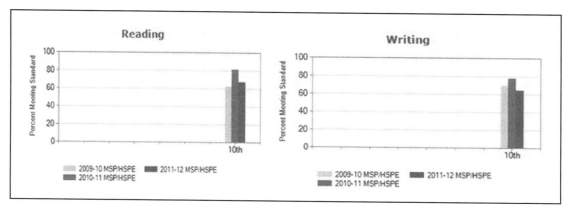

Notice that the scores in both reading and writing went from below average to average in 2010-11. Both he Reading and Writing test scores rose dramatically during the year that WAVA was given the award. But they both fell back down below average the very next year. This indicates that K12 administrators did something to manipulate the test scores in both reading and writing on the 2010-11 test - indicating that WAVA rigged the test in order to get this award.

Because of the potential for rigging scores in order to temporarily raise them, OSPI eliminated the "Improvement" award the year after WAVA Monroe managed to game the system. This kind of conduct is despicable. But this is what we should expect when we allow a Wall Street corporation to bring in a Hollywood marketing firm to fool local parents into sending their kids to this failing program.

How much does K12 INC receive per pupil and what percent goes towards teachers compared to our normal public schools?
The average State funding here in our State is about $6,000 per child. More than 60% of every dollar spent by our normal public schools goes to teacher salaries with the rest spent on all kinds of special programs (including bus transportation) and less than 20% is spent on administrative overhead.

Public school districts have no profit margin and are controlled by a publicly elected school board whose members are not paid anything for their service to the community.

In sharp contrast, K12 INC devotes more than 60% of the tax payer income they receive on salaries and bonuses for their upper management and profit for Wall Street Hedge Fund Managers who own K12INC stock. Last year, **K12 INC reported more than $900 million in revenue and their upper managers were paid millions of dollars each.**

K12 INC gets about $6,000 per student in Washington State because they also get local levy dollars in their contracts with school district. The total currently is about 8000 students. Multiple this times $6,000 per student and it is likely that K12 INC takes $48 million per year out of public schools in our state.

What is happening to K12 INC programs in other States?
There are currently lawsuits in Colorado and Florida with complaints filed in many other States. Virginia just voted to close their statewide K12 INC online school after similar disastrous online student performance in that State. A Tennessee study found their online schools ranked in the bottom 11% of all schools. K12 INC taxpayer-supported, privately operated online schools have been receiving increased public scrutiny, including criticism of their performance and their funding arrangements. Also see the following link for a national study of online school performance:

http://nepc.colorado.edu/newsletter/2013/05/virtual-schools-annual-2013

Calculating the negative impact of K12 INC on students in Washington

There are currently about 8,000 K12 INC students in Washington State – with 4,000 of these students dropping out of the K12 INC programs every year only to be replaced by another 4,000 unsuspecting students and their parents. Assuming that K12 INC gets $6,000 per student from the several school districts which are "hosting" their program, the total loss of funds to our public schools is $48 million per year. The total number of normal public school teachers that have to be fired to make up for this huge loss in revenue is about 800 teachers.

Therefore, if we offered our online students a better program using free open source educational programs, we could rehire 800 teachers – half of whom could be used to support our online education programs in Washington State and the other half of whom could be returned to our normal public schools to reduce class sizes in 400 schools in our State.

A better option... Local Control over a Local Online Educational Program

So far in this report, we have looked mainly at the negative impact of K12 INC on students in Washington State. However, by addressing the shortcomings of the K12 INC program, we could offer an online program which helps students rather than harms them. Some of the changes we should make include:

#1: Warn parents of the actual track record of the K12 INC program.

#2: Offer parents a better alternative than the K12 INC program.

#3: This better alternative would increase the use of a higher number of local public school teachers.

#4: Screen students to insure that only students who have a track record of being able to complete an independent study program are allowed to sign up for more than one online course at any given time.

#5: Provide a training program for online teachers to help them better meet the needs of online students and their parents.

#6: Provide school districts with a list of approved free open source online courses and programs in order to improve the quality of the online curriculum.

#7: Provide multiple types of online learning experiences including not only videos and exercises, but also more and better online interactive books, online student clubs, online forums organized by topic and parent support groups.

What is Next?

Now that we know the drawbacks of the K12 INC scam program, in the next section, we will look at free open source options for those students who really do need an online option for their learning.

4.4 Free Open Source Alternatives to K12 INC

Despite all of the drawbacks of online education, there is a need for some students in some circumstances to take some courses online. However, public schools should not be promoting any private for profit businesses as this leads to massive corruption problems. Instead free public schools should promote and encourage free publicly developed online educational programs. Thankfully, the Washington State Department of Education, called OSPI, is in the process of carrying out some of this work. Their progress is listed on their website: http://digitallearning.k12.wa.us/oer/

Open Educational Resources (OER) are teaching and learning materials that exist in the public domain or have been released under an open license. This means that those resources can be used **free of charge**, distributed widely and are often more up-to-date than textbooks. In most cases, OER can be updated and modified without asking the content creator for permission. OER may be used by any teacher, parent or any student as entire courses, full units, lesson-plan components or supplemental material. Depending on the course, teachers also might be able to download and print a textbook, display video and audio lectures, build and share lesson plans, access free books in the public domain, experience interactive simulations and/or gather and assemble resources like photos, sounds and diagrams. Many open resources may be downloaded in pdf formats and printed on a personal printer or in the case of OER textbooks, sent to a Print on Demand Service such as Lulu or CreateSpace.

In April 2012, the Washington State Legislature passed bill HB2337, directing the Office of the Superintendent of Public Instruction to create a collection of openly licensed course ware aligned to the common-core standards and an associated awareness campaign to inform school districts about these resources. By developing this library of openly licensed course ware and making it available to school districts free of charge, the state and school districts will be able to provide students with curricula and texts while substantially reducing the expenses that districts would otherwise incur in purchasing these materials.

In addition, this library of openly licensed courses provide districts and students with a broader selection of materials, and materials that are more up-to-date." OSPI's OER Project will develop a review process that acts as a model for districts considering the adoption of full-course OER. The results of the review will be a resource for schools and classrooms.

If we cooperate and share, we can build a free online educational program where everyone wins. Teachers have more choices when building their own courses. Teachers and students can work together to solve problems. Students and school districts can reduce cost by reducing the number of expensive and heavy text books. But most important, students learn that access to digital knowledge is a human right and social justice issue. We build a freer and more knowledgeable world. From the OER website, anyone can download complete textbooks and full course materials. There is even a search box where you can enter search terms for presentations, ebooks, videos, lesson plans, text books and full courses. Many other States also have similar free online course resources.

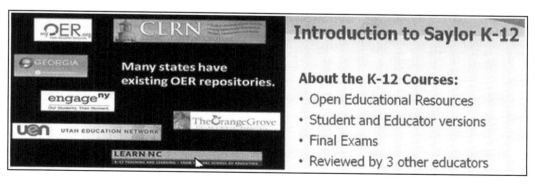

Here is a summary of other free online educational programs and resources taken from the Washington State OSPI website.

OPSI Suggested Sites and Free Open Source Online Learning Resources

California-CLRN: California Learning Resource Network provides educators with a "one-stop" resource for critical information needed for the selection of electronic learning resources aligned to the State Board of Education academic content standards. In addition to publisher material and online courses, free web info links (WIL) are also reviewed.

Connexions: Connexions describes itself as a "digital educational ecosystem." It houses more than 17,000 learning products, and 1,000 + collections of textbooks, journal articles and more. Contributors make a learning module from scratch or re-work an existing Connexions product into a new course.

Curriki: Curriki is a nonprofit K-12 global community for teachers, students, and parents to create, share, and find free learning resources. They currently have 7.7 million users and over 45,000 free resources. Collection may be searched by different criteria including subject, grade level and common core alignment.

Georgia Virtual Learning: Georgia Virtual Learning is the headquarters for online education from the Georgia Department of Education. The content available on the Shared Resources Website is available for anyone to view.

Hippocampus: Free educational resources are provided for middle school, high school and college students and teachers, including video presentations, worked examples interactive simulations, and test prep.

Kansas OER: This webpage prepared by the Kansas Department of Education contains open access resources and digital textbooks that are available within the public domain. They are not copyrighted and may be customized, modified, or combined with other materials.

Maine OER: The Maine Department of Education awarded grants for the identification of on-line educational resources and professional development to assist teachers to develop the skills and knowledge to more fully utilize Maine's rich technological resources to enhance teaching and learning. Check out the specific area landing pages for ELA, social studies, and science.

OER Commons: The Institute for the Study of Knowledge Management in Education (ISKME) created OER Commons to provide support for and build a knowledge base around the use and reuse of open educational resources (OER). As a network for teaching and learning materials, the web site offers engagement with resources in the form of social bookmarking, tagging, rating, and reviewing.

Teachers' Domain: Teachers' Domain is a free digital media service for educational use from public broadcasting and its partners. Here are thousands of media resources, support materials, and tools for classroom lessons, individualized learning programs, and teacher professional learning communities. Non-commercial, educational use only content on the site is made available to users under four levels of permitted uses: online view only, download, download and share, download, share and remix. See specific resource for licensing rules.

OPSI Suggested Sites for Full Online Curriculum Resources

FlexMath: FlexMath is a web-based interactive Algebra I curriculum that provides daily lessons and real-time feedback to help raise student achievement.

Open Course Library: This library of higher education courses is hosted by the State Board of Community and Technical Colleges.

Open High School of Utah: Course materials produced by the Open High School of Utah are licensed under a Creative Commons Attribution 3.0 License. Open educational resources produced by other individuals or organizations that are embedded in Open High School of Utah course materials may be licensed under a different open license.

Additional Open Source Learning Tools which are not yet listed on the Washington State OSPI website

There is an explosion of free open source online educational programs being developed by teachers all over the world. Below are just a few of the more well established examples.

#1: Digital Public Library http://www.openculture.com/freeonlinecourses
A group of top American libraries and academic institutions launched a new centralized research resource, the Digital Public Library of America (DPLA), making millions of resources (books, images, audiovisual resources, etc.) available in digital format.

#2: Edubuntu http://www.edubuntu.org/

Started in 2005, the community-driven Edubuntu project aims to put free and open source software into the hands of children. In doing so, Edubuntu provides children with a flexible and powerful technological environment for learning and experimenting. The Edubuntu project aims to provide the best of everything in Ubuntu—properly tailored for use in schools and as easy to use as possible. Ubuntu is a free operating system that can be installed on any computer and works especially well on inexpensive Google Chromebook computers.

#3: Ubermix http://ubermix.org/

This is another Ubuntu distribution, based on the free Linux Ubuntu operating system which uses a slightly different mix of free open source educational tools. It uses an icon based user interface similar to Apple computers.

#4: Wikibooks http://www.wikibooks.org/

This group is devoted to posting online textbooks. This is important because while some children can learn from videos, others learn better from an online text book or book which can be printed out.

#5: CK12 http://www.ck12.org/student/

This group has all kinds of books, courses and educational programs appropriate for high school students. CK-12 is a non-profit organization dedicated to increasing access to high quality educational materials for K-12 students all over the world.

They offer free high-quality, standards-aligned, open content in the STEM subjects. By providing these free resources, CK-12 is working toward educational equity for all. CK-12 makes it easy for teachers to assemble their own textbooks. You can start from scratch or build from anything the FlexBooks library. Below is a sample text book on High School Earth Science:

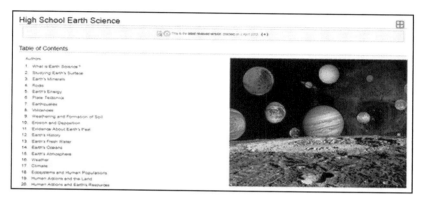

The book is available online and also as a PDF and has been approved by the State of California and the US Department of Education. The program also includes teacher's editions and resource guides for parents and teachers. They use a multi-modal approach – meaning that this program is suited for a broader group of students than programs which merely use online videos.

#6: Coursera https://www.coursera.org/
This program offers 370 courses and has 3.5 million students. A problem with this website is their claim that online learning is "at least as effective as face to face learning." This is simply not true. While online learning is useful for some students in some situations it is not the best choice for most students in most situations. Nevertheless, this website does offer courses on a much broader range of topics than Kahn Academy. For example, they have 21 courses on music. Also, their courses tend to be a higher quality as they are often taught by experienced teachers who are experts in their field. Several university professors have contributed courses to this project.

#7: Udacity https://www.udacity.com/
These are pretty advanced college level courses with economical college credit through San Jose State University.

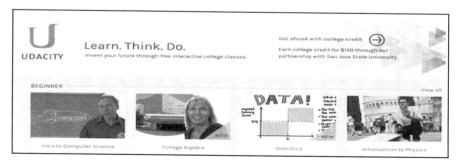

#7: Open Course Ware Consortium... This is MIT's open source courses program. http://www.ocwconsortium.org/en/courses/catalog

There are a lot of courses here. But most appear to be college level courses.

#8: Academic Earth http://www.academicearth.org/
Academic Earth aims to provide everyone with the opportunity to earn a world-class education by offering free online classes and online learning tools. Whether you're looking to advance your career or take classes that interest you, Academic Earth can connect you to the world's top universities and scholars. This group has a well-organized menu of free courses and videos from all kinds of places on all kinds of topics.

#9: Open Learning Initiative http://oli.cmu.edu/
The Open Learning Initiative offers online courses to anyone who wants to learn or teach. Our aim is to combine open, high-quality courses, continuous feedback, and research to improve learning and transform higher education. Basic college level courses in several topics including practice exercises and assessments that provided targeted feedback to students and teachers.

#10 TU Delft Open Course Ware TU Delft
TU Delft offers courses at both the bachelor and master level, arranged by degree program. You will have access to lecture notes, exams, and assignments in a broad range of topics and subjects. It is easy to navigate, free, and requires no sign-in! For a list of 150 free textbooks, click here.

#11 Wake County Public Schools
They have a series of online video lessons called the "Success Series," which provides a review of most of the core subjects and foreign language.

There are obviously more online resources coming online every day. In my opinion, these will never replace a real teacher building a relationship with a real group of students. However, they can offer specific learners specific resources and also supplement normal classroom learning. But it essential that online students and their parents have access to a highly experienced teacher to help them design an appropriate educational program and to monitor this program to make sure the student is able to achieve success.

All of these free State and National online educational programs are better than K12 INC!

The bottom line is that with all of these free online educational programs available, we really do not need K12 INC. We can therefore avoid all of the drawbacks, marketing and lies associated with a private for profit business. Instead of sending our precious tax payer dollars to a private for-profit corporation like K12 INC, there are many free public educational online programs we can offer our students. We can then use the millions of dollars we are spending every year on K12 INC to hire more experienced teachers - and even have local teachers whose only job would be to assist parents and students who want to pursue an online education. Parents and online students would benefit because they would have a local teacher who they could meet with whenever they needed. Our locally elected school boards would be assured that the teacher would not be over-burdened with more than 40 students and we could make sure these students have a teacher with 10 years of experience rather than just one year of experience. These online teachers would be accountable to our publicly elected school board directors – who are in turn accountable to the public. Not one penny would go to Wall Street. If we had more real teachers and less over-crowded schools, we would have fewer unhappy parents and students and less interest in online education.

We wrote this chapter because we want parents to be fully aware of the many serious drawbacks of K12 INC. We want to make it clear that we are not opposed to online educational programs. In fact, we have spent years teaching online courses and building free educational online websites. We are currently building an online educational program for college students and small business owners called **collegeintheclouds.org.** So we are not opposed to innovation. We are only opposed to online educational programs that harm students, mislead parents, exploit teachers and rip off tax payers. We think that online education can work well for some children in some circumstances. It is essential that the student have a parent who is fully available for an online program to work. Our concern is that most parents are not fully available and/or may lack the academic training to actually help their children. This is a problem because the student is unlikely to receive the help they need from poorly trained, inexperienced and over-burdened K12 INC teachers. The only way to truly help struggling children is with local teachers who know the students and can build a relationship with them. This is not possible when the teacher is living far from the student and is responsible for 300 students. Again, while some children may succeed in a Home School environment using the K12 online educational tools, the vast majority of students who are subjected to this program fail terribly. You should consider these facts carefully before enrolling your child in a K12 INC program. There is nearly always a better option available for your child.

What is Next?
Speaking of teachers, in the next chapter, we will explain the benefits of using a real teacher instead of a fake "Teach for America" teacher.

5 Teach for Awhile Fake Teachers

> "American education has a long history of infatuation with fads and Ill-considered ideas. The current obsession with making our schools Work like a business may be the worst of them, for it threatens to Destroy public education. Who will stand up to the tycoons and Politicians and tell them so?" — Dr. Diane Ravitch

Of all of the weapons of mass deception used by the billionaires, Teach for America, more commonly known as TFA is probably the strangest. TFA recruits recent college graduates, gives them five weeks of "training" and then ships them off to inflict their lack of training on innocent and often very young students. The real purpose of TFA, like all of the other weapons of mass deception, is to rob tax payers of billions of dollars and rob children of their future. This fifth chapter is divided into four sections:

5.1 Why Replacing Real Teachers with Fake TFA Teachers Harms Kids

5.2 How TFA Harms Real Teachers

5.3 We Should Not Use Student Test Scores to Fire Teachers

5.4 If You Can Not Measure It, Does It Still Exist?

5.1 Why replacing real teachers with fake TFA teachers harms our kids

> A real teacher has at least 5 years of training.
> Teach for America recruits have only 5 weeks of training.
> Imagine being operated on by a doctor
> With only five weeks of training.

In our last chapter, we looked at how a billionaire funded fake online school called K12 INC, run by Wall Street gamblers, harms millions of students in the US every year. In this chapter, we will look at another billionaire funded scam called Teach For America (TFA). Of all of the weapons of mass deception used by the billionaires, TFA is probably the strangest. TFA recruits recent college graduates, gives them five weeks of "training" - which is really nothing more than a five week pep rally - and then ships them off to school districts nationwide to inflict their lack of training on innocent and often very young students. Just imagine being operated on by a doctor with only 5 weeks of training. Subjecting our kids to fake teachers with only 5 weeks of training is a crime.

Allowing fake TFA teachers with no real training to operate On the minds of young children is no joke... It is a crime!

Within months, many honest TFA recruits quit, leaving the students without a teacher. As with everything else in the corporate raider ed reform scam, using fake teachers is "designed to fail." It really does not matter to the corporate raiders that the TFA recruits quit or if students taught by TFA recruits do poorly on math and reading assessments. All that matters is that this scheme, like Common Core high failure rate tests, charter schools and all of the other weapons of mass deception makes hundreds of millions of dollars for those pushing this snake oil medicine.

Any experienced teacher knows that it takes many years of training and experience to become a good teacher. You have to learn how to construct lessons and design activities in carefully planned year long sequences. You have to learn your content area(s). You have to learn how to think on your feet and develop a broad range of skills that can only come with education and experience. Any one of these skills can take years to learn. It is simply not possible for anyone to learn how to be an effective teacher in only 5 weeks.

The Real Goal of Teach for America is to Bust Teachers Unions

Why would billionaires promote a scam that replaces real teachers who have 5 to 10 years of training with fake teachers who have only 5 weeks of training and typically last less than one year in a classroom before quitting? Why would school administrators waste hundreds of millions of dollars training, paying and replacing thousands of fake teachers when the cost of hiring real teachers is much less? Certainly part of the plan is to make money. TFA makes hundreds of millions of dollars. However, there appears to be another more sinister motive at work. It appears that TFA is being used as a weapon to destroy the teachers union and to destroy teaching as a profession. Why would billionaires want to destroy the teachers union? Perhaps some billionaires see all of the money they could make replacing teachers with computers and computer software. But it is more likely that billionaires see teachers as a threat to their entire privatization plan. It is harder to manipulate teachers with corporate propaganda than it is to manipulate parents. Get rid of the experienced teachers and no one will be left besides already busy parents to oppose the privatization of our public schools.

It is therefore important for both parents and teachers to be aware of the drawbacks of TFA. We will begin with a brief review of the history of this TFA scam and then look at its current harm on our students and public schools.

Follow the TFA Money Trail

TFA was started in 1990 by a person named Wendy Kopp – a person without any training in education or any experience teaching in an actual classroom. Wendy started with about 500 recruits and has managed to raise the number up to about 12,000 fake teachers today – despite the fact that these fake teachers have had a terrible track record since the program started. Currently, Wendy manages to add more than 6,000 new recruits to this scam every year.

Wendy has had the audacity to charge school districts up to $5,000 for every new recruit she supplies them with. Wendy gets her money whether the TFA recruit teaches for a full year or not. Simple math puts the total robbery at about $30 to $60 million per year just from their parasitic relationship with local school districts. But in addition to the millions in State public money Wendy gets every year, Wendy also receives millions more from billionaires who like her style. Billionaire Bill has given millions of dollars to prop up TFA. This is just one of 12 grants from the fake Gates Foundation scam to the fake TFA scam. Bill Gates has given TFA more than $11 million.

> **Teach for America, Inc.**
>
> **Date:** October 2012
> **Purpose:** to support activities in TFA Colorado and TFA Louisiana designed to improve the instructional quality of their corps members through the use of video technology and to increase the leadership development and voice of corps members and alumni
> **Amount:** $1,557,444

In addition, about one third of the money for TFA comes from the US tax payers (you and me) as a result of grants from the federal government via an extremely corrupt US Department of Education. The TFA official operating expenses increased from $10 million per year in 2000 to $114 million per year by 2008 and exploded to $350 million by 2012. TFA currently has assets of more than $420 million. So obviously there is more money coming in to TFA than meets the eye.

TFA Backers have no training in Education or Child Development
Below are some TFA recruits being laugh at shallow jokes and clap for dishonest speeches of TFA recruiters out to brainwash them.

After only 5 weeks of training, these TFA recruits will be sent off to "teach" your kids!

How is this even possible?
In the past, both state and federal law regulated who could teach in our public schools. Teachers were required to have years of training in child development, learning theories, and classroom management. They were also required to complete a several month "practice" teaching experience under the guidance of an experienced teacher. After all of this, they were granted a "Provisional Teachers Certificate" which allowed them to teach. But in most states, additional training during several summers was required to get a permanent teachers certificate.

All of this changed in 2010, when state and federal teaching standards laws were changed in order to allow TFA recruits to qualify as "highly qualified" teachers. It should be obvious that a recruit with only five weeks of training can not possibly be "highly qualified." However, our Congress is so corrupt and so bought off by the billionaires, that on December 21, 2010, Congress amended federal law to change the definition of "highly qualified to include TFA recruits. This was despite the fact that (or because of the fact that) the federal appeals court in California twice ruled that TFA teachers are not highly qualified.

The federal court also ruled that TFA recruits should not be concentrated in districts of high poverty and high disadvantage, where children actually need "highly qualified" teachers, not young college graduates with five weeks to training. For more on this subject, see Renee v. Duncan, decided on September 27, 2010, which struck down Arnie Duncan's crazy regulation that TFA recruits were highly qualified. Any Congress person who voted for this change is corrupt and should be voted out of office.

http://www.ca9.uscourts.gov/datastore/opinions/2010/09/27/08-16661.pdf

TFA Fake Teachers are replacing Real Teachers by the Thousands
TFA uses the false claim that there is a shortage of real qualified teachers to justify their fake teacher scam. Given that there are over 300,000 experienced teachers who are currently unemployed in the US, this claim is absurd. But education reform has never been about the facts. It is about robbing the tax payers of hundreds of millions of dollars while robbing students of their education and their future.

It has been estimated that since the Great Recession began in 2008, more than 300,000 real teachers have lost their jobs to huge State budget cuts. To be exact, according to the Center on Budget and Policy Priorities, between 2009 and 2013, 324,000 education positions in local school districts were eliminated.
http://www.cbpp.org/files/9-12-13sfp.pdf

Total education employees went from 8.1 million in 2009 to 7.8 million in 2013. According to the National Center for Educational Statistics, 3.3 million of these 8.1 million school employees were teachers – dropping to about 3 million full time public school teachers today. http://nces.ed.gov/fastfacts/display.asp?id=372

As the following chart shows, these jobs have not been restored during the claimed "economic recovery."

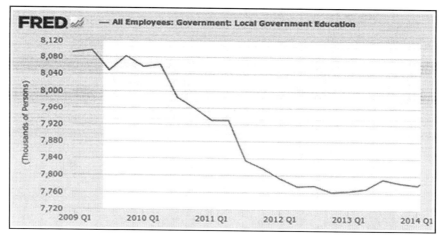

This means that there are currently about 300,000 fully qualified and experienced real teachers without jobs. In addition, another 240,000 novice teachers graduate from Teachers Colleges around the United States each year. Even these novices have 5 years more training than TFA recruits. Given the abundance of real teachers, why would any school administrator, public or private, hire fake TFA teachers?

TFA Cheap, Fake Teachers are a Key Part of the Charter School Scam
TFA's growth depends on and supports the country's corrupt charter school movement. TFA teachers are non-union and work for much less than real teachers. They are therefore a key tactic in reducing the cost of teachers if the goal is making money rather than helping kids learn.

Since the goal of charter schools is making money, it is not surprising that using TFA teachers has become common in charter schools. TFA data shows that 33% of its recruits now teach in charter schools (up from 13% in 2007). Charter schools are almost entirely nonunion, privately run, and can receive millions in private support on top of public funds. TFA has funneled a growing number of new recruits into charters in large urban school districts that have recently laid off hundreds of experienced teachers, including Philadelphia (where 99 percent of TFA recruits teach in charters), Detroit (69 percent) and Chicago (53 percent). According to USA Today, in March 2009, the superintendent of the Charlotte school district claimed that a contract signed with TFA required him to retain 100 TFA teachers despite the fact that the school district was firing hundreds of real school teachers due to budget cuts. Here is a headline from February 2014 about TFA replacing real teachers in New Jersey:

Between 2005 to 2010, New Orleans cut 7,500 school staff, converted its schools to charters, and increased its TFA fake teachers from 85 to 375.

In 2009, TFA came to Seattle Washington. Because of the 2008 economic crash, the Seattle school district has a huge surplus of laid off teachers: 13,800 teachers had applied for just 352 full- and part-time positions. One Seattle elementary school had nearly 800 unemployed teachers applied for a single teacher job. So there are plenty of qualified experienced teachers in Seattle with Masters Degrees in Education. But a corrupt school board elected by billionaires decided to bring in a bunch of TFA recruits. In school board meetings that were sometimes standing room only, dozens of community members — including parents, teachers and students — signed up in record numbers to testify against the district's contract with TFA, urging the administration to hire more experienced local teachers. http://hechingerreport.org/content/teachers-losing-jobs-teach-americas-expanding-whats-wrong_15617/

In 2013, in Connecticut, hundreds of teaching jobs were given to out of state TFA recruits while graduates of Connecticut's 5-Year Teachers College program were not even allowed to apply for these jobs.
http://www.washingtonpost.com/blogs/answer-sheet/wp/2013/08/29/how-teach-for-america-recruits-get-preference-for-teaching-jobs/

An Open Letter to TFA Recruits
In 2013, Chicago closed 48 schools and fired 850 teachers while hiring 350 TFA recruits to replace them. This is an edited version of an article written by a Chicago Special Education teacher called An Open Letter to TFA Recruits:

"We have no teacher shortages. We have teacher surpluses. And yet, TFA is still placing first year novices in places like Chicago. To put it bluntly, the last thing our students undergoing mass school closings, budget cuts, and chaotic school policy need is short-term, poorly-trained novices. Teach for America is not needed in Chicago. If you truly want to help children through teaching, give those future students the greatest chance possible by doing a full preparation program in advance of being left alone in a classroom. Those of us in the teaching profession will welcome bright young beginning teachers with open arms. And if you are not sure teaching is for you, volunteer in a school, tutor, participate in after-school programs. Whatever you do, do not allow TFA to let you learn how to teach on the backs of our neediest children, children living in poverty, children with disabilities, children who are still learning English, children living under oppression, racism, and savage inequalities. All children deserve a fully-prepared teacher for every day of their educational careers. Do not partner with the very people trying to destroy public education for their own personal gain."
Katie Osgood, Special Education Teacher Chicago
http://atthechalkface.com/2013/06/30/an-open-letter-to-new-teach-for-america-recruits/

TFA's Most Famous Ex Fake Teacher... Michelle Rhee
Michelle Rhee, one of the most corrupt and highly paid leaders of the ed Reform scam, attended a private high school and was a TFA recruit in the 1990's. The one and only year teacher reform super star Michelle Rhee actually taught, her Second Grade class was so out of control student and teacher yelling could be heard throughout the building. By her own admission, Michelle decided to put duct tape over the mouths of her students to prevent them from talking while walking to the school lunchroom. After removing the duct tape, skin came off their lips, they were bleeding and she had "thirty-five kids who were crying".
http://voices.washingtonpost.com/dcschools/2010/08/michelle_rhee_first-year_teach.html

How did Michelle's abusive style of controlling young students work?
Michelle Rhee's first year test scores for her abused students showed a precipitous drop: Average math percentile dropped from 64% to 17%. Average reading percentile dropped from 37% to 21%.
https://en.wikipedia.org/wiki/Michelle_A._Rhee

Despite this record of child abuse and low test scores, in 2007, Michelle Rhee was appointed as Chancellor of the Washington D.C. School District. She fired hundreds of teachers and replaced them with TFA teachers. During her three years in charge of DC schools, Michelle fired nearly 1,000 teachers. Videos and articles show that Michelle Rhee took great pride and even joy in firing teachers and closing schools. One time Michelle even invited a PBS news crew to secretly film Michelle firing a school principal.
http://www.democraticunderground.com/1002714439

Here is the link to the Youtube video of this callous 26 second event:
http://www.youtube.com/watch?v=FQ4N6UZbdxA

The result of Michelle firing real teachers? 40% of the teachers in the Washington DC school district are now TFA teachers and test scores are falling.
http://www.washingtonpost.com/wp-dyn/content/article/2011/02/08/AR2011020804813.html

Thankfully, there was a test score cheating scandal during Michelle's brief career that was exposed in USA Today. A new principal discovered that after school, staff members were changing answers on hundreds of tests in order to artificially inflate student scores. With greater security to prevent cheating, test scores at Washington DC schools fell dramatically. Hopefully, this will be the last that young children and their teachers will be exposed to abuse from Michelle Rhee.

Former TFA Recruits agree that the TFA Program is a Scam
Many former TFA recruits have come out against TFA and posted their stories on the Internet. Below are just a few examples.

"When I joined Teach For America I had no idea that my belief in social and economic justice was about to be cynically exploited by the corporate class. Today, seeing how it operates from the inside, I'm convinced that TFA now serves as a critical component of the all-out-effort by corporate elites to privatize one of the last remaining public institutions of our country: our public schools."
http://www.salon.com/2014/01/13/teach_for_americas_pro_corporate_union_busting_agenda_partner/

> MONDAY, JAN 13, 2014 09:33 AM PST
>
> # Teach For America's pro-corporate, union-busting agenda
>
> How TFA uses its vast political influence to boost charter schools and drive down teacher pay (UPDATED)
>
> CHAD SOMMER, EDUSHYSTER.COM

"In Chicago, where I participated in TFA, the organization maintains its own extremely close partnerships with privately managed charter schools. Their relationships are so close, in fact, that earlier this year, after the Chicago Public School system closed forty-nine traditional, unionized public schools, claiming the schools were "underutilized," it was revealed that TFA was working behind the scenes with a number of privately-managed, non-union charter school operators to open 52 new charter schools in Chicago over the next five years.

A Young TFA Recruit Goes to Washington DC

This is a letter from Jesse Hagopian, one of the leaders of Social Equality Educators (SEE) whose goal is to protect public schools from excessive high stakes testing and privatization. He is now a teacher at Garfield High School in Seattle. He was originally a TFA recruit in 2001. Unlike over 90% of TFA recruits, Jesse stayed with teaching. Here is an edited version of his story posted in the Seattle Times on November 15 2010. "

From 2001 to 2003, I "taught for America." After graduating from college, I headed for the Bronx, N.Y., where I underwent Teach for America's (TFA) "teacher boot camp." With just five sleepless weeks of on-the-job training teaching summer school to fourth-graders, I was given the stamp of approval and shipped off to Washington, D.C. At 21, I found myself in a public elementary school in the ghetto of South East Washington, D.C. — in a classroom with a hole in the ceiling that caused my room to flood, destroying the first American history project I ever assigned the students. One lasting memory came on my third day of teaching sixth grade. I had asked the students to bring a meaningful object from home for a show-and-tell activity. We gathered in a circle and the kids sat eagerly waiting to share their mementos. One after another, each and every hand came out of those crumpled brown lunch sacks, clutching a photo of a close family member — usually a dad or an uncle — who was either dead or in jail. TFA didn't prepare me to address these challenges. With only five weeks of training, it wasn't just that I was not equipped to differentiate instruction to meet the needs of students with a wide range of ability levels, create portfolios that accurately assessed student progress, or cultivate qualities of civic courage — it was that I didn't even know that these things were indispensable components of an effective education. If school districts truly want "excellence for all," they will need highly trained teachers who have a lasting commitment to the profession — not the revolving door that has come to be known as "Teach for Awhile."

Here is another 2011 TFA recruit who quit:

"I assumed that I would learn the concrete steps I needed to become a teacher during the training program. Instead I was immersed in a sea of jargon, buzzwords, and touchy-feely exercises. One memorable session began with directions for us to mentally "become" two of our students. After an elaborate, 32-slide reflection guide, we were asked to close the session with a "Vision Collage," for which we were handed pre-scripted reflections.

Typical instructional training included only the most basic framework; one guide to introducing new material told us to "emphasize key points, command student attention, actively involve students, and check for understanding." We were told that "uncommon techniques" included "setting high academic expectations, structuring and delivering your lessons, engaging students in your lessons, communicating high behavioral expectations, and building character and trust." Specific tips included "you provide the answer; the student repeats the answer". After observing and teaching alongside non-TFA teachers at my placement school, I can confidently say that these approaches are not "uncommon."

Once the school year began, I found myself teaching in a 500-student K–5 school with two other corps members and three TFA alumni. The school's other 30 teachers had gone through some version of a traditional teaching program, involving years of studying educational theory and practice, as well as extensive student teaching. As I got to know my new colleagues and some level of trust was established, it didn't take long to discover that TFA's five-week training model was a source of resentment for these teachers. Although I felt bad that TFA had created a system that caused a rift between corps members and traditional teachers, I didn't have much time to worry about that. The truth was, the five-week training program had not prepared me adequately.

I had few insights or resources to draw on when preteen boys decided recess would be the perfect opportunity to beat each other bloody, or when parents all but accused me of being racist during meetings.

I was not alone in my trouble with student behavior. Gary Rubinstein, a 1991 TFA alum and an outspoken critic of the organization, believes **TFA training sets teachers up for failure**: TFA teachers "don't know how to deal with discipline problems, because they've never dealt with a class with more than 10 kids—there's no way to deal with so many potential problems when they've never been practiced."

Although my group was assigned a veteran teacher during Institute, she did not have a substantive role in our training, and halfway through the summer she was implicated in the Atlanta Public Schools cheating scandal. Compared with the experiences of other Teach for America teachers, though, my placement and training were actually fairly lucky. I know more than one Religious Studies major who arrived in Atlanta ready to teach elementary school, only to be told that she was being reassigned to teach high-school mathematics.

When I was once asked to fill in for an absent colleague, one of her second-graders chose to confide in me about his abysmal home life. He explained, with wide and trusting eyes, that his mother's boyfriend enjoyed getting drunk, abusing the family, and shooting at the kids with a BB gun for fun.

I'd been at TFA training, about to head into this system, when the official report on the cheating scandal in the Atlanta Public Schools was released. My immediate reaction was shock that so many teachers could be complicit in something so outrageously dishonest. Midway through the school year, though, I came to understand exactly how it had happened. Atlanta Public Schools teachers spend countless hours teaching to exhaustion, spending their own money on classroom supplies, and buying basic necessities for their poorest students, only to be reminded constantly that their job performance will be judged according to test answers bubbled in by wobbly little fingers barely able to hold a pencil upright." http://www.theatlantic.com/education/archive/2013/09/i-quit-teach-for-america/279724/

Here are comments from another former TFA recruit:
"TFA is notoriously brutal, and the workload is intense. In my first five months as a teacher, I juggled TFA meetings, school meetings, data tracking, a masters degree, and a full-time position as a professional Wrangler of 14-Year-Olds. I was promptly relocated from an under-enrolled charter school to a school bursting at the seams with eighth graders who had already seen two English teachers come and go. I would be their third teacher in six months. There was, I found, a reason for that, one that was not entirely the students' fault.

The city where I taught lives and dies by a lowest-common-denominator standardized test, used primarily as a way to make everyone (administration, faculty, students) miserable. "We aren't teaching to the test," our administrators lied, "we are simply helping students do their very best." The material was lackluster, and despite my best attempts to jazz it up, students were apathetic at best. I couldn't blame them for that. I could, however, blame them for starting a fire in the back of my classroom. I could blame them for vandalizing my classroom. For breaking the door to my room, throwing objects at my head, and instructing me to "shut the fuck up, bitch" so often that I started playing a grim version of Teacher Bingo. I won if I heard it more than twice per period.

My principal, who visited my classroom exactly once, had some helpful advice for me. "Mr. _____ knows how to manage them!" she said, citing the 8th grade team leader, who had been teaching for 29 years, seven years longer than I had been alive. "Why don't you act more like him?" Well. Okay.

The panic attacks began in mid-January. My heart became a percussionist, my entrails contortionists, my thoughts sluggish swimmers in a thick, constant current of dread. I fantasized about crashing my car on purpose.

Already a vegan, I cut out sugar. I cut out gluten. Soon I cut out eating almost completely. I was caffeine and nerves, thrumming like a human electric wire. I didn't think I would ever be happy again.

I joined TFA to be part of the solution. In leaving, I became a part of the problem. TFA's model, predicated on a two-year commitment, is inherently flawed. High teacher turnover contributes to the disorganization, discipline problems, poor academic performance, and low morale of urban schools."
http://thebillfold.com/2012/09/teach-for-america-burned-me-out/

Teach for America also Traumatizes TFA Teachers

As traumatic as having a fake TFA teacher is for students, it can be equally traumatic for an unprepared teacher. The following account has been edited from Rethinking Schools, 2010 by Barbara Miner who interviewed an anonymous former TFA recruit: "One of my good friends (who will remain anonymous for reasons you'll discover below) recently suffered unbelievable physical, mental, and emotional abuse while teaching for an organization called Teach For America (TFA). She has since been diagnosed with Post Traumatic Stress Disorder, and her experience was by no means isolated—TFA cares little about the welfare of those who are trying to better the lives of others by signing up to teach. However, TFA has used every type of threat and scare tactic to prevent stories like this from getting out. Here is the story of this traumatized teacher:

"During my 5 week boot camp I was assigned to teach Algebra, despite my mathematical deficiencies (I got a D+ in the only math class I took in college). I was immediately thrown into a classroom teaching summer school. I hardly slept for those five weeks since every night was spent trying to learn the content and then figure out how to explain a concept I had just taught myself.

Upon going to my assigned region, I found headlines announcing that the school district had **laid off hundreds of employees just weeks before school started.**

Nervous about what this meant for me, I contacted TFA and was assured that I would have a job. **Hundreds of fully certified, experienced teachers were out of jobs, but me, an untrained novice teacher would have a position. It didn't make sense to me. I waited two weeks. School started. And I waited another two weeks. Then the phone call came – I was going to start teaching on Monday, but I would not find out what I would teach until I showed up.**

I did my best to prepare throughout the weekend. I crafted a lesson that could be adapted to multiple grade levels and subjects since the building houses 7-12 grades. But nothing could have prepared me for what I found when I arrived. When I arrived at the school on Monday morning and introduced myself, a man without introduction quickly walked me to a classroom and handed me a slip of paper stating which periods I would have students and that the title of the course was **"Ramp Up Lit 8".** I had no clue what that meant. But before I could ask questions, the man was gone and I was alone in the room.

I surveyed the space, wondering how in the world I was going to make it look and feel like a safe learning environment. The walls and desks were boldly tagged with sexually explicit messages, catching your eye the moment you walked into the room. Most of the cabinets had their handles torn off, and the fronts from all the drawers were missing. The classroom appeared to have been used as a storage room for the school, with half the space being filled with stacks of tables, desks, and chairs. Scattered through the furniture were shards of broken glass, presumably from a fight which had broken out earlier. I quickly went about setting the desks into rows – fixing the upturned furniture and sorting out the broken pieces. Wondering how long I had until students arrived, I realized the classroom was equipped with a clock that could not keep time and was without a phone. I was completely isolated. As students filed in, a nightmare began to unfold. Since school had started two weeks earlier, the students already had their routine down – they had disrespected substitutes and taken control of the room, **turning it into the war zone** I saw when I walked through the door. **I had no class roster,** so I had no way of knowing which students were actually supposed to be in my room or how many to expect. As though rehearsed, when asked for names, each student repeated the same false name and offered explicit commentary on me as a teacher ("I bet your boyfriend loves to f*** you up," "How often does he f*** you?", "I would top that") and what they were going to do to me ("You won't make it a week, we'll make sure of that," "We will run you out one way or another").

During fourth period, things escalated. Nearly 35 students marched into my room (only 24 were registered for the class), each daring me to try to take control. As I started trying to teach, a student slipped out of his desk and turned off the lights in the room. Having no windows, the room became pitch black. Screams and horrific noises immediately filled the air. I ran to the light switch to turn the lights on and discovered a large student standing in front of it that I had to physically fight to turn the lights back on. When I did, I found a scene of chaos.

Students had been throwing desks, punching each other, and had taken everything from my desk and thrown it on the floor. I was outraged and made that clear to my students. However, they were unaffected. Ten minutes later, the exact same scene played out. Unsure what to do, I announced that the rest of the class time would be spent in silence and that students would be dismissed to lunch five minutes late. The class erupted in laughter. There was no silent time. And though I stood in front of the door at the dismissal bell, the students charged out, shoving me out of the way and partially trampling me.

I was determined to make the next day better. I explained what had happened to the principal, and he advised me to **keep my cell phone on me at all times so if a problem arose I could quickly call for security.** Sure enough, a fight broke out the next day. I pulled out my phone, dialed security, and stepped away to break it up. Three large security officers reported to my room. Yet that did nothing but escalate the problem – my students rose to their feet and began yelling at the officers who soon left my room without resolving the conflict. As the door closed behind them, I realized my cell phone had been stolen. Once again I was without protection as the class erupted into chaos. Fortunately, the principal, walking by and hearing the riot within my room, walked in and immediately expelled a student who was throwing a desk.

My third day, I went to the 8th grade administrator's office and told him that I **needed to resign**. When I reported what had happened to TFA, they said they understood me taking the afternoon off but that I had to return to my classroom the next day. I was told that my contract did not make allowance for my requests and I needed to get back to work. Our conversation concluded with me saying I **wanted and needed out of Teach For America.**

I flew home the next day to be with my family. I spent days staring at the wall, terrified to leave my house. I could not handle being alone or being in the dark – I slept with the lights on and woke myself up screaming in response to nightmares of my students finding me. I was destroyed. I decided to write a blog post explaining to my family and friends in accurate detail what had happened. In an unbelievable disregard for my first amendment rights, **TFA threatened to sue me if I didn't remove the blog post immediately.** Suddenly I realized why my initial research of the organization seemed so positive. **TFA also informed me that since I had left the corps without a legitimate reason, I had 30 days to pay back all funds that I had received.** In addition, they said that since I had left the corps, they were in no way responsible for what happened to me and I was on my own. They concluded that I was to blame for my violent classroom. It has now been three weeks since I walked out of my classroom, but I still feel trapped in the situation. The nightmares are real. The constant fear is inhibiting. And I have found that I am not alone in my experience. As documented by Dr. Barbara Torre Veltri in her book, **Learning on Other People's Kids: Becoming a Teach For America Teacher,** hundreds and hundreds of Teach For America recruits have faced the same nightmare as me."

Former TFA Teachers Organize to Warn Potential Recruits of the Dangers

Many former TFA recruits are beginning to realize that they were deceived by TFA recruiters. They are beginning to fight back. . In July 2013 a group of former TFA recruits sponsored an event they called: "Organizing Resistance Against Teach for America and its Role in Privatization".
http://prospect.org/article/teach-americas-civil-war

Their mission is to "challenge the organization's centrality in the corporate-backed, market-driven, testing-oriented movement in urban education.

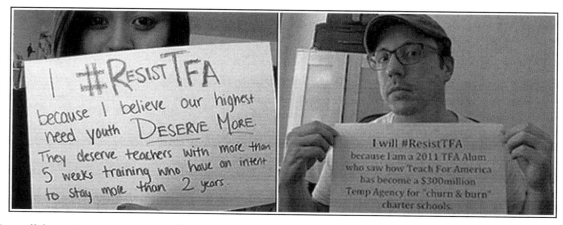

Possible outcomes range from a push for school districts not to contract with TFA to counter-recruitment of potential corps members away from the program. The Chicago summit builds on the gamut of student, teacher, and community resistance to TFA-aligned reform, including recent, successful push back against TFA itself. The summit is intended to be a kind of scaled-up roundtable with a political edge. The organizers emphasize that their purpose is not simply to call out TFA for inadequately training teachers—but to form a space for pushing back on the privatization movement that TFA anchors.

What is Next?

Now that we have seen the harmful effects of the TFA program on TFA teachers and their students, in the next section, we will look at the negative effect that billionaire funded teacher bashing has had on the morale of real teachers.

5.2 How Teacher Bashing has Harmed Real Teachers

> "Teachers are told their jobs depend on imposing Unhealthy ed reform policies. Some resist & are fired. Many retire. Many feign compliance & try to subvert. But many end up going along... with broken hearts"
> Dr. Mark Naison September 2014

In this section, we will look at the harmful effect that TFA and teacher bashing have had on real public school teachers.

How TFA Busts Teachers Unions... The "First Placement" Policy
The alliance between TFA and charter schools is cemented by an arrangement that few people know about outside of TFA. The teacher placement policy of TFA explicitly states in bold letters, **"It is our policy that corps members accept the first position offered to them."** The result of this policy is that TFA recruits have no bargaining position to negotiate wages or benefits, meaning that whatever offer a school makes, the TFA recruit must accept it. The "first placement" policy means that TFA can guarantee charter schools a constant supply of new teachers each year who have no choice but to work for wages and benefits far below those negotiated by the local teachers union at traditional public schools in the same area. While a first year salary for a teacher at a traditional unionized school in Chicago is approximately $45,000, the **starting salary at many of TFA's partner charter schools is nearly 30 percent less at $32,000.**

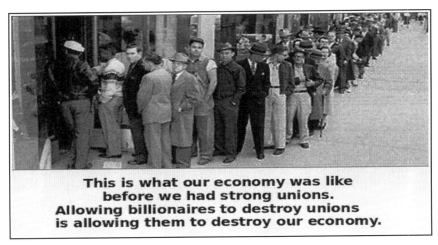

This is what our economy was like before we had strong unions. Allowing billionaires to destroy unions is allowing them to destroy our economy.

Churn and burn is the business model for these schools, and TFA provides a continuous supply of naive young workers who have no choice but to accept their lot. Furthermore, this constant churn of fake TFA teachers who possess zero experience can't possibly be good for the academic or social-emotional development of students who often have little stability in their lives.

"Through its partnerships with charter schools and its mandate that corps members take the first job they're offered, TFA is lowering wages, reducing benefits and worsening the working conditions of teachers. It is increasingly clear that the mission of the corporate class is to destroy teachers unions and remake the teaching profession into a temporary, low paying job. The corporate class is getting all of the help it needs from Teach For America."
Chad Sommer, Former TFA Recruit

Billionaire Attack on Public School Teachers has Severely Harmed the Teaching Profession

Billionaires have been bashing teachers ever since the 1980s. But it was not until the harsh mandatory punishments of No Child Left Behind that the constant stream of abuse has had a negative financial impact on teachers – as thousands of excellent experienced teachers were fired simply for serving at a school that taught low income students.

However, in addition to thousands of teachers being fired, thousands of additional experienced teachers have quit the teaching profession in disgust of all of the ed reform scams being inflicted on students in public schools. This has cause a major shift in the distribution of experienced teachers at our public schools.

Here is what the teacher experience distribution was like 30 years ago:

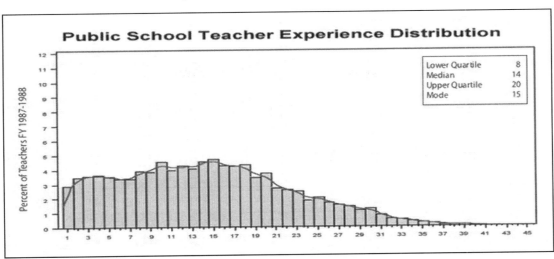

Note the even distribution in years of teaching experience with many more teachers having 10 years of experience than teachers having only one year.

Here is the uneven distribution in teaching experience after 30 years of billionaires constantly bashing public school teachers:

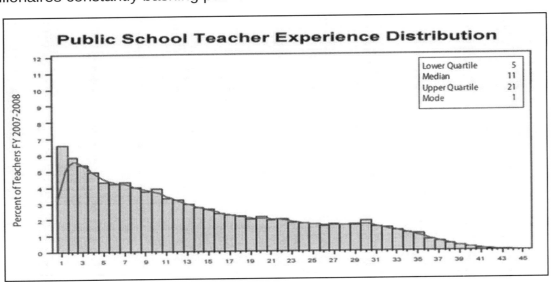

http://nctaf.org/wp-content/uploads/2012/01/NCTAF-Who-Will-Teach-Experience-Matters-2010-Report.pdf

Today, the largest category of teachers are first year teachers -with more than twice the percentage of first year teachers as there was 30 years ago. Every year, more teachers leave in disgust. Instead of helping teachers become better, attacking teachers has led to a huge drop in teacher satisfaction.

A 2010 National Teacher Survey by Met Life found that teacher satisfaction levels have plummeted since stifling Common Core mandates were imposed.
https://www.metlife.com/assets/cao/foundation/MetLife-Teacher-Survey-2012.pdf

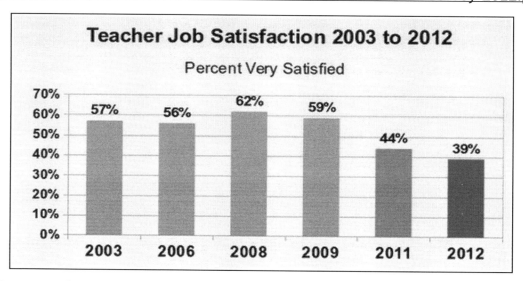

College Students are also Abandoning Teaching as a Profession

With hundreds of thousands of experienced teachers having been fired in the past five years, and Congress deciding that a person with five weeks of training is now "highly qualified," it should come as no surprise that college students are reluctant to train for a career as a teacher. For example, in fall 2004, there were 18,685 students enrolled as education majors at the 14 schools in the Pennsylvania State System of Higher Education. Ten years later, that number had dropped a third to 12,569. It is even worse in California where enrollments in teacher preparation programs have declined dramatically. According to a 2013 report prepared for the California Commission on Teacher Credentialing, 26,446 students were enrolled in teacher preparation programs in 2011-12 – a 66 percent decline from a decade earlier, when 77,700 students were enrolled.

The declining enrollments are echoed by similarly declining numbers of teaching credentials. At the California State University system, only 5,787 credentials were issued in 2011-12 to students in its teacher preparation programs, down from 13,933 in 2003-04. Over the past five years, the teaching profession in California has been devastated by layoffs; some 26,000 teachers lost their jobs as a result of the state's budget crisis. With all of these experienced teachers available, it is very difficult for new teachers coming out of college to even find their first teaching job.

http://edsource.org/2013/enrollment-in-teacher-preparation-programs-plummets-2/63661#.VLYTGHWx3UY

Despite the huge decline in college students enrolling in Education Teacher Prep programs in Pennsylvania and California, and despite the huge numbers of laid off experienced teachers in both States, California and Pennsylvania are among the "leaders" in charter schools, charter school corruption and TFA recruits.

Nine States with the most TFA Teachers
http://nepc.colorado.edu/publication/teach-f0r-america-return

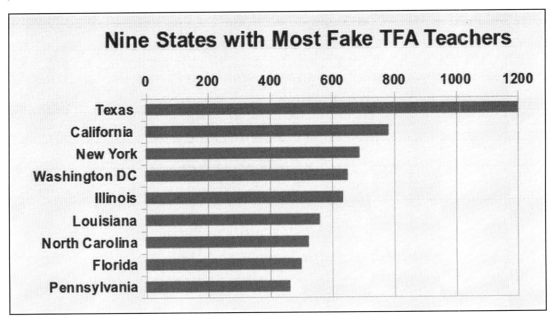

Teacher Turnover TFA Fake Teachers versus Real Teachers

A 2010 study found that "more than 50% of TFA teachers leave after two years and more than 80% leave after three years." By comparison, over 60% of all real teachers - who typically have five years of training – leave after 5 years with most of the remainder staying for more than 10 years. The following chart shows how long TFA recruits remain in the teaching profession.
http://www.greatlakescenter.org/docs/Policy_Briefs/Heilig_TeachForAmerica.pdf

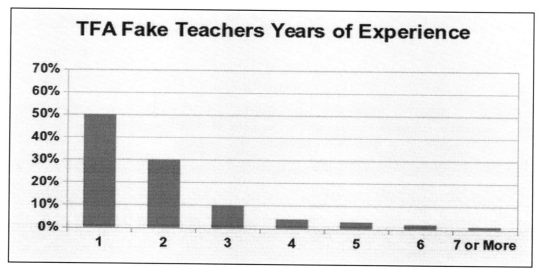

By contrast, this is the experience distribution of real public school teachers using the same scale:

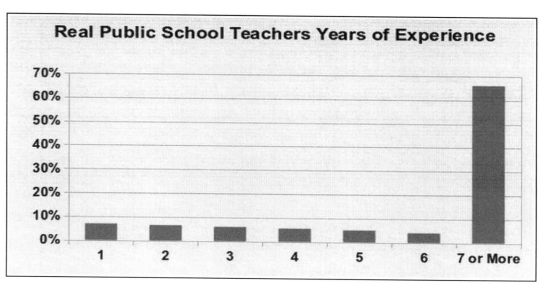

As a result of the huge turnover of TFA teachers at charter schools, students at TFA fed charter schools are taught by an endless stream of first-year teachers. These students and their TFA fake teachers are doomed to failure just so Wendy Kopp can make a few hundred million dollars every year.

The Real Cost of Fake TFA Teachers

In 2007, the National Commission on Teaching and Learning issued a report concluding that Teacher Turnover, including the cost of training new teachers is extremely expensive for school districts – costing over $7 billion per year. This report found that hiring well-prepared teachers reduced first year attrition by 50 percent. Here is a quote from this report:

"Well-prepared teachers possess strong content knowledge; they understand how students learn and demonstrate the teaching skills necessary to help all students meet high standards; they can use a variety of assessment strategies to diagnose student learning needs; and they can reflect on their practices to improve instruction in collaboration with their colleagues."

http://nctaf.org/wp-content/uploads/2012/01/NCTAF-Cost-of-Teacher-Turnover-2007-policy-brief.pdf

Teacher Salaries are Much Lower than Other Professions

Another reason teachers suffer from a much higher turnover than other professions, besides the fact that they are being attacked by billionaires is that are among the lowest paid of all professions.

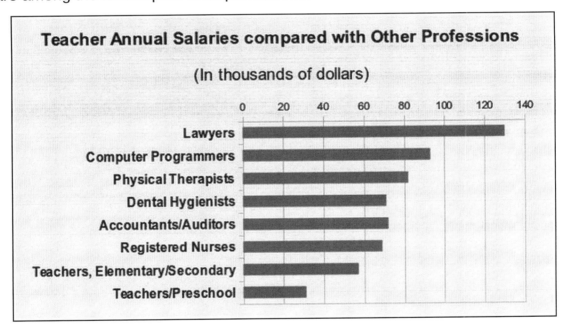

Source: Bureau of Labor Statistics Occupation Employment Statistics

http://www.bls.gov/news.release/pdf/ocwage.pdf

Class Sizes Skyrocket as School Funding Disappears

Another problem inflicted on teachers and students due to the billionaire attack on our schools is huge increases in class sizes. In 1980, at the beginning of the attack on teachers under Reagan, Washington State was 11th in the nation in school funding – spending about 6 cents out of every dollar in income in our State on public schools. By 2000, our state fell down to the national average in spending on public schools which is about 5% of income. By 2012, Washington fell to 47th in the nation in school funding at 4% of state income. As a result, class sizes in Washington state are now among the most overcrowded in the nation. Many math teachers have more than 40 kids per class with 5 classes per day – for a total of 200 kids per day. Is it any wonder our kids are having trouble learning math?

Many math teachers now have more than 40 students per class
With 5 periods per day this is more than 200 students per day.

Meanwhile, Washington state legislators have increased tax breaks for wealthy multinational corporations like Microsoft by more than ten billion dollars per year. The biggest winner of the tax exemption scam is none other than tax evader Bill Gates – who robs of schools of more than one billion dollars per year by refusing to pay his fair share of state taxes.

The Cost of Replacing Exhausted Demoralized Teachers is much Higher than Respecting the Teachers we have

In January 2014, the National Education Policy Center (NEPC) published a study on TFA called **TFA A Return to the Evidence.** They analyzed the total cost of hiring TFA recruits who constantly quit and had to be replaced versus the total cost of hiring and retaining real teachers. The report found that unprepared fake TFA teachers cost school districts four times as much over the long run as real teachers. To be exact, the total cost of the two-year commitment from a TFA recruit can easily exceed $70,000 when including professional development, training and other costs.

Cost Comparison of 100 TFA Teachers versus 100 Real Teachers after 5 years

Due to the high turnover of TFA teachers, the re-occurring costs of hiring 100 TFA recruits is quite high for local school districts—about $6 million more than hiring 100 Non-TFA teachers.

	TFA	Non-TFA
TFA overhead	$5,098,000	0
Salary and Attrition Costs	$1,080,000	$750,000
PD, Mentoring, and Education	$2,016,000	$1,400,000
Total cost to Society after 5 years	$8,194,000	$2,150,000

http://nepc.colorado.edu/publication/teach-f0r-america-return

Real Teachers are Slowly Dying

Susan DuFresne, a real teacher in Washington, wrote an article about her emotionally exhausting life as a teacher. Susan writes:

"What will happen to us as teachers, parents, students, and democracy as we continue to struggle in our mandated race to the top of corporate education reform? As teachers, we are being exploited by the corporate reformers who profit from their failing experiments – and our families are left with nothing but ghosts of who we once were…..It is only December, and yet I I have more second thoughts about continuing my profession and feel closer to succumbing to burn-out than ever before. From the movie, Beyond the Edge: Above 26,000 feet is what we call the death zone…the death zone because you are slowly dying. Just as the mountain above 26,000 feet is uninhabitable – classrooms in public schools across the country have become uninhabitable for human beings – teachers and students alike. With each step further into the world of corporate reform, I become more confused about why I chose this profession and I recognize that a small part of me is dying slowly – as is a small part of each child. Where we once had art, music, creativity, joy, love, learning through play, and autonomy – many of us now have endless testing and data collection, data entry, data analysis, and meetings upon meetings about data. The corporate reformers have sucked the life out of teaching and learning. The real purpose of education is lost in a blizzard of data – numbers entered onto a rubric to become bits of data – trillions of 0's and 1's about each child are flying at high speed, tracked and collecting in data banks like so many feet of snow to be mined for corporate profits – icy cold they create systems of punishment as dangerous crevices – an abyss of corporate created failure – a place devoid of all humanity for children and teachers to try to traverse."

http://www.livingindialogue.com/beyond-edge-climbing-mt-edreform/

Sandra Korn, public school graduate who was a senior at Harvard College in 2013 explained why she was opposed to Teach for America:

"It has become increasingly clear to anyone who thinks critically about teaching that there's something off with TFA's model. After all, TFA alumni repeatedly describe their stints in the American public education system as some of the hardest two years of their lives. Doesn't it bother you to imagine under-trained 22-year-olds standing in front of a crowded classroom and struggling through every class period? However, unpreparedness pales in comparison to the much larger problem with TFA: TFA undermines the American public education system from the very foundation by urging the replacement of experienced career teachers with a neoliberal model of interchangeable educators and standardized testing." http://www.huffingtonpost.com/sandra-korn/why-i-said-no-to-teach-for-america_b_4151764.html

Teachers are Actually Dying due to Attacks by Fake Politicians

No politician in the nation has been more open about his hatred of teachers and their teachers union than billionaire backed Scott Walker. Scott Walker became governor of Wisconsin thanks to millions in hidden money from the billionaire Koch brothers. His first act was governor was to cut funding for public schools.

Gutting of school funding by billionaire backed political hacks like Walker can be extremely upsetting to teachers who devote their lives to helping children. Recently, teachers have committed suicide in several states. Here is one example from Wisconsin.

Wisconsin Teacher in Apparent Suicide, "Distraught" Over Walker's Cuts
By Matthew Rothschild, March 17, 2011 Progressive.org
"Jeri-Lynn Betts, an early childhood teacher in the Watertown, Wisconsin, school district, died on March 8 of an apparent suicide. A colleague says she was "very distraught" over Gov. Scott Walker's attacks on public sector workers and public education. Betts, 56, was a dedicated teacher who was admired in the Watertown community. "She was an amazing person," says the Rev. Terry Larson of the Immanuel Evangelical Lutheran Church in Watertown, where she was a member. "She really put her heart and soul in her work," adds Larson. "She was one of the good guys," says Karen Stefonek, who used to teach with Betts. "She was very, very dedicated, and worked so well with the little special needs children. She just was very, very good with them, and very well respected in the district." In his budget, Walker proposed taking $900 million out of the public schools. "She was definitely very distraught about it," said one of her co-workers, who requested anonymity. " Walker's policies have "shredded the morale of teachers," said Wisconsin State Assemblywoman Sondy Pope-Roberts on March 16. "The cuts to schools districts are going to be drastic."

A former TFA teacher speaks out against TFA

This is what former TFA teacher Gary Rubeinstein said about why he opposed Teach for America: "The organization of TFA is a bit like a pyramid scheme. There are a bunch of VPs who are making a lot of money for a non-profit, certainly six figures. Then there are the majority of staffers, people who work in recruitment, teacher 'effectiveness', even the alumni team, IT, etc., who make much less. But regardless of the status of the TFA staffer, they all have one thing in common: They are all accessories to a $300 million annual fraud funded, in part, by taxpayers, and which has, I'm sorry to say, contributed to the weakening of the public school system which has, in turn, hurt innocent kids and, yes, their hard working teachers. http://garyrubinstein.teachforus.org/2013/11/15/my-advice-to-tfa-staffers-quit-for-america/

This is Gary's advice to TFA recruits:
"TFA is an organization that thrives on greed, deception, and fear. The deception, though, is the thing that is more relevant to you. Part of the deception is that they promote a very oversimplified view of their success. They would have you believe that a good percent of the new CMs [corps members] are way better than the 'average' teacher, mainly because of the high expectations of the CM. They may even say this is aided by the new high expectations of the fancy new common core standards.

Unfortunately, this oversimplified version of reality will lead you to struggle very much your first year, and to fail to be the teacher your students deserve."
https://garyrubinstein.wordpress.com/2014/06/12/advice-to-the-2014-tfa-corps-members/

What will happen to our nation if billionaires succeed in destroying our teachers and their unions?

Simply put, breaking teachers' unions is at the top of the billionaires agenda.

The guy holding the sign About May 1933 must be A History Teacher. He gets an A for Accuracy. The last time there Was this big of an attack On unions was May 1933 When Hitler abolished All unions in Germany. Once unions were gone, Hitler (backed by billionaires) was able to form A Military Dictatorship.

Unions not only protect the rights of teachers, they protect the rights of all of us. Here is what happened after Hitler banned all unions and was able to get complete control over the billionaire backed media and subject the people with massive hate filled propaganda campaigns.

It has always been the tactic of the wealthy few, in order to control others, To monopolize the media, demonize those who oppose them, Divide people against each other and destroy their unions. Hitler disbanded all unions in Germany on May 2, 1933

What is Next?

In the next section, we will at another extremely unfair weapon of mass deception being used by billionaires and their hacks to fire teachers called Value Added Modeling (VAM).

5.3 VAM Scam... Firing Teachers based on Student Test Scores

> Firing teachers based on student test scores
> Is like firing teachers based on a coin toss.
> How would you like it if you could be fired
> Based on a coin toss... Heads you stay. Tails you go!

In this article, we will look at a weapon of mass deception called Value Added Modeling – which is one of the favorite scams being used by billionaires to unfairly rate and then fire teachers. The reason this topic is so important is that Arne Duncan has insisted on using this method to evaluate and fire teachers all across America – and many states are already using VAM to fire teachers!

What is Value Added Modeling (VAM)?
The idea behind value added modeling is that you add up all of the high stakes test scores of a teachers students and compare them to their previous year's test scores. Teachers whose students gained the most are rated as good teachers (they added value to their students). Teachers whose students gained the least are rated bad teachers and are fired.

There are numerous flaws with the using VAM to fire teachers:
First, VAM scores are unfair to teachers working with students from lower income families. Students from higher income homes gain the most on high stakes tests because they did not have to deal with outside problems like living in a homeless shelter. So VAM results in firing teachers in high poverty schools.
Second, VAM scores are not reliable. Because students assigned to any given teacher have backgrounds that vary greatly from year to year, the value added number assigned to a teacher varies greatly from year to year. A teacher rated as one of the best one year under VAM is likely to be rated one of the worst teachers the next year.
Third, VAM scores are not an accurate measure of student learning. High stakes multiple choice tests only measure very low levels of knowledge – like rote memorization of useless facts – rather than a true ability to solve problems.
Fourth, VAM scores vary dramatically depending on the test given to the students. Value added modeling assumes that the students were given a fair test that gave them a fair chance of passing the test. As we have shown in previous articles, Common Core tests are not fair in that they were deliberately designed to fail two thirds of American students even though American students, when adjusted for poverty, do better than any other students in the world.
Fifth, many teachers teach subjects that cannot be measured by a test. For example, it is impossible to measure a music teacher or an art teacher based upon student test scores on music and art. This does not matter that much to Ed Reformers since they want to get rid of music and art anyway.

Sixth, more than 80 research studies have concluded that using VAM to fire teachers is unfair and unreliable.

To better understand the ridiculousness of Value Added Modeling, we will take a brief look at all six of these problems.

#1... VAM scores are unfair to teachers working with students from lower income families.

Students from higher income homes gain the most on high stakes tests because they did not have to deal with outside problems like living in a homeless shelter. So the VAM model results in firing teachers who work in high poverty schools.

What high stakes tests really measure is the income level of the student

"You can not fire your way to Finland."
Dr. Linda Darling-Hammond, 2011

The reason we in the US cannot fire our way to the high test scores in Finland is because Finland has a very low child poverty rate – which is why their students have such high test scores. The only reliable way to raise student test scores in the United States to the level of Finland would be to raise the employment rate among the parents of students in the US and thereby lower the child poverty rate in the US.

Previously, we showed a strong relationship between child poverty and student test performance. This is one of the many charts showing that child poverty is strongly related to student test performance.

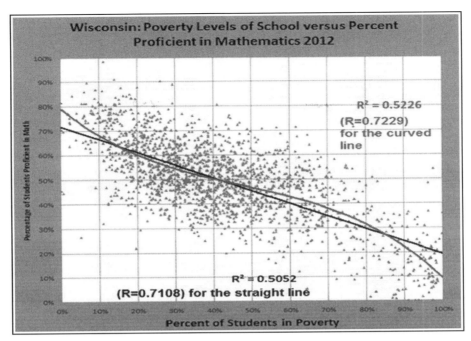

Student test scores are also strongly influenced by school attendance, student health, family mobility, and the influence of neighborhood peers and classmates who may be relatively more or less advantaged.

#2... VAM scores are extremely unreliable

If value added test scores were reliable, we would expect that teachers who have high scores one year would have high scores the next year. In other words, the good teachers would be good teachers from year to year and the bad teachers would be bad teachers from year to year. But this is not what actually happens. Good teachers one year, according to VAM, could be bad teachers the next year. VAM is no better than a coin toss at predicting which teachers are the good teachers. Teachers rated as being in the top third of all teachers one year are often in the bottom third the next year. You can be rated Teacher of the Year one year and be out of a job the next. Imagine if your job evaluation was dependent on the toss of a coin! Heads you stay. Tails you go.

Here is a quote from one teacher in Houston Texas about their experience with three years of VAM evaluations: "I do what I do every year. I teach the way I teach every year. My first year got me pats on the back; my second year got me kicked in the backside. And for year three, my scores were off the charts. I got a huge bonus, and now I am in the top quartile of all the English teachers. What did I do differently? I have no clue." (Amrein- Beardsley & Collins, 2012, p. 15)

Because students assigned to any given teacher have backgrounds that vary greatly from year to year, the value added numbers assigned to teachers varies greatly from year to year. A teacher rated as one of the best one year under VAM is very likely to be rated one of the worst teachers the next year. McCaffrey (2009) did a study of several schools in Florida dividing teachers into five equal groups based on their VAM scores. He found that teachers with the Lowest VAM Scores One Year were likely to have much higher VAM scores the next year

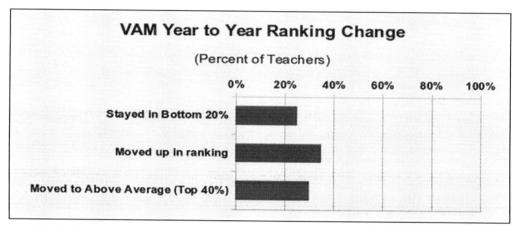

Source: McCaffrey, D. F., Sass, T. R., Lockwood, J. R., & Mihaly, K. (2009). The intertemporal variability of teacher effect estimates. Education Finance and Policy, 4(4), 572–606.

Another study found that across five large urban districts, among teachers who were ranked in the top 20 percent of effectiveness in the first year, fewer than a third were in that top group the next year, and another third moved all the way down to the bottom 40 percent.

Sadly, this problem with VAM being grossly unreliable led to the tragic death of a highly respected 39 year old teacher in the Los Angeles School District. A well liked 5th Grade Teacher committed suicide in 2010 after the Los Angeles Times published the VAM scores of all of the teachers in Los Angeles. This teacher taught at an elementary school with a very high percentage of low income children. Over 60% of the children were Spanish speaking English Language learners. VAM does not make any adjustments for the fact that the students cannot speak English and therefore do poorly on tests that are only printed in English. Naturally, only 5 of 35 teachers were rates by VAM as "average."

The teacher, Mr. Ruelas, had won many awards for being able to work in a bilingual manner to coach and help the children in his classes. But the Los Angeles Times failed to do the research needed to understand that VAM is a SCAM. They published the VAM scores as if they really met something. In our opinion, the Los Angeles Times editors should be prosecuted for reckless manslaughter.

http://www.huffingtonpost.com/2010/09/28/rigoberto-ruelas-suicide-_n_742073.html

#3... VAM scores are not an accurate measure of student learning
High stakes testing is an inaccurate measure of the knowledge of students because it rates them based on how they did on a single day and on a single test rather than on how they did during a full year of work and on many different kinds of assessment methods. Some students who actually learned more during the year may do poorly on multiple choice tests simply because they are bad at taking high stakes tests (called test anxiety). This is why high stakes tests are an inaccurate way of measuring the knowledge of students or the value of teachers.

#4... VAM scores vary dramatically depending on the test given to the students and even the day the test is given to students.
Value added modeling assumes that the students were given a fair test that gave them a fair chance of passing the test. As we have shown in previous articles, Common Core tests are not fair in that they were deliberately designed to fail two thirds of American students even though American students, when adjusted for poverty, do better than any other students in the world.

#5... Many teachers teach subjects that cannot be measured by a test
For example, it is impossible to measure a music teacher or an art teacher based upon student test scores on music and art. This does not matter that much to Ed Reformers since they want to get rid of music and art anyway.

#6... More than 80 research studies have concluded that using VAM to fire teachers is unfair and unreliable
More than 80 studies have been done on using the VAM method to evaluate teachers. They all found that VAM is not a consistent or reliable way to measure teacher performance. Here is a link to a list of these studies.
http://vamboozled.com/recommended-reading/value-added-models/

For example, in 2013, Edward Haertel, a Stanford University researcher, published a detailed report on the lack of reliability of using student test scores to evaluate teachers. http://www.ets.org/Media/Research/pdf/PICANG14.pdf

He concluded that VAM scores were worse than bad. Here is a quote from page 23 of his study: "My first conclusion should come as no surprise: Teacher VAM scores should emphatically not be included as a substantial factor with a fixed weight in consequential teacher personnel decisions. The information they provide is simply not good enough to use in that way. It is not just that the information is noisy. Much more serious is the fact that the scores may be systematically biased for some teachers and against others…High-stakes uses of teacher VAM scores could easily have additional negative consequences for children's education. These include increased pressure to teach to the test, more competition and less cooperation among the teachers within a school, and resentment or avoidance of students who do not score well. In the most successful schools, teachers work together effectively. If teachers are placed in competition with one another for bonuses or even future employment, their collaborative arrangements for the benefit of individual students as well as the supportive peer and mentoring relationships that help beginning teachers learn to teach better may suffer."

A 2010 study by the Economic Policy Institute concluded that student standardized test scores are not reliable indicators of how effective any teacher is in the classroom. The authors of the study, called, "Problems with the Use of Student Test Scores to Evaluate Teachers," included four former presidents of the American Educational Research Association; two former presidents of the National Council on Measurement in Education; the current and two former chairs of the Board of Testing and Assessment of the National Research Council of the National Academy of Sciences; the president-elect of the Association for Public Policy Analysis and Management; the former director of the Educational Testing Service's Policy Information Center; a former associate director of the National Assessment of Educational Progress; a former assistant U.S. secretary of education; a member of the National Assessment Governing Board; and the vice president, a former president, and three other members of the National Academy of Education.
http://epi.3cdn.net/724cd9a1eb91c40ff0_hwm6iij90.pdf

The Board on Testing and Assessment of the National Research Council of the National Academy of Sciences has stated: "VAM estimates of teacher effectiveness should not be used to make operational decisions because such estimates are far too unstable to be considered fair or reliable."

2014 American Statistical Association (ASA) Slams VAM
In 2014, the American Statistical Association issued a statement warning that value-added-measurement VAM) is fraught with error, inaccurate, and unstable. For example, the ratings may change if a different test is used.

The ASA report said: "Ranking teachers by their VAM scores can have unintended consequences that reduce quality." American Statistical Association. (2014). ASA Statement on Using Value-Added Models for Educational Assessment. http://www.amstat.org/policy/pdfs/ASA_VAM_Statement.pdf

Fair Teacher Evaluation
There are other more reliable ways to measure classroom performance. One of the most reliable ways is an actual classroom observation performed by trained administrators. Nearly all teachers are subject to this kind of annual evaluation which is used to identify teachers in the greatest need of improvement.

The Real Reason for Value Added Modeling
Given the overwhelming evidence against using Value Added Modeling to fire teachers, why does Arne Duncan still want to use VAM to evaluate and fire teachers? It is because the goal of VAM is not to fairly evaluate teachers. It is to fire as many teachers as possible in order to create chaos in our public schools and thereby accelerate the movement from public schools to private schools.

Teachers Deserve Fairness

Every classroom should have a well-educated, professional teacher, and every public school district should recruit, prepare and retain teachers who are qualified to do the job. The problem comes in unfairly evaluating and firing teachers rather than helping teachers. Our students and teachers deserve an evaluation system that is fair and accurate. Diane Ravitch is one of our nation's leading educational researchers. Here is what she has to say about using high stakes testing to fire teachers: "No other nation in the world has inflicted so many changes or imposed so many mandates on its teachers and public schools as we have in the past dozen years. No other nation tests every student every year as we do. Our students are the most over-tested in the world. No other nation—at least no high-performing nation—judges the quality of teachers by the test scores of their students. Most researchers agree that this methodology is fundamentally flawed, that it is inaccurate, unreliable, and unstable."

http://www.washingtonpost.com/blogs/answer-sheet/wp/2014/01/18/everything-you-need-to-know-about-common-core-ravitch/

What is Next?

In the next article, we will look at another weapon of mass deception used by billionaires to attack public school teachers. This is the false claim that a teacher having an advanced degree in education has no benefit for helping children in the classroom.

5.4 If you can't measure it, does it still exist?
Why Advanced Degrees in Education still matter.

> If you can not measure something,
> it does not mean it does not exist.
> Instead, it may means that you need to
> Find a better measuring tool.

In the previous section, we look at an unreliable method of using student test scores to rate teachers. We called this method the VAM SCAM because VAM scores varied so wildly that they are no better than a random coin toss. In this article, we will look at how billionaires use the VAM SCAM as the basis for one of the most subtle but vicious attacks on public school teachers... the claim made frequently by billionaires and their political hacks that teacher experience and training have no benefit for student performance. Billionaires would like us to believe that for a teacher to get a Masters Degree in Education has no benefit to their students. To get this Master's Degree, a Teacher has to complete 2 to 3 years of additional studies in learning and child development beyond the 5 years of training required to get their original teachers certificate. If it is really true that an advanced degree in education makes no difference in teacher effectiveness, then perhaps parents should send their kids to a private for profit charter school with a fake TFA teacher – or sit them in front of a computer all day long.

Billionaires Use the VAM SCAM to Claim that Teachers with a Masters Degree in Education Do Not Help Student Performance

Because Bill Gates would like to replace real teachers with computers and fake TFA teachers, he would like us to believe that teacher training and experience have no effect on student performance. So he has spent millions of dollars hiring lots of fake researchers who use unreliable student test scores to assign unreliable VAM ratings to teachers. Since VAM scores vary as wildly as a random coin toss, no relationship can ever been shown between VAM scores and anything. But this does not mean that teacher training and experience do not matter. All it really means is that VAM scores are merely random numbers.

Here is how the first part of the VAM SCAM works:

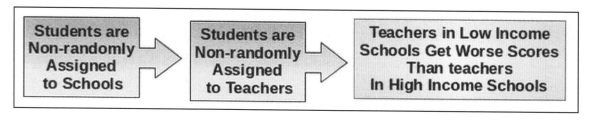

The reason students are not randomly assigned to schools is that some schools have a much higher poverty rate than other schools. Some kids live in rich communities with rich school districts while other kids live in poor communities with poor school districts. The reason that, even in low poverty schools, students are not randomly assigned to teachers is that some children have more difficult learning and behavioral problems than other children. These difficult children are often deliberately assigned to the most experienced and highly trained teachers in the school in an effort to help the children catch up. If you are an administrator with a group of struggling children, the last thing you would want to do is assign them to a rookie teacher. However, even with the best teachers in the school, most struggling children will continue to struggle and not learn as much as the students who do not have learning or behavioral problems. So by being assigned to a group of low income and/or learning challenged students, a teacher will automatically get a lower score than a teacher who is given average or above average students.

But with VAM, it gets worse. Because the scores of students are compared to their previous test scores or the test scores of the teachers previous year of students, the random variability of students from year to year makes it impossible to predict any teachers VAM scores.

Here is how the second part of the VAM SCAM works:

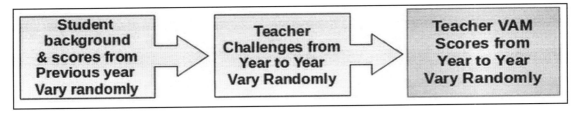

Teachers have no control over the test scores their students had the previous year. Nor do teachers have control over the previous learning experience of students. Teachers do not even have any control over which challenging students will be assigned to their class in any given year. Students are not like cars or computers. Students vary dramatically in their backgrounds and challenges. It is therefore not surprising that a teachers VAM score will vary randomly from year to year.

But because VAM scores are being used to unfairly rate and fire even highly trained and highly experienced teachers, we will provide an example of how VAM scores can adversely effect an actual teacher due to circumstances beyond the teachers control. A friend of ours was one of the most highly trained and most experienced Fifth Grade teachers at a suburban school district near Seattle Washington. She had more than 20 years of teaching experience and held a PHD in child development. The previous year, the local PTA had honored this teacher with the "Teacher of the Year" award for the entire school district.

Parents in this school district asked that their children be assigned to this teacher. However, this relatively affluent elementary school also had a small group of boys who had challenging behavioral problems. The principal of the elementary school rightly assigned these boys to his most experienced and highly trained teacher – hoping she would be able to help these boys in their final year of elementary school. The teacher was able to help some of these boys. But the boys were so disruptive to the rest of the class that the learning experience of her other children was adversely affected.

Had this been a private for profit charter school, the boys would have simply been expelled from the school. However, in Washington State, we have a State Constitution that requires public schools to provide an education for "ALL CHILDREN." Our State Supreme Court has repeatedly ruled that the word ALL means ALL. Public schools are not only required to provide an education for the kids that are easy to teach. They are required to provide an education for all children – including the children who have behavioral problems and are difficult to teach. So the trouble making boys spent lots of time talking with the principal and the school counselor. But they were not kicked out of the school. Amazingly, many of these boys went on to do well in Middle School – and we give a lot of credit to this teacher for not giving up on these boys. But she did tell us it was the **"hardest year of her entire teaching career."**

The point of this story is that this teacher would not get credit under VAM for the future improvement of these boys in Middle School. That credit would unfairly go to some middle school teacher. Instead, under VAM, this teacher would be unfairly punished for the fact that the total scores of all of her students in her class likely declined from the previous year due to the challenging and disruptive boys.

Thankfully, Washington State does not yet use VAM scores. Parents and teachers have fought and won major battles in the legislature to prevent Arne Duncan from forcing VAM on our State. Arne Duncan responded in July 2014 by revoking our State's NCLB waiver – reducing federal funding for our schools by $50 million and requiring that every parent in every school district in our State be send a letter in August 2014 telling parents that their beloved public schools are all failures – simply because our legislature refused to cave into the VAM SCAM.

Billionaires Pay Fake Researchers to Write Fake Studies with Faulty Conclusions Based on the VAM SCAM
To read some of these fake studies, enter this phrase in a search engine, "Teachers Master's Degree in Education, Teacher Effectiveness and Student Test Performance." You will get the following studies:

One of the first result that comes up is an Education Next article: The Mystery of Good Teaching by Dan Goldhaber. http://educationnext.org/the-mystery-of-good-teaching/

Dan's Biography claims he is an expert on Value Added Modeling. This is strange because he does not appear to know that Value Added Modeling has been shown to be a complete scam. Nevertheless, Dan uses Value Added Modeling to claim that neither teacher experience or getting an advanced degree has been shown to improve student performance. This article was funded by the Urban Institute in Washington, D.C.

Do either the Urban Institute or Education Next get funding from the Gates Foundation?

The answer is yes. In July 2013, Harvard got $557,168 to support Education Next promotion of Common Core. This was a followup to $500,000 in March 2011 for Education Next to promote Common Core. The Urban Institute got nearly $15 million to promote Common Core. In total, Bill Gates paid more than $16 million dollars to convince us that teacher experience and training make no difference in the performance of students. Neither the Urban Institute website, Education Next or the author of the fake study disclosed the fact that all of them are working for Bill Gates. In fact, a review of Education Next covers indicates it is nothing but a cheer leader for the billionaire takeover of our public schools – including promoting Online schools despite the fact that they have only a 20% graduation rate:

Another article at the top of the search engine results is also from Education Next. This one is called "The Education School Masters Degree Factory" by Paul Peterson. Paul concluded based on VAM scores that having a Masters degree did not result in higher student test scores. Paul has a PHD in Political Science from the University of Chicago. Naturally, Paul is a big supporter of charter schools and everything else Bill Gates likes.
http://educationnext.org/the-education-school-masters-degree-factory/

The next article was by the Center for Education Compensation Reform. It also used VAM scores to conclude that neither teacher experience or training improve student test scores. This is a government run website with the Department of Education. Most of the staff at the US Department of Education used to work for Bill Gates at the Gates Foundation.
http://cecr.ed.gov/guides/researchSyntheses/Research%20Synthesis_Q%20A2.pdf

The next article was a 2011 September article called Measuring Teacher Effectiveness by Marcus Winters with the Manhattan Institute. The Manhattan Institute got four grants totaling more than $300,000 from the Gates Foundation. Naturally, this article also used Value Added Modeling (VAM) to conclude that teacher training and experience did not improve student test scores.
http://www.manhattan-institute.org/html/ib_10.htm

The next article was by John Schacter with the Milken Family Foundation called Teacher Performance Based Accountability. This was the first study not connected to the Gates Foundation. But that name "Milken" seems to ring a bell. Turns out this is the same billionaire Milken who went to jail for committing fraud in the junk bond market. He later founded K12 INC (See chapter 4 for the horrific story of this outfit). Naturally, this report also used Value Added Modeling and concluded that teacher training and experience are not relevant to student performance on tests.

There are dozens more of these fake studies. But hopefully you can see the pattern. Certainly teacher experience and training do matter to student learning. However, what matters cannot be measured by Value Added Modeling any more than one can determine the quality of a doctor based upon flipping coins in the waiting room.

If VAM is a SCAM, how can we measure teacher effectiveness?
As we have shown in the last section and in previous chapters, the problem with high stakes testing in general and VAM in particular is that student test scores measure the wealth of the students parents. Because students in any class vary from year to year, it is impossible to show a relationship between student test scores and teacher effectiveness. But student test scores are only one of many ways to evaluate teacher effectiveness.

One hundred years ago, the field of Physics went through a case of arrested development due to a theory called Logical Positivism. The claim back then was that "If you can not measure something, it doesn't exist." We have since realized that **if you can not measure something, then you need to find a better measuring tool.** In the case of Physics, the better measuring tool turned out to be Chaos Theory and Fractal Analysis. The math is more complicated, but the results are more real and it allows us to study complex processes (such as real weather) which "did not exist" in traditional Newtonian physics.

We have a similar problem today in the field of education. The claim is that there is no benefit in teachers getting advanced degrees because these advanced degrees do not seem to translate into better student performance on high stakes standardized tests. If there is no measurable gain in student test performance, why should teachers with advanced degrees be paid more than those without? The problem once again lies in the measuring tool. Student performance is almost always measured in terms of paper and pencil or computerized standardized multiple choice tests.

Unfortunately, standardized tests tend to focus on lower levels of learning (such as content) rather than higher levels of learning (such as processes). Seven years ago, one of us (David Spring) had the opportunity to co-author a study at the University of Washington on this exact issue. Our study found that **standardized tests were the least accurate way of measuring higher levels of student learning** (Yeary, Herronkohl & Spring, 2007).

The following are four paragraphs from the Introduction and Conclusion of that 50 page study: "An important concern of scientific research, in any field, is measurement of the object or question one is trying to understand. Standardized objective measurement, in turn, requires the development of measurement tools that can provide the data needed to help one build theoretical models and test competing theories derived from those models. Just as theories are built upon data, data relies upon accurate measurement tools.

Recently, there has been an increased interest in how to improve student learning in science and mathematics. However, understanding how to improve student learning requires the ability to accurately assess student learning. Traditionally, learning was assessed primarily through the use of static paper and pencil tests of low level, content-oriented knowledge. There is now a greater awareness of the need to assess students' higher level process-oriented knowledge.

Static assessments may result in an inaccurate and incomplete picture of such higher level student learning. It is like a yard stick that measures only one dimension of a multi-dimensional building.

We have therefore been studying the benefits of a more holistic assessment tool, suggested by Fredriksen, 2003, which adds two more dimensions to the traditional yard stick of static tests. This article describes how the use of multiple methods of assessment results in a more complete and accurate understanding of student learning."

As stated in Pellegrino, Chudowsky, and Glaser (2001): Traditional testing presents abstract situations, removed from the actual contexts in which people typically use the knowledge being tested. From a situative perspective, there is no reason to expect that people's performance in the abstract testing situation adequately reflects how well they would participate in organized cumulative activities that may hold greater meaning for them (p. 64).

Pellegrino, J., Chudowsky, N., & Glaser, R. (Eds.). (2001). Knowing what students know: The science and design of educational assessment. Washington, DC: National Academy Press.

We consistently found that erroneous inferences may be made when simply reviewing a single, solitary measure of a student's learning. This was particularly true of traditional standardized tests. This finding is troubling given the present reliance in the field of education upon static standardized assessments. The inaccuracy of static tests may be due to "test anxiety" and fear of failure. It may also be due to a lack of social support, or the lack of context, both of which would hide the student's true potential understanding."

Yeary, S., Herronkohl, L. & Spring, D. (2007) Assessing Students Developing Understanding of Science: Case Studies in Holistic Assessment Unpublished Manuscript, University of Washington, Seattle (available from author upon request: email springforschools@aol.com).

One of the primary purposes of the Human Development program at the College of Education at the University of Washington is to move teachers beyond merely teaching lower level "content" using "Lone Ranger" styles of inquiry so dominant in traditional classrooms.

The problem with lower level learning is that it looks great in the short term on standardized tests. But it actually reduces student learning in the long term by limiting the ability of students to solve real world problems. It reinforces bad habits like linear thinking instead of more global problem solving abilities. The goal of advanced training in student learning is to develop multiple instructional strategies in order to assist a broader range of students to achieve their maximum potential. Instead of only using a hammer and treating every student as a nail, the teacher is encouraged to look at every child as an individual with individual strengths and needs. The teacher becomes more of a facilitator and a doctor than a policeman and/or drill sergeant. A broader awareness of potential problems leads to better solutions.

The goal of moving students towards higher levels of understanding is to prepare the student for real life problem solving in which processes play a much more important role than merely answering a content question like what is 6 plus 2. If teachers with higher degrees are teaching higher learning processes, it should be expected that these real gains in higher order student learning would not be accurately "measured" by traditional standardized tests.

Another important goal of the Human Development program at the University of Washington is better understanding of the whole child. Undergraduate courses tend to focus on the "what" or the visible cognitive development of the child. But underlying this cognitive development is the social development of the child. A key difference between humans and other animals is our ability to learn through language. While the traditional classroom is often a one way street from the teacher to the student, real world learning is a two or even three way street. One benefit of smaller class sizes is the ability to permit more two and three way social interactions. The importance of expanding processes to facilitate learning – focusing on the how and not just the what - is one goal of the Human Development program.

A final goal is better understanding of child motivation. Thus, the focus is not merely on the "what" and the "how," but also on the "why" of human development and human learning. If we are to ever improve standardized tests scores of math students, then we need to better understand how to motivate students to do their math homework. Unfortunately, attitudes of students towards math are developed early in life. They are assimilated not just from personal experiences of success or failure, but also from attitudes parents and elementary school teachers hold towards math. If we could expand teacher understanding of the cognitive, social and emotional development of children, we could greatly improve math test scores as well as graduation rates and later performance in college and in life.

But this means **more teachers getting advanced degrees in Education and Child Development, not fewer.** It also means smaller class sizes – because the kind of changes required are simply not possible with 50 kids in a math class.

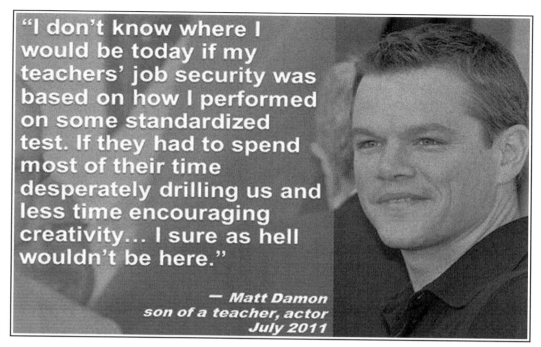

Sadly, what is being discussed in political circles these days is just the opposite. Public schools are being subjected to the corporate model of short term gains and losses without regard to the long term well being and development of the child. Standardized tests reign supreme without regard to their lack of accuracy and inability to measure either social or emotional growth (they are not even very good at measuring cognitive growth).

Why is this? Part of the problem is the Gates Foundation – which funds the bulk of anti-teacher training research – systematically selects and funds researchers who have no awareness of the inaccuracies of standardized tests and no understanding of the complexity of child development. Sadly, Bill Gates never went to public school and dropped out of college. Thus, the folks with the money have a poor understanding of both public schools and higher education.

A good example of this bias was an article in the Seattle Times in 2009. It reported on a study (funded by the Gates Foundation) which included the following unproductive exchange of charges: "There's absolutely no research that says a teacher who takes more course work is more effective in the classroom," said Kate Walsh, president of the National Council on Teacher Quality.
http://seattletimes.com/html/education/2010058256_teacherquality14m.html

Kate failed to mention that she used an unreliable yard stick called VAM to reach her conclusion. She also failed to mention that she had been bribed with more than $10 million grants from the Gates Foundation in order to lie so confidently to the Seattle Times.

GRANTEE	YEAR	ISSUE	PROGRAM	AMOUNT
National Council on Teacher Quality	2013	College-Ready	US Program	$3,688,859
National Council on Teacher Quality	2011	College-Ready	US Program	$2,935,048
National Council on Teacher Quality	2009 and earlier	College-Ready	US Program	$2,565,641
National Council on Teacher Quality	2009 and earlier	Global Policy & Advocacy	US Program	$1,318,239

Another problem is the increasing focus on profit over progress. Our State legislature was sued by dozens of school districts for a failure to fully fund education as is required by our State Constitution. The State called on an expert witness – being paid $80,000 – to tell the judge that "money does not make any difference to student achievement." The State's star witness has never taught in a public school or taken a single course in education or child development and does not even live in our State. Instead, this star witness is from back East and has a degree in Economics. No wonder he doesn't know what he is talking about.

Even complete elimination of Advanced Degrees from the pay scale would only reduce per pupil costs by 3% or about $300 per pupil. Given that 56% of the teachers in Washington State have Advanced Degrees and given that this compensation method is fair, objective and under the control of the teacher and has been negotiated through years of teacher-union contracts, it hardly seems worth the effort of developing an alternate system. We would still be faced with the other 97% of the school funding problem to deal with.

Students would be better served if our legislature spent more time discussing tax reform and less time discussing teacher evaluation. Tax breaks for wealthy multinational corporations have skyrocketed more than 300% in just the past 12 years. The solution to our school funding crisis is not firing experienced teachers – it is in firing legislators who care more about giving tax breaks to billionaires than fair funding to our kids and our schools.

It is not merely students who development cognitively, socially and emotionally. It is also teachers. Forcing our teachers into classrooms of 40 students – where student or teacher success is all but impossible – harms the attitudes of teachers as well as students.

It will take political courage to pass a tax reform measure in Washington State and roll back billions of dollars in unwise corporate tax breaks. But it is the only real solution to our current school funding problem. It is also the only thing that has any real chance of improving student performance and graduation rates.

Why have Billionaires insisted on attacking teachers?

In 2010, Adam Bessie wrote an article called the "Myth of the Bad Teacher." Here is a quote: "The super rich who imploded the economy, manufacturing the recession which now enrages the public, have successfully misdirected the public's justifiable anger away from them and toward teachers." Adam's argument is that it is the billionaires and their concentration of wealth and power that has caused the poverty rate to skyrocket in the US. Fixing childhood poverty would require taking some money away from the billionaires. It is therefore cheaper for them to spend millions of dollars attacking public school teachers.
http://www.truth-out.org/archive/item/92330-the-myth-of-the-bad-teacher

There could be another reason for creating the myth of the bad teacher besides mere distraction. Teachers and their unions are a leading force in protecting public schools against privatization and being taken over by the billionaires. The first step in getting rid of them is to demonize them. The best way to demonize teachers is with Value Added Modeling and the false claim that teacher training and experience have no effect on student outcomes.

As Henry Giroux once said: "Real problems affecting schools such as rising poverty, homelessness, vanishing public services for the disadvantaged, widespread unemployment, massive inequality in wealth and income, overcrowded classrooms and a bankrupt and iniquitous system of school financing disappear in the false claims of the super rich... "The Bad Teacher is an effective myth, a convenient scapegoat for ignoring these greater systemic problems that would require real, substantive reform, reform that would threaten the super rich like Gates and others who are bankrolling the corporatization of public education. This myth, while appealing, stands in the way of real educational reform, by misdirecting the public's attention from the socio-economic conditions that make for a poor learning - and living – environment."
http://truth-out.org/archive/component/k2/item/92120:when-generosity-hurts-bill-gates-public-school-teachers-and-the-politics-of-humiliation

What is next?

In the next chapter, we will take a closer look at Bill Gates and the many front groups he has created to hide his takeover of our public schools.

6 Billionaire Funded Fake Grass Roots

> "The liberty of a democracy is not safe if the people tolerate the Growth of private power to the point where it becomes stronger Than the democratic state itself. That, in its essence, is fascism. Ownership of government by an individual, group or any other Controlling private power."   Franklin D. Roosevelt

In this chapter, we will review how billionaires have carried out their plan to close and privatize our public schools. We will cover where the billionaires got their money and how they use it to control public perception of their scams. This chapter has four sections.

6.1 Billionaire Funded Fake Grass Roots

6.2 Billionaire Controlled Media

6.3 The Gates Foundation... The World's Biggest Tax Evasion Scam

6.4 The Real History of Bill Gates

6.1 Stand for Children Turns into Stand for Billionaires

> "Stand for Children now stands for profits,
> Not for schools and certainly not for children."
> Letter signed by 27 former members of
> Stand for Children, Massachusetts

Given that the programs advocated by the billionaires cause severe harm to millions of students, the real question becomes how are the billionaires able to manipulate public opinion? How do they operate on the ground? What are the tools and tactics they use to leverage their money to control public policy?

Follow the money
Bill Gates controls more than $100 billion in wealth. By strategically deploying his immense wealth through financing fake scientific reports, and fake "Astro Turf" groups, Gates has been able to attack our public schools for over a decade. Previously, we noted that Bill Gates has spent billions of dollars to destroy and privatize our public schools. A huge part of his spending has been the creation of literally hundreds of fake grassroots groups with innocent sounding names like Students First and Parents for Better Schools. These groups often make donations to each other in order to hide the money laundering trail. Below is a chart which attempts to show the interconnections between all of these groups. Go to the link below to see a bigger version of this complex image.

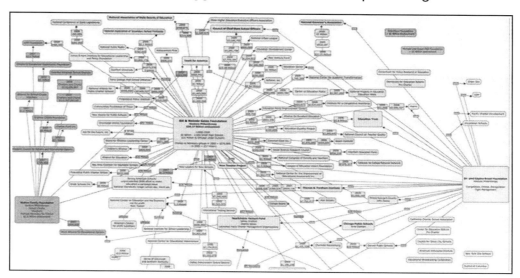

http://2.bp.blogspot.com/_SJpQvXL0IzI/S9n33yt_NnI/AAAAAAAAFSs/oHWSqSz2wyU/s1600/Bill+and+Melinda+Gates+Foundation+-+affiliations+%26+supported+groups.jpg

While Bill Gates has set up hundreds of fake front groups (many shown in the above image), in this article, we will focus on just one of the most notorious and dishonest of these fake grassroots organizations, a group that calls itself Stand for Children (SFC), but should more accurately be called Stand for Billionaires – as it is just a deceptive mouthpiece for Bill Gates and other Billionaires in their drive to privatize schools and destroy teachers unions.

The Beginning of Stand For Children

"Stand for Children" is a fake grassroots organization that is now a front group for Bill Gates and other billionaires. But it was not always a front group for billionaires. When Stand for Children first started in 1996, it actually was a real grassroots group focused on improving children's access to health care. It was created after a rally for children in Washington DC on June 1 1996 organized by Marian Edelman, the head of the Children's Defense Fund. The rally was attended by more than 300,000 people.

The Children's Defense Fund was started in 1973 by Marian Edelman. The motto of the Children's Defense Fund (CDF) was somewhat ominous. It was "Leave No Child Behind" a slogan later used by George Bush to punish children with endless high stakes tests. Also ominous is the fact that CDF is backed by wealthy corporations like CITI Group. Former First Lady Hillary Clinton was a former chair of CDF. According to Open Secrets (dot) org, the Children's Defense Fund has spent more than one million dollars on Congressional lobbyists. Their fund raisers seem to be more about helping the rich feel good about helping the poor while not actually doing much to provide jobs and training for parents of poor children and housing and food for poor children. Meanwhile, the number and percent of poor children has skyrocketed in the past 30 years as the middle class has been destroyed by the billionaires who support CDF.

Stand for Children Turns into Stand for Billionaires

After the 1996 rally in Washington DC, Marion's son Jonah Edelman started a new organization to help children called Stand for Children (SFC). Initially, the focus of SFC was to increase school funding. Their first chapter was in Portland Oregon. SFC members were known for their blue tee shirts. SFC organized parents much like a local PTA into local chapters.

Sadly, in September 2007, STAND began receiving very large multimillion dollar grants from Bill Gates and suddenly the focus of SFC shifted away from school funding and towards firing teachers and privatizing public schools:

> **Stand for Children Leadership Center**
>
> **Date:** September 2007
> **Purpose:** to support the expansion of Stand for Children in Washington State
> **Amount:** $682,565

Since this initial grant, Gates has given SFC nine grants totaling about $7 million - all to advocate for Common Core and High Stakes High Failure Rate tests. After receiving millions of dollars in funding from Bill Gates and the Walton billionaires, SFC changed into a monster that advocates increasing corporate tax breaks, reducing school funding, closing public schools, firing school teachers and replacing them with poorly trained TFA recruits and handing public schools over to private for profit charter school operators – which are also funded by Bill Gates and the Walton billionaires. Even worse, SFC acts as a funnel for billionaires to buy elections for corporate controlled candidates and corrupt politicians.

How SFC Operates

SFC's standard operating procedure is to set up a branch office with professional recruiters who go into a community and spread money and lies around the community in order to deceive and recruit as many parents as possible in an attempt to get them on board as partners. SFC particularly likes to subvert and take over local Parent Teacher Association (PTA) organizations often by giving "jobs" (aka bribes) to local PTA and state wide PTA leaders. SFC also bribes public officials to pass union-busting legislation. SFC has spent massive amounts of money by corporate raiders to buy elections in Arizona, Louisiana, Colorado, California, Illinois, Indiana, Massachusetts, Oregon, Texas, Tennessee, Washington and several other states. Here are a few examples

Stand for Corruption in Oregon

The Bill & Melinda Gates Foundation began by offering SFC in Oregon a relatively modest two-year grant of $80,000 in 2005. In 2007, Gates gave Stand $682,565. In 2009, the point at which Stand's drastically different political agenda became obvious, Gates gave Stand $971,280. In 2010, Gates gave Stand $3,476,300. That is $3.5 million in a single year! SFC used this money to hire and train fake parent "advocates" to give "blame the teacher" slideshows at PTA meetings in several states.

Though Gates remains the biggest donor to SFC, other billionaires have also used SFC to push their school privatization agenda. New Profit Inc. has funded SFC since 2008—to the tune of $1,458,500. The Walton Family Foundation made a 2010 grant of $1,378,527. Several other major funders are tied to Bain Capital, a private equity and venture capital firm founded by Mitt Romney. There are at least a half dozen other billionaires that have consistently support SFC's many fake grassroots (astroturf) campaigns and corrupt political candidates. Thus, Stand can best be described as "Stand for Billionaires" or "Stand for Corruption" or "Stand for Bribery."

Former SFC leader in Oregon, and current member of Parents Across America (PAA) in Oregon, Susan Barrett wrote a ground-breaking post for PAA's blog in 2012, exposing the way a formerly real grass-roots group had been taken over by a fake grassroots group, Stand for Children with an agenda very different from the group's original purpose.

Barrett, Susan. "Stand for Children: A Hometown Perspective of Its Evolution," Parents Across America website: parentsacrossamerica.org/2011/07/stand-for-children-a-hometown-perspective-of-its-evolution

Another former leader of Stand in Oregon was even more blunt in a public letter to Jonah Edelman: "You know and I know that there is not one shred of solid evidence that tougher teacher tenure rules, teacher evaluation using student test scores, or more charter schools (code word "flexibility") will make a damn bit of difference in preparing our kids for future success. You also know, and choose to ignore, the research on the kinds of true capacity building that will make a difference. Yet you continue to push the fads that the millionaires club continues to cheer on and pay for. I will use all the energy I have to fight this growing national threat to public education."

Tom Olson, July 22, 2011 Another Former Stand for Children Member Speaks Out. http://parentsacrossamerica.org/tom-olsen-another-former-stand-for-children-member-speaks-out/

For a video about the Fake Grassroots Organization, Stand for Children, see the following: The Truth behind Stand for Children
http://www.youtube.com/watch?v=j15szpXFJo4&v=4iAjkf99F9c

Stand for Bribery in Illinois
In Illinois, SFC spent more than $3 million in 2010 hiring lobbyists, buying elections and bribing elected officials including Illinois Speaker Michael Madigan. Stand donated $610,000 to nine state campaigns in both major parties in Illinois in a single year. They worked closely with another Bill Gates backed group called "Advance Illinois" to elect Ed Reform candidates. Advance Illinois has received more than $3 million from the Gates Foundation.

> **Advance Illinois NFP**
>
> **Date:** May 2008
> **Purpose:** to promote policies to create a world-class education system in Illinois
> **Amount:** $1,800,000

Gates also gave millions to several other pro-charter school groups in Illinois which also worked to elect the Ed Reform candidates. So while there appeared to be several different groups working on these elections, there was basically one source for all of the funds – Bill Gates. Much of the money was used for radio ads – none of which admitted that they were actually paid for by Bill Gates.

A local community leader, Reverent Robin Hood, reported that the leaders of SFC were disrespectful and arrogant, with dollar signs and union-bashing on their mind. "I found they were anti-union when we met with Stand for Children...I knew they weren't focused on changing things for the children. They were union busting and making money off the backs of our kids... It was all about money, it was nothing about children. We need to educate our kids, not get rich folks richer. These are the same people that don't want you to have a living wage and adequate housing."

Because of aware and active community leaders like Reverend Hood, some of the SFC backed candidates lost. For example, SFC and the billionaires gave $175,000-a record for Illinois- to Republican state House candidate Ryan Higgins, who lost his contest. So money does not always win if a community has informed leaders.

Stand for Billionaires in Colorado
Stand's most significant work in Colorado was their support of Senate Bill 191, a landmark piece of legislation that bases 50 percent of a teacher's evaluation on student achievement data. As Dana Goldstein explained in an American Prospect article, this may lead the state to test every student, in every grade, in every subject—including art, music, and PE. The poisonous debate around the bill vilified those in opposition and demoralized teachers across the state. Given that high stakes testing would have to expand from just a few grades and a few subjects to all grades and all subjects, some have estimated that this will result in a 20 fold increase in testing (and a 20 fold increase in corporate profits associated with designing and giving these high stakes tests). SFC also acted as a money laundering scheme to process campaign funds flowing from billionaires to Colorado school board races. For example, in the 2011 Denver School District school board race, three billionaire funded candidates ran as a "reform slate" for three seats on the seven member school board. Sadly, Colorado does not limit contributions to school board elections, so money from the billionaires poured in.

> "Stand has morphed from an organization with a focus
> On Children's health and school funding to one that
> Focuses on changing teacher contracts, weakening unions
> And pushing corporate-based models of education reform."

SFC Helps Buy Colorado School Board Elections

According to the Colorado Campaign Finance Disclosure website, the reform slate took in $633,807 (an average of $211,269 per candidate). The billionaire funded candidates outspent their opponents by six to one. Just six donors accounted for $293,000. SFC gave the reform slate $88,511 in "non-monetary" contributions of staff support and canvassing services. Put in simple terms, Bill Gates hired a bunch of people to work for SFC. This group then worked to elect the three fake candidates to the Denver Colorado School Board. It was a way for Bill Gates to give money to these corporate candidates without the public knowing he was giving money to these candidates. Even worse, the SFC paid staff appeared to the public to be volunteers when in fact they were paid to help elect the fake candidates. To further hide its involvement, SFC also created another fake non-profit group called "Great Schools for Great Kids" which used a super PAC with the same office as SFC. Two of the three billionaire backed candidates won, allowing the billionaires to maintain a four to three advantage on the Denver School Board. SFC has used a similar strategy to tip school board elections all over the nation.

Stand for Billionaires in Indiana

Stand set up shop in Indiana in early 2011 and began advocating for changes to teacher evaluations as the Republican-controlled legislature passed the most expansive state voucher program in U.S. history, expanded charter schools, restricted collective bargaining, and made serious changes to teacher evaluations. Stand's advocacy for test-based teacher evaluations included statements that were blatantly false, including: "Studies show that a teacher's influence on student achievement is 20 times greater than any other variable, including class size or poverty." What studies have actually showed is that poverty is by far the biggest predictor (constrictor) of child development. Lower class sizes have been shown to help students overcome poverty. Teacher experience does play a role in child development with highly trained highly experienced teachers (those with 5 years of training and 5 years of experience) better able to help children build better internal motivation. However, since Stand advocates for replacing experienced teachers with TFA recruits having only 5 weeks of training and no experience at all, the policies promoted by Stand are not supported by any credible scientific evidence.

Stand for Billionaires in Massachusetts

The same thing happened in Massachusetts, where 39 former SFC activists posted a letter and a petition against an SFC ballot measure that promotes a corporate reform agenda: "Venture capitalists and deep-pocketed corporate foundations, such as Bain Capital and the Walton Family Foundation, are moving aggressively to remake Massachusetts public schools based on their right-wing ideology. They are funding "Stand for Children" to sell a ballot initiative that would undermine our children's learning environment and sharply restrict teacher job protections. Don't let them do in Massachusetts what they did to Illinois!"

The following is the May 17 2012 open letter from former SFC members in Massachusetts warning parents about an "SFC" Ballot Measure. (http://www.citizensforpublicschools.org/editions-of-the-backpack/spring-2012-backpack/an-open-letter-from-former-stand-for-children-activists-about-ballot-measure/)

"As parents, teachers, and community members, we are Massachusetts grassroots activists for education. We read bills, testify at hearings, write letters to the editor, pore over budgets, speak at town meetings, make phone calls, and hold fundraisers. Many of us have done so for years. It was as part of this work and with great hope that we joined Stand for Children. And—initially—Stand helped us do great work.

We cast a critical eye on education bills at the State House and testified as needed. We turned back ballot initiatives that would have gutted education funding. We closely watched local budgets to keep dollars close to classrooms. We put our voices, time, money, and reputations into building Stand for Children.

Because we were united and we spoke from our experience, we were heard. Along the way, we learned a great deal about the legislative process, education funding, and policy. We learned to research our positions, present them, and back them up."

"But in 2009, while we struggled to give voice to the needs of our schools, Stand's staff was turning away from our concerns, announcing that it expected its members to forgo community advocacy in favor of a new, special agenda. This agenda, emerging seemingly out of nowhere, touted more charter schools, more testing, and punishing teachers and schools for low student scores. None of these initiatives arose from the needs of our communities. Indeed, we understood well their dangers. Yet all of them became the positions of Stand for Children. Policy proposals no longer came from the local level. They were dictated from the top. What accounted for this shift? We were mystified at first. But we've since learned that Stand abandoned its own local members – us – to follow the lure of millions of dollars from Bain Capital, the Walton Foundation, Bill Gates, and others who had an agenda in conflict with our previous efforts."

"The ballot initiative brought forward by Stand for Children is just the most recent example. Stand was one group of many at the table when the new Massachusetts educator evaluation system was hammered out. Unions, principals, state officials, parents—all contributed. But when the new regulations were finally announced, one group walked away—Stand for Children."
"Immediately, Stand filed for a ballot initiative and used some of their new corporate money to hire people to collect the signatures. It cost them $3 a signature, but they have plenty more. They are following the master plan revealed in Colorado by their national CEO, Jonah Edelman, a month before it was announced in Massachusetts. The proposed ballot measure attempts to blow up the collaborative work that created the new regulations last spring. It does nothing to improve teaching in our schools. What it does is put the careers of our teachers at the mercy of an untested rating system, violating the recommendations of the people who designed that system. We fear the result would be to drive some of our best teachers away from the schools that need them most. This ballot measure fits the ideology of its corporate sponsors, but it is not what we want for those who teach our children. Most of all, it is not what we want for our children. Therefore we the undersigned, as former members and leaders of Stand for Children, urge Massachusetts voters to oppose this ballot measure."

Stand for Children now stands for profits, not for schools and certainly not for children.

What is Next?
In the next section, we will look at how Bill Gates has also taken over our corporate media which now works with fake groups like Stand for Children to control public opinion.

6.2 The Biggest WMD is the Billionaire Controlled Fake Media

> "To save man from the morass of propaganda is one of
> The chief aims of education. Education must enable one
> To sift and weigh evidence, to discern the truth from
> The false, the real from the unreal & facts from fiction."
> Dr. Martin Luther King The Purpose of Education 1947

If we had an independent media, fake front groups like Stand for Children would be out of business in a week. So would fake scientific reports published by fake journals like Education Next. So would fake teacher groups like Teach for America and fake charter schools and fake Common Core standards and fake high stakes high failure rate tests like SBAC and PARCC. None of these lies would be possible if billionaires did not own the fake news media. Here we will look at how billionaires use the fake media to control public perception of their takeover of our pubic schools.

National Public Radio and the Gates Foundation

To better demonstrate how Bill Gates controls public perception, we will begin with a news group called National Public Radio (NPR) that in the past had been known for unbiased news reporting but has now been completely taken over by Bill Gates. Since 2000, the Gates Foundation has given NPR more than $18 million in 11 separate grants - a rate of more than one million dollars per year.

Grantmaking
AWARDED GRANTS

National Public Radio

Your search for **National Public Radio** returned 11 results.

GRANTEE	YEAR	ISSUE	PROGRAM	AMOUNT
National Public Radio, Inc.	2013	Communications	Communications	$4,500,000
National Public Radio, Inc.	2013	Communications	Communications	$1,800,000
National Public Radio, Inc.	2010	Communications	Communications	$2,390,005

In November 2014, NPR produced a four part series called "Reading in the Common Core Era." Here are links to two of these reports.

http://www.npr.org/blogs/ed/2014/11/11/356357971/common-core-reading-the-new-colossus

http://www.npr.org/blogs/ed/2014/10/27/359334729/common-core-reading-difficult-dahl-repeat

These articles are cleverly written to sound friendly and informative. But in fact, the articles are pure propaganda – filled with lies – designed to convince parents that Common Core will be wonderful for their children. Here is the first sentence of Part One: "The Common Core State Standards are changing what many kids read in school. They're standards, sure — not curriculum. Teachers and districts still have great latitude when it comes to the "how" of reading instruction, but..."

The first sentence is a lie. With Common Core Standards comes Common Core books and Common Core tests. Together, these leave teachers with almost no latitude in how they teach children to read. In fact, teachers are forced to abandon the traditional method of teaching children to read using simple, fictional stories and instead use hard core complex non-fiction – informational text that is way over the head of the brain developmental level of young children. This is why the nation's leading organization of child development specialists have gone on the record as opposing the Common Core standards. Yet there is not one word about the massive opposition to Common Core by the nation's leading experts in child development anywhere in this NPR story.

Here is another quote from the same NPR article: "Common Core English Language Arts Standards call for three major shifts in instruction." The link in this sentence goes to the official website of Common Core called Core Standards (dot) org. The three shifts described on this page are:

#1) Regular practice with complex texts.

#2) Reading, writing, and speaking grounded in evidence from texts.
#3) Building knowledge through nonfiction. In K-5, fulfilling the standards requires a 50-50 balance between informational and literary reading.

Does the above look like "great latitude" to you? All three of these Common Core goals ignore the actual developmental level or ability of young children and ignore one hundred years of research about the brain development and diversity of young children. All children will be forced to fit through the round hole even if they are still a square peg. No more will young children be allowed to linger in a brain development phase called "magical thinking" by allowing children to use 90% fictional text and personal writing to learn how to read and write. Common Core is not "shifting" instruction of children. It is destroying it.

The next 2014 NPR article then goes on to quote a teacher named Aaron Grossman, whose job it is to teach Common Core standards to other teachers. Here is a quote from this article: "The idea of Common Core...is to move away from focusing so much on reading skills and strategies and instead to think more about what kids read and, in particular, to make sure all students are reading text that is at their grade level. In other words, less leveled instruction."

The goal and purpose of "Leveled" reading books is to help kids feel confident about reading by starting them with books that have very short and easy words and gradually moving them up to books with harder and longer words. This is the "leveled" instruction that Aaron Grossman and Common Core want to get rid of. They also want to get rid of the fact that all of these books are fictional books.

The implication of the NPR report is that kids are harmed by "skills and strategies" and "leveled instruction." However, the skills and strategies abandoned by Common Core, one of which is "leveled instruction, were derived from 100 years of research on child development and brain development. This research had concluded that young children in any given classroom in Grades K through 3 vary dramatically in their brain development. Therefore, instructors were given materials that allowed a child to feel success regardless of their brain development level. Human brains do not start becoming more similar until about the 6th Grade. This is why there is a huge difference between Elementary School and Middle School. It is because children are different and can vary greatly from each other and from adults. Young children may look like adults. But their brains think entirely different from adults. Common Core ignores these differences in the brain development of young children and demands that even young children - who are not developmentally ready - be required to read complex non-fiction.

The Right of Every Child to Neurodiversity

Diverse neurological development in children is a normal human difference that should be recognized and respected just as any other human variation.

Most young children should focus on motor development, Spending their days on the monkey bars Rather than sitting in front of a computer.

Because the NPR reporter had no background in child development and because he failed to interview anyone opposed to Common Core, he accepted the nonsense from Aaron Grossman as if it were the truth. What those listening to the report had no way of knowing is that both the reporter and the person he was interviewing were basically on the payroll of the Gates Foundation. The NPR article then goes on to quote a person named David Liben who is from a fake group called "Student Achievement Partners" - who have been paid millions of dollars by the Gates Foundation to write and promote Common Core. Liben shockingly claimed that the former method of teaching reading was discriminatory against low income children. In fact, it is Common Core that has severely harmed low income children by falsely telling them that three out of four of them are failures – even though they are only in the 3rd Grade!

Common Core tests Will unfairly label Three out of four Low income children As Failures. No Third Grader Should EVER be Labeled as a Failure!

Common Core tests will unfairly label millions of American children as failures.

Who is David Liben?

David is a charter school promoter who has a bachelor's degree in Economics and a Masters Degree in School Administration – not a Bachelor's Degree in Education or a Master's Degree in Child Development as do nearly all Elementary School teachers. In 1985, David was the "Assistant Director" at a charter junior high school called New York Prep. In 1991, David started the Family Academy, a school with only one or two teachers where David was the Principal. According to a 1998 New York Times article, David's unique teaching method at the Family Academy was scolding young children to "Put that away before I stuff it in your ear." The threat was directed at a young child who had the audacity of wearing a knit hat into the school.

All of the kids at the Family Academy wear blue and gray military style uniforms. The school uses a competitive game called Jeopardy to motivate students. But competition also turns young children into winners and losers. Jeopardy also values memorizing simple low level facts, such as dates and names, over learning how to think and solve problems. Another New York Times article about the Family Academy said that "the school day ends at 5 pm and the school year is 11 months long." Another article noted that the school starts at 8 am in the morning.

http://www.nytimes.com/1998/03/08/nyregion/teaching-with-a-twist-but-no-magic-formula.html'

The idea of the Family Academy was to combine public funds with private donations. The school was started in 1991 with a $100,000 grant from the "Tiger Foundation." By 1994, grants from the wealthy reached $400,000 per year.

http://www.nytimes.com/1994/01/26/us/school-public-school-harlem-that-takes-time-trouble-be-family.html

How did David Liben's strict teaching style work?

In 1995, four years after David and his wife started their "alternative school," the Family Academy scored dead last out of 700 elementary schools on the New York City Reading test. Less than one in ten kids at the Family Academy scored at or above grade level. The next year, David switched to a phonics based reading program and his kids moved up to 350th out of 700 elementary schools n New York City. The next year, it remained an average elementary school.

How is the Family Academy doing today?

In 2003, the Family Academy became the Family Academy Charter School and moved to the Bronx. The first year budget of $2 million was to serve 162 students. $1.3 million would come from public funds with the other $700,000 from private funds of corporations and foundations.

http://www.regents.nysed.gov/meetings/2002Meetings/September2002/902emsca3.pdf

Currently one in four students at the Family Academy is "proficient" at reading – meaning that this school is still well below the New York City and New York State and National average.
https://k12.niche.com/ps-241---family-academy-new-york-city-ny/

Reading Proficiency

P.S. 241 - Family Academy	24.5%
New York	60.9%
New York City Metro Area	69.7%

One would think with a disastrous record like this, David Liben would have been drummed out of the education field. However, it turns out that David was interviewed by a person named David Coleman while Coleman was looking for "successful" charter schools to promote. Coleman was so impressed with Liben that in 2007, after Coleman got the contract to write the Common Core standards, one of the first people he hired was David Liben. David joined Student Achievement Partners where he was given the impressive title of "Senior Content Specialist of Literacy and the English Language Arts." This is a guy whose teaching methods were an utter failure in New York. Yet thanks to David Coleman, this is the guy who is determining how every child in America should now learn to read! This is how David Liben wound up talking with the clueless NPR reporter in November 2014.

In short, Bill Gates is paying for everyone in media. He pays for the reporter and he pays for the people being interviewed by the reporter. Neither the reporter or the con artist he is interviewing understand anything about child development. Of course, neither does Bill Gates. But the general public does not know that the person being interviewed is a scam artist. Instead, the public thinks this is a person that has a successful track record and knows what he was talking about. Nor does the public know that both NPR and the scam artist are being paid by Bill Gates. The moral here is to find other sources of information that are not being funded by Bill Gates.

Bill Gates writes Educational Programs for Nickelodeon
Sadly, Bill is not limiting himself to fake education reports to NPR. In 2009 the Gates Foundation and Viacom (the world's fourth largest media conglomerate, which includes MTV Networks, BET Networks, Paramount Pictures, Nickelodeon and hundreds of other media properties) made a deal to place Bill Gates messaging in many Viacom programs. Here is a quote from an article in the New York Times: The deal gives Bill Gates "an enormous megaphone. The new partnership, titled Get Schooled, involves consultation between Gates Foundation experts and executives at all Viacom networks that make programming decisions."

Among the programs produced by "Get Schooled" through Paramount Pictures, a subsidiary of Viacom, was a fake documentary called Waiting for Superman, which was really nothing but a promotion for charter schools – filled with lies. Bill was not only the secret funding behind Waiting for Superman, he also paid Participant Media LLC $2 million to promote this film. Here is what an article on Common Dreams had to say about the Getting Schooled program and how it manipulates children that it targets: "In this twisted take on the purpose of education, schooling is narrowed to striving to be a star or faithfully serving those who have reached positions of great wealth and power. There is no mention of becoming a community organizer, public interest attorney, nonprofit leader, or career teacher... The website also encourages viewers to, "Let your elected officials know that you want them to follow the lead of cities like Chicago and New York in making the system work better for students." The two cities, unfortunately, are among the worst school districts in the nation."
http://www.commondreams.org/views/2009/09/08/gates-viacom-and-obama-educational-programming-matters

In 2005, Frederick Hess did a study of 146 educational articles about billionaires written in the national press including analyzing articles written by the New York Times, Los Angeles Times, Washington Post, Chicago Tribune, Newsweek, and Associated Press from 1995 to 2005. His study revealed "thirteen positive articles for every critical account." Specifically, over this 10 year period of time in the nation's five leading newspapers, there were only five articles critical of the billionaires efforts to take over and privatize our public schools. This study was repeated using 140 educational articles from 2006 to 2011. There were only 17 negative articles during this five year period of time. In total, during the past 15 years, 45% of major newspaper articles about billionaire involvement in education has been positive, 47% were neutral and only 8% were critical.
http://www.frederickhess.org/2012/05/media-fawning-a-little-less-when-it-comes-to-edu

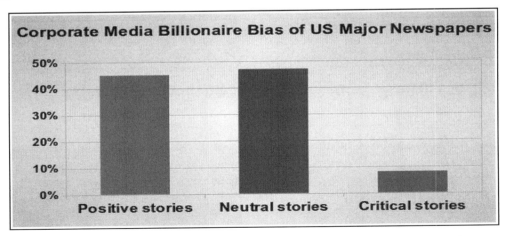

With this kind of media bias, is it any wonder that the majority of Americans think billionaires are doing a wonderful job of helping our schools?

2010 Bill Gates Funds NBC and Education Nation

In September 2010, Bill Gates via the Gates Foundation funded a week long series of programs on NBC and MSNBC called Education Nation. One of the programs, called "Good Apples: How to keep Good Teachers and Throw out Bad Ones" featured Steven Brill, an opponent of teachers unions and a supporter of charter schools. In total, Bill Gates gave Education Nation more than $4 million dollars to support this ongoing scam.

2013 Bill Gates Hides His Bribe of the Seattle Times

In 2013, Bill Gates did a similar fake news scam through the Seattle Times – but he did a better job of hiding where the money came from. This paid advertising program, sold to the public as actual reporting, is ongoing and is called "Education Lab." According to the Seattle Times, it is a joint project between the Seattle Times and a group called "Solution Journalism Network." However, thanks to research by Mercedes Schnieder, we now know that "Solution Journalism Network" is a front for another Bill Gates funded group called "New Ventures Fund" which got $700,000 for this project in July 2013.
http://deutsch29.wordpress.com/2014/08/24/seattle-times-gates-funded-education-lab-blog-experiment/

Here is the grant:

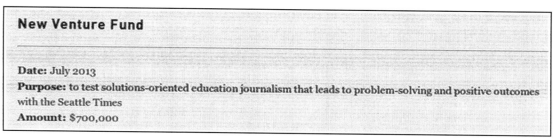

So this is how the money laundering scheme worked:

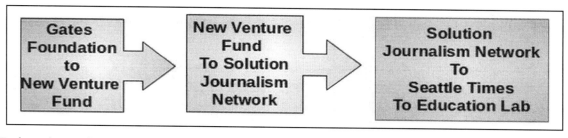

To be clear, the Gates Foundation has used the New Venture Fund to launder a great deal of money for many "projects." The Gates Foundation website shows nearly 50 projects totaling more than $100 million dollars. So this was one of many projects. The first New Venture Fund project started in 2003 with a charter school management organization grant of $22 million:

> **New Schools Fund dba NewSchools Venture Fund**
>
> **Date:** July 2003
> **Purpose:** to support a feasability study, and incubate and support Charter Management Organizations
> **Amount:** $22,262,000

It is also important to note that the Seattle Times is owned by a wealthy family that has long been a promoter of Bill Gates and charter schools. So it likely would have ran pro-billionaire ed reform stories even without the extra money.

One Million Dollars for the "Media Bullpen"

Bill Gates has also given more than one million dollars to a group called the Center for Education Reform to develop an "awareness tool" called "The Bullpen" to provide the corporate media with real time education news analysis.

> **Center for Education Reform**
>
> **Date:** June 2010
> **Purpose:** to support development of a new awareness tool, "The Bullpen", that will offer and analyze real time education news
> **Amount:** $275,000

For those who do not watch baseball, the bullpen is a group of pitchers (or reporters) who come in late in the game if the starting pitcher begins to struggle - and strikes out any batters (or writers) who might try to oppose Bill Gates.

The purpose of the Media Bullpen Mafia is to correct the record whenever any media source accidentally says something bad about the Bill Gates Ed Reform scams.

The actual content for the Media Bullpen will come from the Center for Education Reform which is a bunch of charter school scam artists all paid for by Bill Gates. The Media Bullpen especially focuses on the Internet and Social media – a place where bloggers occasionally say bad things about Bill Gates on their websites and Facebook pages. So look for the Media Bullpen to pretend to be concerned parents in the Comments section of your favorite educational blogs. Sample duties of the Bullpen Media staff include: "Drafting and posting rapid-fire content creation... responses to media stories from daily news feeds (up to 300 stories per staffer/per day)." Job requirements to be a Bullpen reporter include a Bachelor's Degree in Communications. No need for any training in education or child development. But you need to be willing to do "live radio interviews" on NPR!
http://www.schoolsmatter.info/2010/12/media-bullpen.html

Bill Gates Supports Several Online News Programs
In addition to the Bullpen, Bill Gates supports literally dozens of online news websites. These include a $750,000 grant to Editorial Projects in Education Inc (the front group that publishes "Education Week," $400,000 grant to Crosscut Public Media and a one million dollar grant to ProPublica. There are so many grants to so many groups that it would take a lifetime just to figure them all out. None of the groups supported by Bill Gates indicates in their articles that their reporters are actually paid by Bill Gates. But in addition to bribing news groups, as we will see next Bill Gates also controls who even gets to call themselves an "Educational Writer."

Billionaire Bill Also Controls Who is Authorized to Write About Education
In November 2014, Media Matters released a study of interviews on educational issues done by major cable news networks during the preceding 10 months. Out of 185 interviews, only 16 or 8% bothered to include a person with actual experience in education on the panel. This included numerous programs discussing education reform topics like Common Core and Charter Schools. Media Matters defined an educator as "Someone who either is or has been employed as a K-12 teacher, a school administrator such as a principal, a professor of education at the college or university level, or someone with an advanced degree (Master's or Ph.D.) in Education."

Given such a huge bias against teachers, is it any wonder that the public has failed to be told the truth about billionaire led ed reform? http://mediamatters.org/research/2014/11/20/report-only-9-percent-of-guests-discussing-educ/201659

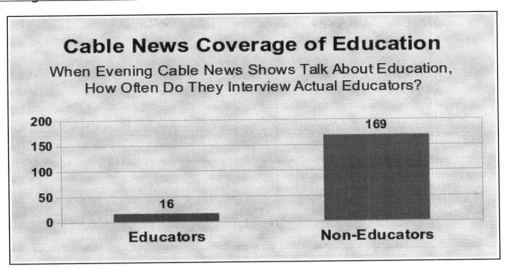

Bill Gates Bribes the Education Writers Association (EWA)
On January 18 2015, award winning education writer, Anthony Cody wrote an article announcing he had been booted out of the Education Writers Association.

http://www.livingindialogue.com/education-writers-association-independent-bloggers-need-apply/

Anthony Cody is a teacher who worked in high poverty schools in Oakland California for 24 years – 18 of them as a middle school science teacher. In 2014, Anthony won a first place prize for writing by the Educational Writers Association. Unfortunately, in 2014, Anthony also wrote a book called "The Educator and the Oligarch" about his attempts to get Bill Gates to reconsider his attack on our public schools. Perhaps because of his book, Anthony is no longer allowed to submit work to EWA. In addition, he was informed that his application to be a journalist member of EWA was rejected. Another important educational writer and researcher, Mercedes Schneider, author of "A Chronicle of Echos", was also rejected. Anthony wrote: "Both Schneider and myself are completely independent. Unlike many of those accepted as journalists by EWA, neither of us are funded by major corporate philanthropies that actively seek to shape news coverage." What could possibly cause EWA to reject the applications of two of the most important educational writers in America? Perhaps it is because the Number One funder of Educational Writers Association is none other than Bill Gates(Gates Foundation) who has paid this group over $3 million. With such a huge network of bribes, the result is that no one in the news media is allowed to disagree with Bill Gates or say anything bad about Common Core, High Stakes tests or Charter Schools.

What is the solution to this problem of Bill Gates controlling the media?

The most important thing we can all do is recognize the massive amount of propaganda that Bill Gates has subjected us to. It is likely that all of us have been affected by this propaganda.

> You don't have journalists [in America] anymore. What they have is public relations people. Two-hundred and fifty thousand people in public relations. And a dwindling number of actual reporters and journalists.
> Robert Crumb, cartoonist, January, 2015

We need to turn off the corporate news and turn to alternative sources of news. Mostly, these will be only found online. The great advantages of online news is that the cost to host a news blog is extremely low. This means writers and researchers do not have to depend on corporate funding to keep them running.

Here are a few better sources of news about the education reform scams:

#1 Diane Ravitch Education Blog: http://dianeravitch.net/

#2 Anthony Cody Education Blog: http://www.livingindialogue.com/

#3 Mercedes Schneider Education Blog: https://deutsch29.wordpress.com/

#4 Parents Across America website: http://parentsacrossamerica.org/

#5 Dora Taylor Education Blog: https://seattleducation2010.wordpress.com/

#6 Network for Public Education: http://www.networkforpubliceducation.org/

#7 National Education Policy Center: http://nepc.colorado.edu/

#8 Jonathan Pelto Education Blog: http://jonathanpelto.com/

#9 Jennifer Berkshire Education Blog: http://edushyster.com/

#10 Mark Weber Education Blog: http://jerseyjazzman.blogspot.com/

#11 Audrey Amrein-Beardsley Education Blog: http://vamboozled.com/

#12 Class Size Matters Education Blog: http://www.classsizematters.org/

What is Next?

In the next article, we will look at the organization behind nearly all of the Education Reform scams – a tax avoidance scam called the Gates Foundation.

6.3 Exposing the Gates Foundation Tax Evasion Scam

"Greed is the Root of all Evil."

The corporate controlled media, which has been bribed with billions of dollars from Bill Gates, repeatedly defends the Gates Foundation by claiming that the Gates Foundation "pours billions of dollars into public education." But this claim is utterly false. In this article, we will explain why the Gates Foundation does not put any money into public education. Instead, the Gates Foundation actually takes billions of dollars per year OUT OF PUBLIC Education. The Gates Foundation is really nothing more than a tax scam for diverting billions of dollars AWAY from public schools and into the pockets of private profit driven corporations like Pearson and Microsoft. Even though the Gates Foundation supposedly gives away more than one billion dollars per year, it's net worth has grown by more than $9 billion in just the past six years from $33 billion to $42 billion:

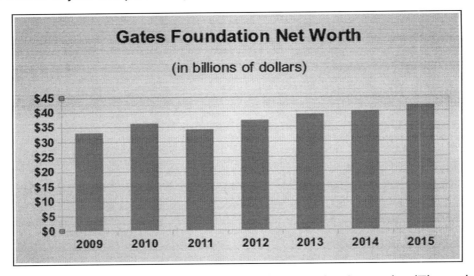

http://www.gatesfoundation.org/Who-We-Are/General-Information/Financials

The Gates Foundation is now more than twice as big as any other foundation in the world. It is important to understand how this massive tax scam works. This begins with figuring out how much Gates has sucked out of our economy since Microsoft began in the 1980's. Forbes indicates that Gates has a net worth of $80.6 billion as of January 2015. But this amount does not include the money Gates has in the Gates Foundation. This is money that Bill Gates retains direct control over and continues to invest in whatever way he wants. Adding $42 billion from the Gates Foundation Net Worth to $80.6 billion gives Bill Gates a real net worth of $122.6 billion.

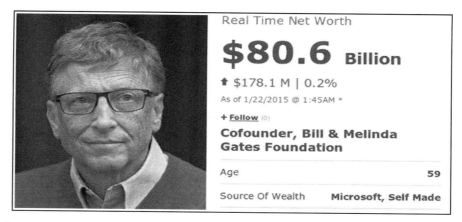

Nearly all of this Gates money came from the Microsoft Monopoly. Leaving aside the problem that this monopoly has three times been ruled to be a violation of the Sherman Antitrust Act, making the whole Microsoft Monopoly as illegal as the Mafia, we will use $120 billion as Gates "income" during the past 30 years. This was about $4 billion per year. Here is the rise in Bill Gates Real Net Worth, with the Gates Foundation added in, since the 2008 Economic Crash.

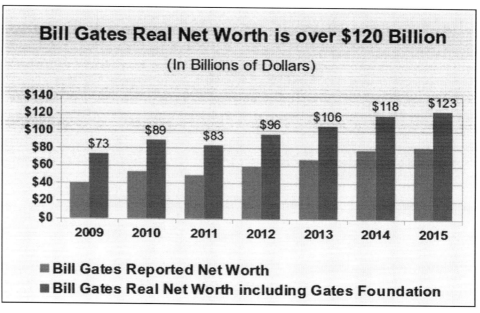

In a sane world, Bill Gates would have to pay federal and state taxes on his $120 billion in profits from the Microsoft Monopoly. For example, back in the days from FDR to Eisenhower, when we had a functioning economy, the federal tax rate on the income of billionaires was 90%. The whole point of the 90% tax rate was to keep money circulating in the economy and prevent a concentration of wealth. This concentration of wealth creates a power so great that it threatens both our economy and our Democracy. In other words, the 90% tax rate had the same purpose as the Sherman Antitrust Act – to prevent a monopoly of wealth and power so great that it threatens our democracy.

Therefore, had Bill Gates paid federal tax at a 90% tax rate, instead of his wealth being $120 billion, he would have paid $108 billion in federal taxes and be left with $12 billion – making him still one of the richest men in the world but with much less of an ability to dominate politics and privatize our public schools.

Bill would have also had to pay his fair share of Washington State taxes. But there is a funny thing about state and federal taxes. People are allowed to deduct their state taxes from their federal taxes. The average state taxes in the United States is about 10 percent of income per year. Ten percent of $120 billion is $12 billion. This would leave $108 billion in income to pay federal taxes on. 90% of $108 billion is $97 billion – leaving Bill with only $11 billion to get by on. That is if we were living in a sane world like we had from 1934 to 1964. Unfortunately, we are now living in a world where elections are bought by billionaires. So instead of paying state and federal taxes, Bill gets to use his billions to bribe politicians and destroy our public schools by turning them into corporate run for profit charter schools.

What Did Bill Gates Really Pay in State and Federal Taxes during the past 30 years?

Thanks to Bill Gates domination of politics in Washington State, Bill has paid much less than one percent in state taxes. According to several studies, Washington State has the most unfair tax structure in America.

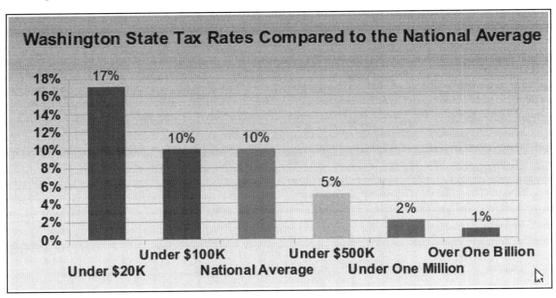

Source: Who Pays? A Distributional Analysis of the Tax Systems in All 50 States January 2015, Fifth Edition, Institute on Taxation & Economic Policy
http://www.itep.org/pdf/whopaysreport.pdf

The above graph shows that those earning less than $20,000 in annual income in Washington State pay 17% of their income in State taxes. Meanwhile, those making more than one billion per year in annual income pay less than 1%.

The main reason Washington State has such an unfair tax system is because our State is one of only three states in the US that does not have a State income tax. In addition, we have among the highest sales taxes and gas taxes in the nation – both of which unfairly target the poor. The net result is that Washington state has become a tax haven for billionaires – who buy elections for politicians who oppose a state income tax in order to keep our state a tax haven for billionaires.

Still one would think that Bill would at least have paid 1% of his $130 billion in income during the past 30 years. But there are at least three tax scams Bill uses to avoid paying anything in state or federal taxes. The first tax scam is the Gates Foundation – which is after all tax deductible.

The second tax scam is offshoring billions of dollars in profits from Microsoft.

In August 2014, Microsoft admitted it is keeping more than $92 billion offshore to avoid paying $29 billion in federal taxes.

http://www.ibtimes.com/microsoft-admits-keeping-92-billion-offshore-avoid-paying-29-billion-us-taxes-1665938

Here is a quote from the above report: U.S. Sen. Carl Levin, D-Mich., said at the time: "Microsoft U.S. avoids U.S. taxes on 47 cents of each dollar of sales revenue it receives from selling its own products right here in this country. The product is developed here. It is sold here, to customers here. And yet Microsoft pays no taxes here on nearly half the income."

This is nothing more than a federal tax evasion scam – made legal because Bill Gates and other billionaires own Congress. Had Microsoft been required to return this money to the US, Bill Gates actual income and net worth would have been much higher – about $30 billion higher and he would have owed both State and federal taxes on $150 billion instead of $120 billion.

The third tax scam is a $600 Million Dollar Per Year tax scam to avoid paying Washington State Business taxes

Instead of having an income tax, Washington State has a State Business and Occupation Tax (B & O tax) of one percent of gross receipts.

This means that Bill"s corporation, Microsoft is supposed to pay one percent of their gross manufacturing receipts in State taxes. Microsoft sales have averaged about $60 billion for the past 14 years. (Microsoft sales are currently about $80 billion per year). This means Microsoft should have paid $600 million in Washington State B & O taxes each year for the past 14 years or $8.4 billion in total B & O taxes. However, 14 years ago, the corrupt Washington State legislature allowed Microsoft to evade paying state taxes by pretending that Microsoft is located in Reno Nevada when in fact the products are produced in Redmond Washington. So Microsoft and Bill Gates owe the people and children of the State of Washington $8.4 billion in 14 years of back taxes plus interest which comes to about $10 billion. If anyone else tried this, they would be put in jail. But because Bill Gates owns the Washington State legislature, he gets away with this tax evasion scam.

So of Bill Gates $150 billion (including $30 billion for his share of the $92 billion Microsoft is holding in offshore tax shelters), $10 billion should have gone to State Business taxes to support our public schools in Washington State, another $15 billion should have gone to paying State Personal taxes to support public schools in Washington State. This entire $25 billion could have been deducted from federal taxes – leaving $125 billion subjected to a 90% federal tax rate – meaning $112 billion should have gone to federal taxes to hire teachers all over the US. This would have left Bill Gates with about $13 billion for his personal living expenses - which is still much more than any person needs to survive or could ever spend in a lifetime – and would still make Bill Gates one of the richest men in the world.

Here is a chart of how much state and federal tax Bill Gates would have paid in a sane, non-corrupt world.

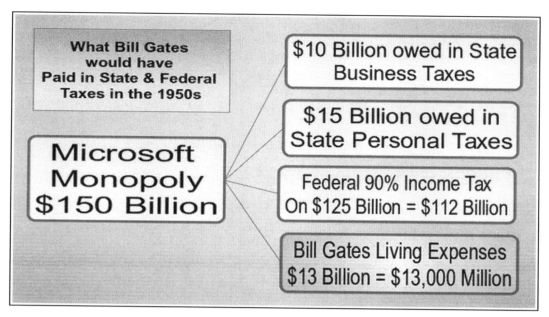

Instead, Bill and his friends bought elections and bribed election officials to change the State and federal tax codes so that they would not have to pay hardly any State or federal taxes. Instead of paying $137 billion in State and federal taxes, Bill simply diverted billions into a series of tax scams including the Gates Foundation, Reno NV and Cayman Island tax dodges – depriving students in Washington State and the US of more than one hundred billion dollars in school funding – enough to hire one million more school teachers in the US. Through scams like the Gates Foundation, our children are robbed twice. First, they are robbed by being deprived of thousands of teachers due to lower federal revenue. Then they are robbed by having this money used to attack and destroy their public schools and their right to a public education.

Result of Bill Gates Tax Evasion on School Funding in Washington State
In 1981, when Bill Gates started Microsoft, Washington State was 11th in the nation in school funding as a percent of income (at about 5% of income). By 1998, thanks to the election of numerous corrupt State legislators over a period of several elections and granting billions in tax breaks to billionaires like Bill Gates, Washington state fell to the national average of about 4.7% of income. Currently, Washington state is 47th in the nation in school funding at about 4% of income – while the national average spending on school funding is about 5% of income. As a result, class sizes in Washington state are among the highest in the nation. Many math classes have over 40 kids per class with 5 sections per day meaning a single teacher is responsible for more than 200 students. Some middle school classes in East King County have had more than one hundred students in a single class!

In addition, one in ten or more than one hundred thousand of Washington State one million students now attend school in temporary particle board boxes because billionaires like Bill Gates refuse to pay their fair share of State taxes so we could build real schools for our students.

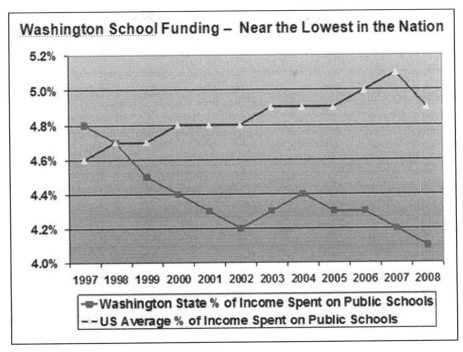

It would take $2 billion per year in additional spending on public schools in Washington state just to return Washington state to the national average in school funding and class sizes. It would take more than $4 billion per year to return Washington state to 11th in the nation in school funding. This is what happens when we allow our State to turn into a tax haven for billionaires.

The US has a Billionaire Problem

Although Washington state has several billionaires, we are not the only state with too many billionaires. Bill did not destroy our country all by himself. The US has about 400 billionaires worth a total of one trillion dollars – including 16 of the richest 25 billionaires. Together, these 400 people are capable of bribing every member of Congress and every State legislature. They are also capable of buying school board races and nearly every newspaper, radio station and TV station in our nation. No other nation in the world allows such a concentration of wealth in the hands of 400 billionaires. In fact, other than France, no other nation in the world has more than one billionaire. Most nations in the world, do not have any billionaires. So the US not only leads the world in child poverty, the US also leads the world in billionaires.

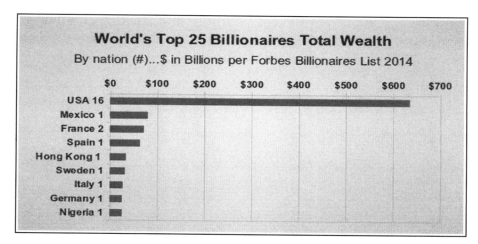

We Must Ban Billionaires to Protect Schools and Democracy

What is needed is a fairer distribution of the wealth in the US. The only way this will ever happen is to remove the influence of extreme wealth from our election system. The only way this will ever happen is to outlaw billionaires by placing a 99% tax on all income over $1 billion. In addition, we need to outlaw allowing billionaires to evade paying state and federal taxes by creating foundations which they control. No foundation should be allowed to control more than one billion in wealth just like no billionaire should be allowed to control more than one billion in wealth. These may seem like extreme measures. But the alternative is not only losing our public schools – it is losing our democracy.

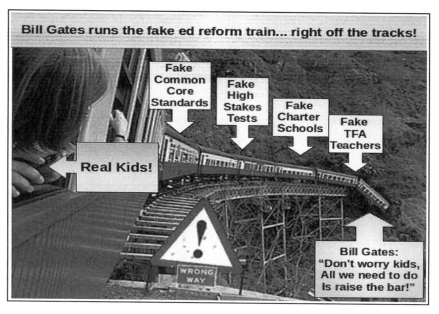

What is Next?

In the next section, we will take a closer look at how Bill Gates got his $150 billion. The number of laws Bill Gates broke in his rise to power makes Al Capone look like a saint.

6.4 Meet the Real Bill Gates

How Bill Gates robs billions of dollars from our children

> "There is something grotesque about the fact that Education reform is being led not by educators, But by Wall Street speculators and billionaires"
> Chris Hedges

Who is that man behind the curtain?
Although there are more than a dozen billionaires responsible for the various weapons of mass deception being used to destroy our public schools, no one is more to blame for the harm being inflicted on our children than the richest man in the world, Bill Gates. Through his fake non-profit organization, the Gates Foundation, Bill has "donated" billions of dollars to hundreds of fake "front" groups in order to create an army of more than one thousand lobbyists who use innocent sounding names like Stand for Children and Students First to spread the myth that our public schools are failing and should be destroyed. The next two leading culprits in this crime wave (Eli Broad and the Walton Family) have "contributed" about five hundred million each to this multi-billion dollar criminal enterprise.

This means that Bill Gates is responsible for over 80% and perhaps more than 90% of the entire war against our public schools. It is not possible to understand any of the weapons of mass deception being used against our public schools without first understanding Bill Gates. How did Bill Gates come to think the things he does? The best predictor of future behavior is past behavior. We will therefore present a history of Bill Gates to show how his current actions to destroy our public schools mirror his past actions to take over computer programming.

Some may be shocked by the information in this article. Most folks have been misled to believe that Bill Gates is a generous billionaire who donated his money to feed the hungry and cure the sick. These beliefs are the result of billions of dollars Bill Gates has spent to control nearly every segment of the media. Sadly, almost nothing in the "legend of Bill Gates" is actually true.

This article builds upon an earlier book we wrote about the many scams Bill Gates used to dominate the computer industry. That book is called "Free Yourself from Microsoft and the NSA." You can download a free copy of this book by going to the following website: freeyourselffrommicrosoftandthensa.org.

For those who do not have the time to read that entire 440 page book, we will present a brief 20 page summary here.

We must learn to avoid projecting our positive values on others who may not share those values

We humans have a natural tendency to believe that others think and feel like we do. Thus, we want to believe that Bill Gates and other billionaires care about our children simply because we care about our children. Sadly, not everyone cares as much about children as they care about money. But many billionaires have learned to pretend that they care about children. A good rule of thumb is to pay more attention to what billionaires do rather than to what billionaires say. Many people have been destroyed because they under-estimated the corruption and depravity of Bill Gates. He is not who you think he is and his goals are far different than what he admits in public. One of the main purposes of our book is to alert readers to the real threat that Bill Gates poses to our public schools. We will therefore go back to the beginning and look at some of the key events in the life of Bill Gates to better understand where Bill Gates is really coming from and why he thinks the way he thinks.

The Unusual Childhood and Youth of Bill Gates

Bill grew up in a family of extreme privilege. His maternal grandfather was the president of a major bank and his dad was one of the leading corporate attorneys in the United States – including advising IBM against antitrust litigation – which was ongoing during Bill's childhood. For some reason, during his childhood, Bill rebelled against his parents which led them to enroll Bill in a private school called Lakeside. Lakeside is a very wealthy private school in Seattle Washington that is a school for the children of the extremely wealthy. Tuition and books for a single year runs $30,000. The total fee for four years of high school is over $120,000 for a single student. Humans tend to become like those they hang around with. We unconsciously adopt the beliefs and values of those around us. Going to a school of the privileged tends to lead to an attitude of entitlement.

Sadly, the primary value Bill absorbed during his childhood was that he was better and smarter than everyone else. This belief goes beyond arrogance. It is almost as if Bill does not even see other people as having value or even counting as humans. For example, Microsoft employs about 90,000 people who Bill drives with almost slave like working conditions. Despite having this huge number of employees, Bill Gates once said that if one eliminated the top 20 people from Microsoft, that the company would soon go broke! Bill thinks only the top matters.

Bill therefore strongly believes that the thoughts and opinions of a very small number of people are more important than the ideas and opinions of tens of thousands of people. He has an unshakable belief in a top down organizational structure. This is why Bill is extremely opposed to unions and why there are no unions at Microsoft. Bill has gone to great lengths to undermine the formation of unions at Microsoft. This is also why he has gone to great lengths to destroy the teachers unions.

A High Stakes Test Proved that Bill Gates is Better than Everyone Else
Bill's evidence that he is better than everyone else began when he scored well on a high stakes test in high school. This is why Bill believes in high stakes tests. When Bill was in high school, he took the SAT test and got a score of 1590 out of a possible 1600. This put him in the top one percent of all SAT testers. We have previously discussed the lack of reliability of SAT tests and that it mainly indicates how wealthy a students parents are. However, this crucial SAT event not only affirmed Bill's belief that he was better than everyone else - it also has led him to believe that high stakes tests are a valid way to determine who is worthy and who is not. There is no point in telling Bill that high stakes tests are unreliable. Bill could never live with such information because it would interfere with his own deluded self image of entitlement. Throughout the following pages, you will see example after example confirming that Bill Gates believes that monopolies and central decision making by a small group of people (basically himself) is the best way to do anything. With that beginning in mind, we will present a brief summary of our previous book, Free Yourself from Microsoft and the NSA. For the links to the actual research, see the website with the same name.

How Bill Gates created the Microsoft Monopoly
The following history shows that Bill Gates did not actually "create" anything. Instead, he stole innovations from others and then mass produced them to create huge profits – profits based on fraud. Naturally, the story begins in Seattle Washington.

Bill Gates commits his first crime... stealing computer time
Anyone who really wants to understand Bill Gates should consider reading a book Hard Drive, published in 1992. While there is a great deal we now know about the real history of Bill Gates that was hidden in 1992, these authors did a good job of describing Bill Gates exploits while he was at Lakeside school in Seattle Washington. By the time Bill entered high school, he already had a million dollar trust fund thanks to his extremely wealthy grandfather James Willard Maxwell who was Vice President of Pacific National Bank (later First Interstate Bank). Willard's dad was the founder of National City Bank in Seattle in 1906 so banking clearly ran in the family. In case the name National City Bank sounds familiar, it is because this was the name of the bank in New York run by Charles Mitchell, a person who ran a Ponzi scheme which led to the Stock Market crash in 1929 – leading eventually to the Great Depression in the 1930s. National City Bank is now just called Citibank. But it is still engaging in Ponzi schemes and causing economic recessions in the US.
http://en.wikipedia.org/wiki/Charles_E._Mitchell

Bill's dad, Bill Gates Senior, was a lead corporate attorney for IBM as there were close ties between IBM and wealthy bankers. Bill's mother, Mary (Maxwell) Gates was also close friends with the head of IBM, John Opel, as both of them served on the national board for United Way.

With Bill's family connections to IBM, it should come as no surprise that the head of IBM, John Opel would eventually sign a deal with young Bill Gates making Bill the richest man in the world. But all of this was in the future. In 1968, Bill Gates was a student at Lakeside school, an exclusive private school for children of the wealthy and powerful, in Seattle. During the beginning of the computer revolution, in 1968, the Lakeside Mothers Club raised $3,000 to rent time on a very expensive Digital Equipment Corporation (DEC) computer called a PDP-10. Within weeks, Bill and his friends had used up the rental time and the Lakeside Mothers had to raise even more money to pay for his expensive habit. Bill eventually taught the computer how to play his favorite game – Monopoly. Bill's other favorite game was called "Risk" - a game of total world domination that Bill Gates is still playing – only for real, and all of us and our kids are the pawns.

On page 27 of the book Hard Drive, the authors describe the first time Bill Gates got caught committing a crime: "Gates and a couple of other boys broke the PDP-10 security system and obtained access to the company's accounting files. They found their personal accounts and substantially reduced the amount of time the computer showed they had used."

Gates got caught for altering the books when he was 13 years old and finishing the 8th Grade. But his only punishment was six weeks of time not being allowed to use the computer.

Also in 1968, Bill Gates met a person named Gary Kildall, who was a computer researcher at the University of Washington working on a "personal computer." Gary, who would later write the operating system that ran personal computers, would often work on the same rental computers that Bill and his friends were working on - some of which were at the University of Washington.

Gary Kildall Creates an Operating System for the First Personal Computer
In 1973, Bill Gates scored 1590 out of 1600 on the SAT, graduated from Lakeside, and was accepted to Harvard. That same year, Gary Kildall, the "father of the personal computer," and graduate of the University of Washington Computer Science PHD program, developed the first operating system for personal computers. He called this program CP/M (Control Program for Microprocessors). It quickly becomes the standard operating system for all personal computers. Gary also developed a "start-up" program to autocratically set the power functions for personal computers. He called his personal computer startup program "BIOS" for Basic Input Output System.

1975... Bill Gates Steals Computer Time on the Harvard Computers
You have probably heard that Bill Gates dropped out of Harvard to start Microsoft. This is not exactly what happened. Here is the real story. Bill dropped out of Harvard after he was threatened with expulsion for having illegally used the school computers for commercial purposes. He and Paul Allen had used the school computers to make private commercial software for the Altair 8800 computer.

This was thus the second of many times when Bill would break the rules. He apparently feels he is above the rules – which only apply to other people. On April 4, 1975 Gates founded Micro-Soft to sell his Altair 8800 computer program – a program he wrote on Harvard computers. The PDP-20 Harvard computer cost several hundred thousand dollars and was part of a secret US military program called DARPA (Defense Advanced Research Projects Agency). Here is a quote from page 81 of "Hard Drive."

"Harvard officials had found out that Bill Gates and Paul Allen had been making extensive use of the university's PDP-10 computer to develop a commercial product. The officials were not pleased... The professor in charge of the computer, Cheatham, refused to talk about the incident. But another professor said Gates was reprimanded and threatened with expulsion."

Gates would soon drop out of Harvard to spend more time working on his new program and his new company Microsoft. In short, Bill Gates and Microsoft began by selling a product called BASIC, that was developed with tax payer funds through a DARPA computer. Thus, because this software was developed with taxpayer money, the product should have been in the public domain. But the crime spree was about to get much worse.

1976 Gary Kildall starts selling DR DOS
In 1976, Gary Kildall started a company called Digital Research to promote his new operating system which he now called DR-DOS (Digital Research Disc Operating System). CP/M (now called DR-DOS) quickly became the dominant personal computer operating system in the late 1970's and early 1980s –selling nearly one million copies.

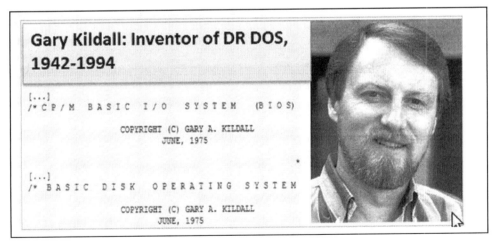

1977 Bill Gates buys a copy of DR DOS

In November 1977, Bill Gates visited Gary Kildall and obtained a license to use CP/M for $50,000 in cash. It was not clear at the time what Bill intended to do with his copy of this extremely important program.

1980 to 1981 Bill Gates steals DR DOS for IBM

In April 1980, a programmer named Tim Paterson with a company called Seattle Computer Products created a clone or copy of Gary Kildall's operating system which Tim called QDOS – which stood for Quick and Dirty Operating System. The first 26 lines of code, called system calls were exactly the same as DR-DOS. It is uncertain where Tim Paterson got his copy of DR-DOS.

Holes in the Legend of How Microsoft took over the computer industry

In July 1980, IBM contacted Bill Gates because they needed an operating system for their newly planned personal computer. The claim that IBM would contact Bill Gates to get an operating system for their personal computer is difficult to believe because Microsoft did not make operating systems for personal computers in 1980. So why would IBM call Bill? Some have suggested that either Bill Gates mom or dad played a role in this – both Bill's mom and dad had connections with those who controlled IBM. Bill Gates dad was an attorney for IBM and Bill Gates mom was friends with the President of IBM through her own father's banking connections.

In the late 1970s, IBM was making more than $30 billion per year but was facing monopoly litigation for claims by the federal government that they were violating the Sherman Antitrust Act. IBM therefore needed someone other than IBM to own the operating system for the new personal computer they were planning to build.

When IBM contacted Bill in July 1980, Bill supposedly told IBM to contact Gary Kildall. This part of the "legend of Microsoft" is also absurd as it expects us to believe that the largest computer maker in the world (IBM) did not know who the largest maker of personal computer operating systems in the world was (Gary Kildall).

The next part of the legend of Microsoft is that IBM and Kildall were unable to agree on terms for a CP/M license. Kildall asked for 10% of the profits from every computer IBM would sell. Some believe IBM did not agree to Gary Kildall's terms because IBM got a "better offer" from Bill Gates. Others believe the fix was in all along and a plan to steal Gary Kildall's personal computer operating system was in place way back in 1977. Here is a quote from page 176 of Hard Drive:

"In late 1978, Gates considered a merger with Digital (Kildall's company)... Gates flew to Monterey and talked about a possible deal over dinner at the Kildall home." However, in 1979, Gates got mad at Kildall for packaging his CP/M operating system with a BASIC program that was competing with Bill Gates BASIC program. Instead of cooperation, Gates would seek revenge.

Some unknown person began to spread the story that Gary Kildall refused to work with IBM in 1980 – that he was off on a wild plane ride when IBM leaders came to talk with him. It was also claimed that Gary had a problem with an IBM contract. In fact, Gary had a cordial meeting with the IBM leaders and had no problem with the contract.

Gary's impression of the meeting was that it had gone well and that he had made a deal with IBM for them to use his operating system on their new personal computer. It was not until the summer of 1981 that a completely different version of what happened began to emerge.

1981 Bill Gates and IBM close the most corrupt deal in history
According to the book Hard Drive, Bill Gates got a copy of Paterson's "Quick and Dirty Operating System" in September 1980 and signed a deal with IBM in October 1980 to supply them with a complete operating system for their new personal computer. Three months later, in January 1981, Microsoft purchased a license to use QDOS from Tim Paterson for $25,000. It was unclear why Microsoft would purchase this license because at the time, they had no products that could use this license. On June 25, 1981 Microsoft reorganized into a privately held corporation with Bill Gates as President and Chairman of the Board, and Paul Allen as Executive Vice President. Microsoft became Microsoft, Inc., an incorporated business in the State of Washington. Then in July 1981, Microsoft Inc. purchased all rights to QDOS from Tim Patterson for $50,000 and renamed it MS-DOS.

On August 12, 1981. IBM released its first personal computer. Microsoft' gave IBM the right to use the MS-DOS operating system on all IBM computers for a mere $50,000 – the same price they had just paid Tim Patterson. But Microsoft (Bill Gates) retained the right to charge IBM competitors for use of MS-DOS. On page 211 of Hard Drive, Bill Gates is quoted in 1981 as saying: "We are going to put Digital Research out of business." On page 212, a friend of Bill's stated: "There was absolute determination on Bill's part to take Digital Research out of the market. It is part of Bill's strategy. You smash people. You either make them line up or you smash them."

Why was Bill Gates so determined to smash Gary Kildall and put Digital Research out of business? This was the first of many times when Bill would take very unusual actions not only to beat competitors – but to drive them out of business – leaving Bill in total control of entire markets – just as if Bill was playing a game of monopoly.

> **In his autobiography, Gary Kildall called MS-DOS "plain and simple theft" because its first 26 system calls worked exactly the same as DR DOS.**

1983 Visicorp and Apple developed the Graphic User Interface
Until 1983, computer screens merely consisted of text and computer programming. Visicorp and Apple developed the modern computer screen that allow the use of multiple open windows at the same time and the ability to transfer data between windows using a visual interface. Steve Jobs made the mistake of showing it to Bill Gates who offered to write some programs for Apple.

1985 Microsoft copies Apple then releases the Windows operating system
In November 1985, Microsoft copied the Apple operating system and released it as the Windows operating system. Apple immediately claimed that Windows was a copy of the Apple Macintosh operating system. Bill Gates then blackmailed Apple into signing an agreement allowing Microsoft to use Apple's software by threatening to not update Microsoft Word and Excel for Mac unless Apple agreed to back down. There was some justice in this since Apple had copied a similar graphic interface created by Xerox years earlier. But instead of Apple and Microsoft sharing the profit, the idea of a graphic interface should have simply been declared to be in the public domain.

1986 Bill Gates takes Microsoft Public
On March 13 1986, Microsoft went public with a stock price of $21 a share and Bill Gates became a multimillionaire worth $234 million (about half the total value of Microsoft) thanks to his theft of Gary Kildall's computer program. This was the first of many thefts Bill would use to dominate the computer industry. Bill had learned that crime pays and big crimes pay really big.

1987 The Microsoft Human Exploitation Department Begins
The year before Microsoft went public and began a major expansion, one of us (David Spring) began teaching adult education courses at Bellevue College – which is only a couple of miles from Microsoft corporate headquarters. For 20 years, until 2004, David taught an average of 20 courses per year with about 10 students per course. About half of his 4,000 students worked at the Microsoft corporate headquarters. A few even worked in the same building as Bill Gates. David therefore knew more about what went on at Microsoft than most Microsoft employees. The stories his students told him were of working conditions at Microsoft that were horrific – a lot like the working conditions inside of a typical charter school. Workers put in very long hours. Often they worked all night and all weekend. Many were forced to travel overseas for months on end. Although many had wives and children, the joke was that their kids thought "daddy" was just a picture on the kitchen refrigerator. Divorce in East King County was rampant. Even worse, even though Bill Gates and Paul Allen were computer programmers from Washington State, and even though there were several world leading computer programmer training programs in Washington State, and a surplus of instate computer programmers looking for jobs, Bill Gates has a strange policy against hiring computer programmers from the local communities – or even from Washington State. One of David's hundreds of friends at Microsoft, who worked in their human relations office, told him that barely one in one hundred Microsoft employees were from Washington State. Put another way, of 90,000 Microsoft employees, less than one thousand of them were from Washington State. This meant that of the two million students who graduated from Washington State high schools and colleges during the past 25 years, less than one in two thousand was hired by Microsoft. Less than half of Microsoft employees were even from the Untied States. Most were from foreign countries.

Some of David's students said they were the only person in their entire department who was from the United States.

1987 Bill Gates becomes the youngest billionaire in the history of the world

Microsoft stock rose quickly to over $90 a share. At the young age of 32, Bill became the world's youngest billionaire. Bill spent the next four years engaging in a series of actions intended to build a computer operating system monopoly – mainly focused on undercutting Gary Kildall and DR DOS by using straightjacket exclusionary contracts. These contracts with computer manufacturers effectively (and illegally) prevented computer manufacturers from offering their customers a choice of operating systems. This was the fourth or fifth time Bill was financially rewarded for illegal activity.

1988 Apple sues Microsoft

In 1988, Apple sued Microsoft, accusing Bill Gates and Microsoft of designing Windows to mimic the Apple Macintosh design. Bill used some of his money from taking Microsoft public to hire literally hundreds of the best lawyers money could buy. Eventually, the Apple lawsuit was tossed out because of the "shotgun" agreement Apple had signed with Microsoft in 1985. This was yet another time Bill was rewarded for illegal activity.

1989 Microsoft releases Microsoft Office

In 1989, Microsoft introduced Microsoft Office which bundled office applications such as Microsoft Word and Excel into one system. The operation of these two programs were very similar to two other popular programs at the time – Word Perfect word processor and Lotus spreadsheets.

1990 Bill Gates sets up the H1B Fake High Tech Worker... a Precursor to the TFA Fake Teacher Program

In an earlier chapter, we reviewed a program called Teach for America that began in 1990 and has replaced tens of thousands of real teachers with fake teachers. Here we will review a similar program that Bill Gates created in 1990 to replace real American high tech workers with fake foreign high tech workers. Despite the fact that there are more than 400,000 unemployed computer programmers in the United States, with thousands more graduating from US colleges every year, in 1990, Bill Gates was able to bribe Congress into passing a grotesque law called the H1B program. The H1-B program allows Microsoft to bring in tens of thousands of temporary computer programmers from other countries every year for the purpose of replacing and/or driving down wages of computer programmers here in the US. These temporary workers are able to stay in the US for up to 6 years at a time – after which they can take their computer jobs back to branch offices of Microsoft located in their host country. Since 1990, an average of 100,000 foreign computer programmers have been allowed to enter the US through this program. At any given year, there are up to 400,000 foreign computer programmers in the US and a nearly equal number of unemployed US computer programmers.

Some of David's students complained that they we forced to train their replacement workers who eventually took over their jobs.
https://en.wikipedia.org/wiki/H1B_visa

An equal number of American High Tech workers have been replaced through a similar program called the L1 visa program. Here is a description of how this scam works: "Through a variety of legal and extra-legal means, American companies have been systematically replacing American workers with foreign workers who are nearly always paid less than those they replace. The L-1 visa system represents the latest legal loophole that is being exploited to the detriment of American workers… These foreign workers are paid only one third of what the laid off American workers had earned… American workers were even required to train the Indian workers who replaced them."
Dan Stein, Executive Director, Federation for American Immigration Reform
http://www.fairus.org/site/PageServer?pagename=leg_legislationb1f2

There is no high tech worker shortfall

In fact, there are 2 new college graduates with a High Tech Bachelors and Master Degree each year for every new hi tech job each year. Thus, there is not a need for a single H1B visa worker. Yet despite the availability of American high tech workers, the amount of foreign workers has been allowed to increase by over 400% in the past 10 years. The constant churn of tens of thousands of foreign workers coming and going has caused severe disruption to schools and communities in East King County. It is similar to another anti-union program that started the same year, Teach for America (more accurately called Teach for Awhile). This fly in and fly out model not only destroys schools, it prevents stable communities. It was not Wendy Kopp who invented the idea of having fake temporary workers taking over the jobs of real permanent workers, it was Bill Gates.

When we see the connection between the underlying goals of H1B and TFA it becomes much easier to see why Bill Gates is one of the biggest supporters of both programs. People who wonder why Bill Gates supports TFA and charter schools simply do not know or understand Bill Gates. This is why we have put this chapter on Bill Gates in our book. We need to learn the truth about the billionaire who is taking over our public schools.

The Microsoft Monopoly costs our public schools billions of dollars

Monopolies are illegal in the United States and most of the world because they lead to "price rigging" which is a two step process in which prices are artificially lowered to unfairly drive competitors out of business. Then once the competition is killed, prices are artificially raised to rip off consumers who now have only one option. In the United States, this one hundred year old law is called the Sherman Antitrust Act. In the 1990's, two federal judges ruled that Microsoft had violated the Sherman Antitrust Act. In June 1990, after constant complaints about illegal actions from Microsoft's few competitors, the Federal Trade Commission launched an investigation into Microsoft monopoly practices in the personal computer software market. Also in 1990, Bill began to build his new home on Lake Washington. It took about 7 years to complete and cost over $100 million.

1991 Bill Gates uses his Monopoly power to kill DR DOS

In the summer of 1991, Gary Kildall sold DR DOS to Novell, a manufacturer of high end computers. Bill Gates recognized this was a threat to his monopoly and immediately tried to buy Novell. When Novell refused to be bought and instead appeared to be working out a deal with IBM to promote DR DOS instead of MS DOS, Microsoft responded in the fall of 1991 by sabotaging their own operating system. The goal of this sabotage was to fool manufacturers and developers into thinking that DR DOS was not reliable and was not compatible with the Microsoft operating system. Bill does not mind lying if it helps he maintain control. On September 30, 1991, a Microsoft senior manager, David Cole, sent out an email defining a plan to sabotage DR DOS:

> "We should surely crash the system... The approach we will take is to detect DR DOS 6 and refuse to load. The error message should be something like 'Invalid device driver interface.'"Maybe there are several very sophisticated checks so competitors get put on a treadmill... aaronr had some pretty wild ideas... The less people know about exactly what gets done the better."

On February 10 1992, an internal Microsoft memo by Brad Silverberg that was released in the 1996 lawsuit explained the purpose of the malicious code:

> "What the guy is supposed to do is feel uncomfortable when he has bugs, suspect the problem is DR-DOS & go buy MS-DOS and not take the risk."

At the 2006 "Comes versus Microsoft" trial, the plaintiffs introduced the following email from Microsoft Manager, Jim Allchin dated September 18 1993.

> "We need to slaughter Novell (DR DOS) before they get stronger....If you're going to kill someone, there isn't much reason to get all worked up about it and angry. You just pull the trigger. Any discussions beforehand are a waste of time. We need to smile at Novell while we pull the trigger."

The attorney for the 2006 Comes versus Microsoft case went on to say... "Microsoft is not just an aggressive competitor. It is a competitor who is willing to break the law to destroy competition. "

On July 11 1994, at the age of 52, Gary Kildall suddenly died. It was reported that he "fell in a bar and hit his head." It was also reported that he "had a heart attack" but the autopsy was unable to determine the exact cause of death. Kildall was buried at Evergreen Washelli cemetery in North Seattle.

1992 Bill Gates becomes the richest man in the world
In 1992, Bill Gates hit the top of Forbes 400 Richest People list, becoming the richest person in the world with $6 billion in personal wealth. Just a mere three years later, Bill's wealth would more than double to $13 billion. Today, Bill is officially worth $80 billion and his private tax free account, the Gates Foundation is worth another $40 billion. But as we explained in a previous section, Bill's real net worth is closer to $150 billion.

1993 Bill Gates uses his Monopoly power to kill Word Perfect
The next challenge to the Microsoft Monopoly was a word processor called Word Perfect – which until 1993 had a higher market share than Microsoft Word. One of the purposes for the constant model changes in Windows was to create incompatibility with Word Perfect. Novell, which owned Word Perfect, brought a lawsuit against Microsoft for this predatory practice.

1994: US Justice Department gives Bill Gates a slap on the wrist
July, 1994 US versus Microsoft (aka Microsoft Act I)

On July 15, 1994, just four days after the sudden death of Gary Kildall, the US Department of Justice (DOJ) sued Microsoft for its predatory actions in using its monopoly position to destroy DR DOS and Word Perfect. Sadly, the DOJ also worked out a 'sweetheart deal" Consent Decree with Microsoft. However, in February, 1995, trial court Judge Stanley Sporkin rejected the sweetheart deal. He found Microsoft guilty of violating several sections of the Sherman Antitrust Act and ordered Microsoft to stop requiring computer manufacturers to enter into straightjacket exclusionary contracts.

1995 Bill Gates uses his Monopoly power to copy and then kill Netscape

On October 13, 1994 Mosaic released Netscape Navigator which quickly became the leading Internet browser. At the time, Bill Gates did not see any value in the internet and did not have anyone even working on a web browser. In January 1995, for some reason Bill's position on web browsers suddenly changed. In May, 1995, Microsoft introduced Internet Explorer which looked and acted almost exactly like a copy of Netscape Navigator. This was yet another time when Bill found it easier to copy an existing successful product than to try and create one of his own. Bill needing to control everything he touched, immediately began work on ways to kill Netscape. This was despite the fact that one judge had already found Bill guilty of violating the Sherman Antitrust Act! In June 1995, the Court of Appeals reversed the trial court's decision, sided with Microsoft and replaced Judge Sporkin with Judge Thomas Penfield Jackson – who was instructed to sign the toothless sweetheart deal that Microsoft had worked out. This deal failed to punish Microsoft for past destructive actions – as long as they promised not to do it again! The ink wasn't yet dry on the agreement when Microsoft was again destroying competitors.

1996 Caldera versus Microsoft

On July 24, 1996, the new owner of DR DOS, called Caldera, sued Microsoft for illegal conduct which "destroyed competition in the computer software industry." The 1996 Caldera lawsuit was based on the 1994 US government lawsuit which found that Microsoft exclusionary contracts violated federal laws. In the 1995 Microsoft consent decree, Microsoft agreed to stop its predatory practices – but continued to use them. The 1996 Caldera lawsuit called the federal consent decree "too little, too late...No single organization should have absolute power."

1997 US versus Microsoft (aka Microsoft Act II)

August 6, 1997. Bill Gates announces $150 million investment (bribe) of Apple. In trade, Apple agreed to replace Netscape Navigator with Internet Explorer. October 27, 1997. The US Department of Justice files a complaint alleging Microsoft has violated its 1995 consent decree by requiring PC manufacturers to bundle the Internet Explorer Web browser with all computers shipped with Windows 95. Despite the Federal District Court's entry of a preliminary injunction on December 11, 1997, Microsoft publicly announced on December 15, 1997 that any computer maker that did not agree to license and distribute Internet Explorer could not obtain a license to use Microsoft's Windows operating system. Microsoft apparently knew that the "fix was in" and whatever the trial court decided would be overturned by the Court of Appeals. In early 1998, just like clockwork, the Court of Appeals reversed the trial court and Microsoft was again free to do whatever it wanted.

1998 US versus Microsoft (aka Microsoft Act III)

On May 18, 1998, the tactics used by Microsoft to kill Netscape led to a lawsuit brought by twenty states against Microsoft.

Bill Gates Laughs and Jokes while testifying at the US Versus Microsoft trial on August 27 1998

Did Bill already know that the "fix was in" regardless of what happened at this trial? According to the 1998 sworn testimony of an Intel employee, in 1995, Bill Gates told him: "This anti-trust thing will blow over. We haven't changed our business practices at all."

At the trial, Microsoft produced video tapes which it later had to admit had been falsified. During the trial, Intel Vice President, Steven McGeady quoted Microsoft Vice President Paul Maritz as stating that Microsoft's intention was to "cut off Netscape's air supply" by giving away a clone of Netscape Navigator for free. Driving Netscape out of business cost Microsoft hundreds of millions of dollars – and eventually even billions of dollars. Netscape's air supply was their revenue. Microsoft was able to use their monopoly power to completely shut off Netscape's revenue in less than 3 years.
http://www.justice.gov/atr/cases/f1900/1999.htm

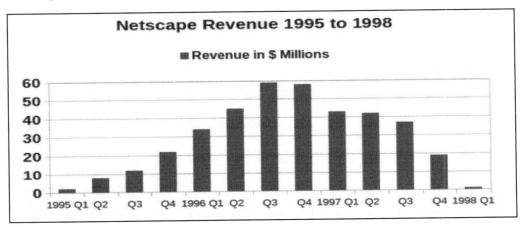

1999 Bill Gates found guilty of violating the Sherman Antitrust Act for the third time

On November 5 1999, federal judge Thomas Penfield Jackson issued more than one hundred pages of findings. This summary of what Microsoft did to Netscape Navigator is a chilling account of the dangers of allowing any company to have monopoly power over any market.
http://www.justice.gov/atr/cases/f3800/msjudgex.htm

1999 Bill Gates net worth reaches $100 billion

In 1999, with Microsoft stock prices at an all time high and the stock splitting eight-fold since 1987, Bill's wealth briefly topped $100 billion. Unfortunately, technology stock prices took a major tumble and his wealth fell back down to a mere $60 billion. Bill learned from this experience that he should diversify and look for other fields to dominate. This may have been one of the reasons he started the Gates foundation shortly after the Dot Com bubble burst.

> "Microsoft enjoys monopoly power" and used that power to "set the price of Windows substantially higher than that which would be charged in a competitive market — without losing so much business as to make the action unprofitable." Judge Thomas Penfield Jackson Nov 1999

On April 3, 2000, Judge Jackson issued his conclusions of law, finding that Microsoft was a monopoly and had violated Sections 1 and 2 of the Sherman Antitrust Act. On June 7, 2000, Judge Jackson ordered a breakup of Microsoft. Microsoft would have had to be broken into two separate units, one to produce the operating system, and one to produce other software components such as Internet Explorer and Office. This would have prevented Microsoft from using a monopoly in some areas to create a monopoly in other areas. Bill Gates confidently appealed this decision to his friends on the Court of Appeals.

2000 Bill Gates starts Gates Foundation to Rebrand Himself
Perhaps it was merely a coincidence, but this same year, Bill Gates rebranded himself as a man of the people by starting the Gates Foundation with initial donations of $16 billion – making it at its inception the world's most wealthy foundation. He soon added another $12 billion making the foundation worth $28 billion. Bill also began giving millions of dollars in grants to National Public Radio supposedly to start covering global health issues. This was just the beginning of a massive multi-billion dollar Gates media campaign that is still going on today.

2001 Microsoft once again wins in the Court of Appeals!
Suprise, Suprise, Surpise. The federal court of appeals in Washington DC – the same group that had overturned the 1995 trial court and replaced Judge Sporkin (by claiming he was biased against Microsoft) with Judge Thomas Penfield Jackson - found that Judge Jackson was also biased against Microsoft. Apparently anyone who rules against Microsoft is automatically biased against them. The federal appeals court therefore remanded the decision to a new judge to determine a new penalty. Perhaps this is why Bill Gates was not worried during the trial. He knew the fix was in and whatever happened at the trial would be overturned on appeal. The "fix" was in as a single corrupt appeals court judge over-ruled the two trial court judges. There were many glaring problems with this decision by the Court of Appeals. Most important, the court of appeals did not find a single fault with any of Judge Jackson's Findings of Fact! Thus, there was no showing of either bias or harm.

Things got even stranger after this. On September 6, 2001, just five days before 9/11 and the attack on the World Trade Center, the US Department of Justice announced that it was no longer seeking to break up Microsoft and would instead seek a lesser antitrust penalty. Microsoft then drafted a toothless settlement proposal. This was like allowing a bank robber to write up their own penalty. Then on November 2, 2001, the Department of Justice reached an agreement with Microsoft to settle the case by basically accepting Microsoft's proposal – a proposal which meant next to nothing in the way of changes for Microsoft. A year later, on November 1, 2002, the new judge who had been appointed by the Court of Appeals, Judge Kollar-Kotelly accepted the proposed toothless settlement. To add insult to injury, Judge Kotelly put "Microsoft Board Members" in charge of monitoring the toothless agreement. Not surprisingly, these Microsoft Board Members have failed to find any further violations.

Nine states (California, Connecticut, Iowa, Florida, Kansas, Minnesota, Utah, Virginia and Massachusetts) did not agree with the settlement, arguing that it did not go far enough to curb Microsoft's anti-competitive business practices. They therefore appealed the decision. However, on June 30, 2004, the DC appeals court unanimously approved the settlement, rejecting objections that the sanctions were inadequate. So after having three times been found to be in violation of the Sherman Antitrust Act (in 1994. 1997 and again in 1999), with over one hundred pages of Findings of Facts about criminal acts on the books against them, Microsoft was given a free ride. Microsoft could continue to use its monopoly power to destroy any potential competitor.

Andrew Chin, an antitrust law professor at the University of North Carolina at Chapel Hill, who had assisted Judge Jackson in writing the Findings of Fact, later wrote that the settlement gave Microsoft "a special antitrust immunity.. under terms that destroy freedom and competition... Microsoft now enjoys illegitimately acquired monopoly power." In a 2005 Wake Forest Law Review article, he wrote "Judge Kotelly's final judgment more closely resembled articles of surrender than a negotiated treaty."

How the Microsoft Monopoly Harms our Public Schools
The Microsoft Monopoly still matters today because some of the biggest expenses of public schools, besides teachers and administrators are computers and computer software. Currently, nearly every school in America spends more than $100 per year per student on computers and computer software. Parents also spend more than $100 per year per student buying computers and software for their kids to use at home.

Since there are about 50 million students in the US, the total cost of $200 per year per student comes to more than $10 billion per year. About half of this or $5 billion per year goes to Bill Gates and Microsoft due to the illegal Microsoft Monopoly.

There is a way for parents and public schools to fight back against the Microsoft Monopoly. If public schools and parents would purchase Google Chromebooks and install a free software program called Linux Mint with LibreOffice on these computers, they can cut the cost of computers and software in half. LibreOffice works almost exactly like Microsoft Office. In many ways, it is much easier for students to learn.

Google Chromebooks are much faster and more reliable than Windows PCs and they have a much longer battery life – making them ideal for use in classrooms. Also, Chromebooks can be bought in bulk for less than $100 each and they last for years. Finally, there are 64,000 free programs you can install on a Google Chromebook, including free image editing and video editing programs, once the Linux Mint operating system has been installed on it. All of our books and all of our websites were made using the Linux Mint operating system and its associated free programs.

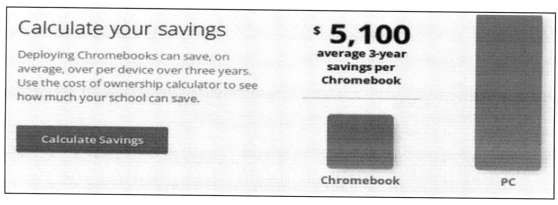

In summary, Bill Gates has been indirectly responsible for the fact that 300,000 teachers have been fired in the past five years and 4,000 public schools have been closed and converted to private for profit schools.

Given that Bill Gates and Microsoft are leading the attack against our public schools, it is unwise for any school district, any teacher or any parent who cares about the future of our children to be using and promoting Microsoft products in our public schools. For more on this subject, see our website, learnlinuxandlibreoffice.org.

What's Next?
In the next chapter, we will look at how Bill Gates and his vast wealth has turned our elections into fake elections and our government into a fake government.

7 Billionaire Controlled Fake Government

> "A handful of billionaires own a significant part of the wealth of America and have enormous control over our economy. What the Supreme Court did in Citizens United is to say to these same billionaires: "You own and control the Economy, you own Wall Street, you own the oil companies. Now, for a very small percentage of your wealth, we're going to give you the opportunity to own the United States government." Senator Bernie Sanders, July 24 2014.

In this chapter, we will review how billionaires have used their extreme wealth to buy elections and take over our state and national governments. We will also cover the Pearson takeover of the GED test – which will permanently harm more than 500,000 low income students every year until it is stopped! Finally, we will cover the marketing slogan "Career and College Ready" and see the actual results of privatizing education for our students and our economy. This chapter has four sections.

7.1 How Billionaires Buy Votes and Win Elections

7.2 Corrupt Corporate Takeover of the GED

7.3 Consequences of the Pearson GED Takeover

7.4 College and Career Ready is a Scam

7.1 How Billionaires Buy Elections

> "Last year, the 25 most successful hedge-fund managers earned a billion dollars each. Call me old fashioned... but I just think it's wrong that a single hedge fund manager earns a billion dollars, when a billion dollars would pay the salaries of 20,000 teachers."
> Robert Reich, Economics Professor, University of California

It is not enough that billionaires like Bill Gates are allowed to create illegal monopolies and overcharge customers and then allowed to evade paying state or federal taxes on their illegal profits through fake money laundering schemes like the Gates Foundation. It is not enough that the main stream media writes garbage fake news articles that favor billionaires by a margin of ten to one. Billionaires also invest directly in marketing campaigns aimed at deceiving voters into trading our public controlled public schools for billionaire controlled charter schools. A good example of this is the 2013 Charter School Initiative in Washington State. We have previously covered the harm and corruption of charter schools. Here we will look at how Bill Gates was able to use his extreme wealth to pass an initiative to bring charter schools here in Washington State.

Bill Gates and his billionaire friends forced charter schools on students in Washington State despite the fact that charter schools in other states have robbed tax payers of billions of dollars in fraud and corruption, despite the fact that diverting public dollars to private for profit charter schools is a clear violation of the Washington State Constitution and despite the fact that charter schools had been previously defeated in public votes in Washington State three times. Bill's charter school initiative eventually prevailed in a very close election in 2012. Here are the election results:

Initiative Measure No. 1240 Concerns creation of a public charter school system	County Results & Map	
Measure	Vote	Vote %
Yes	1,525,807	50.69%
No	1,484,125	49.31%
Total Votes	3,009,932	100%

Out of three million votes cast, Bill was able to fool just enough people to vote for this scam to have it pass by a fraction of one percent of those who bothered to vote in this election. However, the real story was not the outcome of the election, it was how the outcome was obtained. For that story, we first need to go to the Washington State Public Disclosure Commission.

Direct Spending on the Charter School Initiative

Even to get the charter school initiative on the ballot, Bill Gates and his billionaire friends paid petition signature gathers an average of $6 per signature to gather more than 300,000 signatures in June 2012 – for a cost of nearly $2 million.

The "No on Initiative 1240" Campaign raised $26,000 and spent $24,000. The "People for our Public Schools" committee raised $701,000 and spent $701,000. The total spent opposing the Charter School Initiative was $725,000. But this amount was dwarfed by what the billionaires spent to pass the initiative. The "Yes on 1240" group raised and spent $11,401,000. The billionaires outspent teachers and parents by a margin of nearly 16 to 1 just in direct spending. Thus, it was not an election. It was more like a bidding war.

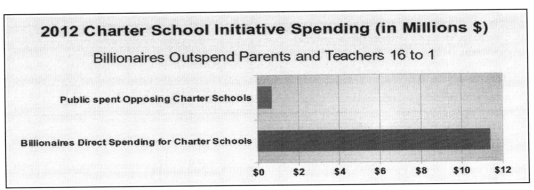

Let's look at the major donors for the charter school initiative. Bill Gates was the biggest promoter tossing in $3.6 million. Another Microsoft billionaire, Paul Allen, tossed in 1.6 million. A few other billionaires including Alice Walton, Nick Hanauer, Steve Ballmer, Mike Bezos, Bruce McCaw and Eli Broad tossed in the rest. Billionaires will always win bidding wars. But even this is the tip of the iceberg compared to what the billionaires really spent to pass this initiative.

Indirect Spending on the Charter Schools Initiative

The billionaire controlled media produced articles in favor of charter school over articles pointing out drawbacks of charter schools by a rate of 20 to 1. This included the State's biggest newspaper, the Seattle Times, endorsing the initiative and pumping out dozens of articles (which were nothing more than "ads") on the benefits of charter schools and/or the shortcomings of public schools. But the real heavy lifting in passing the Charter School Initiative was done by two Bill Gates funded fake "grassroots" groups called the League of Education Voters (LEV) and Stand for Children (SFC). Enter LEV into the Gates Foundation Grants Search Box and you will see **17 grants totaling $12 million.**

What did the $12 million to LEV buy?

LEV used the money to hire dozens of fake "education advocates" who went around Washington state in the two years preceding the Initiative to nearly every one of hundreds of school district PTA groups with slide shows and handouts bashing teachers, condemning public schools and advocating "change."

I attended several of these hour long propaganda sessions. Those giving the presentations claimed to be "concerned parents." They never mentioned that they were paid by Bill Gates through LEV to travel around the state lying to parents. This group also attended PTA regional and statewide conventions and infiltrated and corrupted the Washington State PTA – a group that claims to advocate for and represent more than one million parents and has a massive email list to spread the vicious billionaire propaganda to unsuspecting parents. LEV was not the only front group promoting the charter schools initiative in Washington State in 2012. Enter "Stand for Children" into the Gates Foundation Grant Search box and you will see 10 grants totaling about $10 million

What did the $10 million to SFC buy?
Stand for Children worked side by side with LEV to push Gates propaganda to parents in meetings around Washington State – also focusing on the Washington State, regional and local PTA meetings. The goal was to create a dissatisfaction with public schools in our State. No mention was made at these meetings of the fact that school funding in Washington State had plunged from 11th in the nation to 47th in the nation – or that our State now has the highest class sizes in the nation. Instead, the focus was on "failing schools." Ironically, most parents really liked their own schools and their own teachers. So the real scare tactic was comparing how schools in the US do not "compete" with other schools around the world. The message was that the reason there was no jobs in the US is because our schools were failed to compete on the world market – not because billionaires had outsourced all of our jobs to sweat shops in China.

Just to make sure that LEV and SFC received a warm welcome at Washington State PTA meetings, Bill Gates also bribed the PTA. Enter PTA into the Gates Foundation Search box and you will see 5 donations for about $3 million. Here is one to the Washington State PTA in 2011 – the year before the Charter School Initiative was put on the ballot in Washington State.

Washington State PTA

Date: March 2011
Purpose: to assist with technology communications infrastructure to push for key policies in Washington
Amount: $191,424

The "key policy" Bill Gates was pushing at the Washington State PTA was charter schools. When you add up the $2 million for signature gatherers with the $11.4 million in direct spending and the $12 million to LEV and the $10 million to SFC, the grand total Bill Gates really spent buying the charter school election was about $35 million. Thus, **Bill Gates really outspent parents and teachers by a margin of 50 to 1.**

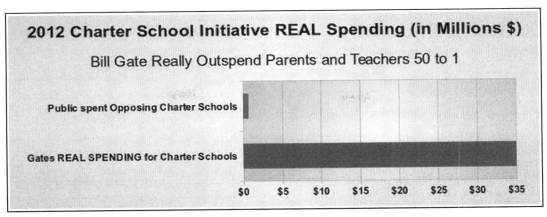

Of course, $35 million was just a drop in the bucket to what Bill Gates was really spending to promote his campaign to privatize our public schools. The really big money was going towards buying our State legislature and our national Congress. When you add in the millions of dollars that Bill Gates and his billionaire friends spend buying elections for corporate candidates in Washington State, the money spent to bring charter schools to Washington State is probably 100 times greater than the money spent opposing them. We do not have space in this book to truly cover all of the political campaigns paid for by Bill Gates. So we will just focus on two Bill Gates aligned politicians here in Washington State to show you how the process works.

Bill Gates Buys Politicians in Both Major Parties
People think that our elections are between the Democratic and Republican parties. But really elections are between the billionaires who own the leadership of both major parties and the people who have almost no one representing their interests and the interest of their children. As an example of this, we will look at two Bill Gates backed politicians here in Washington State, Ross Hunter and Chad Magendanz. Here is a chart comparing the two politicians.

Compare the Candidates	Ross Hunter	Chad Magendanz
Political Party	Democrat	Republican
Used to work for	Microsoft	Microsoft
Supports Charter Schools	Yes	Yes
Supports Common Core	Yes	Yes
Supports High Failure Rate Tests	Yes	Yes
Supports Billions in Corporate Tax Breaks for Microsoft	Yes	Yes
Endorsed by LEV	Yes	Yes
Endorsed by Stand For Children	Yes	Yes
Endorsed by the Seattle Times	Yes	Yes

When you get down to the details, there is really no difference between these two politicians other than the fact that one has a D by his name and the other has an R by his name. They both spend a great deal of time promoting the billionaire agenda at PTA meetings across Washington State – along with their backers from LEV and SFC.

Ross Hunter worked as a Manager for Microsoft for 17 years Now works as a lobbyist for Bill Gates Promoting Charter Schools and Billions in Microsoft Tax Breaks In the Washington State Legislature

They also both took an oath to "uphold the Washington State Constitution." And they both were found guilty of violating our State Constitution by the Washington State Supreme Court in September 2014. They both voted to divert billions of dollars away from public schools and into billions of dollars in corporate tax breaks. The prime beneficiary of these corporate tax breaks is none other than Bill Gates.

Chad Magendanz worked as a Manager at Microsoft for 10 years Now works as a lobbyist for Bill Gates Promoting Charter Schools and Billions in Microsoft Tax Breaks In the Washington State Legislature

Chad's background is working on nuclear submarines while his opponent in the 2010 and 2012 elections, David Spring, has a background in education and child development. During his campaign against Chad, David often said: "Putting Chad in charge of the education of our children is as dangerous as putting me in charge of a nuclear submarine!"

But because Ross and Chad have a huge amount of money to pay for their re-election campaigns and the endorsement of the Seattle Times and dozens of paid campaign staff members paid for by Bill Gates through LEV and SFC, both Ross and Chad manage to be re-elected and stay in office.

Chad and his "Stand for Children" Campaign Crew... Paid for by Bill Gates!... These same people helped pass The Charter School Initiative. It's a small world.

Bill Gates does not have to write a check to Ross Hunter or Chad Magendanz to help them win elections. When you have as much money as Bill Gates, you simply buy an entire organization (or two) with dozens of staff -such as LEV and SFC - to elect your cronies to the legislature.

Charter School Chad shaking hands With his boss Billionaire Bill Gates

Bill Gates uses his extreme wealth to buy elections in his quest for total control over our public schools.

This is how Bill's Cycle of Bribery, Corruption and Kickbacks works:

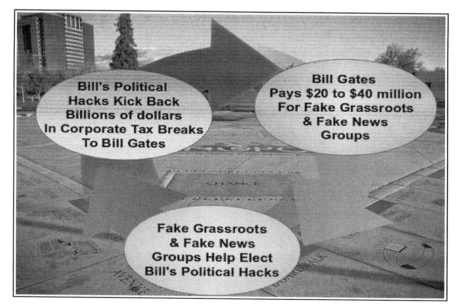

Washington Superintendent Randy Dorn turns to the dark side

In 2008, the voters in Washington State booted out the former Superintendent of Public Instruction, Terry Bergeson and elected Randy Dorn based on his promise to get rid of the unfair and hated WASL test and replace it with a fairer and shorter Measurement of Student Progress (MSP) test. Unfortunately, after only a couple of years with the MSP test, Randy was persuaded to adopt the Common Core SBAC test – which is even worse than the old WASL monster in terms of the number of students it will unfairly label as failures.

Perhaps Randy's change in position had something to do with Randy being appointed to a trade group called CCSSO – a group that Bill Gates has given more than $50 million to "help promote Common Core.". It is hard to turn down that kind of money. Randy now says he is worried about the one percent of kids who move from one state to another having consistent standards. What he fails to mention is that this change to Common Core and SBAC will severely harm the other 99 percent of our kids who now will be severely harmed by having our standards written by Wall Street consultants rather than Washington State teachers.

But what is more troubling to understand is the sudden change in Randy Dorn's position on charter schools. Before and during the 2012 charter school election, while Randy was running for re-election, Randy repeatedly said that "the charter school initiative was contrary to the Washington State constitution." Randy also assured those of us who supported him that he would file a lawsuit to overturn the initiative if it passed. Naturally, after the charter school initiative barely passed by the slimmest of margins in November, 2012, those of us who supported Randy assumed he would file a lawsuit. But on January 8 2013, days after Randy was sworn in for a second term, he announced that he had decided against filing a lawsuit. Then in an interview on July 28th and again on September 4 2014, Dorn said that he was now in favor of charter schools!
http://www.washingtonpolicy.org/blog/post/superintendent-dorn-changes-stance-charter-schools

In the 2012 election, Randy Dorn stated He opposed charter schools Because they were unconstitutional & Because they robbed public schools Of urgently needed funds. Randy now favors charter schools!

This left the teachers union as the only group that sued to enforce our State Constitution. In December 2013, a King County judge agreed with the teachers union that charter schools are contrary to the Washington State Constitution because the Washington State Constitution limits spending tax dollars on normal public schools under the control of the Superintendent of Public Instruction and a locally elected school board. On October 28 2014, the Washington Supreme Court accepted the issue and will make a ruling whether to uphold the trial court sometime in 2015. For the issues in this case, see League of Women Voters et al versus State of Washington.

http://www.courts.wa.gov/content/Briefs/A08/89714-0%20Brief%20of%20Appellants.pdf

Dorn also supports using unreliable student test scores to fire teachers
Perhaps the most shocking part of the corporate takeover of public schools is the use of unreliable student test scores to rate and fire teachers. The research against this is overwhelming. It is unfair to teachers and unfair to students. Yet in 2014 and again in 2015, Randy Dorn promoted bills in the Washington State legislature to require the use of student test scores in ranking and firing teachers. State law already says that student test data must be used as part of teacher and principal evaluations, but school districts can choose which tests they will use: school-based, classroom-based, district-based or statewide. After the Legislature failed to make using state tests mandatory, U.S. Secretary of Education Arne Duncan pulled Washington's waiver. Dorn said he plans to push legislation in 2015 that would say school districts must use applicable state testing data in teacher evaluations. Randy Dorn, Tacoma News Tribute November 30 2014

The WEA said this about Randy Dorn's Teacher Evaluation bill:
"WEA members believe the top-down, unproven approach to teacher evaluations promoted by Sen. Litzow, Supt. Dorn and US Education Secretary Arne Duncan is driven by political considerations rather than what research shows – and teachers know – will benefit students and teachers. Instead of playing politics with our kids' education, the politicians should focus on what would really benefit students – fully funding K-12 education."
http://ourvoicewashingtonea.org/wp-content/uploads/2014/02/WEA-Evaluation-Principles-v2.pdf

Will Washington State suffer the same fate as California, Illinois, and Ohio and see our public schools destroyed by the cancer of charter schools?
The first charter school to start in Washington, in September 2014, has suffered from a series of disasters. This will hopefully help voters better understand that charter schools are not the miracle cure their promoters have claimed they are. Because parents and teachers are turning away from Common Core and high stakes high failure rate tests, there is the hope they will see that these scams are connected to the Charter school scam and eventually turn against the entire corporate ed reform program. Finally, the dramatic turn of the Superintendent Dorn in favor of the SBAC test – a test that will fail 60% to 70% of all Washington students – makes it likely that the public will support a replacement in the 2016 election. One can only hope that the replacement will show more concern for the well being of our children and less concern for the well being of Bill Gates.

What is Next?
We will next look at the scam that led to the start of this book – the Pearson Takeover of the GED Test. Why should public school parents care about a private for profit takeover of the GED? The first reason is that Pearson is using the same bait and switch Common Core testing scams that will soon be inflicted on K12 kids. The second reason is that Pearson "raising the bar" on high school drop outs will increase the number of prison inmates by more than 50,000 in the US – costing US tax payers hundreds of millions of dollars in additional prison costs.

7.2 Corrupt Corporate Takeover of the GED Exam

> "Please, someone, time for in-depth journalism that Documents how Pearson bought American education And what it means to our children."
>
> Diane Ravitch November 26 2012

We agree. In the next three sections, we will take a closer look at a huge corporation called Pearson and their role in destroying the GED exam, destroying our schools and destroying the self esteem of our children and young adults – all to increase corporate profits. Pearson is a private for profit corporation that in 2012 made more than one billion dollars leaching off of our public schools. In the first and second chapters of our book, we showed that Common Core standards are not as complete as the prior Washington State learning standards. We also showed that whoever wrote the Common Core standards knew nothing about child development. We also showed that the Common Core "high failure rate" tests have very little to do with Common Core standards. The whole goal of the new tests is not to measure Common Core standards. Instead, the purpose of the SBAC and PARCC tests are to artificially increase the failure rate of students in order to accelerate the transition of $700 billion in public taxpayer money to private Wall Street corporations. In this article, we will show that the new Common Core GED test, called the Pearson GED test, is also designed to artificially increase the failure rate. The reason is the same. Pearson, the provider of the 2014 Common Core GED test stands to make billions of dollars selling educational products to students who fail the new GED test.

Why Should Public School Parents Care about Changes to the GED?
The GED exam, also called the General Education Development exam, is a test that can be given to high school dropouts to determine if they have academic skills and abilities similar to a graduating high school senior. If a person can pass this GED test, they are given a GED certificate which allows them to apply for a good job or get financial aid to go to a good college. The first reason we should all care about the GED is that the Pearson 2014 GED is the "Canary in the Coal Mine." What happened to GED candidates in 2014 is now happening to K12 public school students all around the nation in 2015. Just as the Common Core tests in Kentucky and New York unfairly labeled 70% of their students as failures, the 2014 Pearson GED test unfairly labeled over 80% of GED candidates as failures – and the 2015 Common Core tests (SBAC and PARCC) will use similar tactics to unfairly label 60% to 70% of the students who take those tests as failures in 2015. It is important to see how all of the Common Core tests are related to each other even though none of them are actually related to the Common Core standards.

The second reason we need to pay attention to what is happening with the Pearson "Common Core" GED test is that in denying about 500,000 low income young adults of a GED certificate every year, more than 10 percent of these low income people will wind up committing major crimes and going to prison. This will increase prison populations in states around the US by more than 50,000 inmates. At an average cost of $50,000 per year per inmate, the increased cost to US tax payers will be more than $2.5 billion. Most of this is money that will be robbed from public schools causing the loss of tens of thousands of public school teachers. We therefore all need to pay attention to the corrupt corporate takeover the GED exam. The change from the 2013 GED test to the Pearson 2014 "Common Core" GED test in 2014 has resulted in 10,000 fewer students passing the GED test in Washington state and 500,000 fewer students passing the GED test in the United States compared to previous years. This is tragic because the GED is not merely a second chance for students who dropped out of high school. For many struggling young adults, the GED is their last and only chance to get a good paying job and have a decent life. It is also necessary for people to have a GED or a high school credential to apply for financial aid to go to college. Taking this final chance away from millions of young adults, essentially closing doors to them, is a crime because it unfairly labels hundreds of thousands of young adults as "failures" when they would have been able to pass the previous more fairly constructed GED test. The Pearson GED test robs people not only of their hope and dignity, it robs them of their future.

How did the Pearson Takeover of the GED occur

We will begin by looking at the history of the GED and how it was taken over by Pearson. The first GED exam was created in 1942 by the non-profit American Council on Education (ACE) to help World War II veterans. Since then the exam has been updated three times – in 1978, 1988 and 2002. More than 17 million people have earned their GED certificate through this program.

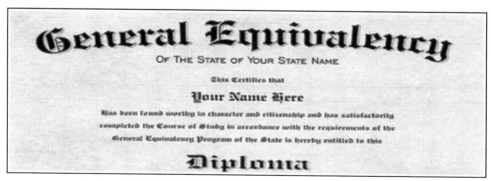

A new update of the GED was scheduled for 2012, but then it was postponed because of major changes in US curriculum due to a Gates Foundation backed scam called Common Core. In 2011, a for-profit corporation called Pearson took over the GED and created a Common Core version of the GED which they released in January 2014.

The chief difference between the Pearson GED test and the prior ACE GED tests was not that it was "aligned with Common Core." Rather, it was that the difficulty of the GED test questions were increased to such a point that the average high school senior could no longer pass the test. It is therefore not a high school equivalency test. It is simply a high failure rate test.

Why We Need to Restore GED Fairness
When we first saw the math portion of the 2014 Pearson GED test in March 2014, we were surprised by the difficulty of its math test. One of us, Elizabeth, had taught GED classes several years ago, and the Pearson GED math test was nothing like the math test her students had taken in the past. Elizabeth took the Pearson GED math test in March 2014 and flunked. She asked around at other colleges and found that very few students were able to earn their GED in many Washington colleges during winter quarter 2014. Elizabeth wondered why Pearson changed the GED test to make it so difficult? Do students really need to be able to answer two-step probability questions to get training to be a hair stylist or a nursing assistant? We both started doing research which is what our website, "**Restore GED Fairness (dot) org**" is all about. Elizabeth gave a sample GED math tests of 5 questions to 50 people with college degrees and only 4 people could pass the test. Of the 4 who passed, two were engineers and one was a math major. We have been working hard to get a fairer GED test in Washington State ever since.

What difference does it make if the GED test is owned by a nonprofit agency or a for-profit corporation?
The GED test has historically been a gateway to college and better employment opportunities for countless out of school youth and adults. The keys to that gateway are now controlled by a for- profit organization.

Pearson is the largest private for profit educational corporation in the world. In 2013, Pearson made nearly two billion dollars in profits on ten billion dollars in sales. They have literally dozens of brands making it appear like there are lots of options – when nearly all of the brands are actually Pearson.

Often the same book is put out by their "different" publishers with only slightly different formatting. In 2000, Pearson bought out Simon & Schuster's education businesses and opened a new, overarching company—Pearson Education. Two years later, in 2002, Pearson acquired the Minnesota-based testing company National Computer Systems for $2.5 billion and began expanding into assessments. Pearson has it all—and all of it has a price. For example, for statewide testing in Texas alone, the company holds a five-year contract worth nearly $500 million to create and administer exams. If students should fail those tests, Pearson offers a series of remedial-learning products to help them pass. Thus Pearson makes money when students prepare to take a test, more money when they take a test and even more money when students fail a test.

Money, Money, Money

Pearson has a well documented record of bribing politicians. In 2011, Pearson spent close to $700,000 lobbying in four key states. On April 27, 2011, the Pearson Foundation announced its partnership with the Bill & Melinda Gates Foundation to create 24 online courses to teach the Common Core Standards for Math and English in our public schools. Because profit is important to corporations, the cost of taking the new Pearson GED test versus older 2002 version of the GED has approximately doubled. That's what happens when for-profit corporations are in charge. Education now is seen as simply another economic domain slating to be milked for profit.

The Pearson Monopoly

In a scary article called "The Pearson Monopoly" posted in November 2012 by Jennifer Job, a Professor with the University of North Carolina, we learn that Pearson bought Harcourt, another publishing company, in 2008. This allows Pearson to monopolize both the curriculum and assessment markets. This gives Pearson both a horizontal and a vertical monopoly. For comparison, Microsoft is a horizontal monopoly while Apple is a vertical monopoly. Pearson is both. Here is a quote from the Pearson Monopoly article:

"To grow into the multibillion-dollar corporation they are today, Pearson blurs every line among for profit, nonprofit, and government systems. They have prominently partnered with University of Phoenix, whose parent company's CEO also sits on the board of Teach for America... Pearson's advocates for education reform were instrumental in the development of the Race to the Top initiative, from which they have benefited in numerous ways. For example, Race to the Top requires significant data accumulation, and thus Pearson partnered with the Gates Foundation to be the ones to store the data."

Surely, we don't want to have one corporation Pearson with Gates Foundation backing controlling our students' learning, assessment, their private data and our teacher evaluations. According to Diane Ravitch in a 2012 blogpost: "It (Pearson) receives billions of dollars to test millions of students. Its scores will be used to calculate the value of teachers. It has a deal with the Gates Foundation to store all the student-level data collected at the behest of Race to the Top.

It recently purchased Connections Academy, thus giving it a foothold in the online charter industry. And it recently added the GED to its portfolio." The Koch brothers have connection to Pearson, as does Teach For America and they all have plenty of money to bribe our elected leaders. The more Pearson acts, the fewer choices we have over education in our towns and cities.

How was the Pearson High Failure Rate GED Test Created?
Having spent many years as a math instructor and a math tutor, one of us (David Spring) was aware that math questions do not just fall out of the sky. In the past, math questions were very carefully generated and scientifically studied. For each math content area, the questions were specifically designed to range from "easy" questions which most students could answer to "hard" or challenging questions which very few students could answer. When we reviewed the math questions on the 2014 GED test, we found that the new GED questions had almost nothing to do with the new Common Core standards. Some standards were covered with several questions while other standards were not covered by any questions. Instead, the questions appear to be specifically written to make it impossible for struggling math students to pass the test. In short, the 2014 GED test has also been designed to fail. We wondered who would do such a thing and why would they do it?

We then learned that the GED test was recently taken over by a private for profit corporation called Pearson. This is the same corporation that designed the Common Core PARCC tests which huge numbers of students failed in Kentucky in 2012 and 2013 and in New York in 2013.

We began to wonder where the Common Core math questions were coming from and why they were really chosen. This led us to study our nation's most studied math questions... many of which are found in the National Assessment of Educational Progress database. You can do the same study if you want. Just go to the new NAEP home page. http://nces.ed.gov/nationsreportcard/

Then click on **Main NAEP Assessment.**

Then click on **Sample Questions, Analyze Data and More** in the side menu. Then click on **NAEP Questions Tool**. Then click the "Questions Tool... Explore the Database" box. Then click on the "Mathematics" box. This will bring up the following side menu box.

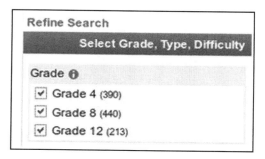

As we are interested in evaluating the difficulty of the Pearson 2014 GED Math test questions – which claim to be an equivalency test for the math knowledge of high school seniors, uncheck the 4th and 8th grade boxes. This will bring up a table of the most recent NAEP 12th grade publicly released math questions. There are three levels of NAEP math questions. Easy, Medium and Hard. Easy questions were answered correctly by about three in four 12th graders. Medium questions were answered correctly by about half of the 12th graders and hard questions were answered correctly by about one in four 12th graders.

How to create a math test that the majority of high school students will fail
We have also studied the Easy and Medium questions. But let's assume for the moment that you work for Pearson and you have been given the task of coming up with math questions that the majority of students will fail.

The way to do this is to un-check the Easy and Medium Questions. This leaves 100 hard questions from the 2001, 2005, 2009 and 2013 NAEP exams.

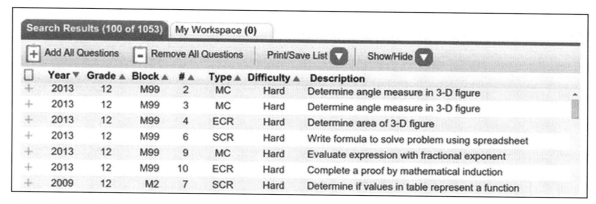

Check **Add All Questions** to add all of these questions to My Workspace. Then click on the **My Workspace** tab.

Next, check all four boxes in the Select Content side menu.

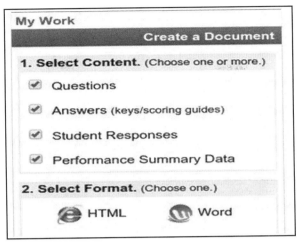

Then click on **HTML** to view the questions and performance summary data in a web browser. You can then copy paste any content you want from the web browser to other documents. We looked at all 100 items. But here we will only look at 2 of them and compare them to nearly identical questions on the Pearson 2014 GED test.

Sample NAEP 2009 Hard Question #1... Determine if values in a table represent a function (This is the very first 2009 "hard" question in the NAEP table above).

The table below shows ordered pairs (x, y) that define a relationship between the variables x and y.

x	y
−2	3
−1	0
0	−1
1	0
2	3
3	8

Is y a function of x? Yes or No. Give a reason for your answer: _____.

To answer this question, in two minutes or less, the student needs to create a two dimensional graph with an X and Y axis and plot these six points on the graph. The student must then recognize that the shape of the curve formed by the six dots on the graph is a parabola which is a type of function of the form y = (x)(x) -1. The correct answer is Yes and the reason is that it is a parabola.

According to years of NAEP data, this question is classified as a "hard" question because **only 14% of high school seniors are able to answer this question correctly.** Put another way, if you ask 100 high school seniors this question, 86 of them will fail to get the right answer. This is not a fault of the students. Nor is it a fault of the question. It is simply **a question that is designed to fail.**

It does what it is intended to do which is separate students who are very good with math from students who are not very good with math. Here is the Pearson 2014 GED version of this same question.

Which table of values represents a function?

A.

x	y
-4	7
-3	5
1	7
4	-1

B.

x	y
-2	-5
-2	-3
-1	0
0	1

C.

x	y
1	-2
2	-3
2	1
3	4

D.

x	y
3	-2
3	0
3	2
3	5

This Pearson question is actually more difficult than the related NAEP question in that to answer the Pearson question the student needs to create FOUR two dimensional graphs and plot a total of 16 points on these four graphs in less than two minutes. Alternately, they can remember that a general definition of a function is that there is only one value of y for every value of X. Since A is the only option above that meets this definition, A is the answer.

However, students are also taught in high school math courses that the definition of a **quadratic function** is a function of the form $y = a(x)(x) + b(x) + c$ and (x) is not equal to zero. This is extremely important for two reasons. First, the NAEP question did use a quadratic function of the kind high school students might be familiar with. Second, with the Pearson question, while Option A above is a technically a function in the loosest sense of the term "function", it is **NOT a quadratic function.** A student who understands quadratic functions could therefore reasonably conclude that the above Pearson problem has no correct solution. Needless to say, it is likely that the vast majority of high school seniors will get this Pearson question wrong. And that is the goal of the Pearson 2014 GED test. It is not about improving math instruction and it is not about Common Core standards. It is about creating a test which is "designed to fail." As the above question is so abstract that it may be hard for a non-math major to understand what I am talking about, let's look at another more real world example.

Sample NAEP Hard Question #2...

Bob is going on a trip. He will be taking a taxi, a flight, and then a train. Bob chose the following three companies based on their claims.

- Tom's Taxi Service claims that it is on time 95 percent of the time.
- Friendly Flyer Airlines claims that it is on time 93 percent of the time.
- Rapid Railways claims that it is on time 98 percent of the time.

Based on the three companies' claims, what is the approximate probability that all three parts of Bob's trip will be on time, assuming that all three probabilities are independent?

Answer_____

The key to this question is to recognize that the probability of each event is independent from the probability of the remaining two events. The solution is therefore in two minutes or less to multiply the three probabilities times each other. 0.95 x 0.98 x 0.93 = 0.865 = about 0.87. In many years of testing 12th graders on this complex probability questions, only 12% of 12th graders got the correct answer. Again, this was not the fault of the 12th graders or the fault of the question. It is simply a question which is designed to fail the majority of 12th graders who are asked the question.

Here is the Pearson 2014 GED version of this same question.

A snack stand is open each day that there is a ball game. There is a 70% probability that a ball game will take place on any given day. To the nearest whole percent, what is the probability the snack stand will be open Monday through Friday this week? Enter the exact answer to the nearest whole percent (no options given).

This question also involves recognizing that the event (rain) is independent for each of the five days. Thus, the answer is 0.7 x 0.7 x 0.7 x 0.7 x 0.7 = about 17%. But the Pearson question is harder than the NAEP question for two reasons. First, the fact that the events are independent is hidden because the event itself (rain) is the same each day. Second, the Pearson question asks about five events while the NAEP question asks about only three events.

It is therefore likely that less than ten percent of all high school seniors can answer the Pearson question correctly. Once again, that is the goal of the Pearson 2014 GED test. It is not about improving math instruction and it is not about Common Core standards. It is about creating a test which is "designed to fail."

What is Next?

Now that we better understand how the Pearson GED "Designed to Fail" test was created, in the next section, we will take a look at the consequences of that test for students in Washington state and around the nation.

7.3 Consequences of the Pearson Takeover of the GED Test

For the past decade, an average of 13,300 low income young adults per year passed this GED test in Washington State – allowing them to seek better opportunities with employers and qualify for better college opportunities. However, in January 2014, a multinational for profit corporation called Pearson, took over the GED name and changed the GED test to an unfair test that was not related to the academic skills and abilities of the average high school senior. The Pearson GED test, currently the only GED test students can take in Washington State, was substantially more difficult to pass than the prior GED test. As a result, the number of candidates who passed the new Pearson GED test **in 2014 in Washington State fell to only 2,850 – a decline of more than 10,000 students from the average of previous years.**

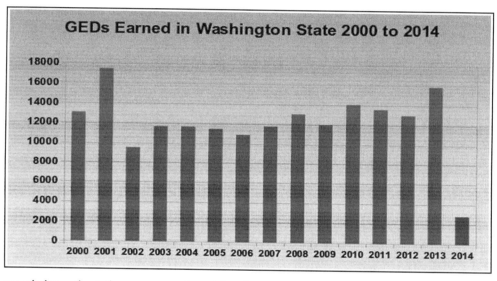

Pearson claims that the reason for this change is to align the GED test with Common Core College Ready standards. However, the purpose of a GED certificate is not to determine whether a young adult is college ready. It is merely to determine if a person has the academic skills comparable to the average high school senior. Pearson also claims that the former GED test, called the 2002 GED test, was too easy and could be passed by "90 percent of high school seniors." In fact, a norming verification study done by the American Council of Education (ACE) in 2007 comparing thousands of graduating high school seniors to thousands of GED test completers reached a surprising conclusion about the 2002 version of the GED test: **"GED Test candidates who completed the test – regardless of whether they passed – performed better than graduating high school seniors... 75% of GED Test candidates versus 69 percent of seniors earned an average score of 550 on the test... GED test passers correctly answered 5 to 16 percent more items than graduating seniors."**
http://www.gedtestingservice.com/uploads/files/d0ade443cadf10b859e3467fcfe85757.pdf

Those who completed the 2002 GED test did better than the average high school senior – even if they did not pass the test! In other words, the 2002 version of the GED was already too hard for the average high school senior to pass. The 2014 GED is the 2002 GED on steroids. The claim by Pearson that the test needs to be made harder in order to better match high school seniors is completely absurd.

The Pearson test also suffers from numerous other drawbacks. The cost of the Pearson GED is twice the cost of the prior test ($120 versus $60). The Pearson GED requires access to a computer and keyboarding skills and can only be taken online. This limits who can take the test and where the test can be given.

This GED student wants to attend cosmetology school.

The old GED would have taken her 3 to 6 months.

The new Person GED Test will take her two years.

Will she persist in learning complex algebra...

or will she give up?

There is a less expensive option called the HiSET test, which only costs $60, can be taken with paper and pencil if needed and is more fairly normed to the match the actually abilities of graduating high school seniors. In the spring of 2015, we therefore promoted a bill in the Washington state legislature to restore GED fairness. Our bill was Washington state House Bill 1743 and companion Senate Bill 5676. This bill would allow GED instructors in Washington State to offer students a fairer, less expensive and more accessible High School Equivalency test, called the HiSET test, and thereby end the Pearson GED test monopoly in Washington State. To support the need for this bill, we provided legislators with Pearson and HiSET test results from Washington, Kansas, and Missouri to conclude that had the Washington State Board for Community and Technical Colleges (SBCTC) chosen the fairer HiSET test instead of the unfair Pearson GED test in 2014, an additional 8,000 students would have passed the test and received their high school equivalency diploma in Washington State in 2014.

A national study indicates the low income young adults without a GED or high school diploma, who lack access to a good job or chance to attend a good college, are 14% more likely to commit a major crime and wind up in prison. Thus, the failure to offer our low income young adults a fair GED test in 2014 is likely to result in about 1,000 additional inmates in Washington State prisons. Another study indicated that the total cost of keeping a person in prison in Washington State is about $50,000 per year. Assuming an average prison term of one year, this means that the failure of SBCTC to insure access to a fair GED test will cost Washington State tax payers an additional $50 million dollars per year – making the decision by SBCTC one of the most costly errors in Washington State history – both in terms of human cost as well as cost to the tax payers. We therefore hoped our State legislature would pass House Bill 1743 and companion Senate Bill 5676. Below is a summary of this information.

Comparing the HiSET Pass Rate to the Pearson GED Pass Rate
The annual GED reports for past years are found at the following link:
http://www.gedtestingservice.com/educators/historical-testing-data

These reports were used to construct the following graph.

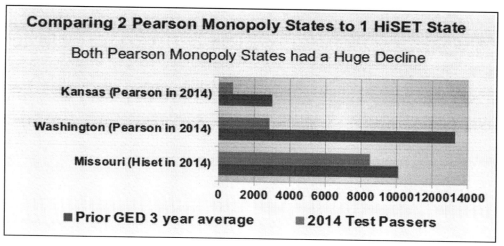

Washington was not the only Pearson GED monopoly state to suffer a huge drop in the number of GED test passers. Kansas had an average of 3,000 passers per year prior to 2014. There were only 806 students who could pass the unfair Pearson GED test in 2014 – a decline of 73%. Here is a graph comparing the 2 Pearson Monopoly states to the HiSET State of Missouri.

Why the Sharp Decline in the Pearson Monopoly States?
This sharp decline in the pass rate in Washington and Kansas is due primarily to the fact that the Pearson GED test uses NAEP Hard Questions whereas the 2002 GED test and the HiSET test use NAEP medium questions. In addition, the Pearson test can only be taken on computer whereas HiSET can be taken without a computer. Finally, the Pearson test requires $120 while the HiSET test costs only $60.

Because of the drawbacks of the Pearson GED test, 18 states now offer their students an alternative High School Equivalency test:

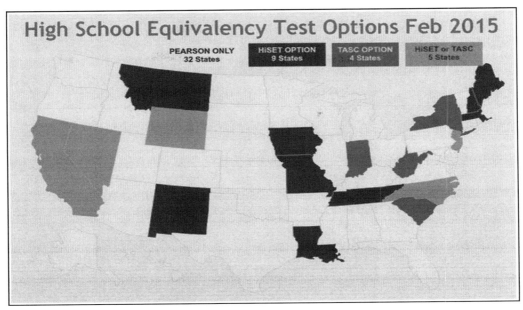

GED Marketplace... Turning Personal Tragedy into Pearson Profits
Pearson makes hundreds of millions of dollars in profit by deliberately and unfairly maximizing the failure rate on the Pearson GED test. If you go to the Pearson GED Test Prep store, called the GED Marketplace, you will see dozens of Pearson GED test prep products for sale. http://www.gedmarketplace.com/

Click on GED Test Prep in the left side menu to reach this page:
http://www.gedmarketplace.com/Articles.asp?ID=252&category=testprep

Pearson offers 73 products to prepare for the Pearson GED test. Those who fail the GED test, and parents of those who fail the GED, are likely to order many of these products in a desperate attempt to pass the Pearson GED test. Some of the items are not sold but rented by the month. For example, the first item costs $50 per month. There are 30 products on the first page with a total price of about $1,000. The total for all 73 Pearson GED test prep items is about $2,000.
Pearson profit from the GED Marketplace is about $500 million per year!

How much will the Pearson monopoly - destroying the lives of 8,322 mostly low income young adults per year - cost Washington State tax payers?

High school dropouts who do not get a GED are as much as three times more likely to commit a crime as those who do have a high school diploma or GED. Here is a quote from a recent study: "Nearly 1 of every 10 young male high school dropouts was institutionalized versus fewer than 1 of 33 young male high school graduates." "The Consequences of Dropping Out of School, Joblessness and Jailing for High School Dropouts" October 2009

The Role of the GED in Breaking the Cycle of Poverty and Prison

Poverty creates prisoners and prisons in turn fuel poverty. Once a person has been incarcerated, the experience limits their lifetime earning power and their ability to climb out of poverty even decades after their release. This sets up a vicious inter-generational cycle of poverty and prison. Over one third of prison inmates—37 percent in 2003—do not have a high school diploma or a GED certificate. With a prison record and no certificate, few jobs are available.

In 2002, the U.S. Bureau of Justice Statistics reported that 67% of inmates released from state prisons in 1994 committed at least one serious crime in the three years following their release. A GED certificate is a "last chance" to break this cycle of poverty and prison.

Offenders under the age of 21 who earned their GED diploma were 14% less likely to return to prison within three years. Without a GED to help them get a job, 54% of young offenders return to prison within three years.
http://www.passged.com/media/pdf/research/The_Effect_of_Earning_a_GED_on_Recidivisim_Rates.pdf

Making the GED much more difficult to pass will reduce the number of High School Dropouts and Prison inmates who can pass the test. Fewer GEDs and fewer jobs will increase the prison population

Calculating the Cost to Tax Payers of 8,322 mostly low income young adults not being able to pass the GED due to the Unfair Pearson Test

Given that having a GED has resulted in a 14% drop in committing crimes and given that the prison population passes the GED test at the same rate as the non-prison High school drop out population, we can predict that had 8,322 low income young adults been given a fair chance at passing the GED test so they could get a decent job of go to college, the rate in this group committing crimes would be 14% less. This would be about 1,165 fewer low income young adults committing crimes and going to prison in Washington State. According to a 2012 study, the annual cost to Washington State tax payers to house and feed a single prisoner is over $50,000. This does not include the cost to victims from crimes, the cost in police to catch law breakers and the cost to courts in legal fees. Assuming a one year jail term, **the cost of one thousand extra prisoners is at least an additional $50 million per year**. Washington State had an average daily prison population of over 16,000 in 2012. Most did not have a GED certificate. Adding another 1,000 prisoners would represent a 6% increase in the prison population and in the cost of prisons which is currently just under one billion dollars per year. http://www.vera.org/files/price-of-prisons-washington-fact-sheet.pdf

A mother of three kids learned that she passed the old GED test on the final day of 2013. She said she needed her GED so she could go to college and become a social worker or an advocate for children with special needs. She was lucky.
But what about the next young mom who needs to pass the GED?

The Poverty to Prison Money Machine

Putting Pearson profits above the need of students who need a GED certificate is despicable enough. But there is an even more sinister aspect of preventing high school drop outs from getting their GED - the billions of dollars to be made running private prisons – filled with young men who failed to pass the GED test.

Poverty to Prison Pipeline... America's new growth industry

According to a 2011 ACLU report called "Banking on Bondage", the United States has 2.3 million citizens behind bars, more than any other nation. The United States has less than 5 percent of the world's population. But it has almost a quarter of the world's prisoners. It hasn't always been this way. Up until 1970, the US was at the world average of one in one thousand citizens being locked up. https://www.aclu.org/files/assets/bankingonbondage_20111102.pdf

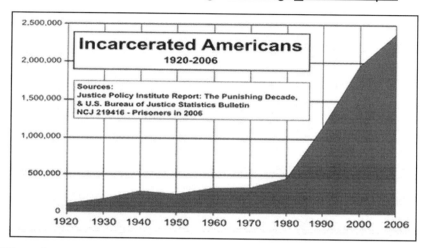

Then the billionaires began their takeover of our media and our State legislatures and national Congress. One of their first actions, besides taking over our public airwaves and getting rid of the "Fairness Doctrine" was to pass laws putting many more people behind bars. This "war on the poor" movement really took off after the election of Ronald Reagan in 1980. Many States now spend more on locking people up in prisons than on funding higher education. Here is the graph for the State of California spending on both as a Percent of State General Funds:

Spending on Prisons (Green) compared to Spending on Higher Education

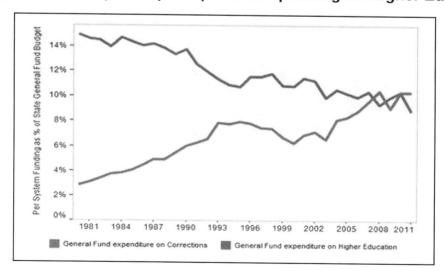

"Since 1980, higher education spending has decreased by 13 percent in inflation adjusted dollars, whereas spending on California's prisons and associated correctional programs has skyrocketed by 436 percent. The state now shells out more money from its general fund for the prison system than the higher education system." http://www.huffingtonpost.com/2012/09/06/california-prisons-colleges_n_1863101.html

On reason states have had to cut support for higher education and raise tuition has been to pay for all of the prisons. The rise in tuition has led to an explosion in student debt. **Both corrections spending and student debt hit $1 trillion dollar milestones in 2012.**

What is the real harm with high stakes high failure rate testing?
A 2013 study found a significant relationship between high-stakes testing and the school-to-prison pipeline, with students who fail high stakes testing exams 12 percent more likely to face incarceration. http://therealnews.com/t2/index.php?option=com_content&task=view&id=31&Itemid=74&jumival=10458

This is a 12 minute video on High stakes test failure linked to winding up in prison
https://www.youtube.com/watch?v=9sWw9Y77y5A

The School-to-Prison Pipeline Exposed, a new study has revealed that in states that use high-stakes exit exams, students who fail these tests were more than 12 percent more likely to face incarceration and had lower graduation rates than states without exit exams. Meanwhile, the study found no consistent effects of exit exams on employment or the distribution of wages.

"This school-to-prison pipeline is a catastrophe in communities across the nation, and it's being fueled by this high-stakes testing regime. We are the only country in the world that is so obsessed with these high-stakes standardized tests."
Jesse Hagopain, Teacher Garfield High School, Seattle Washington

Bill Gates makes a Profit from the Poverty to Prison Pipeline
The most well-known prison profiteers in the United States are the Corrections Corporation of America (CCA) and the GEO Group. Between them, these two firms pulled in about $3.3 billion last year running scores of private prisons and immigration detention centers.
http://billmoyers.com/2015/01/21/five-corporations-youve-never-heard-making-millions-mass-incarceration/

The world's largest operator of private prisons and detention centers, GEO runs 59 facilities across the country. The Gates Foundation, chaired by Bill Gates, invests $2.2 million in the GEO Group. Gates is a stockholder in both GEO private prisons and G4S global security. G4S is the same company that profiteers from buses along the Arizona border searching for migrants to transport into detention. Bill Gates is one of the top shareholders in the notorious prison profiteer G4S. http://www.g4s.com/en/Investors/Investor%20Relations%20Information/Major%20Shareholdings/

Immigrant justice campaigners and prison divestment advocates delivered 10,000 petition signatures demanding immediately withdraw its investment in the GEO Group: "GEO Group makes billions of dollars putting people in cages — and they drive profits by lobbying to put more people behind bars for minor crimes," said Arturo Carmona, Executive Director of Presente.org. "With Latinos now the largest group in federal prisons and detention centers—mostly for minor or non-existent crimes—the Gates' investment is particularly galling for us. Unless they divest, the Gates Foundation will drag their legacy into the mud of wasteful, overcrowded and abusive immigrant prisons."

Corruption Kills House Bill 1743 and Senate Bill 5676

Given that the Pearson GED monopoly will likely cost Washington State taxpayers more than $50 million dollars per year in additional prison costs per year, one would think that our State legislature would quickly approve of a fairer and less expensive high school equivalency test option like the HiSET test. Unfortunately, Bill Gates has bought not only many members of our state legislature but also the Washington State Board of Community and Technical Colleges (SBCTC) – who have been given more than $13 million in grants and bribes by the Gates Foundation. As a consequence, the director of the State Board Marty Brown, was able to convince the chairs of the House Higher Education Committee, Drew Hanson and the Senate Ways and Means Committee, Andy Hill, to kill the bill.

Washington State Board for Community & Technical Colleges	2012	Strategic Partnerships	US Program	$4,029,394
Washington State Board for Community & Technical Colleges	2009 and earlier	Postsecondary Success	US Program	$5,295,000
Washington State Board for Community & Technical Colleges	2009 and earlier	College-Ready	US Program	$3,775,000
Washington State Board for Community & Technical Colleges	2009 and earlier	College-Ready	US Program	$423,500

There is an important reason why Common Core promoters do not want a fair GED test. It is because once students understood how unfair the SBAC test was, they would opt for the fair GED test instead.

It therefore was necessary for the Ed Reform scammers to close the GED escape hatch before adding the unfair SBAC test.

As a consequence of Common Core advocates blocking a fair GED test option, GED candidates in Washington state will continue to fail the Pearson GED test in record numbers for yet another year – increasing Pearson's record profits while driving thousands more low income young adults into our state prison system – increasing profits for Bill Gates. We will continue our campaign for a fair GED test in Washington state. Our plan is to travel across our state exposing this problem. But our efforts will not do much good as long as Bill Gates is allowed to use his billions to control our state legislature. What we really need is a more honest state legislature which will require that in the 2016 election more honest people run for the state legislature. So in addition to campaigning for GED fairness, we will be seeking our teachers and parents and young adults willing to run for office. We plan on helping train them and building a network of parents and teachers interested in protecting our public schools. We hope you will join us! See our website for additional information on our efforts to restore GED fairness in Washington state and across the US, visit our website on this topic: http://restoregedfairness.org/

What is Next?
The billionaire takeover of our government has not only corrupted the GED process, it has corrupted our entire economic system. In the next section, we will look at how young adults in the US have almost no job prospects even if they are "college and career ready."

7.4 The College and Career Ready Marketing Slogan is a Scam

> Telling millions of low income students all they need to do to get a good job is "learn to pass a more difficult test" is like telling someone hit by a tidal wave all they need to Do to keep their head above water is "learn to swim faster."

We have shown that Common Core tests, including the SBAC test, the PARCC test and the Pearson GED test, are more difficult to to pass not because of the change to Common Core standards, but because they use NAEP "Hard" questions instead of NAEP "Medium" questions. This artificial increase in difficulty insures that the vast majority of students will fail Common Core tests. The typical reason given for dramatically increasing the difficulty of high stakes tests is to prepare students to be "career and college ready." In this section, we will expose the fact that even if students are able to pass Common Core tests, most will not have a high paying high tech job waiting for them at the end of this grueling marathon. For example, we already have many more high tech workers than high tech jobs. Swimming faster is not the solution to this problem when the problem is that wealth is concentrated in the hands of a few billionaires. Instead of expecting kids to swim faster, we need to stop the tidal wave of wealth being transferred from the poor to the rich.

It is difficult to understand how failing 80% of the students who take the GED is going to better help them prepare for jobs flipping burgers at McDonald's – when they will not even be able to apply for these jobs since they do not have their GED because Pearson made it impossible for them to pass the GED test!

Comparing US High Stakes Tests to China

One of us (Elizabeth Hanson) has been working as an ESL instructor – including working with students from China - for 30 years. Asian kids come to study in the U.S. because either they did not do well enough on their high stakes tests to enter university in China, or their parents did not want their kids to suffer the massive amount of studying required to pass the Gao Kao – a two day test given to seniors in China. Only half the students who take the Gao Kao pass it. The cut score, the score determining if you pass a test or not, is set by the Chinese government. http://factsanddetails.com/china/cat13/sub82/item1649.html

Students in China spend years studying for the Gao Kao Test... Is this what we want for Our students in the US?

What is the real reason for "College and Career Ready" testing?

What seems to be going on is this: Some billionaire-corporate types started a myth that Americans were falling behind the rest of the world, and then they stepped in with the solution: copy-written educational standards, tests, curricula and materials and a system for data-mining to write reports to justify the whole mess. Look at Pearson Publishing, a UK company, which owns the GED and publishes high stakes tests and curricula. They earn $4 billion in sales annually in North America from solving the "problem" of our kids not being "College and Career Ready". What is happening to our education system is very simple and very devious... **Create a problem and create a market to solve the problem.**

How Designed to Fail Tests are Related to our Designed to Fail Economy

It would be one thing if we as a people really were failing- if we had somehow become less creative, less productive. It would be one thing if we had a real demand for workers and didn't have enough workers to fill that demand. But those aren't the problems. The problem is that we've off-shored and out sourced our jobs. We don't have much of an economy for the bottom 60% of Americans. And public education with its budget of $750 billion a year is in the corporate sights. Our kids have become commodities. The ed-refomers have created an industry with "designed to fail" tests. Let's turn to the real problem: the economy which has also been "designed to fail."

Free Trade versus Fair Trade

Let's take a look at this robust economy that we are preparing our kids for when they get College and Career Ready. Where are all of those great "Career Ready" jobs going to be? What ever happened to Detroit and Camden and Pittsburgh and other formerly great cities in the U.S? Due to "free trade" agreements, 30 million jobs have been lost in the U.S. since 1992 and with more trade agreements in the wings - the TPP and TTIP - many more jobs are sure to be off-shored and out-sourced. If our government really cared about the people, would they have allowed free trade agreements to go through? Our students are forced to struggle with high stakes tests where many of the questions are years above their reading ability – and after all of this high failure rate testing, all they get from it is a failed economy that results in a dead-end future So much for college and career ready.

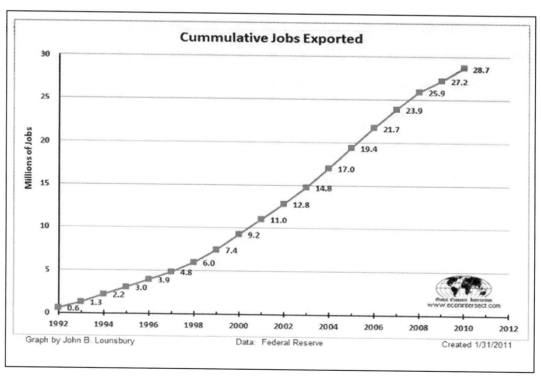

We need more real jobs not more fake tests

Billionaires claim that we need to get our kids college and career ready to be prepared to work in this new high tech economy. But there is no truth to this claim. According to the Bureau of Labor statistics, of the 30 jobs which will have the most demand and openings in the U.S.- from now until 2022 - 2/3 won't even require a college degree. Examples of the jobs we will have are store clerks, food service workers, nursing assistants, day laborers... those jobs will be in high demand. (http://www.bls.gov/news.release/ecopro.t05.htm)

Many of the fastest growing Careers such as health care Will not require more than a two year College Degree & will not require more than a minimal Background in math!

What about STEM jobs?

STEM jobs pay well. However, according to the Census bureau, only 1 in 4 Stem graduates are working at a STEM job that requires their degree. The others are working at jobs that don't require their degree.
(http://www.census.gov/newsroom/press-releases/2014/cb14-130.html)
Moreover, look at the low growth in STEM jobs.

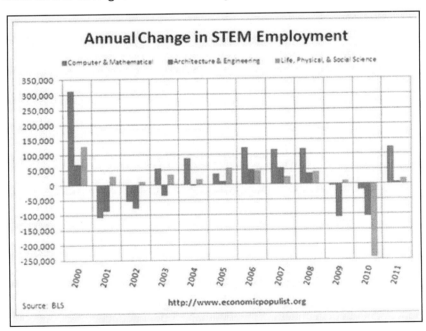

http://www.economicpopulist.org/content/congress-betrays-us-stem-worker-once-again

Where are these math jobs?
The biggest myth we need to refute is the claim that there are "millions of good paying job openings" just waiting to be filled if only we could somehow raise the math ability of high school dropouts (or high school seniors, or college seniors). The claim is that the skills of the current labor pool are "not aligned" with the available jobs. These phony claims sound good and have been repeated so often in the corporate media, that many people believe they must be true. But the "millions of jobs awaiting those with better math skills" claim is not supported by any actual facts. For example, there are already hundreds of thousands of unemployed high tech workers in the United States. In addition, the 2010 US Census confirmed there are 1.8 million unemployed engineers in the US.

Hundreds of thousands of unemployed high tech workers in the US
According to an article on ComputerWorld.com, there are already more than **241,000 unemployed U.S. high tech workers – all of them with very good math skills.** High tech jobs have been outsourced to H1B foreign workers not because there are not enough workers in the US to fill these positions – but rather because wealthy multinational corporations can find cheaper workers in other countries to do high tech jobs due to the lower standard of living in other countries. There was a special report on this scam on the PBS News Hour on July 24 2013:
http://www.pbs.org/newshour/making-sense/the-bogus-high-tech-worker-sho/

Close to half of all recent college graduates are working at jobs that don't require a college degree, jobs like nursing assistant, store clerk office worker, food service, and on top of that they are on average $30,000 in debt.
http://www.usnews.com/news/articles/2014/11/13/average-student-loan-debt-hits-30-000

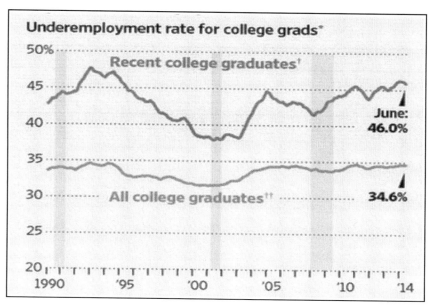

Here is a quote from the PBS report: "High-tech industries are now using guest workers to fill two-thirds of new IT jobs. At the same time, U.S. colleges are graduating more than twice as many science, technology, engineering and math (STEM) graduates than the number of STEM openings generated by our economy each year... Only half of engineering graduates find engineering jobs."

Tech industry insiders have admitted at conferences that most of the high tech jobs listed are fake jobs that do not even exist. The only purpose in listing these fake jobs is to fool the US Congress into increasing the number of foreign workers allowed into the US. A survey of college graduates by the National Center for Educational Statistics confirmed that only two-thirds of computer science graduates went into IT jobs in 2009. One third reported there were no IT jobs available.

Currently, U.S. colleges graduate far more scientists and engineers than find employment in those fields every year — about 200,000 more STEM graduates than STEM jobs per year. These are all people with a high school diploma and a college diploma and excellent math skills that cannot find a job. If these highly qualified college graduates cannot find jobs, how is pushing a high school drop out into learning advanced algebra going to help them find a job?

Corporate Outsourcing of Jobs and Wealth

Corporate propaganda has falsely claimed that we do not have enough skilled workers in America and we therefore have to import H1B visa workers from overseas. **But the truth is that there is no shortage of skilled American workers.** Often dozens of qualified Americans apply for every job. In fact, the workers imported to replace American Hi Tech workers often had LESS training than the workers they were replacing.

So the truth is that wealthy corporations are simply bringing in foreign workers to drive down wages and train workers to outsource jobs overseas.

"These foreign workers are paid only one third of what the laid off American workers had earned… American workers were even required to train the Indian workers who replaced them."

Dan Stein, Executive Director, Federation for American Immigration Reform
http://www.fairus.org/site/PageServer?pagename=leg_legislationb1f2

Despite the availability of American workers, the amount of foreign workers has been allowed to increase by over 400% in the past 10 years. The result of this corporate corruption is that hundreds of thousands of US workers have been displaced by cheaper foreign workers who are themselves abused in order to drive down wages in the US computer industry. Many H1B workers are being paid only $10 an hour. In some cases H1B workers were paid only $18,000 for a year of work. Eventually, these same jobs are outsourced overseas as these guest workers, trained by US computer programmers, take themselves and the jobs back to their home country.

But what about all of the ads in the paper for good paying computer jobs?
Nearly all of these ads are for fake jobs that do not actually exist. The purpose of the ads is simply to create the illusion of demand as an excuse to bring in even more low paid and low skilled H1B workers. In the youtube video below immigration attorneys from Cohen & Grigsby explain how they assist employers in running classified ads with the goal of NOT finding any qualified applicants; and the steps they go through to disqualify even the most qualified Americans in order to secure green cards for H-1B workers. Watch in the video what corporations and Congress really mean by a "shortage of skilled U.S. workers". Microsoft, Oracle, Hewlett-Packard and thousands of other companies are **running fake ads for fake workers for fake jobs in Sunday newspapers across the country each week.**
http://www.youtube.com/watch?feature=player_embedded&v=TCbFEgFajGU

There is a 30 day period of time in which Americans can submit resumes for these fake jobs. However, this marketing firm supplies employers with a chart of all of the possible ways to reject the US applicants.

If a US applicant is so qualified that they cannot be rejected based on their resume, they are brought in for an interview for the sole purpose of finding a "legal basis to disqualify them" and reject their application. There is not a requirement that all qualified US applicants actually be interviewed.

So maybe there are not a bunch of Hi Tech Jobs... Where are any jobs?
Not only are there no jobs requiring advanced math skills. There are no almost jobs at all. While job growth averaged 30% per decade from 1940 to 1980, it fell to 20% per decade for 20 years, and then disappeared completely since 2001:

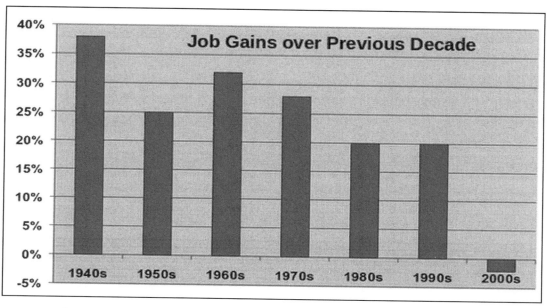

Report on the American Workforce Table 12
http://www.bls.gov/opub/rtaw/stattab2.htm

After 40 years of employment growing with the population, the past decade has seen no employment growth at all. The difference between the growing work force and the stagnating jobs growth is now more than 33 million jobs – for a real unemployment rate of 25%. Washington State has 4 million workers, but only 3 million jobs. This is a real unemployment rate of 25%. The unemployment rate among those under the age of 25 is approaching 50% - and is getting worse every month!

Never in our nation's history have so many been unemployed for so long in order to create wealth for so few. The percentage of long term unemployed (out of work for more than half of a year) has risen from 10% in 2000 to nearly 50% today.

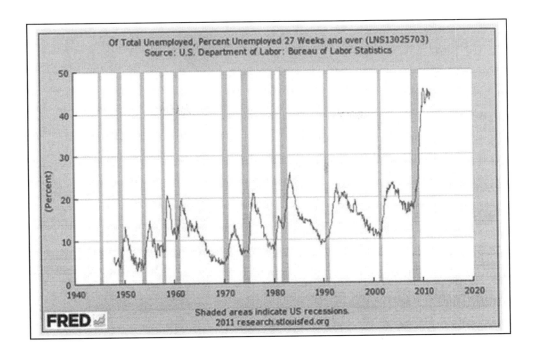

According to the Moyers PBS report, more workers have been out of work longer than at any point since statistics have been recorded, with over six million now unemployed for over six months. A record 20 million Americans qualified for unemployment insurance benefits last year, causing 27 states to run out of funds, with seven more also expected to go into the red within the next few months. Do all of the people below simply need to improve their math skills in order to get a job? Will increasing the difficulty of the GED or the SBAC or PARCC test create even a single job?

What about the corporate media claim that there are jobs and people simply need to be retrained to qualify for these jobs?
A 2011 Survey done by the Washington State Employment Security Department of thousands of long term unemployed workers – unemployed more than 2 years - found that three in four had not been able to find a job despite years of looking. The reason they could not find a job was not lack of training. In fact, many were over-qualified for the jobs they were applying for. Instead, most felt the biggest obstacle was their age. Most employers simply do not want to hire older workers.

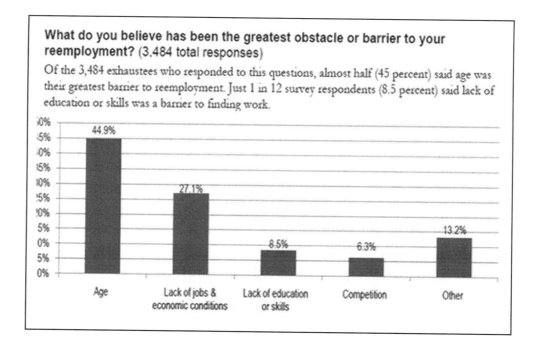

Less than one in ten felt it was a lack of education. Instead, it was a lack of jobs. More than 600 unemployed teachers applied for a single teaching job.

What is needed is not more training. It is more jobs!
We have a jobs crisis worse than the Great Depression and yet we have insane administrators claiming that the solution to this problem is to flunk more kids trying to get their GED. What we really need to do is stop listening to the billionaires and stop giving the billionaires billions of dollars in tax breaks and start enforcing a fair tax structure and hire back all of the teachers. We also need to put a few of the billionaires in jail for tax evasion and for bribing our elected officials.

Why about the 4 million jobs that go unfilled?
Let's look at some of these invisible job openings. The biggest BS group is called the Bureau of Labor Statistics. (BLS). According to the May 2014 BLS report, the number of positions waiting to be filled was 4 million in March 2014 and also 4 million in February 2014. But what the BLS fails to mention is that none of these were new jobs. Instead, there are always 4 million jobs waiting to be filled!
http://www.bls.gov/news.release/archives/jolts_05092014.htm

What is relevant is that there were about 2.6 unemployed people vying for every opening in March, up from about 1.8 when the last recession began in December 2007. So if the GED test takers get better at math, the best they can hope for is to get in line with all of the rest of the highly qualified people who are unable to get jobs – regardless of their training. But even if they did get jobs, the odds are extremely high that their job would only be a low paying part time job.

Nearly all current available jobs are low wage part time jobs that do not require advanced math skills

According the BLS Household survey, of 1 million jobs created in 2013, 77% were part time jobs. Compared with December 2007, when the recession officially began, there are 5.8 million fewer Americans working full time. In that same period, there has been an increase of 2.8 million working part time. In the past, before the corporate takeover of our government, the ratio of full time to part time jobs was about 1 to 1. Currently, the ratio of part time to full time new jobs is 4 to 1 and rising. The problem with unemployment has nothing to do with qualifications of workers and everything to do with greed and corruption of billionaires. Trickle down economics simply does not work.

Will even having a full time job provide a living wage?

Even if one was lucky enough to have a full time job, the average worker is working 34 hours per week. The average wage is $10 per hour.
http://www.bls.gov/data/#employment

That is $340 per week or about $1400 per month. Given that rent averages $1,000 per month and food averages $400 per month, it is pretty obvious that there is a problem here even if a person does manage to get a job.

Corporate Profits now at a Record High of $1.7 Trillion per Year

Meanwhile, half of Americans say they couldn't come up with $2,000 in 30 days without selling some of their possessions.

Half of all Americans earn less than $35,000 a year, half of all students are eligible for free and reduced lunches, and a record 50 million Americans are on food stamps – all while billionaires are making record profits. So what is the point of creating a college and career high stakes system that only stresses out students, teachers and parents?

What is the Solution to the Record Unemployment Problem?

We do not need to flunk kids on the GED test. Instead, we need a fair tax structure – requiring billionaires like Bill Gates to pay their fair share of State and federal taxes - so we can create a full employment economy. Essentially this means turning all of our unemployment offices into employment offices and making sure people get employment checks instead of unemployment checks. The cost of a Full Employment program would be almost nothing. According to Learning from the New Deal, http://www.philipharvey.info/newdeal.pdf, a 2010 paper written by Rutgers University professor of law and economics Philip Harvey, a full employment program would pay for itself over the course of a business cycle.

His proposal is that instead of giving nearly a trillion dollars to the super rich and then hoping the benefit will trickle down in the form of jobs for the rest of us, that we eliminate the greedy Wall Street banker – middle men and simply create direct public employment jobs. We have learned from the 2009 stimulus package that when you give money to billionaires all they do with it is engage in stock market speculation – leading to the current jobless "recovery." The problem is that without jobs, there can be no recovery – only another economic collapse once the Wall Street gamblers have blown away the money Congress gave them. Rather than being an "Employer of Last Resort" (ELR) program, the intention of the program is not merely to provide jobs for those in need, but to serve a useful and beneficial public service – such as education, child care, health care, senior care and the creation of efficient public energy in the communities where those in need live. "In short, communities would be encouraged to view their unemployed members as an untapped resource rather than as a burden." (Harvey, Page 23)

What is significant about the above study is the conclusion that **a direct jobs program would provide 5 to 6 times the number of jobs as a program which merely gives tax breaks to the super rich with the hope that the jobs will trickle down to the rest of us.** Having everyone working increases tax revenue and saves billions of dollars on the cost of unemployment insurance, food stamps and other safety net programs. These public workers will spend their earnings on local community businesses creating even more jobs. The bottom line is a **Full employment is cheaper than rampant unemployment.**

In closing, we each need to do research about the state of our economy. We need to demand an economy which has jobs for everyone. The media is saying that our public schools, teachers and students are the problem when they are not. Corporate propaganda is the problem; an off-shoring of our economy is the problem; too big to fail and deregulated banks are the problem. We need to focus on solving the real problems, not the fake problems which serve only to demean the people and increase corporate profit and power for the billionaires. We need to elect leaders who are willing to face and solve real problems. We need to all join together to turn this ship around.

8 Real Education Reform... Options for a Better Future

> "We have known for a long time that policies such as using high stakes testing to flunk struggling students sound good and Make political points – but end up as very costly failures.
> It is time that we held accountable public officials who continually Exploit these popular but failed ideas."
> — Dr. Gary Orfield, Harvard University

In this chapter, we will provide a series of specific steps each of us can take to protect our public schools against the war being waged by billionaires. This chapter has four sections.

8.1 Twelve Steps to Real Education Reform

8.2 How to get your State Party to Pass a Resolution Against Common Core

8.3 How to Pass a Bill in your State legislature

8.4 Active Activism... Join the Fight to Protect our Public Schools

8.1 Twelve Steps to Achieve Real Education Reform

> This final chapter may be the most important chapter of Our book. Here we go beyond merely complaining about The problem to offering real actions we can take to create A better future for our kids, our economy & our democracy.

In previous chapters, we have described the billionaires war against our public schools. These attacks threaten not only the future of 50 million children, but also the future of our economy and our democracy. In this final chapter, we will look at steps each of us can take to achieve real education reform.

Real Actions versus False Hopes
There have been many previous books over the past 20 years to warn parents and teachers of the harm being inflicted on our public schools. These books typically end with vague advice to "sign a petition or call your Congressman." The problem with such advice is that it does not ultimately lead to solving the problem. It is the illusion of action. Billionaires do not care if you sign a petition or call your Congressman. It is likely that they paid for your Congressman's election and he or she will vote for what is best for billionaires and not what is best for our children. We need to recognize that we are in a war and the enemy, the billionaires, have already occupied our nation's capital – just as surely as the British occupied it in 1812. Billionaires have also taken over most State legislatures and most school boards - just as they have taken over most TV stations, radio stations and newspapers. It will take aggressive action on the part of parents and teachers and all of us if we are to restore and protect our public schools and the future of our children.

The first step in this process is getting better informed. This is in part why we wrote this book. The first step in solving any problem is becoming more fully informed about the underlying cause of the problem. Our conclusion is that the problem is not merely privatization of our public schools, it is concentration of wealth and power in the hands of a few billionaires. The second step is forming a shared vision of what would really help our schools. It is not enough to be merely against Common Core, Charter Schools and High Failure rate tests. We also need to have a clear vision and be able to express what we are for. That is the purpose of this first section. But we must not end there. The challenge we face is about more than what reforms would lead to better public schools. It is also about how to organize politically to take back our democracy. Therefore in the next three sections we will talk about how to organize politically to take back our political parties, take back our school board elections, take back our legislative district elections and ultimately take back our Congress.

A Shared Vision of Real Education Reform: Promoting What Actually Works

To provide a better future for our children, our public schools can and should be improved. But they should be improved with the kinds of reforms that are supported by the scientific research on child development. We will therefore briefly review what the scientific research has concluded would help children have a better chance at success in life. We will cover not only what works, but why it works. The following 12 steps represent a broader, more effective approach to educating our children for greater success in life. Much of the data cited below comes from a report called Poverty and Potential, Out of School Factors and School Success, by Dr. David Berliner, Arizona State University http://nepc.colorado.edu/files/PB-Berliner-NON-SCHOOL.pdf

#1 Reduce Child Poverty by Making Sure their Parents Have Good Jobs

Children are not isolated machines. They are not like computers. What happens to a child inside of school is strongly influenced by what happens to the child outside of school. Children are a reflection of their families and communities. In addition to investing in our public schools, children will only succeed if we also invest in helping all families succeed and invest in strengthening our local businesses and local communities. The issue with students in poverty is that they are in poverty. They don't need their schools closed. They need their parents to have jobs. It is tough for a kid to do well in school when they are hungry and living in the back seat of a car. The problem with poverty is that it causes chronic stress in the lives of children. The stresses low income children experience include loss of their home, frequent relocations, lack of food, stressed out impatient punishing caregivers, lack of health care, lack of books and toys and many other problems. These chronic adverse events harm the child's development by causing the child to see the world as a dangerous place.

The stress associated with poverty harms a child's ability to learn because learning requires trust.

Children who live in poverty are far more likely to have adverse outcomes, such as dropping out of school, taking drugs and committing crimes. Sadly, with the concentration of wealth in America, many American families now live at or below the poverty line. One in four children live in poverty and one in two children live near the poverty line. The most important thing we can do for children is to make sure their parents have meaningful living wage jobs. Sadly, our current political leaders place more importance on increasing corporate profits than increasing living wage jobs. As a consequence, parents now face record unemployment.

#2 Make Sure All Families have a Stable Home

Children need a secure base with a consistent regular predictable schedule. Sadly, our State and nation are forcing millions of children out of their homes due to an economic crisis created by the same Wall Street gamblers who are now threatening our public schools by funding fake charter school groups. Children will not do well in school when they are living in the back of a car or frequently moving to a new school where they do not know any of the other children. The Superintendent of Public Instruction reported in December 2011 that 24,000 Washington state school children were homeless in Washington State in 2010. This is a 56 percent increase from 2006. These figures suffer from under-reporting due to the reluctance of many families to admit their circumstances. The real number of homeless children is likely to be double the reported number. Homelessness is a crime against our children. We should put an immediate halt on all home foreclosures involving children. We should also put families back into all of the boarded up houses and charge them rent based on their ability to pay.

#3 Make Sure All Parents have Access to Parent Education

For children to form a secure attitude toward learning, children need caregivers who are consistent, sensitive and responsive to their needs. Parent education is the best way to help children develop a more positive attitude toward learning. Ideally, parent education should include prenatal care and courses as the most crucial time in any child's development is the first few months of life. Like everything else that actually helps children, funding for such programs is being cut when it should be expanded.

#4 Provide All Children with Free Real Health Care

Children with hearing and vision problem, and many other medical problems will have a much harder time learning. As much learning occurs early in life, the sooner these problems are addressed, the more likely a child is to succeed. Sadly, 50 million Americans are without health insurance. This number does not include the poor who have policies but cannot afford the co-payments and therefore cannot get the health care their children need.

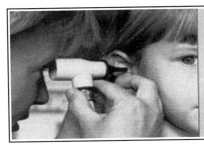

Many low income families Even with health insurance Do not seek health care For their children Because they cannot Afford the co-payments.

As just one example of how lack of health care harms learning, among school age children living at or near the poverty level, 32% had cavities and tooth aches – but had not seen a doctor in more than one year. As most health insurance in America comes from employment, record unemployment makes this problem much worse.

#5 Provide All Children with Adequate Food

It is estimated that one in ten children in the US suffers from food insecurity meaning that they often do not get enough food to eat. One in four children lives in poverty and one in two children in many cities now qualify for food stamps. With the record high unemployment, a record number of 46 million Americans are now on food stamps as their primary source of food.

Sadly, the food stamp program does not give enough food to meet the recommended daily allowance of the Thrifty Food Plan (TFP). There have also been cut backs in school breakfast and lunch programs. Schools have learned that giving children a high calorie meal on the days the children take high-stakes testing can increase test scores 4 to 7% - an indication that children are not getting adequate calories on non-test days. A better solution would be to make sure all parents had jobs which would increase the chances of children having enough to eat on weekends and summers as well as when they are at school.

"I wish my mom had a better job so we could have more food. But I'm not angry about it because I know my mom Is trying."
Libby

#6 Provide All Children with Quality Preschool Education

If we truly want to improve outcomes for all children, then we must help children at every point of their development. Preschool education helps prepare children for elementary school at a time when children are learning emotional regulation and crucial social skills. Quality daycare also allows parents to go to work knowing their children are well cared for. Sadly, in the past few years, the Washington State legislature has cut millions of dollars from the Work First program. This cut preschool funding for more than 20,000 low income children at the same time that their parents were losing their jobs and losing their homes.

#7 Full Day Kindergarten Helps Children

The legislature is supposedly moving to all-day kindergarten by 2018. Sadly, they have not provided any funding for it. Also, they have not provided funding for the dozens of elementary schools that will have to be built for the 80,000 Kindergarten children who will be moving from half day to full day Kindergarten. This is the equivalent of adding 40,000 children to our public schools.

At 500 students per elementary school, we will need 80 new elementary schools to have the classrooms for all of these kids. At $20 million per elementary school, the estimated cost of construction is $160 million. In addition to doubling the number of kindergarten classrooms, we will also need to double the number of kindergarten teachers. At 20 kids per Kindergarten class, or 50 teachers per thousand children, we will need 50 x 40 or 2,000 more teachers.

#8 Lower Class Sizes Helps Children

As we discuss elsewhere, our students are subjected to some of the highest class sizes in the nation. It would take more than $2 billion annually to lower school class sizes down to the national average and another billion annually to build the extra classrooms needed for national average school class sizes.

#9 Experienced Teachers Help Children

Research shows it takes 5 years of training and another 5 years of actual teaching experienced for most teachers to finally be able to effectively teach higher order reasoning and problem solving skills. Sadly, the charter school reformers think it is perfectly fine to put someone in charge of a classroom with only 5 weeks of training. These fake teachers usually quit during their first year – causing even more harm to the children who blame themselves for the loss of their teacher. The best way to retain quality teachers is to give them reasonable sized classrooms and make sure the children come to their class room with positive attitudes ready to learn. This includes making sure the child got adequate sleep in a safe home the night before class and adequate food before starting their school day.

#10 Provide Free School and After School Social and Sports Programs

Many children need help with their homework. Many have parents have jobs and are unable to pick them up until several hours after school closes. Many children are highly motivated by sports or other social based after school programs. Sadly, all of these programs are being cut as school districts can no longer afford to provide them. In many school districts, even modest user fees leads to a huge reduction in student participation in after school recreational programs. The low income children who need the extra attention the most are the very children who no longer have access to it. This crucial programs need to be restored or our entire community will suffer.

Our nation's children are suffering an epidemic of obesity at the same time that schools are discontinuing PE and recess to spend more time drilling children for high stakes tests. Sitting in a chair too long is harmful to a child's brain and physical development. Our kids need more physical activity, not less.

#11 Reducing School Violence Helps Children

Children need to feel safe on the bus going to school and they need to feel safe while they are at school. Sadly, over-crowded schools and over-crowded, high pressure classrooms foster the very conditions that lead to bullying, drug abuse and school drop outs. We should increase programs which teach children problem solving and conflict resolution skills.

#12 Greater Parent Participation in Public Schools Helps Children

Parents are not only the most knowledgeable about their children, but seeing parents in school helps their child feel good about attending school and motivates the child to do better in school.

There should be more opportunities for parent involvement in the classroom, in the lunchroom, on the playground and in after school activities. The opinions of parents should also be given greater weight at school board meetings and PTA meetings regarding policies that affect them and their children.

It is ironic that, instead of pursuing these 12 known effective strategies, the corporate education reformers are instead focusing in on strategies that are doomed to failure. This shows that the ed reform movement is not about helping kids. It is about increasing corporate profits.

What is Next?

Now that we have presented a shared vision of real education reform, in the next section, we will introduce the topic of political organizing, which is the only way we will ever be able to take back our public schools from the billionaires.

8.2 How to Get Your State Party to Oppose Common Core

> "Never doubt that a small group of thoughtful, committed citizens can change the world. Indeed, it is the only thing that ever has."
> Margaret Mead

On January 24, 2015, a miracle happened in Washington State. The Washington State Democratic Party became the first Democratic State Party in the nation to pass a resolution opposing Common Core! This is huge because Washington State is not only the home state of Bill Gates, it is also the home state for the SBAC Common Core test. If Washington state pulls out of Common Core, it could bring the entire project crashing to the ground.

We realize that several Republican controlled states have already rejected Common Core. But it is much easier for a Republican controlled state to reject Common Core than it is for a Democratic controlled State to reject Common Core. All Republicans have to do is call it "ObamaCore" and blame the entire thing on those "Damn Democrats" and Republicans will jump at the chance to get rid of Common Core. For example, the Washington State Republican Party passed a resolution opposing Common Core over a year ago.

But not all states are Republican states. Nor do children come with D's or R's stamped on their foreheads. For a Democratic state to pass a Resolution opposing Common Core requires going against a sitting Democratic President and also going against nearly your entire Democratic Party political leadership – who are all aligned with Obama and Arne Duncan just as Common Core tests and Common Core books are (supposed to be) aligned with Common Core standards.

A Brief Lesson in Political Organizing

For parents and teachers living in Democratic controlled states and wanting to escape from the death grip of Common Core, we would like to explain how this miracle happened – so that you can use this process to pass a similar resolution in your state. First, we have been working on this issue for nearly a year. So it will take a lot of patience and determination to overcome the wealthy billionaire controlled wing of the Democratic (or Republican) Party. Do not expect overnight success. You should write a well organized resolution that takes no more than one page. Our successful resolution is at the end of this article if you would like to read it. Feel free to copy it. Unlike Common Core, it is not Copyrighted!

Shawn DuFresne Shows off His Sign Shortly after The Washington State Democratic Party Voted to Oppose Common Core.

Second, it is helpful if at least some members of your group are already members of your state's Democratic Party. One of us, David, has been a Precinct Committee Officer (PCO) in the Democratic Party for more than 14 years in East King County, near Seattle Washington. The other of us, Elizabeth, is a new PCO for a different legislative district in North Seattle, Washington. Even if you do not like politics, you should join your local Democratic or Republican party and start attending monthly party meetings in your legislative district. You will find that most people in grass roots politics care about our kids and about the future of our country just like you.

Third, it is helpful if you have passed other resolutions at various levels of the Democratic or Republican Party in the past and have at least some idea of how the process works. We have previously passed SIX resolutions in the State Democratic Party before the Common Core Resolution. These include resolutions in favor of a State Public Bank, restoration of Glass Steagall Banking Regulations, Getting the Money out of Politics, and Restoring a Fairer GED test. So this was our seventh successful resolution. But it was also by far the hardest to pass. So try to connect with people who know how the resolution process works.

It is essential to start at the legislative district level. Start with your own legislative district. Attend several monthly meetings. Get to know the other folks attending the monthly meetings.

Fourth, find parents and teachers whose kids are struggling with Common Core. Most kids are having a terrible time. Ask these parents and teachers to help you pass a resolution in your legislative district. After you pass a resolution in your legislative district, work on passing the resolution in neighboring legislative districts. Eventually, we were able to get the Resolution Opposing Common Core passed in four legislative districts in Washington state.

Teachers Susan DuFresne And Don Bunger Show off Their Signs Just before the Washington State Democratic Party Meeting

Fifth, also join your State Party Progressive Caucus or some other statewide caucus in your political party. Look for folks who really support public schools and are opposed to the billionaires privatizing and taking over public schools. The more wealthy democrats are called "New Democrats." These are the folks who are in it for the money and are paid off by the billionaires. The benefit of having the resolution passed by the Progressive Wing of the Democratic Party is that these folks are often extremely long time Democrats and they really know the ropes and how to get things done – despite the opposition of the corporate or "New Dems" wing of the Democratic Party. Many are also on the County and /or State Resolutions Committees.

Sixth, the next task is to get the resolution considered by the County Resolutions Committee. It is helpful if you have friends on this committee and/or can get to know the members of this committee.

Seventh, the next task is to get the resolution considered by the State Resolutions Committee. This group only meets three or four times per year. There are lots of rules that have to be met to get a resolution considered by the county committee or the state committee. These rules are usually posted on the County Democratic Party website and/or the State Democratic Party website.

Eighth, get to know your progressive State Party leaders. These are elected representatives who care more about kids and parents and teachers than about keeping billionaires happy. We are lucky in our State to have State Senator Maralyn Chase in our corner. Having a well respected leader of the State Party on your side will help because the billionaires will certainly have some state party leaders on their side.

Teacher, Susan DuFresne, Washington State Senator Maralyn Chase And Chair of the Washington State Progressive Caucus Brian Gunn All played Huge Roles in Passing the Resolution Opposing Common Core.

Ninth, get some upset parents and upset teachers on your side. We were very lucky to meet a group of upset teachers called Washington Bad Ass Teachers, who understood that Common Core is very bad for kids. These parents and teachers played a crucial role in helping us get the last few votes we needed to get the resolution passed because thankfully teachers are still highly respected in our state and state delegates were willing to listen to these teachers talk about how Common Core harms kids.

Tenth, build a website where parents, teachers and State Party delegates can go to learn more about why they should support your resolution. We built a website called "Weapons of Mass Deception (dot) org. To learn more about how to build your own website using a free platform called Joomla, visit one of our other websites: http://buildyourownbusinesswebsite.org/

Strategy At the State Party Meeting

After getting the resolution passed at a legislative district meeting and or a county meeting, it is forwarded to the state party for consideration at the next state party meeting. You need to go to this meeting a day in advance – because the State Resolutions Committee usually considers resolutions the evening before the main state party meeting. Bring a one page flier of no more than ten reasons why those on the resolutions committee should vote for your resolution. Arrive to the committee meeting early and make sure that everyone on the committee gets a copy of your handout. In Washington State, there is usually about 30 people on the resolutions committee. Your state may be bigger or smaller than our state.

The first task of the resolutions committee is to "clean up" your "poorly written" resolution. Do not argue with them. They have been writing resolutions and cleaning up resolutions for years. Let them fix your resolution. They know what they are doing. The second task of the resolutions committee is to decide whether to recommend that the main group "pass" or "not pass" or "table" the resolution or send it to the main body "without recommendation" so it can be debated by the main body.

Because Common Core is very controversial in Democratic states, do not be surprised if it is passed to the main body without recommendation.

That was what happened to us. The state resolutions committee usually meets on a Friday night and the main State Party meeting is the following afternoon from 1 to 4 pm. We prepared about 300 handouts to pass out. These were 40 for the Resolutions Committee plus 60 for the Progressive caucus meeting on Saturday morning plus 200 to place on chairs at the main state party meeting 30 minutes before the meeting is scheduled to start. After attending the progressive caucus meeting on Saturday morning, meet with your group of parents and teachers. Hopefully, they will have signs and their own handouts to pass out at the main meeting. Hopefully someone experienced with the process should explain what will happen at the state party meeting.

David Spring and Elizabeth Hanson Preparing for the State Party delegates To arrive Just before the Main State Democratic Party meeting.

The goal is to get your team to the meeting before it begins and pass out the fliers with one on every chair. Then have parents and teachers on your team circulate around the big room as the state delegates begin to arrive. The goal of each parent and teacher is to talk with just a few delegates before the main meeting is called to order. You will have about 20 minutes after the delegates arrive. There were 8 of us and with each talking to about five delegates for about 4 minutes each. Together, we were able to share our stories with about 40 out of the 200 delegates. Our goal was simply to "tip" a close vote in our favor. As you approach a delegate, ask them if they have heard of Common Core and if they have decided how they will vote on the resolution.

Most delegates will be undecided and will usually give you a couple of minutes to explain to them why they should vote for the resolution. If a delegate has already decided, then move out to someone who is undecided. Do not waste these precious minutes trying to convert someone whose mind is already made up. If a delegate does not support the resolution, then just chalk it up to "Bill Gates and his billions in corporate propaganda."

Two retired Teachers, Keitha Bryson And Don Bunger, Shown with Brian Gunn, Played important Roles in talking with State Party Delegates Before the State Party Meeting

You also need to meet with the State party delegates who will each give a two minute speech in favor of the resolution. You need at least two and hopefully three speakers qualified to speak. These folks will likely be state committee delegates from the legislative districts that passed your resolution earlier in the year. They need to not only know about the drawbacks of Common Core, they also need to be able to speak clearly. It is also helpful if they are well known and well respected by other members of the Democratic Party. So choose wisely. We were lucky to get Sarajane Siegfriedt, the chair of the King County Legislative Action Committee and member of the State Resolutions Committee to speak in favor of the motion. We were also lucky to get Brian Gunn, the chair of the State Progressive Caucus to speak in favor of the motion. Brian said, "Corporations are looking at our children as commodities. We're allowing corporations that produce these materials and sponsor these tests to treat our children as sources of income...a source of profit. And that source of profit is our own children."

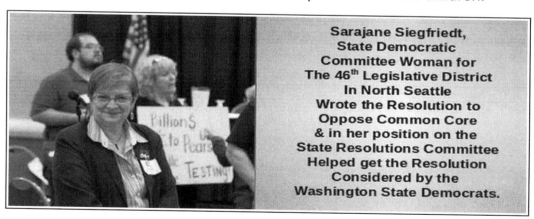

Sarajane Siegfriedt, State Democratic Committee Woman for The 46th Legislative District In North Seattle Wrote the Resolution to Oppose Common Core & in her position on the State Resolutions Committee Helped get the Resolution Considered by the Washington State Democrats.

Our final speaker was Richard May, a leader of the Whatcom County Democrats who is also a parent. Richard spoke of the negative impact Common Core had on his two daughters.

Richard said that "Common Core sucks... All of the parents and teachers in Bellingham hate it."

Parent, Richard May, Shown here with his Wife Melanie And daughters Tily and Ruby, Told the State Delegates "Common Core Sucks."

Do not be surprised if the wealthy wing of the party tries to sabotage the issue. In our case, the leaders of the party read a letter from a well known state senator urging the group to vote against the resolution. She warned the group that should this resolution pass, it would make passing a state budget and getting school funding much more difficult. This of course was a lie. Common Core costs our state more than one billion extra dollars for the tests and books. But the goal of the billionaires is not to tell the truth. It is simply to deceive the public.

Next was the big vote. We thought it would be very close – especially after the letter from one of the leaders of the democratic party was read. As it turned out, we won the vote by a two to one margin – with more than 120 state party delegates voting to ignore their own state party leaders and ignore their own President and support our resolution. This huge landslide victory proves that Democrats care just as much about the well being of our children as Republicans.

The other good news is now that Common Core is officially opposed by both the Republican and Democratic Party in Washington State (perhaps the first time we have ever agreed on anything), there will be a bill introduced in the state legislature halt Common Core in Washington State. In our opinion, the most crucial element of our success was the presence of real parents and real teachers speaking from their hearts about how Common Core harms their kids.

The other important factor was the year we spent building our team and building support one person at a time and one legislative district at a time within the Democratic Party. Common Core is an extremely complex issue that has billions in marketing used to fool parents. It takes one on one talks to overcome this marketing blitz. But we proved it can be done. We hope you have as much success in your state as we had in ours. Below is a copy of our successful Common Core resolution. Be sure to visit our website to learn more about the drawbacks of Common Core. Here is the link.
http://weaponsofmassdeception.org/

Resolution Opposing Common Core State Standards

WHEREAS the copyrighted (and therefore unchangeable) Common Core State Standards are a set of controversial top-down K-12 academic standards that were promulgated by wealthy private interests without research-based evidence of validity and are developmentally inappropriate in the lowest grades; and

WHEREAS, as a means of avoiding the U.S. Constitution's 10th Amendment prohibition against federal meddling in state education policy, two unaccountable private trade associations--the National Governors Association (NGA) and the Council of Chief State School Officers (CCSSO)--have received millions of dollars in funding from the Gates Foundation and others to create the CCSS; and

WHEREAS the U.S. Department of Education improperly pressured state legislatures into adopting the Common Core State Standards and high-stakes standardized testing based on them as a condition of competing for federal Race to the Top (RTTT) stimulus funds that should have been based on need; and

WHEREAS as a result of Washington State Senate Bill 6669, which passed the State legislature on March 11, 2010, the Office of the Superintendent of Instruction (OSPI) adopted Common Core State Standards on July 20, 2011; and

WHEREAS this adoption effectively transfers control over public school standardized testing from locally elected school boards to unaccountable corporate interests who stand to profit substantially from CCSS; and

WHEREAS the Washington State Constitution also calls for public education to be controlled by the State of Washington through our elected State legislature, our elected State Superintendent of Public Instruction and our elected local school boards; and

WHEREAS implementation of CCSS will cost local school districts hundreds of millions of dollars to pay for standardized computer-based tests, new technology, new curricula and teacher training at a time when Washington is already insufficiently funding K-12 Basic Education without proven benefit to students; and WHEREAS some states have already withdrawn from CCSS;

THEREFORE BE IT RESOLVED that we call upon the Washington State legislature and the Superintendent of Public Instruction to withdraw from the CCSS and keep K-12 education student-centered and accountable to the people of Washington State.

What is Next?
Once you have managed to change the official position of your state party, the next step is to write and pass a law in your state legislature to match the intent of the resolution. That is the subject of our next section.

8.3 How to pass a bill in your State legislature

In our last article, we explained how to get a resolution passed by your State political party. But passing a resolution does not do much good unless you follow it up by passing a bill in your State legislature. In this article, we will explain the process for passing a bill here in Washington State. The process is similar in most other states.

Step One... Make a Long Term Plan for Passing Your Bill
Many people will be surprised that this article is about passing a GED Fairness bill, when our previous article was about passing a Resolution to Oppose Common Core. We do intend to submit a Common Core bill during this session, but there are several reasons we do not think it will pass this year - and that it is more likely we will pass the GED Fairness bill. The biggest reason is that we have documentation showing the harm of the 2014 Pearson GED – but the major harm of the Common Core SBAC test will not come until the summer of 2015 when 60% or more of Washington State students will be declared failures due to the grossly unfair SBAC test. We believe we will need much more support from teachers and parents if we are to pass a bill withdrawing Washington State from Common Core. This is why we wrote a book called "Weapons of Mass Deception" to explain the harm of Common Core to parents and teachers. Our goal is to talk to parents and teachers all over the State in the coming year with the hope of building a large enough coalition to pass a bill opposing Common Core in 2016. The other reason we believe we are more likely to pass a GED fairness bill in this session is that we can show that depriving more than 8,000 low income young adults of a GED greatly increases the number of people committing crimes and going to prisons – which will cost our state as much as $50 million in extra prison costs each year. So there is a financial reason for legislators to support our GED Fairness bill. We understand that Common Core and SBAC will cost our State more than one billion extra dollars to implement. But this cost is carried by local school districts rather than the state legislature. So this money is more easily hidden and ignored by the legislature. It will help more than 8,000 low income young adults in Washington State if we can get the GED Fairness bill passed this year. So that is our current goal.

Step Two... Write a Rough Draft of the Bill you would like to Pass
Legislators tend to be very busy with hundreds and perhaps thousands of people asking them to change one law or another. Some legislators respond to as many as one thousand emails and phone calls per day. Actually, it is their legislative assistants who do most of this triage work, but you are more likely to pass a bill if you can send your legislators a rough draft of the bill. What? You say you have never written a bill before? The process is not that hard. All you need to do is a google search on similar bills that have been filed in other states that accomplish what you want done. I usually get about five bills and then compare them, using the sentences I like and ignoring the rest.

Then to make the bill work for your state, you will need to look up the state laws in your own state that you want to amend with your bill. In Washington, these are called the RCW (Revised Code of Washington) and are found by subject at leg.wa.gov. http://leg.wa.gov/LawsAndAgencyRules/Pages/default.aspx

Plan on taking a day to write the rough draft. But don't worry if it is not perfect. Legislators will go through and make their own changes. Then any legislator can send any bill to the "Code Revisers Office". The Code Reviser will double check every sentence and every law to make sure the correct laws are being revised.

Step Three... Find some legislators willing to sponsor your bill

This is where it helps to be a member of a major political party and attend monthly party meetings in your legislative district and get to know your State legislators. In politics, it often is not what you know or how good your bill is – it is who you know and whether your bill has political support. One way to get political support is to spend a year getting your political party to pass a resolution supporting your issue. A legislator is much more likely to sponsor a bill if they think that the members of their party want them to sponsor the bill. One option is to ask your local legislator to sponsor the bill. But it is often better to guess what committee the bill might be assigned to and then ask a member of that committee to sponsor your bill. Committees for the Washington State House and Senate are listed at this link:

http://leg.wa.gov/legislature/Pages/CommitteeListing.aspx

The bill we are currently working on passing is House Bill 1743.

"Concerning the acceptance of additional high school equivalency tests."

It is a bill to restore GED Fairness in Washington State. See our website Restore GED Fairness (dot) org for more information on this bill. We had a resolution passed in favor of the bill at the September 2014 meeting of the Washington State Democratic Party and have worked with Representatives and Senators for months drafting and submitting the bill. This bill has sponsors and has been referred to House Higher Education Committee. There is an identical companion bill in the Senate. Senate Bill 5676 which has been referred to the Senate Higher Education Committee.

Step Four... Get a Hearing for your Bill

For a bill to become a law, it needs to pass both the House and the Senate and then be signed by the Governor. But before it can be voted on in either the House or the Senate, it needs to be approved in a vote by the majority of a committee. Before it can be voted on by a committee, it needs to have held a public hearing. Because there is only a limited amount of time to hold hearings, not all bills get hearings. Most bills "die in committee." The person who decides which bills get a hearing is the Chair of the Committee. That person usually will only hold hearings for bills that are supported by several Committee members.

So as not to put all of your eggs in one basket (or one chairperson), you need to focus on getting the support of committee members and the committee chair in both the House and the Senate.

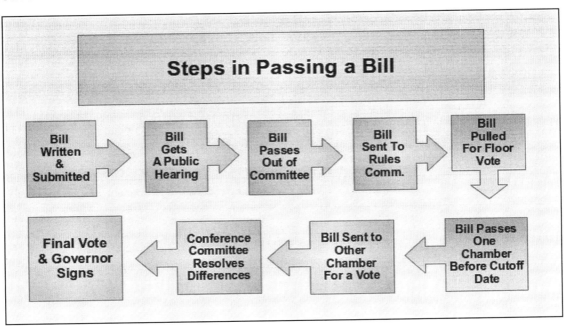

The next step is to call, email and visit every member of the House Higher Education Committee and Senate Higher Education Committee to encourage them to support the bill and answer any questions they may have about the bill. If you can not get an appointment with the legislator, get an appointment to speak with their legislative aide. Lists of who is on each committee along with their contact information are available on the legislatures main website.

Be Aware of Bill Cutoff Dates
There are many firm deadlines. The first is the committee cutoff date (except fiscal bills). This year, it is February 20, 2015. The bill must be heard and voted out of committee by this date. But since bills are scheduled for committee hearings more than one week in advance, the real committee cut off date is about February 10 2015. The second deadline is is the Ways and Means Committee cutoff date for bills with a fiscal note. This is typically one week after the original committee cutoff – or this year it was February 27, 2015. The final cut off to vote out of the House of origin is March 11 2015. In addition, it is important to always get your article to the chair of the committee and their assistants. If you have time, you should consider making a 15 minute appointment with each of these important people and/or their assistants and personally hand them the article you wrote with a cover letter. If you have time, email your article and cover letter to every member of this committee – including members who have already sponsored the bill with a cover letter thanking them for sponsoring the bill. What? You do not have an article and cover letter? That is the next step.

Step Five... Write your article and cover letter
It is very important that you clearly and briefly outline the problems with the current law and how your proposed bill will address those problems. Add information on what is happening in other states regarding this issue. Add, if possible an estimate of how much your bill will save the tax payers. Then post your article on your website and include a link to the article in case legislators would rather read the article online. Finally, email key legislators a PDF of your article and use the body of the email as your cover letter. Be sure to include the Bill Number and Title of the Bill in your cover letter. This means you will have one cover letter with the House Bill number to email State Representatives and another cover letter with the Senate Bill number to email State Senators. Here is a brief cover email we sent to legislators asking them to cosponsor the GED Fairness Bill.

Email Topic Line: Please Support HB 1743 (SB 5676) to Restore GED Fairness

Dear Representative (LAST NAME HERE),

We are hoping you will consider cosponsoring and supporting House Bill 1743 (Senate Bill 5676) "Concerning the acceptance of additional high school equivalency tests." This bill has been referred to the Higher Education Committee and would restore GED fairness by ending the Pearson Test Monopoly here in Washington State. In 2014, Pearson introduced a new GED test that is much more difficult to pass than the prior GED test. As a consequence, the number of candidates who received a GED fell from an annual average of 13,300 to only 2,850 in 2014 – **depriving more than 10,000 students of a GED certificate needed to get a good job or go to college.**

Also, without a GED certificate, low income young adults are much more likely to commit crimes and wind up in prison. Our estimate is that the unfair Pearson GED test will increase our state's prison population by more than 1,000 additional inmates per year – c**osting our state's tax payers more than $50 million in additional prison costs per year.**

Thankfully, there is an alternative GED test called HiSET which is less expensive than the Pearson test, more accessible to those without computers and is more fairly normed to the actual skills and abilities of high school seniors. House Bill 1743 and Senate Bill 5676 would offer students the option of taking this fairer, less expensive and more accessible High School Equivalency test. For more information on the benefits of this bill, please see the attached 15 page report. You can also view this report online by going to the following link on our website: http://restoregedfairness.org/latest-news/46-support-house-bill-1743-restore-ged-fairness-by-ending-the-pearson-test-monopoly.

If you have any questions, feel free to email us.

Sincerely,
Elizabeth Hanson, M. Ed. & David Spring M. Ed.
Restore GED Fairness (dot) org

Making a List and Checking it Twice

Keep a careful checklist of all of the Representatives and Senators you emailed and the date you emailed them and whether they responded to your email and/or have decided to cosponsor your bill. After a few days, you can call their legislative assistant to set up an appointment. With a cut off of February 20th 2015, all of this needs to be done by February 10th. Here are the status codes we use with our table of legislators:

Status: (a) sent email; (b) made phone call to legislative assistant; (c) agreed to support bill; (d) agreed to cosponsor bill; (e) appointment set in Olympia

Step Six... Email a group of supporters with the same PDF article and a similar cover letter and ask them to contact this same group of key legislators

While it is always helpful to contact every Representative and every Senator and ask them to cosponsor your bill, the reality is that unless there is a public hearing in at least one committee in the House or the Senate and unless the bill is passed out of committee, the bill will never come up for a vote on the floor. We once had a bill with 50 sponsors in the House – enough to pass the bill in the House. But because the bill failed to come out of the committee, there was never a vote. In that case, the chair of the committee blocked a committee vote on the bill. Hopefully, during the months in the year before the bill is considered, you have been working on building an email list of supporters willing to contact legislators with their own reasons for wanting the bill to be approved.

Among the folks we sent emails to support our GED Fairness bill were GED instructors, the American Federation of Teachers (AFT), the Washington Education Association (WEA), Parents Across America (PAA), Social Equity Educators (SEE) and Washington Bad Ass Teachers (WA BATS) and several other groups of retired teachers, retired Americans, union members and Democratic Party organizations.

Step Seven... Plan for a Day or Two at your State Capital
State legislators get hundreds of phone calls and emails every day. It can sometimes be difficult to get their attention even for a very important bill. One way to get their attention is by setting up a series of short 15 minute appointments a couple of weeks in advance with key legislators and/or their legislative assistants. The purpose of these personal meetings is not only to help you pass your current bill, but also build a personal relationship for helping to pass future bills. Setting up a meeting is best done by calling their legislative assistants – or even driving down to Olympia a couple of weeks in advance and talking directly to their legislative assistants. This can be difficult if you work during the week. But if your bill is important enough, you may want to consider taking a day off work to drive down to Olympia and meet with as many legislators and their assistants as you can. Even if a legislator is busy, which they often are in serving on several committees and going to many caucus meetings, meeting with their legislative assistant can be very important. Legislators often meet with their assistants in the evening. If you can convince a legislative aide that a bill is worth supporting, they can often convince their boss to support your bill. During your appointment, give them a copy of your bill report. Limit your comments to no more than 5 minutes. Allow plenty of time to answer any questions or concerns they may have about the bill. End the meeting by asking whether they will consider supporting the bill and if there is anything you can do or anyone else you can talk with to help pass the bill. Then thank them for taking the time to meet with you and leave early to get ready for your next appointment. Occasionally, your next appointment will have a cancellation and can give you this extra time.

Step Eight... Keep checking with bill sponsors for the date of the hearing and make plans for you and your supporters to attend the hearing to speak in favor of the bill
This is important. You need several people willing to go to Olympia and speak in favor of the bill if it gets a committee hearing – even if this means you and they have to take a day off from work! Prepare a brief three minute speech as this is the most time you will be given. Also prepare a two minute speech and a one minute speech as often the public is limited to only one minute each. I strongly recommend bringing written comments that explain more fully why you are hoping they will vote in favor of the bill. Keep the written comments to under four pages. Make 30 copies of your written comments. Give 10 to 20 comments to the committee staff before the meeting starts.

The rest can be passed out to others speaking in favor of the bill before the hearing. Be early in order to be first on the list to speak. Be prepared to stay for hours as other bills may be heard first. Arrive at the committee hearing at least 30 minutes before it starts in order to add your name to the list of people wanting to speak in favor of the bill.

Step Nine... Getting your bill pulled from the Rules Committee
Assuming your bill is passed out of the Education committee, it will be sent to the Ways and Means Committee if it has a fiscal note. Otherwise, it will be sent directly to the Rules Committee. This is a group of legislators who decide what bills actually go to the floor for a vote. Just because your bill passed the committee does not mean it will get a floor vote. Someone on the Rules Committee needs to "pull" your bill from the long list of bills sitting in the Rules Committee. You therefore need a list of legislators on the House and/or Senate Rules Committee. Usually, bills are pulled in groups through a negotiation process... you vote to pull my bill and I will vote to pull a bill you want.

Step Ten... The Floor Vote
If a bill is pulled for a vote before the Floor Cutoff on March 11th, there will then be a floor vote often the very next day. You can sign up for a list of bills being pulled from the Rules committee with an order of which they will be voted on the next day. Each Senator and Representative gets the list of bills about to be considered in case they want to study them and propose amendments. There is no question that Pearson will have paid lobbyists who do not like our bill and will try to kill it either in the Higher Education Committee, the Rules Committee or on the floor vote. One way to gut a bill that appears popular and likely to pass is to attach Poison Pill Amendments that change the purpose of the bill or add innocent sounding loopholes. This is where it is important to send emails to everyone in the House or Senate the day before the bill is being considered and urging them to support the bill as written.

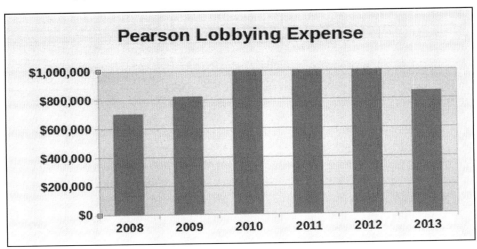

https://www.opensecrets.org/lobby/clientsum.php?id=D000036571

Step Eleven... Consideration by the other Chamber

If the bill manages to get out of the House in one piece, it still needs to pass the Senate. This will take more urging and education of Senators on the Higher Education Committee and on the Rules Committee. Be ready to attend a Senate Public hearing if it is held and have more written comments to pass out to Senators. This is the time to reach out to all Senators, especially those on the Senate Rules committee with the hope of getting the bill voted on in the Senate.

Step Twelve... Contact the Governors Office for Support

It is worth setting up an appointment with one of the Governor's staff once the bill passes out of either chamber and looks like it may pass the other chamber. The Governor's staff need to understand why this bill is needed or the Governor may veto the bill. Bring a written article explaining the problems with the current law and how your bill solves those problems. The aide may actually bring it to the Governor to read or summarize it for the Governor. The Governor rarely vetoes a bill. But it can happen especially if he does not understand what it is about and why it is needed.

Step Thirteen... The Signing Ceremony

If the bill passes, there may be a signing ceremony. Ask the bill sponsors when this might be and encourage all of your friends and supporters to come with you for this bring event. Hopefully once you pass your first bill, it will give you the confidence you need and the relationships you need with members of the House and Senate to pass other harder bills in the future.

What is Next?

In the final section, we will take about how to use free modern communication tools such as video conferencing and website Enewsletters to organize a local or national grassroots movement on an extremely low budget.

8.4 Active Activism... Join the Fight to Protect our Public Schools

In this final section, we want to provide some ideas for political organizing. With the future of our children at stake, we need to go beyond merely attending PTA meetings and writing our legislators. If we care about our kids, our economy, our country and our future, we all need to recognize that there is a well-financed war being waged against our public schools – and our children are being used as pawns in this battle. It is time to look behind the curtain and expose those who are waging this war. It is time to examine the real reasons for this attack on our public schools. It is time to admit that we are currently losing this war. We therefore need to develop greater awareness of the tactics of those who are out to destroy our public schools and develop more effective strategies for responding to these attacks. Until we see this war for what it is, things will only get worse for our kids, our economy and our country.

It does no good to point out that the educational reforms harm students. Those advocating for reform do not care about the harm their reforms inflict on children. All they care about is money and power. If billionaires cared about our children they would not be going to such great lengths to evade paying their fair share of State and federal taxes. Nor would they be spending millions of dollars working to divert billions of dollars away from public schools and into private for profit corporations. Certainly, reading the articles and watching the videos on this website are a good start. But this alone will not protect our public schools from being taken over by the billionaires. We need to organize. Therefore, in addition to writing this book, we have started a new organization to fight back against this insanity. It is called the Coalition to Protect our Public Schools.

To join this free group, simply go to our website, **Coalition to Protect our Public Schools (dot) org** and click on the Join Now button.

Active Activism
Writing letters and signing petitions to corrupt leaders does us and our children no good. Rather than wasting time writing corrupt officials, we should spend time our talking with our friends and neighbors to help them understand how they are being misled by the billionaires. There is only one solution to this problem and that is for parents and teachers to first get informed about the problems and solutions - and then run for office. Run for your local PTA. Run for the School Board. Run for the City Council. Run to be a representative in your union. Run to be a Precinct Committee Officer in the political party of your choice. Run for the State legislature. Join the campaign of another parent or teacher running for office. Even if you do not win, it will give you an excuse to go door to door talking with other parents about the danger of turning over our public schools to a few greedy billionaires. In fact, run for ANY elected office and use it as an opportunity to talk with your neighbors about the need to protect our public schools from corporate raiders. You may not win the first time. But at least you can challenge the status quo and get incumbents thinking about either funding schools or getting voted out.

Learn how to use modern mass communication tools
One of the underlying problems in protecting our public schools is that the billionaires have taken over the news media in the US. This gives the billionaires the ability to deceive and manipulate parents into helping them privatize and destroy our public schools. The only way to beat the billionaires is not fall for the lies. Instead, learn the truth and then stand up and speak out. Thankfully, there are some free and very powerful modern tools that we can use to help us organize at a very low or even no cost. We have built a website to explain how these tools can be used. The website is called Free Casting (dot) US.

How do we learn what we learn and know what we know?
In the past, folks relied upon the town crier to share important news. The printing press brought us the town newspaper. Radio brought us the FDR fireside chats and Edward R. Murrow. The television gave use Walter Cronkite and the Evening News. In the 1980's, as these traditional media sources were taken over by a handful of billionaires, active learners began seeking out new sources of information. First, there were alternative news websites like Counter Punch and Common Dreams. Then there were audio podcasts like Thom Hartmann. Recently there has been an emergence of video web cast alternative news channels like Democracy Now and the Real News Network. All of these information sharing tools required huge investments of time and money. There is a saying that the news is controlled by the person who owns the printing press.

What is Free Casting?
Now there is a new option for sharing information that we call FreeCasting. FreeCasting allows anyone with a modern computer and a high speed internet connection to start their own broadcasting channel and share information with others for almost no cost and with no need to know computer programming.

Welcome to FreeCasting.Us
The Power of Free Broadcasting in the Hands of Everyone

This new option allows for the free and open exchange of ideas using free open source tools. These tools include the free Linux operating system and the LibreOffice document sharing program for your computer. They also include free Ebook creation and publishing tools and free website building tools. Most important, they include free video conferencing and video sharing programs. Our mission at College in the Clouds is to help you learn how to use these free open source tools to gain your freedom from the billionaire controlled mass media. Our conviction is that the sharing of information should be free just as a public library is free and our public schools are free. These free online tools can benefit any teacher, any parent and any student. These tools allow groups of as few as two or as many as a thousand to interact in a very efficient way that is ideal for sharing knowledge and building relationships.

FreeCasting includes video creation by a panel of experts that is shared live and also posted on an organization's YouTube channel allowing it to be shared with millions of people – who can then post questions on the organizations website for panel experts to answer – empowering local citizens to national leaders.

FreeCasting can be used as a tool to build and organize a national movement. Guests on a national panel can be come hosts on a regional panel. Guests on a regional panel can become hosts on a State panel. Guests on a State panel can become hosts on a Local panel. Guests on a Local panel can interact directly with parents and teachers to provide feedback that is then shared with the entire organization through interconnected local, State and National websites.

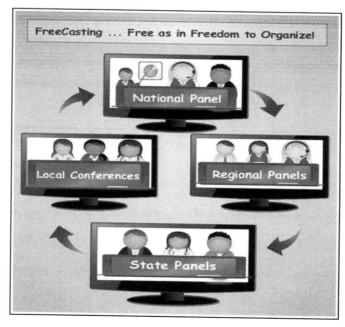

Freedom to learn, freedom to share and freedom to organize lead to freedom to act. The same free tools that help folks learn, share and organize can also be used to plan and carry out events.

Use Free Casting to Build a Grassroots National Movement

One obstacle facing any low budget social or political organization was how to grow their movement without any money. Here we will explain how free Google Video Conferencing combined with a free YouTube channel can help you grow your movement from a few people with a common cause to a national organization with millions of people. WE will use the example of a group of teachers and parents who want to form a national group to protect our public schools from being destroyed and replaced with billionaire driven private schools.

The following structure is based on the organizational structure and practices of other large national political organizations such as the Democratic Party and the Parent Teachers Organization with three important differences. First, this new organization would be non-partisan and include members of any existing party and endorse candidates of any political party willing to truly support and protect our public schools.

Second, the members of this new political movement would be trained and be able to use free web based organizational tools such as Google Hangouts to conduct National, Regional, State, County and Local meetings and exchange information without the need to travel to a physical location. Third, candidates endorsed by this political movement would be offered access to and training in the use of free customized websites, sample fliers and other materials to promote their political campaigns.

Eventual Size of an Effective National Political Movement

While the actual size of a national movement may begin with as few as six members, the eventual goal of a successful national political movement should be one million or more members paying dues of $20 per year which would be split between county, State, regional and national divisions of the organization to pay for a small staff to maintain the database and other structures of the organization (see table below). Just as with the Democratic Party or PTA, the vast majority of the work would be handled by local volunteers with the support and training of a small paid staff.

Local Websites and National Database Organization

Just as with the PTA and/or Democratic Party, each school district group, county group, State group, Regional Group as well as the national group should have their own websites with all websites linked together through a national database and all website managers and group coordinators trained on how to build and use their own websites. Ideally, all websites should use the same web building tools and database management tools to facilitate transfer of data from local and state groups to the national group and from the national and state groups to the local groups.

Evolution and Organic Growth of a National Political Movement

Research on group dynamics has repeatedly concluded that the most effective group size is 6 to 12 people. Less than 6 people leaves too few people to get the work of the group done and more than 20 people makes it difficult to impossible to conduct an efficient meeting and/or make decisions based on group consensus. It becomes difficult to allow all members to participate and all voices to be heard. Therefore, the goal of an effective video conference should be to have no more than 10 to 15 people be speakers on the video conference panel and no more than 100 people to be able to call in with questions for the panel speakers. The remaining members of the group can watch the conference via live streaming from the group websites. Google Hangouts is ideal for this purpose. Teachers have also found that Google Hangouts is very useful for working online with groups of students and networking with other teachers. Parents have found that Google Hangouts is ideal for visiting with friends and relatives who live in other communities. So it is worth the time for parents and teachers to learn this skill. As a video conference group reaches a size of 15 speakers, the group should split into two groups of 8 and then continue to meet and grow from there.

How does the interaction of Google Hangouts with Joomla websites fit into the movement building process?

It is common to think that if you have one hundred people in your group, you need to set up a video conference to invite all one hundred people. Folks therefore dismiss Google Hangouts as an option because Google limits the number of participants to ten people (a limit that can be raised to 15 by clicking on a few buttons to get a free Google Apps EDU account). But the reality is that it is difficult to conduct or even watch an efficient meeting where more than ten people are presenting. A far better process is to have ten experts, guests or team leaders participate on a video conference "panel" with the person who arranged the video call acting as the host, moderator or facilitator of the video conference call. The rest of the group can watch on YouTube or on your website if you have one. Viewers can also email in questions for the panel and/or post questions and comments on a social media page or website forum page. The best option here is a website forum page where the questions and comments can automatically be organized by topic for later viewing by those who were not able to listen to the conference live. The video(s) can even be posted on several websites – each belonging to a different division of the bigger group and each ran by local leaders. This way a million people can be involved and relationships can be build within local communities even when discussing a nation event. After the main video conference, each of the team leaders can turn into hosts and set up their own video conferences with up to ten more guests – either taped and posted to YouTube – or through a simple Google Hangouts video conference which is not taped and therefore may allow more open discussion of ideas. Then each of these guests can host their own video conferences with their local community.

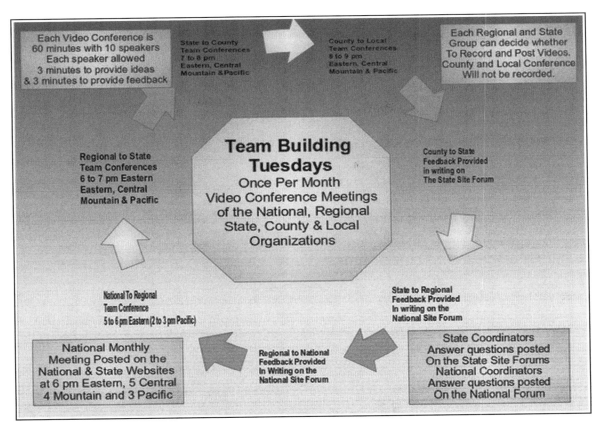

All of these groups can then exchange information through the use of a coordinated series of Google Hangout recorded and non recorded video conferences. For example, one might have a national leader start a hangout video conference with a panel of national leaders and regional leaders as guest speakers – inviting everyone in the nation to watch the event. At the end of the national presentation, each of the Regional Leaders can have Google Hangout hangout Regional video conferences with State leaders recruited from those in various State who watched the national event. Parents and teachers in each region can be directed to a link to watch their own regional video conference. The State leaders can then hold their own State video conferences with a panel of county leaders who can then be trained to offer their own county video conferences who can then be trained to offer their own school district video conferences – with the goal that each State organization can help elect better leaders to the State legislature and each county and school district organization can help elect better leaders to each local school board.

This is bottom up democracy in action and it is a tool that is now available to those willing to learn how to use it. I believe that parents and teachers concerned about the attack on their kids and their local tools will be willing to take the time to learn how to use this new, free and extremely powerful tool – as long as there is a clear and concise training manual that they can follow.

How Joomla web building tools can help structure a national movement
This will eventually require maintaining interlocking websites coordinated by the national organization website database. This is where a well organized website management system and forum system like Joomla excel. The Joomla log in, menu structure and articles structure can allow each state to have its own set of web pages all organized under the national website with a single national registration process for all users. Each State and local organization could generate their own email lists and newsletters. The only limitation is that the organizational structure of the website categories and database divisions would need to be set up from the beginning. Put another way, each State, County and local school district organization could have its own website, forum, email and newsletter service provided free of charge by the national organization as long as the foundation of the national website was structured to provide it.

Email Newsletter Sending Options
Another crucial tool for modern group communication is an email newsletter program. Joomla offers a free mail newsletter program, called AcyMailing, that is better than any of the commercial email newsletter programs. For example, the annual cost for an email newsletter list with 6,000 email addresses is free with AcyMailing. However, it costs $660 with Mail Chimp, $840 with Nation Builder and $1,020 with Constant Contact.

Free newsletter tools are one of dozens of reasons to build your community organization with the help of a Joomla website. Joomla also offers free form building tools, free video display tools, free community forum tools, free shopping cart tools, and thousand of other free tools. To learn how to build a Joomla website and use many of these free tools, visit our website:
http://buildyourownbusinesswebsite.org/

For more information on how to get started in video conferencing and building your own YouTube channel, visit our website:
http://createyourownvideochannel.org/

Conclusion... It is Up to Each of Us to Fight Back
There is a war of lies, greed and corruption going on. It is a war against our kids and our schools. It has been going on since at least the publication of the fake report called "Nation at Risk" in 1983. The real question is when will parents and teachers finally start to rise up, speak out and fighting back?

When we started this book, our goal was to provide parents and teachers with information about the many weapons of mass deception used by billionaires to take over and destroy our public schools. Our hope was to inspire at least some parents and teachers to get more politically active, and to start attending more school board meetings and political party meetings each month – and possibly even run for office and/or join us to help build a national movement to actively oppose the billionaire takeover of our public schools. We can win this war but only if more parents and teachers are willing to become much more active.

There are four specific things you can do to help our movement grow.

The first is to share information about this book with your friends, neighbors and other parents and teachers. Send an email to anyone you think is interested giving them a link to the website for this book:
http://weaponsofmassdeception.org/

Second, join our our Coalition to Protect our Public Schools. Our goal is to eventually have a chapter in every major city and every school district in the nation. To form a chapter for your community, go to website:
http://coalitiontoprotectourpublicschools.org/

Third, opt your children out of high stakes, toxic tests. For more information on the latest developments in the Opt Out movement and to download a form on how to opt your students out of toxic tests, visit **http://optoutwashington.org/**

Fourth, attend the monthly meetings for your local PTA. Meet other parents and teachers and form a group to resist the billionaire takeover of our public schools.

Fourth, and perhaps most important, help us take back both major political parties by becoming a PCO for your community. The political parties are the groups who actually write the laws and change the laws. Becoming more politically active is something that will only require one evening per month of your time. But it is the only way we have any hope of protecting our schools and restoring our democracy. There is very likely a local branch of the Republican and/or Democratic party in your Legislative District and/or county. Find out what evening they meet each month and where they meet. You should also find out what "precinct" your home or apartment is in – where you are registered to vote. Your county election department can tell you what precinct you are in. It will have a Name and/or a Number, like North Bend 068.

Then attend the next monthly meeting of either political party. Even if you hate both parties, join one of them anyway and start attending the meetings. Find out if your precinct has a "precinct committee officer" - more commonly called a PCO. Most precincts do not have one. If your precinct lacks a PCO, volunteer to be a PCO. If it already has a PCO, volunteer to "adopt" a different precinct near your home. You do not need to wait for an election to become the PCO for your neighborhood. Once you are an appointed PCO, you will have a vote at the next meeting. Bring other parents and/or teachers with you to form a voting block. Talk with other parents and teachers at the meeting who are already PCOs and come up with a plan to pass a resolution opposing the billionaire takeover of our schools. Eventually, run to be the elected PCO of your precinct and run to be on the Board of your legislative district and/or county organization. Then run for State party office. If every concerned parent and teacher would invest 12 nights per year to attend political party meetings, within 2 years, we could take back control of both major political parties! Together, we can provide a better future for our children and all children. Thanks for reading. See you on the battlefield!

About The Authors

We are two community college instructors who care deeply about all students getting a good education. Both of us have Master's Degrees in Education and have taught at community colleges in Washington State for more than 20 years.

David was a 7th Grade Math teacher and has a Major in Science Education. His Master's Degree was in Child Development. He has spent years studying how chronic stress, such as from high stakes tests, can severely harm a child's ability to learn. David is the Director of College in the Clouds, an online non-profit educational program. David also teaches courses in Website Design. See **Collegeintheclouds.org** and **Buildyourownbusinesswebsite.org** for more information about these programs.

Elizabeth has taught English as a Second Language since 1985. Earlier in her career, Elizabeth was a GED instructor. Some of her friends are GED instructors. They alerted us to the harmful changes in the 2014 GED. We therefore decided someone needed to do something to offer struggling students a fairer chance at a better future. We hope you will join us in working to restore GED fairness and end Common Core, High Stakes testing in Washington State and across the US.

To help build a grassroots community to restore sanity to public education, we have started a group called the **Coalition to Protect our Public Schools (dot) org**. Here is the link: http://coalitiontoprotectourpublicschools.org/

Our website has a **Latest News** section for ongoing events in the fight to protect our public schools and a **Community Forum** section where parents and teachers can ask questions about the issues raised in this book and how they can organize politically in their own communities.

If you would like to join us, click on the **Join Now** link. If you have any questions or information you would like to share with us, click on **Contact Us** in the main menu. You can also email us privately at springforschools@aol.com

Made in the USA
Middletown, DE
12 March 2015